The First English Novelists

# The First English Novelists:

Tennessee Studies in Literature Volume 29

# Essays in Understanding

Edited by J. M. Armistead

*honoring the retirement of Percy G. Adams*

The University of Tennessee Press / Knoxville

Frontispiece: "The Overturned Coach," watercolor drawing by
Thomas Rowlandson,
from the Albert H. Wiggin Collection.
Courtesy of the Print Department, Boston Public Library.

Publication of this book has been aided by a grant from The Better
English Fund, established by John C. Hodges at The University of
Tennessee, Knoxville.

Since its inception in 1956, the distinguished series, "Tennessee
Studies in Literature," sponsored by the Department of English at
the University of Tennessee, Knoxville, published 26 volumes.
Beginning with Volume 27, the series presents a new format. Each
book deals with a specific theme, period, or genre, for which the
editor of that volume has invited contributions from leading
scholars in the field. No longer an annual series, the volumes will
be published as they are ready. As with all University of Tennessee
Press books, the "Tennessee Studies in Literature" volumes are
printed on paper that meets the guidelines for permanence and
durability of the Committee on Production Guidelines for Book
Longevity of the Council on Library Resources, and binding
materials are chosen for strength and durability.

**Library of Congress Cataloging in Publication Data**
Main entry under title:

The First English novelists.

(Tennessee studies in literature ; v. 29)
Includes index.
1. English fiction—18th century—History and criticism
—Addresses, essays, lectures. 2. Adams, Percy G.
I. Adams, Percy G. II. Armistead, J. M. III. Series.
PR851.F57 1985 813'.5 85-3153
ISBN 0-87049-468-6

# Tennessee Studies in Literature

*Editor*
J. M. Armistead

*Editorial Board*
Allison R. Ensor        Norman Sanders
Thomas J. Heffernan     Jon Manchip White
B.J. Leggett

Inquiries concerning this series should be addressed to the Editor, *Tennessee Studies in Literature*, Department of English, The University of Tennessee, Knoxville, Tennessee 37996-0430. Those desiring to purchase additional copies of this issue or copies of back issues should address The University of Tennessee Press, 293 Communications Building, Knoxville, Tennessee 37996-0325.

# Editor's Preface

Few topics of specialized research remain as pertinent to classroom teaching as does the rise of the English novel. Paradoxically, this may be because early prose fiction can still be readily comprehended without recourse to scholarly underpinning. To enjoy most other forms of eighteenth-century literature—say, poetry or drama—one must know more than a little about the social and intellectual contexts within which it was originally created; novels of the period, on the other hand, carry little worlds with them through the centuries, defining themselves largely through details of ordinary life. Even their philosophical and moral bases are usually conveyed in terms that their characters, "non-specialists" of a sort, can understand. Thus, modern critics and commentators need not exhaust their skills just to get us in the door. We are already inside, wanting to know more about the House of Fiction.

And yet, once inside, we often want to get out again, to see the early novels with some degree of critical detachment, to ponder their seemingly artless art and to connect their fictions with their authors' (and audiences') realities. In an effort to prime this critical sensibility, I have assembled a distinguished group of specialists whose common trait is the ability to communicate with generalists, students, and casual readers. I have asked each of these contributors to write a unified introduction to the major works of one or a small group of the most influential early novelists. The goal is not a "companion" to eighteenth-century fiction, but rather a series of broadly aimed interpretations based on the latest research. Each chapter should help the modern reader to grasp key literary achievements in a certain way, the way of a trained critic who is attuned not only to the interplay of text and context, writer and culture, but also to the working-out of central meanings within the text itself.

If this effort succeeds in giving ordinary readers access to the findings of serious criticism and scholarship, it will have accomplished another objective as well—the objective of honoring the retirement of Percy G. Adams. For many years Percy has resisted the tendency of pedagogy and scholarly study to fly apart like galaxies in an expanding universe of intellectual disciplines. In his own professional life, he shows how scholarship can be stimulated by classroom instruction and how the quality of instruction can be enriched by ongoing research. This volume is dedicated to him, then, not merely as a form of flattery, but in the hope that it will help to perpetuate the ideal of scholar-teacher for which he has served as both spokesman and model.

J. M. Armistead

# Acknowledgments

For the index to this volume I am indebted to Mr. Daniel Pigg, an advanced graduate student at the University of Tennessee, and for reliable professional advice I am grateful to J. Paul Hunter of the University of Rochester. The idea of creating a book such as this was stimulated by discussions with my students, who for years have needed more guidance than I could give them as they read the early works of prose fiction in English.

J.M.A.

# Contents

Editor's Preface                          *page* vii
     J. M. Armistead

Acknowledgments                         ix

For Percy G. Adams                   xiii
     Donald Kay

Introduction                            xxi
     James E. Gill

Popular Narrative in the Early Eighteenth Century:
     Formats and Formulas                    3
     John Richetti

Defoe and the Geography of the Mind      41
     Paula R. Backscheider

Saying "No," Saying "Yes": The Novels of Samuel
     Richardson                             67
     Margaret A. Doody

Fielding: The Comic Reality of Fiction      109
     Sheridan Baker

Smollett's Art: The Novel as "Picture"      143
     Jerry C. Beasley

Structure, Language, Experience in the Novels of
     Laurence Sterne                         185
     Howard Anderson

Jane Austen's Accommodations            225
     Alistair M. Duckworth

Books about the Early English Novel: A Survey and
     a List                                 269
     Jack D. Durant

Contributors                               285

Index of Names and Titles              288

# Donald Kay

## For Percy G. Adams

This is no time to be modest in praise, and there is no need to be. Percy G. Adams, in whose honor these essays were written upon the occasion of his retirement from the faculty of the University of Tennessee, Knoxville, is indeed one of the giants of our profession of letters, one of the most dedicated, generous, and searching scholars of his generation.* Assuredly, he was, and remains, a teacher of rare skill, primarily, it has been said, because he seemed to act on the assumption that the undergraduate and graduate students who came to him knew little but wanted to know everything. A former student put it this way: "He always treated us with courtesy, respect, and good humor—in short, like colleagues—but he taught us every single thing from basics to esoterica in the clearest, most professional manner possible." He expected the best, and he understood the fundamental reality that students enrolled in courses to learn, and that only those who needed instruction, required inspiration, wanted his guidance, would be sitting before or around him.

One of the hallmarks of his teaching philosophy was that he always—in courses from the freshman to the doctoral level—believed the primary text was more important for study than the secondary criticism about it, although what others had to say was naturally to be considered and could be overlooked only at one's peril in class. And in those classes and seminars, where discussion was choice, Percy had the knack to make a student feel comfortable, not in his or her ignorance but in the ability to make judgments. He had the gift to instill, as well, an enthusiasm and joy for reading and writing in his charges and to extract the last ounce of energy and commitment from those who often thought of themselves (later) as

*I am indebted for information in this introductory commentary on Percy G. Adams's life and career to a number of individuals, foremost among whom are his colleagues Kenneth Curry, Edward W. Bratton, and Bain Tate Stewart—and, of course, to Polly Adams. The bibliography of his published works, not intended to be exhaustive, has been obtained from the files of the University of Tennessee Department of English.

"Percy's Brigade." Even those who moaned at having to write the legend-ary three-page-and-not-one-word-more paper for every seminar meeting soon came to an appreciation of the discipline in both analysis and rhetori-cal skills engendered by such a practice.

In retrospect it is clear that Percy G. Adams must have had this ability to teach from almost the very beginning of his life in Beeville, Texas, where he was born on 16 December 1914. The diversity of his interests is equally evident (and it mirrors the diversity of literary genres he loved from the literature of the 1700s), for after graduating in 1933 from Texas A&I with a major in mathematics and chemistry he began to teach, at the ripe age of eighteen, first in a county school and then at Kingsville High School from 1934 to 1940; it was during this latter tenure that as coach he twice guided the basketball team to a regional championship. Contrary to received legend, Percy did not go to school on an athletic scholarship, though he did letter in both tennis and basketball in college. During these years of teaching high school mathematics and English, he worked in the sum-mers toward an M.A. in English and French (received in 1937) from the University of Texas; and after leaving high school teaching in 1940, he taught at the University of Texas at Austin before joining the U.S. Naval Air Corps in 1943. He was discharged in 1946 as a lieutenant, and in that same year he was awarded the Ph.D. degree in English, American liter-ature, and French from the University of Texas.

It was in Austin during these years that he developed fully his interest in travel literature, and his doctoral dissertation on St. Jean de Crèvecoeur's *Voyage dans la haute Pensylvanie et dans l'état de New York*, directed by Theodore Hornberger, was later expanded into a book, *Crèvecoeur's Eigh-teenth-Century Travels in Pennsylvania and New York* (University Press of Kentucky, 1961), and at least six articles. Much of his course work at Texas was with R.H. Griffith, and it was the stimulation provided by Griffith that helped to fuel Percy's lifelong passion for things British as well as those belletristic contributions of France and America.

It was in 1946 that Percy really began the career of university teaching and literary criticism that has led to his current position as Lindsay Young Professor of English at the University of Tennessee, Knoxville, and all along the way he has been accompanied by Pauline Serger Adams, whom he married in 1941. After a brief time at Ohio State University (1946–48), he devoted himself chiefly to building the fabric of the University of Tennessee Department of English, save for a period from 1966 to 1970 as Professor of English and Director of Graduate Studies in English at Loui-siana State University. At Tennessee he worked hand in glove with schol-ars like John C. Hodges, Kenneth Knickerbocker, Kenneth Curry, Richard

Beale Davis, Alwin Thaler, Nathalia Wright, Bain Tate Stewart, and Norman Sanders to establish and promote a curriculum of outstanding merit. From 1974 to about 1982 he was Director of Graduate Studies, and he also found time to serve as Visiting Professor of Comparative Literature at the University of Southern California and Fulbright Professor at Aix-en-Provence and Grenoble. His tracks always seemed to end up in France—that early Texas passion for French literature never diminished—and he has always valued his work with Professor Charles Dedeyan and others at the Sorbonne and the Bibliothèque Nationale (most of which was accomplished without a great deal of financial aid from university sources).

It is difficult to catalog the sense of activity, of movement, that characterizes Percy's superb career as teacher and scholar, but to note his direction of at least thirty Ph.D. dissertations and approximately two hundred M.A. theses and to recognize him as author and editor of numerous seminal essays and books is to be impressed and to have no doubt that this honorific volume is his due.

That others have previously recognized his contributions has led to his being appointed to the editorial board of *Early American Literature* (1969–71), elected as the first President of the Southeastern American Society for Eighteenth-Century Studies (1974–75), selected as Chairman of the South Atlantic Graduate English Association (1975–76), chosen as Senior Fellow of the National Endowment for the Humanities (1976–77), and elected to the Executive Committee of the South Atlantic Modern Language Association (1980–83). There is, finally, no surprise, only rejoicing, that his career has been capped by the magnificently rich *Travel Literature and the Evolution of the Novel* (1983), in some respects the culmination of the work that led to his published dissertation (1961), his *Travelers and Travel Liars* (1962; paperback ed., 1979), and his general editorship of the Dover Publications travel series. Like his previous books, most recently *Graces of Harmony* (1977), this new one is a model of style and substance; all those students he has taught, all those colleagues he has instructed, and readers in America, France, and Great Britain especially (and, one imagines, even one or two of those Kingsville High School basketball players) are in his debt for having brought it all together for us.

For these reasons this volume of essays, edited by Jack Armistead and provided by Percy's friends and professional colleagues, is being published by the University of Tennessee Press in his honor. The contributions he has made to our knowledge of the novel, both in America and in Europe, and those many additional works he has inspired are his living endowment to his favorite main-traveled road in the realm of literary studies. Thank you, Percy, for everything.

# Publications by Percy G. Adams

1941. "Voltaire and Shakespeare." *Shakespeare Association Bulletin* (April).

1942. "Poe, Critic of Voltaire." *Modern Language Notes* (April).

1947. "Crèvecoeur and Franklin." *Pennsylvania History* 14, no. 4 (October), 273-80.

1948. "Notes on Crèvecoeur." *American Literature* 20 (November), 327-33.

1949. "Crèvecoeur—Realist or Romanticist." *French American Review* (July-September), 115-34.

1953. "The Historical Value of Crèvecoeur's *Voyage dans la haute Pensylvanie et dans New York*." *American Literature* 25 (May), 152-69.

1956. "The Real Author of William Byrd's *Natural History of Virginia*." *American Literature* 28 (May), 211-20.

1957. "John Lawson's Alter-Ego Dr.—John Brickell." *North Carolina Historical Review* 24 (July), 313-27.

1958. "A Fake Eighteenth-Century Traveler: Francois Corcal." *Newberry Library Bulletin* 4, no. 8 (April), 239-53.

1960. "Crèvecoeur, St. Jean de." *Encyclopaedia Britannica*.

———. "The Franco-American Faulkner." *Tennessee Studies in Literature* 5, pp. 1-15.

1961. "American Literature in the Universities of France." *Studies in Honor of John C. Hodges and Alwin Thaler, Tennessee Studies in Literature*, spec. no., 175-84.

———. "Benjamin Franklin's Defense of the De Fonte Hoax." *Princeton University Library Chronicle* 22, no. 3 (Spring), 133-41.

———. *Crèvecoeur's Eighteenth-Century Travels in Pennsylvania and New York*. Lexington: Univ. Press of Kentucky.

———. "Young Henry James and the Lesson of His Master Balzac." *Revue de Litterature Comparée* 25, pp. 458-68.

1962. "The French 'Image' of the United States." *Mississippi Quarterly* 15, pp. 35-47.

———. *Travelers and Travel-Liars, 1660-1800.* Berkeley: Univ. of California Press.

1964. "Humor as Structure and Theme in Faulkner's Trilogy." *Wisconsin Studies in Contemporary Literature* 5, pp. 204-13.

1965. "The Case of Swaine versus Drage: An Eighteenth-Century Publishing Mystery Solved." In *Essays in History and Literature Presented by Fellows of the Newberry Library to Stanley Pargellis*, ed. Heinz Bluhm. Chicago: Newberry Library.

1967. " 'Harmony of Numbers': Dryden's Alliteration, Consonance, Assonance." *Texas Studies in Literature and Language* 9, pp. 333-43.

———. Introduction to John Esquemeling, *The Buccaneers of America.* New York: Dover.

———. Introduction to William Byrd, *Histories of the Dividing Line betwixt Virginia and North Carolina.* New York: Dover.

1968. Introduction to William Dampier, *A New Voyage Round the World.* New York: Dover.

———. "Pope's Concern With Assonance." *Texas Studies in Literature and Language* 9, pp. 493-502.

1969. Introduction to Woodes Rogers, *A Cruising Voyage Round the World.* New York: Dover.

1970. "What Happened in Olivia's Bedroom? or Ambiguity in *The Plain Dealer.*" In Thomas A. Kirby and William J. Olive, eds., *Essays in Honor of Esmond Linworth Marilla.* Baton Rouge: Louisiana State Univ. Press.

———. Editor, Louisiana State University Humanities Series: *The Poems of William Smith*, ed. Lawrence A. Sasek.

1971. Editor, Louisiana State University Humanities Series: Gresdna Ann Doty, *The Career of Mrs. Anne Brunton Merry in the American Theatre.*

———. Editor, Special Southern Issue of *Early American Literature* 6.

———. Introduction to *The Explorations of Captain Cook in the Pacific As Told By Selections of His Own Journals, 1768–1779.* New York: Dover.

1972. "Chaucer's Assonance." *Journal of English and Germanic Philology* 71, pp. 527-40.

1973. "The Epic Tradition and the Novel," *Southern Review* 9, pp. 300-11.

———. "Faulkner, French Literature, and 'Eternal Verities.' " In *Proceedings of the Comparative Literature Symposium, January 24-27, Texas Tech University.* Lubbock: Texas Tech Univ. Press.

———. "The Historical Importance of Assonance to Poets." *PMLA* 88, pp. 9-19.

———. Introduction to *Anson's Voyage Round the World.* New York: Dover.

1974. Editor, Special Eighteenth-Century Issue of *Tennessee Studies in Literature* 18 (1974).

1976. "The Anti-Hero in Eighteenth-Century Fiction." *Studies in the Literary Imagination* 9, pp. 29-53.

———. "Benjamin Franklin and the Travel-Writing Tradition." In J.A. Leo Lemay, ed., *The Oldest Revolutionary: Essays on Benjamin Franklin.* Philadelphia: Univ. of Pennsylvania Press.

———. "European Renaissance Literature and Discovery of the New World." *Comparative Literature Studies* 13, pp. 100-16 (originally an address at a conference, First Images of America, in Los Angeles; subsequently videotaped and used on educational TV in California).

1977. *Graces of Harmony: Alliteration, Assonance, Consonance in Eighteenth-Century Poetry.* Athens: Univ. of Georgia Press.

1978. "The Achievements of Captain James Cook and His Associates in Perspective." Opening address of the Captain Cook Bicentenary Celebration for Alaska.

———. "The Coach Motif in Eighteenth-Century Fiction." *Modern Language Studies* 8, pp. 17-27.

———. "Seventeenth- and Eighteenth-Century Travel Literature: A Review of Recent Approaches." *Texas Studies in Literature and Language* 20 (Fall), 489-575.

1979. Introduction to *The Dramatic Works of James Thomson.* New York: Garland.

1983. *Travel Literature and the Evolution of the Novel.* Lexington: Univ. Press of Kentucky.

xx

Forth-
coming  "Misconceptions and Travel Lies About the North American Indian." In *The North American Indian*, 26 vols., ed. William Sturtevant (Washington, D.C.: Smithsonian Institution).

————. "Perception and the Eighteenth-Century Traveler." *The Eighteenth Century: Theory and Interpretation.*

————. "Three Recent Scientific Travel Books of the Eighteenth Century." *The Eighteenth Century: Theory and Interpretation.*

————. "William Wycherley." In *Collier's Encyclopedia of Literature.*

# James E. Gill

# Introduction

From its inception this collection of essays has been planned for the audience which has most often concerned Percy Adams during his career—not the expert but the serious collegiate student of eighteenth-century literature, here represented by the early English novel. The contributors to this volume, themselves experts and master teachers, have diversely and sensitively and generously set their hands to the task of communicating vast worlds of thought; for as these splendid essays show, the early masters of English fiction and the milieu which fostered their novels are complicated topics, and no amount of skillful summary, no amount of searching for clever approaches or new angles of vision can make even this wonderful subject at once delightful and simple to understand. The great scholarly work that synthesizes all our knowledge of it seems a remote dream, and no one following current critical developments could hope for a less diverse and rich harvest of thought.

Under these circumstances, essays that introduce and summarize, that take well-informed and clearly articulated stands about early fiction and do not at the same time oversimplify—such essays are of great value to the student. But because of its complexity and the wealth of data and opinion about the subject, it has been thought advisable also to provide for the reader some brief guide to these studies, one that endeavors to appreciate the fineness of their perceptions, to summarize what appear to be their major points, and to identify where possible the tendencies of their arguments. The aim of this introduction, then, is to make these studies as useful as possible by providing the student with a guide and checklist as he or she moves through them.

In the first essay the admirable John Richetti discusses the eruption—not the evolution—of the eighteenth-century novel in a set of forms or formats and possibilities which the great novelists of the century could and did transcend. In short, he studies "a necessary provocation" to their genius in the "artistically insignificant . . . forgotten fiction that precedes and surrounds the eighteenth-century masters." The literary "junk" of an era has at the least a profound historical significance and helps to highlight the artistic choices of its great writers.

The number of kinds of popular narratives practiced during the eighteenth century is astonishingly large, and the range of interests is enormous. The aristocratic romance and *Pilgrim's Progress* define only the extremes between which the more "factual" types burgeoned—memoir, history, life, voyage, adventure, tale, letters, and journal. However crude or absurdly plotted, books that claimed factuality seem to have appealed most. Reports of crimes and trials continued to have an immediate vogue during the early decades of the century, issued as they were early in the morning after verdicts or executions. And though these accounts utilized earlier rogue literature forms, they inspired a detailed and specific interest that is significant in the emergence and appeal of the novel—perhaps because, according to Richetti, "the criminal increasingly represented an apt expression of certain feelings of isolation and marginality to which [readers] could respond"; it may be that the malefactor's "attractiveness lay in his or her subversive individuality." Underworld life tended to balance two contradictory patterns of behavior: in one the criminal is victim; in the other he achieves "self-defining freedom." Some criminal narratives—notably "pirate history" like Defoe's—skillfully blend real data with the fantastic.

Travel narratives, another popular type, also embody this pattern: they are blends of "objective" data, the exciting or dangerous, affirmations of providential designs, and expressions of the myths of European imperialism. In short, such narratives offer "solid emotional and ideological satisfactions to willing readers." Even so, some shorter travel and adventure narratives also serve the radically different purpose of presenting older, satiric attitudes.

Most numerous in the fiction of 1700–40, according to Richetti, are amatory narratives, so-called histories or secret histories or memoirs which sought to replace their less "realistic" and lengthier French predecessors. Mary Manley's preface to *Queen Zarah* (1705) justifies this type of narrative, characterized by a central and significant confusion of purpose—its appeal to vicarious excitement or pleasure and its didactic pretensions. The result is, as Richetti says, a shift from "edifying scene and moralizing discourse" to an early luxuriating in emotion. In general, such novels move quickly toward "a world of sexual fantasy and thrilling moral melodrama." In them contemporary gossip is accommodated to a satirical picture of a corrupt society in which the "power of love is irresistible." The topical satiric content of these novels aside, they create a mythical world of "female innocence . . . exploited by male corruption"—a world marked by a "recurrent erotic moment, a soft-core rape-seduction extravaganza," and energetic denunciations of "intrigue, lust, betrayal, and even crime."

Her successor, Eliza Haywood, "refined and developed this formula by stripping it of political content and all but the most general satiric purpose. At the center of her "genteel, euphemistic pornography" is the destructive and forbidden (but undeniable) power of love. Richetti's description of a typical climactic scene is hilarious, and his isolation from such novels of a "vigorously insistent" version of "the crisis of subjectivity" is brilliant. Here "psychological interiority" becomes "*the* defining female trait" as women are helpless in the face of male exploitation and are betrayed by "their own irresistible, wayward sexuality."

Mrs. Haywood's balanced blend of eroticism with psychological consolation explains her popularity, Richetti believes, and he accounts for the successes or failures of other eighteenth-century amatory novels by their adherence to or deviation from Mrs. Haywood's formulas. In general, stories veering toward the brutal and more explicit, or toward the woman's fierce dying denunciation of her seducer, violated the profound cultural norms embodied in the Haywood formulas and failed of success. At the other extreme, simple, transparently moralizing stories were equally unsuccessful.

Too numerous to summarize here are Richetti's many valuable synopses and comments on such matters as expressive form vs. format, on technique and style, and on unique early experiments in fiction. His wide knowledge of the popular fiction of the period is seldom matched, and his ability to find clear paths in dense thickets of popular literature is exemplary. As he acknowledges, feminist criticism has contributed much to our understanding of the early novel, and feminist critics will find this essay especially interesting.

In her essay on Daniel Defoe, Paula Backscheider appears to concentrate on *Robinson Crusoe* as the secure foundation of Defoe's lasting fame, but in reality she uses her discussion of the book as a basis for comment on Defoe's other novels. Through *Crusoe* she describes the central situation in a Defoe novel, in which a character presents himself as immersed in the circumstantial *and also* "appears in one archetypal incident after another" in a series of "what if" fantasies. The question of bare survival is succeeded by questions of the mysterious ground of existence and the hidden causes of things. The consciousness of the physical is inevitably joined with feelings and issues which experience awakened in the eigh-

teenth-century mind—questions of political rights, economic development, moral obligation, and providential plan. In fact, Ms. Backscheider
argues, the twentieth century has come to see Defoe's novels as a complex
blend of genres, into which he absorbed a great number of broad interests,
intellectual debates, and journalistic devices. Thus critics are beginning to
understand his complex amalgamation of "simpler" fictional structures
and techniques: "Defoe transformed basically mono-referential forms
into vehicles that satisfied readers' desires for adventure and for emotional
exploration." As the great Defoe scholars have shown, into the service of
the novel Defoe pressed travel literature, history, spiritual autobiography,
"Providences," conduct books, economic essays, and the journalistic and
fictional accounts of rogues.

Her examinations of such mixtures of structures and themes contain
some of Ms. Backscheider's best commentary, for she shows that Defoe is
not merely a "cut-and-paste" artist: the blend of rogue biography and
spiritual autobiography, for example, produces curious and different perspectives. In *Moll Flanders* the reader joins not the "initiated, experienced" character but the naive one whose simplicity is highlighted but
not undercut by the ironic or cynical awareness of adults. Though she is
both naive and vain, the young Moll is also hard-working and is in any case
innocent of the crasser duplicities which surround her. Thus she is set
apart at first so that behind the sly rogue and fierce predator who she
becomes, there "lives the girl who wanted independence, respect, and a
constant love."

One detects in such comments and analysis the beginnings of an interesting deconstructionist approach to Defoe's novels—works which have
often stubbornly resisted detailed formalist and structuralist analysis.
Since 1970, Ms. Backscheider shows, there has been less study of the way
that the novels themselves illuminate Defoe's work and greater attention
to the ways in which Defoe's very full participation in the intellectual,
political, religious, and economic life of his times illuminates his artistry.
Thus Defoe is seen to have exploited and integrated into his novels ideas
and structures which he knew or used elsewhere—ideas about a bewildering array of important topics such as the almost overwhelming issues of
Providence and uncertainty. Such ideas have a powerful effect on character, and because Defoe grasped the dynamic relationships of the issues that
impassioned his age, he was able to create gripping fictions from them.

In addition, and perhaps conversely, critics since 1970 have also seen
how Defoe's nonfiction works are themselves "fictional" and "partake of
the mainstream techniques and themes of the novel." Here the great
organizing themes are the uniting of money and marriage; the recognition

of the power of the past—of the past of the individual as well as of history; and the conflict between the individual and society. In all these areas, Defoe clearly apprehends psychological truths, historical trends, and complex relationships. In turn, Defoe's fiction, "shaped both by his own imagination and by the lively publishing world in which he worked," seems to consist of "deliberate experiments drawing with increasing self-consciousness upon fictional structures and strategies." Thus one can see in his later novels a more confident reliance on "incident, metaphor, and symbol" than in *Crusoe*—which is "more traditionally biblical, more repetitious, and more expository" than, say, *Roxana*.

Yet, as Ms. Backscheider concludes, Defoe is ever the master of the particular, a fact which contributes to the "subjectivity and structural disorder" of the novels and which leads him to chronological presentation, to the "representational" rather than to the "illustrative." Even so, as she observes of Paul Alkon's study of Defoe, the critic can demonstrate in Defoe's fiction the writer's control of such factors and techniques as pace, tempo, space, repetition, and cross-referencing to achieve effects and to develop readers' expectations. In ways that are as certain as they are difficult to describe, Defoe shaped—as surely as Richardson, Fielding, and Sterne—the course of the English novel.

Margaret Doody's sensitive essay on the novels of Samuel Richardson emphasizes Richardson's development of his characters, in whom the novelist said he lost himself and in doing so "raised the novel as a form with philosophical implications." "Islands in time, stuck in the 'now,' and lacking a known past, Richardson's characters mirror each of us in the process of living." Such realism, according to Doody, dwarfs mere verisimilitude. Since in their conflicts, such characters assault one another's views of life, they call attention to matters of style and structure, and hence Richardson's novels early attracted the attention of "new-style" critics—structuralist and deconstructionist. Even those critics who have attacked Richardson are responding strongly to his characters and are thereby revealing an intense belief in them. And because he deals with the groundwork of human existence—with personal desire, with sex, and with the roles imposed by society—Richardson has also stimulated Marxist and feminist critics. The strong feelings which he provokes have, in short, led many kinds of readers to accept his great artistic innovations.

Ms. Doody conjectures that Richardson shows from the beginning "a tendency to confuse or question set hierarchies," including moral and aesthetic ones, perhaps because he himself was not a member of the "establishment." His first heroine, Pamela, leaves a simple home to enter a world where struggle and heroism may not be elegant or dignified—a world both nightmarish and comic. Mr. B_____'s tricks and Mrs. Jewkes's brutish voyeurism both partake of this mixed quality. And what horrifies Pamela at one time inspires a full range of other responses at other times.

One can see Richardson's concern with both matter and form as Pamela's growth and her increasing interiority are fostered by her isolation and by the fact that her letters to others become a journal in which she "queries and dodges herself." Such a procedure, while it does not conceal her vanity, misperceptions, and duplicities, marks her real growth and endows "a powerless teenager with undeniable aesthetic and moral authority," which as the novel progresses everyone is forced to acknowledge.

Ms. Doody's commentary on *Pamela II* provides not only a concise introduction to that often unread sequel (in itself a boon to students) but also an interesting point of departure for her discussion of *Clarissa*, where Richardson developed what he began in the second *Pamela*—multiple correspondents and more than one dominant point of view.

The brilliant discussion of *Clarissa* makes the student aware of the novel's deep concern with social class and family rivalry as well as with the intensive analysis of one character's feelings and language by others, both confidante and antagonist. Lovelace's "game" to trick and seduce Clarissa is grounded then in deeper games of language and relationship. And his game also mimics art and stage as he becomes a kind of grand director. Set against this background is Clarissa's "painful dereliction," decline, and re-creation of herself—of a *new* completeness "out of a great depth of madness and sorrow." Ms. Doody's account reinforces our sense of both Richardson's and Clarissa's ability to win true meaning through true art out of the omnipresent tendency to debase art and distort meaning.

In these terms Ms. Doody is able to confront, in some of the essay's best discussion, the "darkness" perceptible in the novel, the charges that Richardson was at bottom a sadist or a pious pornographer, and the feeling that *Clarissa* presents chiefly "a violent and dark social and psychic landscape."

In contrast, Ms. Doody shows, the world of Richardson's last novel, *Sir Charles Grandison*, is one in which "everything is salvageable"—a world in which men have been "redeemed from perversity" and a woman "may safely love." The chief problems of this world are those of loving women who must modestly appeal to scrupulous men or who suffer the guilt of repressed desire. Yet the novel flows past its eventual weddings into spats and pregnancies, "the consequences of saying 'Yes,' " and Grandison Hall stands "an abode of happy affirmatives resting on the right to consciousness."

Sheridan Baker's lively essay on Fielding presents him as the son of the great Scriblerians, a conservative devoted to hierarchy, and an admirer of the Ancients. Fielding served his apprenticeship in the modern theater, and in his novels he replaced the drama as a dominant form, transformed neoclassical practice into a "new poetics of prose," and explored in *Amelia* "a new and modern indeterminacy of character." Truly creative, Fielding is of his age, of that earlier world of classical humanism, and of our age also. Yet as Professor Baker shows, the inventive Fielding's work is of a piece throughout despite its diversity. His first play, *Love in Several Masks* (1728), "forecasts *Tom Jones* in surprising detail," and its characters can be seen as Slipslops, Lady Boobys and Bellastons, Sophias and Allworthys in the bud. And in his earliest rehearsal-farce, *The Author's Farce*, Fielding "discovered his autobiographical authorship of comic romances, a comic double self-portraiture in hero and author alike." All in all, he created "nine commenting authors on the stage" before he turned to writing political journalism and novels.

One of the great pleasures of this treatment of Fielding's career is that while Baker clearly delineates the unity of Fielding's concerns, he also perceives and accounts for Fielding's growth and deepening. Thus he points out that while the *Champion* continues the drama's attack on Walpole, Fielding also writes thoughtfully of the duties and conditions of the clergy: his attacks on religious abuses are related to his views of other matters, and his criticism of Whitefield's self-centered piety are of a piece with his ridicule of Cibber's conceit. And these are one with Shamela's hypocritical piety and Pamela's militant humility. All point up by contrast the center of Fielding's religion—"selfless charity."

Baker sees in *Shamela* the blending of hilarious obscenities (some in need of explanation to the modern reader) with delicious portrayal of the comic hypocrisies of civilized people in whom hidden desire struggles against propriety. And these concerns forecast *Joseph Andrews* just as Parson Oliver's comments on Richardson's pious lubricity point toward the moral of the still-to-be-written *Tom Jones*.

The discussion of Fielding's novels is thus based on but not limited to the background that Baker provides. His treatment of *Joseph Andrews* skillfully demonstrates Fielding's way with many of his sources and blends this discussion with exposition of the novel's central concerns. The result is an adept portrayal of the writer's integrity and growth—an account clearly but unobtrusively combining many of the best observations of modern readers.

Baker finds that "*Tom Jones,* though philosophically positive, is morally cautionary. . . . In this cautionary balance and wiser view, Fielding culminated the Augustan perspective." Here Baker seems to follow the straightforward providentialist reading of the novel, according to which "Fielding the novelist plays God to the world of his creation, illustrating God's ways to man." The inexperienced student needs at this point also to scrutinize Baker's notes, in which he very fairly lists critics who give other readings of this important novel—some of them, like that of John Preston, extremely interesting and provocative.

*Amelia,* Fielding's last novel, is one in which, according to Baker, "the realities darken beyond comic affirmation." Again Baker approaches the novel through analogies found in its sources—the *Aeneid* and three of Fielding's plays, among other works—and he concludes that "this is a new age; subjective consciousness breaks through Augustan order and objectivity. . . . Hume's solipsistic feeling has overturned reason, and Hume is clearly Fielding's unmentioned antagonist as he attempts to adjust the new philosophy to the providential Christianity it so profoundly unsettled."

Baker's Fielding is an admirable, complex author who often plundered his own works as he constantly rethought in ever more complex ways some of the central problems of his age.

Other novelistic strategies are described by Jerry Beasley, who likens Smollett's novels not to the beautifully plotted and designed *Tom Jones* but to a series of interconnected dramatic paintings like those of Hogarth. Smollett cares less for conventional laws of causality and process than for "wonderfully eccentric" and abrasive characters and for vivid, dramatic, surprising "self-contained episodes occurring in hurried succession." The scenes do "eventually add up to a whole, but by a method more cumulative than linear." The endings of the novels are marked by the reader's and the protagonist's understanding of manifold adventures, and "with understanding comes redemption . . . and happiness and repose." Although such endings are "always providentially contrived," they are never "quite gratuitously so," since Smollett, while quite capable of cynicism and bitterness, ultimately subscribes to a "generally optimistic Christian [and comic] interpretation of history."

Smollett's first novel, *Roderick Random,* is built of episodes that emulate many of the author's own vivid experiences, but *Roderick* is also a fresh blend of several popular narrative forms: rogue biography, travel tale, "sentimental novel of love and intrigue," and "romance of disinheritance and dicovery." Imitating the picaresque adventure tale, Smollett excels here and in succeeding works in focusing on the way experience is "registered by consciousness of the character who must live it" and who eventually must make sense of it. Indeed, so powerful is this sense of immediacy that it has led some readers to confuse Smollett's voice with that of Roderick; such sympathy owing to immediacy sometimes threatens the reader's critical detachment and may implicate him, for example, in the hero's failings as he responds to a brutal world.

Beasley sees the novels of Smollett's middle years—*Peregrine Pickle, Ferdinand Count Fathom,* and *Sir Lancelot Greaves*—as "lively and sometimes bold new experiments" in the art of fiction. *Peregrine Pickle* sprawls over Europe in what seems to be a comprehensive study of Western society through scores of episodes rich in clever portraits. So varied is the menu that the novel may be thought diffuse. Though its hero is a lively impish picaro, the third-person narrator of *Pickle* does not provoke, despite its brilliant comic portraiture, the reader involvement which *Roderick* urges; and the subsequent failure led Smollett "to a different, more restrained, and less brashly topical approach" to fiction in his third novel, *Ferdinand Count Fathom*. In a new kind of experiment in depicting the criminal intelligence in action, Fathom's satiric and villainous actions are balanced by the "providential" appearances of his helpful friend, the virtuous Renaldo, who eventually triumphs as Fathom is undone, is brought to repentance, and sinks into obscurity. One character's actions throw the other's into sharp relief and thus define one of Smollett's main broad but effective techniques.

Beasley also discusses another important aspect of Smollett's art prominent in *Fathom*—the author's topicality, his inclusion of historical event and character in his novels. These often represent the author's effort to develop "important and unusually subtle relationships" between the fictional world and the "enduringly relevant facts of the real world."

Smollett's last novels, according to Beasley, mark "a new mellowness" in his works. *Sir Launcelot Greaves* (1760) is chiefly interesting today as a close imitation of *Don Quixote*. The direct antithesis of Fathom, Greaves wanders about, reforms through benevolence, and successfully resists collapsing into cynicism despite numerous provocations.

Smollett's last novel and masterpiece, *Humphry Clinker*, is a comic romance in the epistolary style. Both "cleverly conventional and profoundly original," *Clinker* combines epistolary narrative, travel account, biographical narrative, satiric vignette, and farce. It is, in addition, a "spoof of the new cult of sensibility" and "a fable of passage." The novel gradually reconciles and harmonizes the tensions and oppositions that arise within it as Matthew Bramble's traveling group grows from "fragmentation to wholeness." The complex macrocosm depicted in *Clinker* reflects the dynamics of the microcosm of travelers as it draws them into it, and by this "reflexive process" the principal characters come to know themselves, both privately and with respect to the world.

Beasley's account of this gradual process is excellent as he shows that Smollett "was able to give his story a form exactly suited both to his own talent and to the vibrating complexity of his extraordinarily ambitious subject." *Clinker*, marked by a "radical eclecticism," is the "culminating manifestation of the theory of novelistic composition laid down . . . in the dedication to *Ferdinand Count Fathom*."

The purpose of Howard Anderson's "Structure, Language, Experience in the Novels of Laurence Sterne" is to show how Sterne's novels come to matter to the reader. Admitting that the narrator's beginnings or openings are gambits as likely to alienate as to attract, Anderson argues that many readers never recover from the sense that Tristram, for example, has played fast and loose with their sensibilities, but those who do learn to appreciate the narrator's playfulness probably do so because of the self-recognition and self-knowledge inculcated by these zany storytellers: "Questioning Tristram's judgment leads us to question our own." Tristram teaches us how to read his unconventional book, and as we take his course, we reflect also on reading and on our relation to experience outside of books.

Sterne, according to Anderson, typically piques the reader's desires in the following sequence: he provokes our craving for meaning, our searching for contexts as providers of meaning, and our looking to conversational intercourse as the means to context. "This is the pattern of the experience Sterne engages us in and of what he has to teach us." Such a pattern requires patience, tolerance, and good humor—it requires "sentiment," for without sentiment there is no genuine communication: it is not facts which are important but what one makes of them. Hence Tristram's work is not only progressive but digressive, not merely an arbitrary movement from birth through assorted misfortunes toward death but an expressive, comic nourishing of self. Similarly, *A Sentimental Journey* parodies the straightforward *factual* travel book with its collection of sometimes sordid facts by blending pathos with elegance, not in responding to the usual sights but in seeking out new ones—the living human beings and their ways viewed with acceptance and sympathy if with some amusement.

The digressions in both works, then, are connective. Tristram's carry him toward those who make up his past and toward the reader. In the later novel Yorick's impulses are similarly communicative and reflexive.

Anderson also studies the part that Sterne's "conscious *view* of language
. . . plays in the integrative 'experience' . . . embodied in the digressive
progress of his two novels." Among these devices is Sterne's "verbal
associationism"—especially his notorious double-entendres, "hobbyhorsical" and otherwise. Tristram's sensitivity to the wayward potency of
words is one way in which he is connected with his forebears Walter and
Toby. But through it and through the unavoidable creation of images,
Sterne also attacks the view that language is or ought to be almost purely
denotative. Instead, he justifies and practices the method of *wit* implicit in
his view of language. Judgment alone is insufficient; it must be answered
by wit, and all argument is "radically dependent on the figurative power of
language." Sterne's sensitivity here reveals wit to have a critical function:
it exposes shallow theory, imposture, and selfish egotism. His concern for
language and his exploitation of wit enable him also to explore with the
reader the connections between mind and body. His technique is not
simply reductive, however, for the reader becomes aware of the "wonder
and subtlety" of these connections as well as their absurdities. And what
goes for words also applies to body language, to gestures.

Another crucial element in Sterne's narratives is the metaphor of the
journey. In *Tristram* it is as important as that of the hobbyhorse, and it is
the central image "figuring spiritual development" in *A Sentimental
Journey.* In the former the grand tour is a means of eluding and discomfit-
ing death; in the latter the journey is a way of coming to love the world.

Anderson points out that Sterne's peculiar themes and techniques—his
digressive structure and his witty language—are, as phenomenological
critics have shown, well designed to appeal to a fellowship of sentiment in
the reader and, as it were, to engage him in conversation. His ultimate aim
is to delineate what one critic has defined as the "close relation between
understanding an 'other'—person, event, text, or tradition—and understanding oneself." Thus the narrator's quest to understand himself has
ontological implications for the reader also: when does the individual's
existence begin? how variously do we apprehend the brevity of our own
existences? how are body and mind to be reconciled? These topics and
others are the subjects of Tristram's conversations, which engage the
reader and demand his participation. Tristram's comic vision, his efforts to
evade "the ultimate danger . . . is precisely the opposite of ignoring the
threat's reality." And this matter is intensified by the tendency of various
voices in Sterne to flow into one another. These are Sterne's means to
make his books matter to the reader.

Studying deftly and sensitively Jane Austen's exquisite sense of place as
a means of delineating "the predicament of the single woman in a matc-

rialistic world," Alistair Duckworth sees the happy endings of her novels as "subtle and complex negotiations with the facts of her social experience, as these may be accommodated to inherited fictional traditions." Plot being traditionally "the accomplice of desire," Jane Austen, according to Duckworth, "sought to bring her dreams into acceptable conformity with the exigencies of real life." Implying that integrity and intelligence will be rewarded with "a fitting domestic establishment," she also sought to render her vision of virtue rewarded authentic by presenting also in one way or another the other alternative—the "unaccommodated" woman.

Weaving his way between the facts of Jane Austen's life and her fiction, Duckworth explores her class's sense of country, of family, of the place of women, of house and manor, and even of carriages as they impinged on her awareness. As he observes, "her Tory ideology is nowhere more evident than in the ideal settings," the "final accommodations of her heroines," as they "imply traditional cultural values of continuity, growth, and the interdependence of church and land." And "although her accommodations differ somewhat from novel to novel, they are the result of authentic searches . . . and not mere capitulations to conventions." Her ideal accommodation is the "self-subsistent community," "an organic social community," in which "religious principles, morals, and manners" exist in relations of mutual reciprocity.

The success of each of the novels in conservatively accommodating individual and social claims varies considerably, as Duckworth's detailed analyses reveal. The unfinished novel *The Watsons* is marked by a sense of bitterness and oppression, traits that also mark *Sense and Sensibility*. This work, like *Mansfield Park*, can be called a "problem" novel, whereas *Pride and Prejudice* and *Emma* are "accommodative" novels: they "successfully contain their criticisms of society's venality within an affirmation of a worthy cultural heritage." The discussions of *Mansfield Park* and *Persuasion* will be especially rewarding to the student, for these include Jane Austen's most mature and detailed examinations of women whose prospects of accommodation are slender and who are often made aware of their own "nothingness." In *Persuasion*, for example, Duckworth finds Jane Austen seeking new and fresh forms of accommodation, now symbolized not by ancestral estates or dignified parsonages but by the vigor, economy, and elasticity of mind seen, for example, in the novel's "naval" couples, the Crofts and the Harvilles, people who have traveled the world. These, despite their lack of "technical" gentility, manifest "morally informed manners"; and *Persuasion* also indicates other "new possibilities of accommodation for the marginal woman," as Anne Elliott "before her rapprochement with Wentworth showed stoicism, self-reliance, and above all, 'usefulness' in her social relations." And here external nature becomes more than a place to be responsibly and charitably inhabited, for its scenes now provide a "disciplined and emotional consolation."

Duckworth's comments on each novel are well worth the student's close attention, for they contain valuable hints about themes, devices, and rhythms not specifically developed but demanding further thought. The essay itself is throughout a fine attempt to view the author handsomely accommodated in her works.

These splendid tributes to the early English novelists and to Percy Adams are concluded by the useful recapitulation of major themes by Jack D. Durant, who provides a brief but helpful "Survey and List" of important studies of the early novel—studies of influences, trends, forms and formal procedures, reading publics, character types, and bibliographical resources. Ninety-one crucial works are listed with one-sentence summaries. These annotations suggest also what is not treated in the essays in this volume—the products of the gothic craze, some of the early novels of sensibility, and important minor novelists such as Sarah Fielding, Elizabeth Barbauld, and Fanny Burney, to name only a few.

The depth and polish of the essays in this study, and the wealth of criticism to which they refer, may lead the student to believe mistakenly that all that is worth saying about the traditions of early English fiction has in fact been said. But the studies of the great novelists here are full of suggestions of topics needing further exploration and of exciting critical approaches; Durant's essay fittingly provides a useful guide to ways of filling out the picture here boldly if briefly sketched.

The First English Novelists

# John Richetti

## Popular Narrative in the Early Eighteenth Century: Formats and Formulas

Like most narrative, literary history is drawn to an organic metaphor, the useful analogy whereby literary forms can be thought of as engendered, nourished, and developed toward strength and eventual maturity by just those circumstances historians seek to delineate. Perhaps more than other genres, the eighteenth-century English novel seems especially well served by such an analogy, since the qualities often said to define it—social and psychological realism, moral complexity, narrative self-consciousness—represent for modern criticism a sort of evolutionary pinnacle of narrative achievement.[1]

At the same time, however, the evolutionary analogy has been accompanied by another, almost contradictory, emphasis in literary history that stresses the uniqueness of the major eighteenth-century novelists and identifies their work as a radically new beginning for narrative, recognized as such by the novelists themselves.[2] On the one hand, the eighteenth-century novel seems best and most fully understood within a rich complex of generating circumstances, and literary history like other sorts of history is committed to genetic explanations. And some of the narratives published in England in the late seventeenth and the early eighteenth century do resemble in themes and techniques the works of the masters. On the other hand, as modern readers of those narratives have generally agreed, there are no meaningful precursors in them of those same masters. In a now discarded exercise, literary historians used to sift patiently through such material, looking hopefully for small signs of development toward the social and psychological realism, moral complexity, narrative control, and technical sophistication achieved by Defoe, Richardson, and Fielding.[3] They found so pathetically little evidence of evolution that it now seems safe to assert that there are no missing links and that the major English eighteenth-century novelists, in effect, created the genre *ex nihilo*, by sheer force of genius and imagination. Or, to put the case less dramatically and to give the literary historian something to do, Defoe, Richardson, and Fielding transcended their predecessors, not simply refin-

4

ing, extending, or adapting but transforming the narrative themes and techniques available to them. Their crude contemporaries and immediate predecessors, then, serve chiefly to dramatize the force and profound originality of the major novelists.[4]

But these crude materials also acquire from this perspective two kinds of related significance. First, they represent an essential stage for the eruption (if not the evolution) of the eighteenth-century novel, a set of forms (or at least formats) and possibilities that the major novelists could transcend, a necessarily inferior provocation to their genius. Second, and more specifically, these books are evidence of an emerging, crucial shift in the nature and purpose of narrative that affects and indeed promotes the appearance of the major novelists themselves. Minor eighteenth-century narratives point by their very features to a new sort of audience and a changing set of social circumstances surrounding the production and consumption of narrative literature.

Artistically insignificant, then, the forgotten fiction that precedes and surrounds the eighteenth-century masters has at least a sociological relevance for a genre whose emergence is inseparable from changing social conditions. During the early decades of the eighteenth century, certainly, there is a busy, expanding market for prose fiction, and that bookseller's product provokes in different ways, as the century continues, the works of Defoe, Richardson, Fielding, and other novelists: Defoe to serve or exploit some of the market's needs; Richardson to improve, refine, indeed exalt some of those needs; and Fielding to parody and then to transform some of them. What, then, was that market like? What sorts of needs did it serve? Did those needs represent something new for prose fiction? Is the presence of such needs a significant factor in the emergence of the novel in something like its modern form in the early eighteenth century?

To ask such questions and to grant a limited genetic importance to the minor fiction of the early eighteenth century should not obscure the simplified artificiality of our scheme. Then, as now, a variety of narrative formats and purposes competed for attention and served different audiences, and it is a mistake to think in terms of the clear dominance of one particular form of narrative. For example, as Ian Watt points out, the popularity of religious narrative continued unabated. By 1792, Bunyan's *Pilgrim's Progress* had gone through 160 editions, and religious and didactic works remained hugely popular throughout the century.[5] At the other end of narrative possibility, Sidney's *Arcadia* appeared in its fourteenth edition in 1725 and in the same year in a rewritten modern English form.[6] Popular religious allegory and aristocratic romance such as these books represent, however, were both giving way in the early years of the eighteenth century, or at least sharing the stage with a number of other narrative types—some just as traditional, others newer, some modified and modernized versions of romance and religious allegory.[7] To some extent, popular narrative in the early eighteenth century can be said to veer away from the extremes represented by religious allegory and aristocratic romance toward a center of secular factuality, although generalization of this sort is risky and needs immediate qualification. Obviously, Bunyan's enduring popularity stems from his grounding of Christian allegory in the felt experience of that rural working-class life he lived in all its difficulty.

What seems undeniable is that overt fictionality or artificiality ceased to be an attractive or profitable feature, at least in narratives that claimed to be current. In his bibliographic survey of prose narratives published in England from 1700 to 1739, W.H. McBurney found only one *new* English work deliberately labeled a romance. However improbable or conventionally fictional the events within a book might be, McBurney notes, booksellers favored descriptive titles that claimed factuality: history, memoirs, life, voyage (trip, travels, discovery), adventures, tale, letters, and account (journal, relation). Most such books seem patently fictional to a modern reader, and the ones labeled "novels" were really only shorter, often crudely simplified versions of the elaborate plots of romance.[8] For whatever cultural reasons, many readers seem to have wanted at least the claim of factuality attached to narrative.

In part and at times, this claim was valid; a good deal of narrative from the first half of the century has at least some documentary validity. Given the absence of modern newspapers and other information media, there was a traditional market for news of a sensational sort, notably the lives of criminals, including pirates and prostitutes. Pamphlets, broadsides, even topical ballads for spreading sensational news or rumors are as old as the hills, but the expansion of the English printing industry in the early eighteenth century and the accompanying growth of a reading public (whether cause or effect of the former) enabled more elaborate publication of such "news."[9] Following a practice stretching back to the late sixteenth century, short pamphlet accounts of sensational crimes and domestic violence were still popular in the early decades of the eighteenth, reflecting the perennial fascination of tabloid journalism. Three examples will illustrate not just the lurid attractions of these pamphlets but the journalistic particularity that is an important part of their appeal:

*An Account of a most Barbarous and Bloody Murther Committed on Sunday last, by Mr.James Smith . . . on the Body of one Mr Cuff . . . With an Account of how he mangled his Body in a most Barbarous manner, Cut off his Left Hand, and Stabb'd him in several places of the Body, leaving him Dead upon the place, with other particulars relating to the occasion of that Inhuman Action* (1703).

*The Tryal and Conviction of several Reputed Sodomites, before the Right Honourable the Lord Mayor, and Recorder of London, at Guild-Hall, the 20th Day of October, 1709.*

*The Cruel Mother. Being a strange and unheard-of Account of one Mrs. Elizabeth Cole, a Childs Coatmaker in the Minories, that threw her own Child into the Thames on Sunday Night last, a Girl of about Five Years of Age. With the manner how the poor Child begg'd of her Mother not to drown her. . . . Also, an Account of one Sarah Taylor a Maid-Servant, near Ratcliff-Cross, that Hang'd her self on Tuesday last at her Masters, for the Love of a Young Man* (1708).

Much of the material in such pamphlets came from more sober accounts of criminal trials at the Old Bailey, published in the Sessions Papers. The most popular and presumably authentic accounts of notorious criminals were the pamphlets issued by Paul Lorrain, the ordinary (chaplain) of Newgate prison from 1698 to 1719, whose office made him privy to the last, normally repentant, hours of the condemned. These pamphlets had an immediate appeal, issued as they were at eight in the morning following the execution.[10] *The Ordinary of Newgate's Account of the Life, Conversation, Birth and Education, of Thomas Ellis, and Mary Goddard. Who were Executed at Tyburn, on Wednesday, the Third of March, 1708. With the most Remarkable Passages of their whole Lives and Wicked Actions, from the time of their Birth, to their untimely Death; as also their Tryal, Examination, Conviction and Condemnation, at the Old-Bayly, their Behaviour in Newgate, their Confession, and True Dying-Speeches, at the Place of Execution* (1708) is a typical sample of Lorrain's apparently popular enterprise. Sensational and pious, circumstantial and evangelically generalized, such pamphlets exploited the traditional drama of sin, repentance, death, and salvation and intensified the appeal of that spectacle by local details, yesterday's events, and ordinary folk caught in the eternal struggle between good and evil.[11]

By 1730, according to F.W. Chandler, the popularity of such crude pamphlets had declined, giving way to more sophisticated criminal biographies (*Moll Flanders* is the most well-known example, but there were various lives of actual offenders like Jonathan Wild and Jack Sheppard) and to more elaborate collections of criminal biography, like the very popular *History of the Lives and Robberies of the Most Noted Highway-Men, Foot-Pads, House-Breakers, Shop-Lifts and Cheats of both Sexes in and about London and Westminster* (1713) by one Captain Alexander Smith.[12] As

Chandler pointed out long ago, much of this criminal "journalism" is rooted in traditional rogue stories, the local and sensational details supplemented or indeed guided by patterns inherited from the myth of the "trickster" figure and passed on through various subliterary and literary embodiments like Elizabethan ballads and chapbooks, Spanish picaresque fiction, and its French imitators such as Paul Scarron.[13]

And yet in spite of such sources, in spite of the perennial appeal of criminal heroes, it can be argued that the increasingly detailed and specific interest in criminal narrative in the late seventeenth and early eighteenth centuries is significant for the emergence of the novel. Perhaps the criminal increasingly represented an apt expression for many readers of certain feelings of isolation and marginality to which they could respond; perhaps the criminal's attractiveness lay in his or her subversive individuality, an exaggerated or simplified version of what many readers presumably admired or feared. Certainly, such possibilities are exploited in Defoe's pseudo-memoirs of Moll Flanders and Colonel Jacque and in his monumental compilation, *A General History of the Robberies and Murders of the most notorious Pyrates* (1724), where many of the buccaneers are hugely attractive, glamorous, and powerful figures, quasi-mythic embodiments of a ruthless acquisitive individualism.[14]

At the least, criminal narrative, from Paul Lorrain's brief pamphlets to Defoe's extended narratives, suggests a preoccupation with the patterning of individual lives, the connections between individuals and various forms of social environment. Criminal narrative tends to balance two contradictory explanations of behavior: the criminal, a prisoner of circumstance, has either been led astray, or has consciously and horribly deviated from moral norms. Such a life can highlight dramatically both the coercive force of circumstance and the individual's self-defining freedom. Although later fiction is more self-conscious about these issues, some version of such ideological ambiguity is at the heart of most novels.

Lennard Davis has recently underlined and complicated the significance of criminal narrative for the emergence of the novel. Following Michel Foucault's view, Davis sees the criminal, at the moment of execution or in the truthful rendering of his life in print, as a figure of what he calls the novel's "double discourse." This is to say, the novel "is a reaction against social repression" (depicting free and self-defining individuals who are of interest to narrative precisely because of their deviation from social norms), but the novel "also authorizes that very power of repression at the same time" (the criminal tells his story only because he is about to be executed or is repentant, or his story assumes its meaningful shape only in the moment of capitulation to a necessity greater than himself).[15]

Davis's "double discourse" is a provocative notion, pointing to other contradictions at the heart of the novel that are highlighted by criminal narrative. For example, the novelist in the early eighteenth century claims to tell the truth but in fact invents a lie to bring the reader to some sort of moral truth. Like the criminal, says Davis, the novelist is both an "example and dis-example"; the novelist's lies are like the criminal's transgressions, immoral preconditions to a moral end.[16]

To be sure, such critical paradoxes have their limitations, since the early eighteenth-century literary marketplace includes other sorts of popular narrative featuring less controversial characters. The traveler, like the criminal, is a figure of perennial interest and, like the early novelist, something of a liar. The loose mixture of fact, exaggeration, and plain invention in the enormous mass of travel literature from the seventeenth and early eighteenth centuries has been charted by various scholars, notably P.G. Adams.[17] The pirate, of course, is the traveler as criminal, and the popularity of Defoe's *History of the Pyrates*, a book that effectively establishes the buccaneer as a mythical figure who is still a part of the popular imagination, points to the force of the combination. Defoe surrounds his pirates with impressive documentation—biographical details, statistics, casualties, judicial proceedings, etc.—but the accounts of some of them, like "Blackbeard" (Captain Edward Teach), Bartho Roberts, and Captain Misson, serve purposes that run counter to historical realism. They provide, for example, exotic locales, stirring adventure, daring exploits, thrilling cruelties, and moral-satiric commentary on ordinary society. In short, pirate biography can be both real and fantastic; it is defined much of the time in Defoe's book by a combination of carefully documented actuality and an imaginative rendition of the extraordinary.[18]

Something like that combination animates other apparently fictional narratives featuring travelers who stay within the law. *Robinson Crusoe* (1719) is the most subtle and well known of such narratives, and it provoked various imitators throughout the eighteenth century. A convenient example is William Chetwood's *The Voyages, Dangerous Adventures, and imminent Escapes of Captain Richard Falconer: Containing the Laws, Customs, and Manners of the Indians of America . . . Intermix'd with the Voyages and Adventures of Thomas Randal, of Cork, Pilot: with his Shipwreck in the Baltick . . . Written by Himself, now alive* (1720).[19] Titles like this advertise the complementary satisfactions of travel adventure narrative: educational and informative, providing facts about other cultures gathered first-hand by an actual person, the book is also exciting and unusual, full of "imminent Escapes" and "Dangerous Adventures." Falconer's story is an adventure-travelogue, a series of near-disasters (shipwrecks, encounters with hostile natives and pirates, captivities, ingenious and daring escapes) and commercial transactions. Like *Robinson Crusoe*, on which it is clearly modeled, it features regular affirmations of providential design in the middle of all this tremendous variety of incident and locale, the religious moments acting as a sort of ideological check to the ingenuity, daring, and self-reliance of the heroes.

*The Voyages of Captain Falconer* is a clumsy book, clearly a hasty attempt to exploit the pattern of adventure stories just made popular by Defoe. But it is also an energetic, entertaining narrative, hardly as penetrating psychologically as Defoe's best work but less pious than *Crusoe* and immensely readable. Martin Green has seen in Defoe's adventure novels (and he could have included spirited imitations like *Falconer*) a rival tradition to what he calls the "novel of courtship" or domestic realism that came to dominate the English narrative tradition. Green proposes an elaborate cultural theory to account for the demotion of the adventure novel to the rank of popular or children's literature, the essence of which is that the adventure novel expresses rather too overtly a myth of European imperialism that literary intellectuals felt uncomfortable with, preferring an opposite "myth" of domestic order and an interiorized psychological-moral adventure in place of the crudely external travel adventure story.[20] Part of Green's thesis makes good sense if we look at one sequence in *Falconer*.

Near the end of his adventures, Falconer is separated from his shipmates while on shore getting wood and water. Captured by Indians, he is made a member of the tribe and given a wife. "But I had no great Stomach to my Bride, although a young, well-featur'd Woman, yet her Complexion did not like me." She proves lovable, however: "Loving and Courteous, and nothing like the rest of the Savage Crew, who were prone to all manner of Wickedness . . . I really began to love her and only wish'd she had been my Wife in the usual Forms." One day when Falconer wanders into a vale that his wife has warned him he must not enter, he is seized and bound to a stake by Indians from a rival tribe. In a scene depicted on the frontispiece of the first edition, these Indians "set fire to the Wood which enclos'd me" and dance around him in various grotesque and threatening postures as he looks up past palm trees and high mountains to a dark sky, confident and untrembling, an English St. Sebastian. A storm breaks and extinguishes the flames; another group of Indians appears and defeats Falconer's captors; his wife rushes in and frees him, but she is killed as they attempt to run away. In the end, Falconer escapes, taking an Indian who has been his friend and guide and who becomes his servant when they settle in England.

This sequence offers solid emotional and ideological satisfactions to willing readers: action in an exotic locale, a brave and resourceful hero who also trusts in providential pattern, the titillation of miscegenation with a racist solution in self-sacrificing love, suspense and pleasing dread in the presence of the savage non-European "other," and the eventual defeat and rejection of the exotic culture we have sampled. Unlike Swift's parodic reversal in *Gulliver's Travels*, travel adventure like this implicitly confirms the superiority of home; it validates the ordinary by allowing its readers to exhaust and indeed to domesticate the extraordinary. In its confused variety of scene and action, *Falconer* has little time for psychological development. The emphasis in travel adventure tends naturally away from seeking the depths of personality in experience to depicting breadth and extent of experience. Even Defoe's *Colonel Jacque*, a rather more specific and historical and less melodramatic narrative, promises its readers the same sort of pleasures as *Falconer*; witness its charming title page: *The History and Remarkable Life of the Truly Honourable Col. Jacque. . . . Who was Born a Gentleman, put 'Prentice to a Pick-Pocket, was Six and Twenty Years a Thief, and then Kidnapp'd to Virginia. Came back a Merchant, married four Wives, and five of them prov'd Whores; went into the Wars, behav'd bravely, got Preferment, was made Colonel of a Regiment, came over, and fled with the Chevalier, and is now abroad, compleating a Life of Wonders, and resolves to dye a General* (1722).

A review of the English fiction that survives from 1700 to 1739 yields only a few examples of such extended and unified travel adventure narratives.[21] Variety of scene and action was, however, an advertised feature of more traditional anthologies of shorter narratives. Charles Gildon's *The Golden Spy: or, A Political Journal of the British Nights Entertainments of War and Peace, and Love and Politicks: Wherein are laid open, The Secret Miraculous Power and Progress of Gold, in the Courts of Europe. Intermix'd with Delightful Intrigues, Memoirs, Tales, and Adventures Serious and Comical* (1709) initiates a narrative tradition of using an inanimate object to tell a story.[22] But as the title page makes clear, these stories have more in common with Chaucer or Boccaccio than Defoe. The "golden spy" is a French gold coin (a *louis d'or*) who was part of Jove's golden shower in the rape of Danae, is now in the author's purse, and relates all the scandalous events he has seen. Various other coins, including an English guinea, take part in telling lascivious satirical tales, mostly of comic adultery and other sexual escapades. Supervising these rough-and-ready entertainments is a satiric leveling and comic reduction of rank and pretense. The narrator asks the golden spy for news of "the *Camp* and the *Court*, which were places I had but little acquaintance with." The coin invokes the comic inevitability of the ordinary, a theme repeated in many of the stories:

> You must not (replied he) expect to find Princes and Great Men such Gods as their Flatterers and Idolaters make 'em, or so exalted in Wisdom and Virtue as in Riches or Degree. Alas! their Failings and Follies, as well as Vices, are as numerous as those of other Men: Nay, I who have been admitted into their closets, have been Witness of such Transactions as the meanest of their Subjects would have blush'd at. These Demi-gods, whom some Men reverence as things of a superior nature in many particulars, in all Ages, have discover'd themselves to be much less than Men. (pp. 31– 32)

The old satiric attitude that all men, seen up close, are morally equal can also point to a newer interest in the ordinary or the domestic or the grossly material and biological as the only valid categories of experience. At first glance, this newer domestic or reductive realism is more prominent in Gildon's other narrative anthology, *The Post-Man Robb'd of his Mail: or, the Packet broke open* (1719).[23] The author-editor, Sir Roger de Whimsey, echoes Addison and Steele's Sir Roger de Coverley and claims in his preface to follow in their wake: "I find most Readers are of my Mind, and love not to dwell long on any thing. This gave Success to the *Tatlers*, the *Spectators*, the *Lay-Monk*, and the like, which are a Sort of Epistles to the Publick, such as I now present, tho' not in the same Form." The book consists of commentary on letters stolen by the members of the club, a series of essayistic, generalized discussions of set satirical situations illustrating moral topics such as the lewdness of women, the avarice of old men, the cupidity of lawyers, the intellectual pride of irreligious wits, and so on. Behind their jocular pretense to journalistic veracity, Gildon's energetic collections exemplify an older, less intense, less specific mode of narration, overtly committed to moral and satiric patterns and taking pleasure in the priority of exemplary moral types over particular personages. Popular as this mode of narration remained (it is, of course, preserved in novelists like Fielding), its essayistic moral manner is less prominent in the popular market of the time than the amatory novella, a much more involving and less sophisticated sort of narrative.

In terms of numbers, at least, the market for fiction in the first forty years or so of the eighteenth century was clearly dominated by amatory fiction, narratives (mostly short, novella length) often subtitled histories or secret histories or memoirs, sometimes original English productions, often translations of foreign authors. "A small tale, generally of love," is

Johnson's definition of "novel" in his *Dictionary of the English Language* (1755), and he was thinking of the short amatory narratives that seem to have replaced as main purveyors of this theme the enormous and elaborate French heroic romances of the seventeenth century. The latter had enjoyed a considerable vogue in the late seventeenth century, but even then their English translators felt it necessary to defend them against "the charge of unreality."[24] Indeed, a recurring theme in various early eighteenth-century comments on fiction is the need for rejecting an unreal artificiality, represented by just these French romances, and for developing a native truthful simplicity and naturalness.[25]

In the preface to her *Secret History of Queen Zarah and the Zarazians* (1705), Mary Manley notes that the French romances have been replaced by books such as "the little Histories" she offers for sale. The virtue of such "histories," she says, lies essentially in eliminating those features of the romances that have "given a distaste to persons of good sense," their "prodigious length . . . the mixture of so many extraordinary adventures, and the great number of actors that appear on the stage, and the likeness which is so little managed."[26] Manley goes on to recommend a moderate realism, involving consistent and probable characters with "passions, virtues, or vices, which resemble humanity" and a moral neutrality in which the author "ought neither to praise nor blame those he speaks of . . . contented with exposing the actions, leaving an entire liberty to the reader to judge as he pleases" (pp. 24, 25).

Manley's preface is not entirely consistent, for she also emphasizes two sorts of authorial manipulation. First, she tends to stress the reader's involvement when the author achieves characters and actions that are familiar. The result is a "curiosity and a certain impatient desire to see the end of the accidents, the reading of which causes an exquisite pleasure when they are nicely handled" (p. 24). At the same time, Manley pays lip service throughout to conventional eighteenth-century didactic notions, and she concludes her preface by reaffirming her commitment to recommend virtue and discourage vice. But the reader she evokes is caught up in events and personalities, instructed by a powerful involvement in the narrative.

> 'Tis an indispensable necessity to end a story to satisfy the
> disquiets of the reader, who is engaged to the fortunes of those
> people whose adventures are described to him; 'tis depriving him
> of a most delicate pleasure when he is hindered from seeing the
> event of an intrigue which has caused some emotion in him,
> whose discovery he expects, be it either happy or unhappy. The

chief end of History is to instruct and inspire into men the love of
virtue and abhorrence of vice by the examples proposed to them;
therefore the conclusion of a story ought to have some tract of
morality which may engage virtue. Those people who have a
more refined virtue are not always the most happy, but yet their
misfortunes excite the readers' pity and affects them. Although
vice be not always punished, yet 'tis described with reasons which
shew its deformity and make it enough known to be worthy of
nothing but chastisements.   (pp. 26–27)

This passage deserves quotation because, in spite of Manley's attempt to
voice a modest moral realism, she points to the central and significant
confusion behind a good deal of the amatory fiction of the early eighteenth
century. The reader's excited participation ("pleasure" is Manley's recurrent term) is in fact what matters for her in such fiction; didactic clarity is
subordinated in practice to the emotional needs of the reader, who learns
about virtue and vice chiefly by inspiration and engagement rather than
"moral reflections, maxims, and sentences"—which are "more proper in
discourses for instructions than in Historical Novels" (p. 26). In the fiction
Manley and others actually wrote, the traditional literary ideal of moral
instruction shifts strongly away from a combination of edifying scene and
moralizing discourse toward a proto-sentimentalism that is in practice as
morally confused as it is emotionally intense and ideologically coherent.
By and large, the popular amatory novella quickly disregards its claims to
domestic moral realism and constructs a world of sexual fantasy and
thrilling moral melodrama, a world where persecuted female innocence is
exploited by male corruption, sexual and financial. As we shall see, there
are a few exceptions, witty and well-shaped moral tales, but they prove the
popular rule.

Manley's preface is totally inconsistent in its defense of sense, clarity,
and probability, for *Queen Zarah*'s characters are monsters of vice, their
language rhetorically swollen, and the scenes and actions wildly exaggerated. In fact, the book is not a collection of "little Histories" but a
*chronique scandaleuse* attacking Sarah, Duchess of Marlborough. As a
narrative format, the scandal chronicle has a long, dishonorable ped-
igree.[27] Collections of rumor, libel, and scandal about prominent people,
these "secret histories" began to be especially popular in England during
the late seventeenth century. Manley achieved special notoriety and tremendous popularity a few years after *Queen Zarah* with *Secret Memoirs
and Manners of several Persons of Quality, of Both Sexes from the New
Atalantis, an Island in the Mediterranean* (1709).[28]

Like *Queen Zarah, The New Atalantis* is a collection of scurrilous, often nearly pornographic incidents involving Whig nobles and politicians, notably the Duke and Duchess of Marlborough. The stories have some small basis in fact, and the book was designed as Tory propaganda to undermine public confidence in the Whig ministry, which fell from power in 1710. Manley's enormous success is easy enough to explain: her scandals were mostly sexual (usually false or grotesquely exaggerated), and she had a talent for vividly rendering what the eighteenth century often called "warm scenes." Like other such narratives, *The New Atalantis* has an elaborate moral structure and claims to be an outraged satiric attack on the corruption of the times. It is actually a lubriciously delighted version of life at the English court from the Restoration to the early years of the reign of Queen Anne. Manley begins Part II by calling her book a satire "on different Subjects, Tales, Stories, and Characters of Invention, after the Manner of Lucian, who copy'd from Varro." For a modern reader, the best parts of the book are precisely the satiric ones, those recurring energetic denunciations that add up to a lively, often grotesque panorama of intrigue, lust, betrayal, and even crime. *The New Atalantis* was reprinted several times until 1736, long after its scandals had faded, suggesting that Manley's real achievement was the effective imagining of a mythical world of corruption and immorality in which readers found satisfactions that were neither satiric nor political.

One incident from the book will serve as an example of how Manley's gossip is accommodated to the imaginative world of the melodramatic amatory novella. Near the end, we are introduced to Lady Diana, married to the old and rich Conde de Bedamore but desired by Don Tomasio Rodriquez (the "Key" to the book identifies these characters as Lady Diana Cecil, Lord Scudamore, and Lord Coningsby). Manley's description of Lady Diana is a set piece, an almost abstract and totally formulaic evocation of female desire.

> Her Person lovely, as the most lovely Imagination could form it.
> The darting Lustre of her Eyes, were like the Lightnings Flash, so
> awful and so piercing. But having cast the dazling Death, they
> roul'd into a rest from Fire, and gave the Gazers an Alternative of
> pleasing Pain, with leave to wonder at their various Beauty, for
> Languishments would take their turn, and show the Mine of Love
> within. A mine which threw abroad such Sparkles of desire, as
> spoke the amorous Temper of the Fair: She was the Queen of Love
> herself, in all her Attributes! so bright, so soft, so warming, so
> enviting, so envited, as if she languish'd for a part of that Delight,

which her Beauties must necessarily inspire into the Hearts of her Beholders.[29]

Such writing is deliberately indifferent to anything but the reader's capacity for erotic fantasy; indeed, it presupposes an eager reader able to construct a picture of desire from this formulaic sketch. The "power of love" (which was Manley's title for a collection of amatory novellas she published in 1720) is irresistible, and this outline of the signs and effects of desire prepares readers for the inevitable warm scene between Diana and Don Tomasio. He, naturally, is also married, but "no sooner did he see the Day of Madame de Bedamore's Eyes; but he thought to himself he had hitherto wander'd in unaccountable Darkness!" (p. 221).

Since the Conde de Bedamore has agreed to rebuild his country house to suit his wife's continental taste, Tomasio offers part of his house to the couple, and to Diana he offers his passion. She resists, and resolves not to see him. He feigns departure, but returns on a day when her husband is away and finds Diana in the garden. What follows is Manley's recurrent erotic moment, the soft-core rape-seduction extravaganza that was her signature as a popular narrator.

> It was the Evening of an excessive hot Day, she got into a shade of Orange Flowers and Jessamine, the Blossoms that were fallen cover'd all beneath with a profusion of Sweets. A Canal runs by, which made that retreat delightful as 'twas fragrant. Diana, full of the uneasiness of Mind that Love occasion'd, threw her self under the pleasing Canopy, apprehensive of no Acteon to invade with forbidden Curiosity, her as numerous perfect Beauties, as had the Goddess. Supinely laid on that repose of Sweets, the dazling Lustre of her Bosom stood reveal'd, her polish'd Limbs all careless and extended show'd the Artful Work of Nature. . . . [Tomasio] vow'd he wou'd not make himself possessor of one Charm without her willing leave; he sighed, he look'd with dying! wishing! Soft-regards! The lovely she grew calm and tender! The Rhetorick of one belov'd, his strange bewitching Force; she suffer'd all the glowing pressures of his roving Hand; that Hand, which with a Luxury of Joy, wander'd through all the rich Meanders of her Bosom; she suffer'd him to drink her dazling naked Beauties at his Eyes! to gaze! to burn! to press her with unbounded Rapture! taking by intervals a thousand eager short-breath'd Kisses. Whilst Diana, lull'd by the enchanting Poison Love had diffus'd throughout her form, lay still, and charm'd as he!—she thought no more!—she could not think!—let Love and

16

Nature plead the weighty Cause!—let them excuse the beautous Frailty!—Diana was become a Votary to Venus!—obedient to the Dictates of the Goddess. (pp. 227–29)

Tomasio's wife discovers them *in flagrante* and vows to reveal all, and at last Tomasio returns to her, leaving Diana to the forgiveness of her husband. This resolution is quite tame. Many of Manley's swollen anecdotes are much more violent and melodramatic, involving outright rape, incest, fake marriages, and suicide. But sensational violence is always subordinate to voyeurism, to pseudo-elegant evocation of sexual fantasy like the one above. *The New Atalantis* is necessarily indifferent to narrative values such as individuality and depth of characterization, complexity of scene and plot, and linguistic self-consciousness. Characters and narrator inhabit without embarrassment a stylized world of moral and emotional simplicity, indeed a narrative world in which the chief attraction is the utterly predictable repetition of character, scene, and language.

That there is always a large and eager audience for formula fiction of this sort is evident from the career of Eliza Haywood, Manley's successor in the 1720s as the chief purveyor of sensational amatory fiction. Haywood produced a highly successful imitation of Manley's secret history in her *Memoirs of a Certain Island Adjacent to the Kingdom of Utopia* (1725). The satiric occasion for the book's denunciations of the rich and powerful was the so-called "South-Sea Bubble" financial disaster of 1722, but the book's main appeal was the near-pornographic intensity and lurid melodrama of its recurring sexual scenes. Unlike Manley, Haywood was not a political writer, and her tremendous output of popular narrative during the 1720s repeats tirelessly the formulas of the amatory novella, occasionally extended to novel length (several hundred pages).

Haywood began her career in 1719–20 with *Love in Excess; or, the Fatal Enquiry,* a novel in three parts, a great success that reached a seventh edition in 1732. During the decade that followed she published some thirty-eight original works, translated a number of French novellas, and wrote three plays.[30] In stories such as *Idalia: or, the Unfortunate Mistress* (1723), *Lasselia; or, the Self-Abandon'd* (1723), *The Injur'd Husband: or, the Mistaken Resentment* (1723), *The Fatal Secret; or, Constancy in Distress* (1724), *The Force of Nature: or, the Lucky Disappointment* (1725), *The Distress'd Orphan; or, Love in a Mad House* (1726), *Philidore and Placentia: or, L'Amour trop Delicat* (1727), and *Love-Letters on All Occasions Lately passed between Persons of Distinction* (1730), Haywood rehearsed with unfailing energy and only slight variations the popular formula promised in her titles: a format highlighting genteel, euphemistic but effectively pornographic descriptions of female passion and male lust, and featuring most of the time aristocratic elegance and corruption.[31] Typically, a young girl is pursued by a treacherous suitor in a complicated social or moral situation that sometimes includes incest as well as adultery. Seduction or outright rape is standard, and terrible consequences invariably follow, even violent death and sometimes grim revenge on the seducer. At the center of all this operatic melodrama is the "power of love," an irresistible but, for women, a destructive urge whose thrilling, forbidden intensities and pathetically satisfying tragic aftermath Haywood's stories were designed to elaborate. A prefatory poem in her 1732 collected *Secret Histories, Novels and Poems* identifies her methods and certifies her success: "Persuasion waits on all your bright Designs,/And when you point the Varying Soul Inclines:/See! Love and Friendship, the fair Theme inspires,/We glow with Zeal, we melt in soft Desires!"

A scene like this one from her first novel, *Love in Excess*, is entirely representative of her style and method and recalls the scene I have quoted from *The New Atalantis*. The virginal heroine, Melliora, is asleep: her "Gown and the rest of her Garments were white, all ungirt, and loosely flowing, discover'd a Thousand Beauties, which modish Formalities conceal." Melliora dreams of her guardian (to whom she was entrusted by her dying father), the handsome Count D'Elmont, and he enters to steal a chaste goodnight kiss. But the scene erupts with Haywoodian eroticism complicated by the moral melodrama of near-incest. D'Elmont hesitates as he gazes on the luscious but innocent Melliora; he thinks "it pity even to wake her, but more to wrong such Innocence." But as he stoops to her, she embraces him as part of her dream, and we are off:

> He tore open his Waistcoat, and joyn'd his panting Breast to hers, with such a Tumultuous Eagerness! Seiz'd her with such a Rapidity of Transported hope Crown'd Passion, as immediately wak'd her from an imaginary Felicity, to the Approaches of a Solid one. Where have I been? (said she, just opening her Eyes) where am I?—(And then coming more perfectly to her self) Heaven! What's this?—I am D'Elmont (Cry'd the O'erjoy'd Count) the happy D'Elmont! Melliora's, the Charming Melliora's D'Elmont! O, all ye Saints, (Resum'd the surpriz'd Trembling fair) ye Ministring Angels! Whose Business 'tis to guard the Innocent! Protect and Shield my Virtue! . . . Come, come no more Reluctance (Continu'd he, gathering Kisses from her soft Snowy Breast at every Word). Damp not the fires thou hast rais'd with seeming Coiness! I know thou art mine! All mine! And thus I—

Yet think (said she Interrupting him, and Strugling in his Arms)
think what 'tis you would do, nor for a Moments Joy, hazard your
Peace for Ever. By Heaven, cry'd he: I will this Night be Master of
my Wishes, no matter what to Morrow may bring forth.[32]

The simple structural principle in *Love in Excess* is delayed rape, a
protracted eroticism or extended foreplay intensified by the crudest sort of
moral melodrama. But one detail in this scene is especially revealing.
Melliora finds to her confusion no clear distinction between dream and
reality; in fact, the latter is even more compelling and confusing for her
than the former. Haywood's novels of the 1720s are virtually unreadable
nowadays, but they are an important expression of a vigorously insistent
sort of the crisis of subjectivity that becomes in due course the central
theme of much serious fiction. Women in eighteenth-century popular
fiction, as Ruth Perry observes, are "imprisoned, seduced, abducted, raped,
abandoned, and their passively outraged responses to these developments
are carefully detailed." By and large, Perry suggests, the only act granted
women in this fiction is self-examination, bewildered observation of their
own psychological instability and social marginality.[33] Even (or perhaps
especially) in Haywood's formula fiction, women are symbolic figures
who enact in melodramatic fashion the marginal status and limited basis
of female identity that many eighteenth-century readers seem to have
found truthful and moving (or perhaps simply reassuring). The popularity
of formula fiction like Haywood's, in short, points to a definition of
psychosexual differences that is of profound importance in the development of the novel with its particular notions of personality. Women in the
psychological novel that develops eventually, as Myra Jehlen shrewdly
proposes, "define themselves and have power" only in the "interior life,"
and androgyny becomes "a male trait enabling men to act from their male
side and feel from their female side."[34]

However pathetically helpless she made her heroines, of course, Haywood herself seems to have been an independent, successful writer, and
there is an implicit feminist awareness in her works that flares out occasionally: in *The British Recluse* (1722), two women find they have been
violated by the same man and resolve to live together in the country,
"happy in the real friendship of each other."[35] But even a plot resolution
like this bears out Jehlen's point that psychological interiority is *the*
defining female trait in such fiction, a source of strength but simultaneously a capitulation to and affirmation of the division of psychosocial
reality along the patriarchal lines that generate in the first place the
harrowing plots of female formula fiction.

Contemplative rejection of the male world rather than defiance of it, then—self-absorption and examination as the defining and compensatory female acts—is what Haywood dramatizes here and makes explicit in, for example, the dedication to *The Fatal Secret* (1724). This is a defiant sort of apology for the subject matter of the novel that makes a virtue of her limitations: "But as I am a Woman, and consequently depriv'd of those Advantages of Education which the other Sex enjoy, I cannot so far flatter my Desires, as to imagine it in my Power to soar to any Subject higher than that which Nature is not negligent to teach us." To write about love, she continues, "requires no Aids of Learning, no general Conversation, no Application; a shady Grove and purling Stream are all Things that's necessary to give us an Idea of the tender Passion." But this sleep of reason that female authors like Haywood allow to possess them produces monsters, male and female, whose active/passive sadomasochistic intertwinings look forward to Richardson's intense dramatization of a similar relationship in *Clarissa*.

Consider in this regard Haywood's *The Mercenary Lover: or, The Unfortunate Heiresses. Being a True, Secret History of a City Amour* (1726). The story looks interesting at first glance for its nod to local realism, its attention to money as well as love. Clitander, a "Trader" but a "Master of Accomplishments rare to be found in a Man of his Station," marries a rich country heiress, Miranda.[36] Quickly tiring of her and anxious to secure the other half of the family fortune, which her sister holds, he sets out to seduce Althea, plying her with "certain gay Treatises which insensibly melt down the Soul, and make it fit for amorous Impressions, such as the Works of *Ovid*, the late celebrated *Rochester*, and many other of more modern Date" (p. 17). Ludicrous enough, such a strategy for seduction points to an interesting contradiction in the standard amatory plot. Otherwise intelligent female characters like Althea are manipulated by seducers like Clitander, who exploit their helpless ignorance of psychosexual fundamentals obvious, one would think, to anyone past puberty. When female passion explodes, it is mysterious and irresistible, grounded in this disabling female ignorance. Haywood defers to Althea's inexpressible confusion:

> But with what Words is it possible to represent the mingled
> Passions of *Althea's* Soul, now perfectly instructed in his
> Meaning; Fear, Shame, and Wonder combating with the softer
> Inclinations, made such a wild Confusion in her Mind, that as she
> was about to utter the Dictates of the one, the other rose with
> contradicting Force, and stop'd the Accents e're she cou'd form

them into Speech; in broken Sentences she sometimes seem'd to
favour, then to discourage his Attempts, but all dissolv'd and
melted down by that superior Passion, of which herself till now
was ignorant she had entertain'd, never had Courage to repel the
growing Boldness, with which he every Moment encroach'd upon
her Modesty . . . *Action* was now his Business, and in this Hury of
her Spirits, all unprepared, incapable of Defence, half yielding,
half reluctant, and scarce sensible of what she suffer'd, he bore
her trembling to the Bed, and perpetrated the cruel Purpose he
had long since contriv'd.  (pp. 23–24)

Eventually, Clitander poisons Althea, who dies in agonies physical and
spiritual, "Ravings so horrible and shocking, that they imprinted a Terror
on the Minds of those present, which for a great while they were not able to
wear off" (p. 54).

*The Mercenary Lover* is a painful book to read, as melodramatic as
anything Haywood wrote but convincing as an image of female hope-
lessness in the face of male power and guile. Popular eighteenth-century
female fantasy seems drawn to elaborated self-hatred and destruction,
fascinated evocations of rape and murder. Although happy endings and
imposed moral symmetries are often employed to negate the pain of such
imagining, Haywood's artless dreaming of what "Nature is not negligent
to teach" reveals a sort of cartoon version of women's psychological
complicity in their double oppression: exploited sexually and econom-
ically by men, and betrayed into that exploitation by their own irresistible,
wayward sexuality.[37]

Haywood's successful formula, then, is not simply a careless, thrilling
blend of sex and violence; rather, it is thrilling precisely because it is a
balance of erotic effects and psychological consolations with profound
cultural implications. This conclusion is reinforced by brief consideration
of some representative examples of similar amatory tales that appeared
during the period of her great popularity. Some are variations from the
Haywoodian norm that seem to have been relative failures. Others conform more exactly to the pattern and were slightly more successful.

The audience for the amatory novella seems not to have been attracted
by the bluntly sensational brutality that sold so well in some criminal
biographies. A collection of uncompromisingly brutal stories, *Lovers
Tales: In Several New Surprising and Diverting Stories* (1722), apparently
did not reach a second edition, in spite of what is to a modern view a fairly
concise and realistic presentation and a refreshing lack of moral posturing:
"The relations are concise, and 'tis hoped will prove diverting to the

Reader, which is the only Aim of the Author."[38] Some of these are rough-and-tumble stories, fairly free of the pathetic, full of violence and sex of a straightforward, traditional kind. In the first of them, for example, a rich old man marries a young girl. She acquires a lover, her husband's nephew, who not only tricks the old man but manages to inherit his fortune. Similar in its rough cuckold baiting is "The Pleasant Adventure of the Doctor and the Scholar, about the Art of making Love," in which the clerk receives lessons on seduction from the doctor. The woman on whom this quick scholar practices the art turns out to be the doctor's wife. The old doctor is not only cuckolded but beaten and bound in chains. Perhaps all this is too close to the simple amorality of the folk-tale for the pseudo-sophisticated audience that bought Haywood's hugely moralistic love tragedies.

Haywood's persecuted maiden is nowhere in sight in the next story, "The Cruel Revenge of a young Lady on a Gentleman who promised her Marriage, but deceiv'd her." Hector, a young Venetian nobleman, promises Leonice that he will marry her and is, on the strength of this, admitted to her bed. After a time, Hector reconsiders; it is soon announced that he is to marry Clelia, a lady of suitable wealth and position. Leonice persuades Hector to visit her again, drugs him, ties him up, and then dismembers him with ritualistic cries, a female avenging angel of a horrible sort:

> Infamous Man, said she, it is now that at the Peril of my own Life
> I come to revenge the Affront thou hast done me. Thou hast
> ravished from me my Honour, and I will take from thee thy
> Life. . . . I will begin thy Punishment with that deceitful Tongue,
> which hath been one of the first Instruments of my Disgrace. No
> sooner had she pronounced these words, but she took a Razor and
> slit his Tongue in the middle.   (pp. 42–43)

She then pulls out his eyes, cuts off his genitals, and stabs him in the heart. To complete the story, she takes poison and denounces Hector with her dying breath before the Venetian court.

Having read Haywood, we know that this spectacular vengeance violates the central moral precept of the formula story. Leonice begins as a pragmatist who agrees to marriage and, worse, to premarital sex before she loves Hector. Only after she gives herself to Hector does she come to love him, which may be psychologically accurate but is past forgiveness within the ideology of the amatory novella. The ritual murder, obviously, is a further violation, offending as much by its shocking aggressiveness as by its extravagance. Heroines may kill seducers occasionally, but only by an involuntary reflex when fate provides the circumstances.

22

This collection looks like an uncertain attempt to please a public taste that in 1722 could confer enormous success on both *Love in Excess* and *Moll Flanders*. The sensationally specific journalistic titles and the gory crimes depicted point to an attempted compromise between the novella and the criminal pamphlet or novel. But the brutality must have been excessive for the audience that bought love tales. As the third decade of the century wore on, Haywood's dominance continued; her amazing production held steadily until about 1727, and her influence and popularity were plain until well after that.[39] Two anonymous novellas from the late 1720s will serve to illustrate the persistence of her formula and, by comparison, the special skill with which she exploited it.

All of the moral simplifications of the Haywoodian tale are packed into a novella short enough to be an epitome of the fable of endangered innocence, *The Treacherous Confident; or, Fortune's Change* (1728). Allegorical simplicity and moral melodrama are the main values here, as innocence is threatened and rescued miraculously within twenty-two pages. We are in Castile, where Syphon, an eminent nobleman, has retired to the country with his only daughter, Almiana. She is a paragon of "Virtue, Sense and Beauty," and is in love with Thetes, himself a "generally belov'd and admir'd" noble youth now in exile owing to the king's unjust displeasure with him. Almiana continues to love and even glories in misfortune, "to make her Love the more apparently Great and Constant; and resolv'd to persevere in her Affection, or wait the Event of Time, and sink with her Love."[40] Further afflictions and a specific adversary are provided in the person of Scomes, a treacherous courtier who petitions the king for Almiana's hand. She declares that she loves Thetes, and Scomes resolves to murder Thetes. The latter is saved when he deviates from his route to save a lady from a ravisher. This lady turns out to be the king's niece. The narrator pauses to remind us of the moral implications of these fortunate accidents: "How omnipotent is the Preservation of the Almighty Being! which protects the Innocent and Meritorious from the Snares of the Envious and Cruel" (p. 16). Scomes does shoot a traveler he mistakes for Thetes and announces his death to Almiana and her father. Then Thetes arrives, and the divine purpose in all this is evident. Syphon draws the tale to a close with still another reminder of the unique perfection and distinction of the match: not just a happy marriage but the triumph of virtue. "Since the Gods have thus countenanced the Loves of this joyful Pair! and have thus declar'd themselves instrumental in preserving this noble youth! to the Joy of us all, and the Rescue of my Daughter's Life: Let us give 'em Thanks, and join the Couple, which is miraculously distinguish'd to be their Will" (p. 22).

Such transparent simplicity is foreign to Haywood's novels, and this is a simple-minded provincial imitation. By her standards, the heroine's distress is too artificial and open to charges of superficiality because it is so deliberate and articulate. The quasi-physiological details of passionate awakening are missing. The plot lacks intricacy; there are no complications and subplots. The style is too clear and simple, lacking those swellings of anguish, pain, and confused desire that should accompany love and provide sexual excitement. In other words, this novella has a moral simplicity and bare unreality foreign to Haywood's tangled narratives, where endless moral complication and elaborate fantasy are the rule.

But even exaggeration can be overdone. Using Haywood's novels as a norm, we can see that an extravagant novella like *The Forced Virgin; or, the Unnatural Mother* (1730) goes too far perhaps. Written in a style even more tumid than Haywood's, it describes a sexual encounter and an ultimate disaster that make Haywood's big scenes look decorous and staid. Here, for example, is the heroine, Lominia, kidnaped out of the arms of her lover, Arastes, by the minions of his spurned rival, Lysanor. She is taken to a secret cave where Lysanor awaits her.

Thus they dragg'd the beautiful Innocent in; forcing her thro' many dark Turnings to a Room, in Appearance, more like a Palace, than a Place of so villainous a Retreat; where she again saw, seated on a Purple Couch, the hated Lysanor. . . . Lysanor, impatient of Delay, already prepared for the direful Act, came hasty in; from forth his burning Orbs the destructive Light'ning flew;—His whole Frame shook with boiling Joy; Lust, not Love, sway'd his Soul, and nothing less than Lominia's Ruin possessed his Brain. The Door at his first Entrance he secured, when with a sudden Turn he seized the trembling Maid;—The beautous Fair, press'd in his rough and harden'd Arms, by more than manly Force he bore with Pleasure to his stately Bed: in vain she prayed, his Lust had shut his Ears to such Intreaties.—In vain she strove to stay his raging Flames; regard to her Virtue, or Fear of future Punishment, could make no room for a Moment's Delay; he had her now in full Possession, and was resolved to use the wished-for Hour; with one Hand intangled in her Hair, he held the Maiden down; while the other furthered him to compleat his hellish Purpose. . . . "Nor Heaven nor Hell, (cry'd he) shall share my Joy, or participate with me in my good Fortune.—I'll make one continual Riot of the much-desired Feast, nor shall fear of any Punishment rob my swelling Love.—My Soul's on the Wing! O

Enjoyment! unable for Expression,—I melt,—I die,—I live,—I feel
your Charms; the balmy Bliss revives my dropping Soul, and I'm
all Ecstacy!"[41]

This passage has a ponderousness missing in Haywood's lubricious cadences. "In full possession" and other similar phrases are almost clinical
descriptions when we recall Haywood's breathless euphemisms. The picture evoked by the foaming assailant holding Lominia down with one
hand in her hair, "while the other furthered him to compleat his hellish
Purpose," has a crude graphic directness she never allows herself. Moreover, there is an unequivocal violence about this rape that she carefully
avoids, preferring seducers who are ambiguously attractive, constructed
to encourage the participation and identification that are the key values of
formula fiction. Lominia's distress lacks the erotic subtlety Haywood
evokes in the cornered maiden; there is no reciprocal and tangled complication of masculine force and reluctant feminine desire. There is too
much simple terror here for the special kind of pity Haywood delivered.

The rest of the plot seems, as well, an unsuccessful variant of stock
tragedy. Lominia escapes but soon grows pregnant from "Lysanor's filthy
embraces." She has already shown her capacity for action by stabbing
Lysanor with his own knife just as he finishes raping her. She now resolves
to abort and does. Such strength of purpose is a bad sign. Heroines usually
do abort ill-begotten babes but because of involuntary agitation. Lominia
seeks the abortion actively and, without actually submitting to a medical
operation, causes it—wills it we are assured. There follows a series of
complications, at the end of which Lominia kills her child, fathered she
thinks by Lysanor (but actually by Arastes). About to be tried for this
crime, she kills herself.[42] All these details are merely horrible rather than
pathetic; the author has miscalculated and allowed his heroine to go past
distress into criminal insanity. As the Haywoodian novella makes clear, it
is quite correct to have the heroine possessed by mysterious impulses, but
these should render her passive and helpless. In *The Forced Virgin* the
standard combination of sex and violence is unbalanced, tilted toward an
unacceptable explicitness and aggressiveness.

There can be little doubt that Haywood's blend of these ingredients was
the most popular recipe. Even after her vogue was past, we can see a clear
attempt to market the same confection in an elaborately presented and
expensive book published in 1732, *The Happy Unfortunate: or, the Female Page* by Elizabeth Boyd.[43] This book concerns not one but a series of
unhappy heroines, tied together by simple narrative links that lead to
endless interwoven complications and relationships between their vari-

ous stories. But such variety is superficial. The stories are all the same; the masculine world makes every woman's story tragic, and Boyd uncovers the expected facts relentlessly, with no hesitation or embarrassment at the repetition.

The central female character is Amanda, who is posing as a page (Florio) in the Duke Bellfond's household. In this sort of formula fiction, country houses burst at the seams with amorous intrigue and hiss with illicit desires; this book is clearly no exception. Amanda-Florio is in love with the Duke but is loved by the Duchess and her maid. The Duke has come to the country in order to pursue still another lady, Amira, whose tragic story is the first of several we are told. Although betrothed to a rich old man who died and left her his fortune, Amira had been in love all along with Marcus La-Motte, declared unsuitable by her father, who preferred the avaricious Zemo. In what reads almost like a parody of Haywood's overheated style, we hear how Zemo parted the lovers just as they were to marry:

> Zemo, observant, watch'd the cautious Lovers, and on the very Day assign'd for Hymen, parted them, far [sic] obliging La-Motte to hasty leave the Shore; the Hour unnotic'd, nor a Cause declar'd, nor ever made La-Motte the Cyprian Isle [the setting is Cyprus], whilst three long Annals roll'd their yearly Circuit, the Time he found Amira at the Duke's.  (p. 90)

Meanwhile, the Duke seems especially friendly to the young page, and Amanda-Florio is set ablaze by his seemingly innocent intimacies. He bids the page lie with him that night for warmth and there reveals his knowledge of Amanda's identity. Readers are invited to imagine the specific erotic turbulence of a situation rendered in very general terms: "Let those who know a fierce unbounded Passion, smothered by Awe, Respect and Modesty, a long, long Term, and but imagin'd found, judge of her Thoughts" (p. 48). Repression of and extended resistance to desire are the prerequisites for intensity, and Amanda runs away the next day, pursued by the Duke (who surrenders Amira—remember her?—to La-Motte). Bellfond plies Amanda with sophistical arguments for free love as opposed to sordid marriage, but she hesitates virtuously, clinging to a purer vision of "the Nuptial State" as "the State of Angels" (as she calls it later in this long novel when she is still unmarried). A sort of rescue from these torments comes when Bellfond's mistress—by whom he has two sons— dies, and he sails off to find forgetfulness. Amanda retires to the country with her brother Felix and his new bride, Elaira. Then Luvania comes along and tells them the most involved and incredible of all the female tragedies in the book.

Predictably, Luvania has been married at fourteen to a man of fourscore and got with child by Carlo, a young courtier. Her husband forgives her and accepts the child. When he dies, however, she is imprisoned by her husband's relatives, escapes, and is then restored to her former privileges. She resolves to return to Spain where she was born and enter a convent. As she bids farewell to her son and to the world, the narrator pauses and asks familiar questions:

> What now could injure the All-happy Fair, divinely beautiful, divinely good: but what is certain in a Mortal State? This lower world, govern'd by unseen Springs, bears nothing perfect, lest it become a God. From the bold Vigilance of one fallen Star, how many weep, even old in Bitterness: Thus well-inclin'd, thus as all thought past Fate, the lovely new-made Nun, form'd to be wretched (for Beauty is but rare sublimely bless'd) was in a surly Minute robb'd of Peace. (p. 164)

Her old seducer, Carlo, arrives; he fires the convent, and ravishes Luvania. Unlike Haywood's novels, *The Happy Unfortunate* is sparse in erotic details, and the assault is rendered in general terms. It is worth noting, however, that even as Carlo violates her amid the flames of the convent and she pleads with him to cease, "a thousand Terrors made the Villain hated, whilst yet a thousand Softs pleaded within: So true it is, where once we love, 'tis difficult to hate" (p. 164). But worse follows. Easily sated, Carlo ships her off to Persia in the hands of an infidel captain, who makes her his slave and concubine. She is saved by Osorio, a young Neapolitan who has loved her ever since he saw her enter the convent and who happens to be on the voyage to redeem his brother from slavery. He persuades the "Sophy's" vizir to buy her, and when the Sophy dies, she and Osorio run away.

The indefatigable Carlo is soon at her again, but when she threatens to expose his crimes, he turns his attention to Amanda and to Elaira, Felix's wife. Treachery and countertreachery too complicated to summarize ensue, and Carlo is finally captured and tried for his crimes in Spain. He confesses but implicates Luvania falsely. This perjury, the last of his assaults on the long-suffering fair (and I have omitted a number of her ordeals), proves fatal. Shipwrecked, she lands back in Spain, where she is put on trial and convicted of the crimes of which Carlo has accused her. Her execution is truly spectacular, a tragic apotheosis beyond anything Haywood ever contrived, a *via dolorosa* for the persecuted maiden that in its quasi-blasphemy comes close to making explicit the buried analogy in this sort of fiction between the female victim and the Christian martyr.

Distrest Luvania, was condemn'd to walk wrapt in a Sheet,
branded with the vile Name of an Apostate, with lighted Tapers,
naked legg'd and footed, three tedious Miles, by the Priest's rigid
Sentence, o'er snowy Mounts and Bars of burning Steel, but that
the Royal Goodness would not suffer; in Lieu of which, she was
adjudg'd to walk thrice three Times slowly on snow-cold Irons,
and repeat her Crimes, the Circuit of the Courts of Judicature,
from thence was to be led to the left Convent Altar [i.e., the
convent Carlo set afire and kidnaped her from], there to be stript
and excommunicated, then to be drest as an Apostate Nun, in
Black and Veil'd, which as a Hieroglyphick of her Choice, was
stain'd with Blood of the most Salvage-Wolves, then to be drove in
a black open Chariot, to a retir'd Palace of the Kings, there on a
Scaffold hung with mournful Sables, with a Sharp Axe to lose her
Head; and Being; after which her Body was destin'd to be burn'd
to Ashes, and mingled with inhumane Carlo's Dust, scatter'd over
some wide, unfathom'd Sea, and be deny'd the sacred Rites of
Burial. (pp. 326–27)

Amanda hears of this in a letter from Luvania's son, also named Carlo.
She herself is suffering intolerably, besieged by would-be seducers on all
sides. Bellfond's brother, married unhappily, has resorted to violence in his
attempts at her, and she has just heard that the Prince of Cyprus is
enamored of her. This prince, having listened to calumnies, has banished
Duke Bellfond, but not before Amanda finds herself pregnant by the still-
married Duke. Luvania's spectacular expiation changes the course of the
novel abruptly. No explicit connection is made, but the relationship is
clear: the gods can now relent, for Boyd's readers have had their tragic
catastrophe and can proceed to the happier possibilities of the story of
persecuted female innocence.

The Duchess dies suddenly, and Bellfond is free to marry, the prince
having discovered his innocence. The marriage is prefaced by Amanda's
denial that this is the end of love, the end of intensity and excitement. She
warns Bellfond not to marry her out of a sense of duty; this is to be a free act
and to continue the bliss of love without the guilt.

If ever I am wedded to Bellfond, let Love alone make up the
solemn Contract, it is that Doubt, my Lord, makes me uneasy; I
would be Bellfond's Wife, but for the Dutchess would not lose the
Lover. . . . But if you love like me this Moment wed me, and let us
be the Wonder of gay Cyprus, for it is now almost a Miracle to see

> a Great Man marry her he loves, or she that loves him, tho'
> mutual Love is all we know of Heaven.   (p. 337)

Such trenchant separation from the world of lust and avarice is a satisfying
if abrupt and implausible conclusion to a series of events that has demonstrated the impossibility of escape from that world's complicated net-
works of disaster. Love descends and rewards its faithful devotees by its
magic simplifications.

Simplicity, in fact, is the key to the erotic-pathetic formula. The trick in
such fiction is to twist events, characters, and scenes into a tightly tangled
mess whose unraveling is accomplished by the recurring simplicity of
personality and motive in characters who are rigidly confined to psychosexual stereotypes. The audience assumed by *The Happy Unfortunate*
expects and enjoys disaster, and the author's skill as a popular entertainer
is in playing heightened variations upon that convention of danger and
disaster or near-disaster. Complexity of character, particularity of scene, or
narrative self-consciousness has no place in such fiction, because any of
them would interrupt the immediate pleasure of formula recognition.
Character, especially, conforms to the preexisting pattern, and the reader's
pleasure is precisely in tracing the narrative's quick assertions of the
inevitability of the pattern, which invokes an unavoidable, often destructive psychosexual destiny for all concerned. It is difficult to say exactly
what the popularity of such fiction tells us about its audience, especially
since something very like that formula is still a part of contemporary pulp
romances. In any event, as I have suggested above, the emergence and
insistence of the formula in the early eighteenth century must signify
something about the way readers responded to the issue of female identity
and destiny.

But is this mass of popular amatory narrative nothing but humorless
pulp, interesting perhaps for the literary historian but virtually unreadable
otherwise? Not quite. Within the repetitive sameness of amatory formulas there are, after all, a small number of genuine minor precursors of
the masters.[44] "Precursors" is, however, a misleading term that appears to
justify the untenable evolutionary model of literary history. Instead of
looking forward to what did not yet exist, these books refined or rejected
existing narrative formulas, modifying their extravagance and unreality,
adding especially a certain consistency of character that avoids the melodramatic moral and psychological simplicities of the amatory novella.
One obvious importance thus granted to formula fiction is that it
provoked these refinements, dramatizing by its popularity the significance of its themes and challenging some writers to appropriate those

themes for audiences more attuned to sophisticated narrative values. To be sure, there were other ways of rejecting or improving the Haywoodian formula. Pious female writers like Jane Barker, Penelope Aubin, and Elizabeth Rowe produced stories that shifted the thematic emphasis of the novella toward virtuous and ultimately victorious resistance to the power of love, providing most of the thrills of watching beleaguered virtue but avoiding the violence and lubricity that usually supplemented them.[45] What separates early eighteenth-century fiction still worth reading from these moral tales is technique, management of narrative so that it yields a truthful complexity—moral, psychological, or social.

Robert A. Day calls *The Perfidious P* (1702) "the best epistolary novel before Richardson."[46] By such praise he means that its epistolary technique is an expressive form rather than merely a format, that its letters serve to differentiate and define characters, that the reader is made aware of individualized characters writing letters rather than simply being made to speak through them. In formula fiction, as a strict rule, language is transparent, a vehicle for whatever emotional and ideological satisfactions are being delivered by the narrative: hence the unembarrassed repetition and eager reception of clichés that are crucial to its effects. More sophisticated narration tends to stress the functionality of language for revealing character and describing setting and action. That stress on language as a medium, manipulated openly by characters or by authors, points at times to its inadequacy for rendering the truth, the latter emphasis helping to establish the mode of narration we call "realistic." *The Perfidious P* in one sense is a banal tale of amorous betrayal, but it is redeemed by moments when such manipulation is highly visible, when characters implicitly reveal their uneasiness with amatory language and the world it invokes.

Corydon, a nobleman, has sent his mistress, Clarinda, to the country while he is at court in London. Writing to Corydon, Clarinda reminds her lover of his extravagant promises. She finds his previous letter written in "too loose a Stile for my Heroick Love; with more Care and greater Study you made your first Approaches to my Virgin-Heart."[47] Clarinda's suspicion, then, begins in textual alertness, as a modern critic might like to put it—in an analysis of her lover's writing that causes her to extend that analysis back to his seductive speeches. In its protestations, Corydon's response verifies Clarinda's suspicions, as he denies his old rhetoric even while affirming his feelings. For amatory hyperbole, Corydon substitutes homely and potentially reductive analogies, turning his letter into a self-conscious display of verbal virtuosity, preferring his own wit to meaningful reassurance for Clarinda.

Why all these Doubts and Fears, my Love? Why this needless
Repetition? Does my *Clarinda* think I am grown so stupid, so
lifeless, for so I must be when I forget the least Particular of what
has past between us, those soft Embraces, moaning Sighs and
melting Tears, which were too precious to fall unobserv'd, are still
fresh in the Memory of *Corydon*. What shall I say more? I think
there is nothing more of consequence to say, except I entertain
you with Truths obvious to every eye; as, that 'tis Day when the
Sun shines, and when he's gone 'tis Night; or, that I love you
dearer than all the Women in the World, as great a Truth as either
of the former, and ought to be as well known to you. For my part,
I think the telling of this over and over, as some Men do their
Passions, ought to be tiresome to Women of your Nicety, and as
nauseous to the Mind, as Meat often drest to the Stomach: for to
be always in the high Road of making Love, a Man must Bake,
Boil, Roast, Hash, and Mince his Love, to find Variety for his
Mistress, who perhaps does not think, because 'tis brought warm
to her, it has so often been cool'd by another, and only tost up
again for her Palate. . . . I am now in haste, being just going to
wait upon the King; yet you see I prefer Love to all, and stay to
write this long Letter, when it might be easie for me to tear what I
have done, then tell you wittily, this Letter is an Emblem of my
Heart rent and torn for you—Meer trifling, and ought no more to
pass for Love than Childrens Toys for Riches, or a gilded lump of
base Metal for true Sterling. (pp. 13–16)

Corydon visits Lucina, Clarinda's friend and confidante, and soon falls
in love with her. Knowing this, the reader can see revelations in Corydon
and Lucina's letters to Clarinda that she cannot, and again the book's
interest turns on the simultaneous duplicity and truthfulness of language.
After the betrayal is known to her, Clarinda writes in conventional ranting
fashion, calling herself a dreadful warning to her sex not to listen to man's
"bewitching Tale, for if you hear like me, you surely are undone" (p. 132).
Melodramatically desperate enough, Clarinda is still aware just how rhetoric did her in and begins her sad summary with a specific warning against
listening to love's language rather than falling in love. Especially in the
context of Clarinda's passion, such awareness marks the technical sophistication of *The Perfidious P.*

There is another kind of self-consciousness about language and another
sort of protorealism in the novels of Mary Davys.[48] *The Reform'd Coquet*
(1724), to my mind her best work, stands nearly alone in early eighteenth-

century domestic narrative for its humor. Numbering among its subscribers Martha Blount, Alexander Pope, and John Gay, *The Reform'd Coquet* is a genuinely witty book about the education through experience of a young lady, her conversion into a woman of good sense as well as a happy wife.

Amoranda's father is a nobleman whose estate has been eaten up by the excesses of his father. His younger brother, a rich East India merchant, redeems the estate; when her father dies without male issue and her mother soon after, Amoranda becomes an orphan heiress, much sought after, spoiled and self-indulgent but essentially strong and sensible rather than weakly pathetic and quiveringly susceptible like the typical heroine of the Haywoodian novella.

The ensuing complicated plot has a richly theatrical inventiveness, as Davys manages an ironic, controlled distance from actors and events, her narrative a balance of the standard entanglements of the amatory novella and witty moral observations. In a stylish anticipation of Fielding's manner, Davys invites her readers to the contemplation of ironically inevitable moral complications and the enjoyment of the twists of fictional artifice required to resolve them, rather than to the amatory novella's excited participation in events and enthralling identification with characters. From the beginning, Davys displays a narrative control that balances events and witty moral observation. Here, for example, is her rendering of the financial and sexual excitement that threatens the newly orphaned heiress before her uncle can send a substitute guardian.

> During this Interregnum, *Amoranda* was address'd by all the Country round, from the old Justice to the young Rake; and, I dare say, my Reader will believe she was a Toast in every House for ten Parishes round. The very Excrescencies of her Temper, were now become Graces, and it was not possible for one single Fault to be joined to three thousand Pounds a Year; her Levee was daily crowded with almost all sorts, and (she pleased to be admir'd) tho' she lov'd none, was complaisant to all.[49]

Amoranda's various suitors provide occasion for a comic version of the novella's melodramatic sexual aggression, and Davys' bantering dialogue shows her knowledge of stage models. When Lord Lofty swears he is entangled in her charms, Amoranda pretends to misunderstand him:

> Well, I'll swear, my Lord, said Amoranda, that's a pity; methinks a Man of your Gallantry should never marry. Marry! said my Lord in great Surprize, no, I hope I shall never have so little love for any Lady as to marry her: Oons! the very Word has put me into a

32

Sweat, the Marriage-Bed is to Love, what a cold Bed is to Melon-
Seed, it starves it to death infallibly.   (p. 26)

As on the eighteenth-century stage, such bantering easily turns brutal and
sordid. Two of Amoranda's other suitors, Callid and Froth, plot to kidnap
her and force a marriage. Pleased and amused even by foolish admirers
who prove dangerous, Amoranda is saved by Formator, a middle-aged
friend sent by her uncle to protect her. Formator and a footman, disguised
as Amoranda and her maid, thrash Callid and Froth soundly. (They quarrel
subsequently, and in Davys' wicked summary, "tho' they liv'd like Scoun-
drels, they went off like Gentlemen, and the first Pass they made, took
each other's Life" [pp. 52–53].) Formator then institutes a program of
moral improvement for Amoranda. "His constant Care was to divert her
from all the Follies of Life, and as she had a Soul capable of Improvement,
and a flexible good Temper to be dealt with, he made no doubt but one day
he should see her the most accomplish'd of her Sex" (p. 53).

A stranger appears soon after and reveals herself as Altamira, a woman
driven out of her home by her incestuously minded brother, only to be
seduced by Lord Lofty, who has tricked her with a written contract of
marriage. Amoranda is as quick as her new guardian; she arranges to meet
Lord Lofty for a secret wedding and to substitute for herself the wronged
Altamira. Matters seem to be resolving themselves with perfect romantic
symmetry, as Altamira's brother marries Lofty's sister, when Amoranda is
kidnaped by one Biranthus, a visitor who has arrived in female disguise.
Lurid melodrama takes over: Amoranda strikes the poses of the persecuted maiden, and her virtue hangs by a thread:

No, base Biranthus, said she, if Providence had design'd me a Prey
for such a Villain, I should have fallen into your first Snare, but I
was delivered from you then, and so I shall be again. Before I
would consent to be a wife to such a Monster, I would tear out the
Tongue by the roots that was willing to pronounce my Doom. I
would suffer these Arms to be extended on a Rack, till every
Sinew, every Vein and Nerve should crack, rather than embrace, or
so much as touch a Viper like thyself. Then hear, said he, and
tremble at thy approaching Fate. This minute, by the help of thy
own Servant, I will enjoy thee; and then, by the assistance of my
Arm, he shall do so too. Thou lyest, false Traitor, said she, Heaven
will never suffer such Wickedness.   (pp. 112–13)

And heaven, of course, does not. A passing gentleman, Alanthus, rescues
her and becomes her suitor, Formator informing her that this in fact is the

man her uncle has selected for her. But there is one last revelatory twist to the plot. Alanthus and Formator turn out to be one and the same, and both are actually Lord Marquis of W, who was unwilling to force Amoranda into marriage by her uncle's command and has resorted to elaborate subterfuge to improve her and win her love.

The Reform'd Coquet strikes a balance, clearly, between the extravagance of the amatory novella and the moral realism of stage comedy, but it does not renounce the lurid thematics and moral melodrama of the novella. Although the theory can hardly be proved, it seems as if the emergence of what we now recognize as novelistic narrative in these early years of the eighteenth century takes place precisely because of the force of those crude, popular thematics. What this survey of the market for fiction in the century's first four decades or so may suggest is that the popularity of the amatory novella expresses or responds to the radical separation of middle- and upper-class women from public economic life. That is Ruth Perry's point when she insists that the novel as a crucial literary form coincides with the separation of urban literate women "from the active concerns of life into a pretend world of romantic love and fantasy relationships."[50]

I would prefer a slightly broader conclusion. Suffering and confused female characters in eighteenth-century popular fiction enact, we may say, a cultural crisis and enormous ideological transition, the privatization and fragmentation of experience for men and women. This is a theme the major writers both accept and attempt to revise by means of the technical control and moral coherence they bring to bear on the formulas of popular fiction.

### Notes

1. The evolutionary analogy has been challenged by many critics lately. Henry K. Miller, for example, ridicules it elegantly by speaking of the "gloriously self-serving" teleology of nineteenth-century literary history. Miller also admits that the last two hundred years really have produced something new and remarkable in narrative, "and this has made the invocation of an evolutionary or teleological pattern considerably more plausible" ("Augustan Prose Fiction and the Romance Tradition," in Studies in the Eighteenth Century, ed. R.F. Brissenden and J.C. Eade [Toronto: Univ. of Toronto Press, 1976], 241–42).

2. And modern criticism has simply followed the eighteenth-century view of Richardson's and Fielding's originality. As William Park summarizes it ("What Was New about the 'New Species of Writing'?" Studies in the Novel 2 (1970), 113–14), Richardson and his coterie stressed three factors in his work that were without real precedent: "writing to the moment," by which a new intensity and realism were added to romance; the depiction of a "familiar" everyday life rather than the unrealities of "high" life (as in romance) or the sordid details of "low" life (as in criminal and picaresque narrative); a moral control and coherence

whereby moral values were actually exemplified in characters and events rather than merely stated at the beginning or the end of the narrative. In his preface to *Joseph Andrews,* Fielding claimed to be introducing a new narrative genre into England, "the comic epic in prose," and in *Tom Jones* he speaks of himself as the founder of a "new province of writing." Eighteenth-century readers, Park points out, awarded the two novelists different kinds of originality but saw their works "as but two versions of the 'modern romance,' a familiar, natural, and moral species which had 'exploded' the old improbable one."

3. In *Factual Fictions: The Origins of the English Novel* (New York: Columbia Univ. Press, 1983), 7, Lennard Davis rejects what he defines as three "models" literary historians have used to account for the English novel: evolution, osmosis, and convergence. While most traditional literary history has employed the first of these, Davis calls Ian Watt's *Rise of the Novel* (Berkeley: Univ. of California Press, 1957) "osmotic" because it posits a connection between cultural change and the emergence of the novel, a sort of osmosis in which shifts in philosophical perspective and social structure permeate narrative structures. Watt's attempt fails, says Davis, because the "micro connection between, say, a larger, middle-class reading public and a structural change in narrative" is missing. In the "convergence" model, the novel is simply the result of all the narrative forms that preceded it, "taking on the best features of disparate forms such as the essay, the history, and so on." In the place of such models, Davis proposes Michel Foucault's notion of "discourse"; that is, the novel should be understood as part of a "larger ensemble of written texts," including not only novels and literary criticism but "parliamentary statutes, newspapers, advertisements, printer's records, handbills, letters, and so on." Like Foucault, Davis boldly rejects the question of origins, since the shift to that "discourse" of which the novel is a part is a "rupture" or a "transformation" rather than part of a linear progression in which one can properly speak of causes and effects. The novel, in this latest attempt to account for it, is part of the effort by seventeenth- and eighteenth-century European man to dominate and administer the world. Just how superior such a formulation is to the older ones that Davis rejects is an unresolved issue.

4. Ernest A. Baker (*The History of the English Novel,* 10 vols. [1929; rpt. New York: Barnes & Noble, 1959], III:107) made the case for the minor novelists very clearly: "The service they rendered was to have kept up a supply of novels and stories, which habituated a larger and larger public to find their amusement in the reading of fiction, and which poor in quality as they were, provided the original form for the eighteenth-century novel of manners. Defoe, for the most part, took a line of his own; yet he was not entirely out of their debt. Richardson and Fielding were less innovators than is usually supposed; in turning to novel-writing, they entered upon an established and thriving business, and they adopted many tricks of the trade from these humble precursors."

One of the problems students of the novel have faced is the difficulty of reading what posterity has willingly let die. Eighteenth-century popular narrative of the sort that precedes and surrounds the major writers has hitherto been available only in major research libraries. That situation has been remedied lately by the Garland Press series, Foundations of the Novel, "a collection of 100 rare titles reprinted in photo-facsimile in 71 volumes," compiled and edited by

Michael F. Shugrue (New York: Garland, 1973). Most of the works discussed in this essay are reprinted in that series.

5. Watt, *Rise of the Novel*, 50.

6. Maurice Evans, Introduction to *Arcadia* (New York: Penguin, 1977), 9.

7. Earl Wasserman pointed out that the prose fiction of the Renaissance enjoyed steady popularity through the eighteenth century, as did medieval romances and other traditional narratives adapted into popular and modern idiom as chapbooks for the barely literate (*Elizabethan Poetry in the Eighteenth Century* [Urbana: Univ. of Illinois Press, 1947], 253). Henry K. Miller recalls for us that Sterne's Uncle Toby remembers "when Guy, Earl of *Warwick*, and *Parismus* and *Valentine* and *Orson*, and the *Seven Champions of England* were handed around the school" (*Tristram Shandy*, VI,xxxii) ("Augustan Prose Fiction," 249).

8. W.H. McBurney, comp., *A Check List of English Prose Fiction, 1700–1739* (Cambridge, Mass.: Harvard Univ. Press, 1960), vii–viii.

9. Marjorie Plant, *The English Book Trade*, 2d ed. (1939; rpt. London: Allen and Unwin, 1965), 56–58.

10. See the article on Paul Lorrain by Thomas Seccombe in the *Dictionary of National Biography* (XXXIV:140).

11. See my *Popular Fiction before Richardson: Narrative Patterns, 1700–1739* (Oxford: Clarendon Press, 1969), 27–29, for more detailed discussion of the issues raised by these pamphlets.

12. For an extended discussion of this and other similar works, see ibid., 45–59. "Smith" produced several other collections like this one, as well as one devoted to female offenders: *The School of Venus, or Cupid restor'd to Sight; being A History of Cuckold and Cuckold-makers* (1715–16).

13. F.W. Chandler, *The Literature of Roguery* (New York: Houghton Mifflin, 1907), 173–74. For a discussion of *The Scotch Rogue: or, the Life and Actions of Donald Macdonald A High-Land Scot* (1706) and *Tom Merryman* (1725) as works that exemplify this combination of criminal journalism and folktale features, see *Popular Fiction before Richardson*, 41–43.

14. Manuel Schonhorn has edited Defoe's work and provided a full and illuminating introduction. His conclusion summarizes Defoe's achievement and the importance of the book: "In its narrative vigor, its emotional balance, and its creative reconstruction of dim events elevated at times to a dramatic universality, it has remained the indispensable record of English piracy in the first quarter of the eighteenth century and a classic in the literature of the sea" (*A General History of the Pyrates* [Columbia: Univ. of South Carolina Press, 1972], xl).

15. Davis, *Factual Fictions*, 136.

16. Ibid., 132.

17. P.G. Adams concludes his study by emphasizing the intellectual importance of travel writing for an age of expanding enlightenment, and he points to the philosophical and scientific implications of travel narratives that, collectively, "taught that each nation had a distinctive, even appropriate, way of life." But Adams also notes that the improbability of many accounts of foreign parts was apparent from the beginning: "That travelers were eyed askance is proved not only by the hesitant acceptance accorded them, but ironically by the great necessity they all—truthful and untruthful—felt to profess their innocence,

as if they had been caught in a company of shady characters" (*Travelers and Travel-Liars 1660–1800* [Berkeley: Univ. of California Press, 1962], 224, 228).

18. For a discussion of some of these pirate lives, see my *Popular Fiction before Richardson*, 64–84.

19. Like so many other producers of early eighteenth-century popular narrative, Chetwood was a member of the subculture referred to as "Grub Street," part of a number of struggling "hack" writers and publishers associated with the neighborhood around that now vanished London street. He was the publisher of many of Eliza Haywood's works, and she and Chetwood are numbered among the dunces in Pope's *Dunciad*. Bookseller, dramatist, and miscellaneous writer, he was the prompter at Drury Lane theater for many years. See James Sutherland's biographical appendix to his volume of the Twickenham edition of Pope's *Dunciad* (London: Methuen, 1943), 433. On Grub Street, see Pat Rogers, *Grub Street: Studies in a Subculture* (London: Methuen, 1972).

20. Taking a broad historical overview beginning with the seventeenth century, Martin Green sees a "moral revolution" in England sponsored by the "merchant caste" that appropriated literature and culture. "This moral revolution redirected spiritual intensity toward home life, marriage, and sex; away from older objects of devotion, like the liturgical life of the church, and the cults of the aristomilitary caste. When the spiritual religion came out of the monastery, to adapt a famous phrase, it settled in the home as well as in the market place, making its altar the bedroom and the bed. Indeed, as far as the serious novelists were concerned, it was the home and *not* the market that was important" (*Dreams of Adventure, Deeds of Empire* [New York: Basic Books, 1979], 63).

21. McBurney's *Check List* shows sixteen original English narratives published during those years that qualify in my judgment as travel adventure stories. I exclude the novels of Penelope Aubin, who combines the pattern of the amatory novella with the geographical diversity of the adventure story. For an account of her works, see *Popular Fiction before Richardson*, 216–29, and W.H. McBurney, "Mrs. Penelope Aubin and the Early Eighteenth-Century English Novel," *HLQ* 20 (May 1957), 245–67.

22. Malcolm Bosse, Introduction to the Garland edition of *The Golden Spy*, 5.

23. Gildon's original version of this anthology dates to 1692, when John Dunton printed *The Post-boy rob'd of his Mail: or, the Pacquet Broke Open. Consisting of Five Hundred Letters to Persons of Several Qualities and Conditions.* As Robert A. Day notes, this was partly translated from Italian and French models (*Told in Letters: Epistolary Fiction before Richardson* [Ann Arbor: Univ. of Michigan Press, 1966], 243).

24. J.B. Heidler, "The History, from 1700 to 1800, of English Criticism of Prose Fiction," *University of Illinois Studies in Language and Literature*, no. 13 (Urbana: Univ. of Illinois Press, 1928), 17.

25. For a discussion of these and other issues surrounding the romance tradition in the early eighteenth century, see Miller, "Augustan Prose Fiction," 245–46.

26. "To the Reader," in *Eighteenth-Century British Novelists on the Novel*, ed. George L. Barnett (New York: Appleton-Century-Crofts, 1968), 22. References in the text are to this edition.

27. According to A.J. Tieje, the *chronique scandaleuse* became a formal type in 1660 with the appearance of Bussy-Rabutin's *Histoire amoureuse des Gaules*

("The Theory of Characterization in Prose Fiction Prior to 1740," *University of Minnesota Studies in Language and Literature*, No. 5 (Minneapolis: Univ. of Minnesota Press, 1916), 54. An English translation of Bussy-Rabutin's book appeared in 1725, and such translations were popular and frequent during the early decades of the century. As James Sutherland points out in *English Literature of the Late Seventeenth Century* (Oxford: Clarendon Press, 1969), 209–10, English secret histories began to flourish in the climate of partisan politics after James II's abdication.

28. See *Popular Fiction before Richardson*, 119–52, for a discussion of Manley's popularity.

29. *Secret Memoirs and Manners of several Persons of Quality, of Both Sexes from the New Atalantis, an Island in the Mediteranean* [sic]. *Written Originally in Italian* (London: Printed for John Morphew and J. Woodward, 1709), p. 217. References in the text are to this edition.

30. See G.F. Whicher, *The Life and Romances of Mrs. Eliza Haywood* (New York: Columbia Univ. Press, 1915); Mary Anne Schofield, *Quiet Rebellion: The Fictional Heroines of Eliza Fowler Haywood* (Washington D.C.: University Press of America, 1982).

31. *The Force of Nature, Lasselia,* and *The Injur'd Husband* have been reprinted in facsimile recently by Mary Anne Schofield (*Four Novels of Eliza Haywood* [Delmar, N.Y.: Scholars' Facsimiles and Reprints, 1983]). *Philidore and Placentia* can be read in W.H. McBurney's *Four before Richardson: Selected English Novels, 1720–1727* (Lincoln: Univ. of Nebraska Press, 1963.) Many of Haywood's novels are also available in facsimile reprints in the Garland series, Foundations of the Novel.

32. *Love in Excess* is divided into three parts, the first two published separately in 1719, the third in 1720. This passage is from Part II, pp. 48–49 (Garland edition). For an extended analysis of the book, see *Popular Fiction before Richardson*, 183–207. Melliora, it is worth noting, escapes D'Elmont here, and consummation of their love is delayed through many ordeals and temptations until the happy ending in Part III.

33. Ruth Perry, *Women, Letters and the Novel* (New York: AMS Press, 1980), 22–23.

34. Myra Jehlen, "Archimedes and the Paradox of Feminist Criticism," in *The Signs Reader: Women, Gender and Scholarship*, ed. Elizabeth Abel and Emily K. Abel (Chicago: Univ. of Chicago Press, 1983), 90.

35. See *Popular Fiction before Richardson*, 210, for a discussion of this work.

36. Garland edition, p. 10. References in the text are to this edition.

37. In some ways, eighteenth-century amatory formula fiction resembles what John G. Cawelti calls "social melodrama," which he defines as a synthesis of the archetype of melodrama "with a particular set of current events or social institutions." The result looks like social criticism but is in fact an affirmation of the status quo. "The appeal of this synthesis combines the escapist satisfactions of melodrama—in particular, its fantasy of a moral universe following conventional social values—with the pleasurable feeling that we are learning something important about reality" (*Adventure, Mystery, and Romance: Formula Stories as Art and Popular Culture* [Chicago: Univ. of Chicago Press, 1976], 261).

38. It had rather stiff competition in 1722. Defoe's *Colonel Jacque* appeared then, and *Moll Flanders* reached a third edition in the year of its publication. Haywood's *The British Recluse* went through two editions, and Penelope Aubin published two of her novels that year.

39. In 1727, Haywood published six books, including the notorious secret history *The Court of Caramania*, which is one of the books borne by the donkey in the frontispiece to Pope's *Dunciad* (along with "Haywood's Novels"). A collected edition also appeared that year, bringing together *Secret Histories, etc. Written or translated by Mrs. Eliza Haywood. Printed since the Publication of the four Volumes of her Works* (see McBurney, *Check List*, 74). Those four volumes referred to were reissued in a third edition in 1732.

40. *The Treacherous Confident* (Dublin: Printed by S. Powell, for Sylvanus Pepyat and Thomas Benson, 1728), 8. Page references are to this edition.

41. *The Forced Virgin; or, the Unnatural Mother. A True Secret History* (London: printed for W. Trott, 1730), pp. 11–16. References in the text are to this edition.

42. To summarize briefly: Lominia does abort Lysanor's child, but is then made pregnant again by Arastes, who drugs her wine and takes her in her sleep. As far as she knows, then, the child she feels in her must be Lysanor's. She has her maid expose the child when it is born, but Arastes is watching; he takes the child into the country and has it cared for. Arastes and Lominia come upon the child by accident while walking in the country some years later, and Arastes reveals that he saw her maid expose this child but does not say he is the father. Lominia comes back later and kills the child.

43. According to Robert A. Day, Elizabeth Boyd issued in 1732 a proposal for printing her novel by subscription. Day cites these interesting figures: 328 subscribers, 188 men and 140 women; 92 subscribers belonged to the nobility (*Told in Letters*, 74). The bound book cost five shillings but was obtainable in quires for three shillings. It was reissued in 1737 as *The Female Page: A Genuine and Entertaining History, Relating to Some Persons of Distinction*. All references in the text are to the 1732 edition.

*The Happy Unfortunate* is prefaced by some verses exalting Boyd as Haywood's successor:

> Yield Haywood yield, yield all whose tender Strains,
> Inspire the Dreams of Maids and lovesick Swains,
> Who taint the unripen'd Girl with amorous Fire,
> And hint the first faint Dawnings of Desire:
> Wing each Love-Atom, that in Embryo lies,
> And teach young Parthenissa's Breasts to rise.
>
> A new Elisa writes—by her the Young
> Instructed, shall avoid the busy Throng,
> Retire to Groves, by murmuring Fountains sigh,
> Expire in Vision, and in Emblem die.

The hint of humor in the last line is confirmed by lines that predict the novel's effects on its male readers:

> Rough Country 'Squires, the Glory of our Isle:

Soft Billet-doux, shall in kind Accents write,
And wafted Vows from Cornwall wing their Flight.
No more on Dunkirk, or the Nations Debt,
Old Hackney'd Themes, our Senators shall meet,
But o'er a gilt Romance enamour'd hang,
Sit on a Leer, or on a Sigh Harrangue:
And Love's own Monosyllables apply
To their due Province restor'd, No, and Ay.

Such genial humor disappears in the novel itself.

44. Robert A. Day finds four epistolary novels that "represent the highest development of letter fiction before Richardson": *The Perfidious P* (1702), *Lindamira* (1702), *Olinda's Adventures* (1693), and Mary Davys' *Familiar Letters Betwixt a Gentleman and a Lady* (1725). Day praises these "highly promising experimental" books for their varying degrees of technical competence and for the resulting verisimilitude of scene and character but calls them "fragmentary and tentative," lacking the "significance and depth" of Richardson and later novelists (*Told in Letters*, 177, 191). On the issue of technical achievement, see Benjamin Boyce's introduction to his edition of *The Adventures of Lindamira* (Minneapolis: Univ. of Minnesota Press, 1949) and my discussion of *Lindamira* in *Popular Fiction before Richardson*, 170–73.

45. For an extended analysis of the works of these three writers, see ch. 6, "The Novel as Pious Polemic," of *Popular Fiction before Richardson*, 211–61.

46. *Told in Letters*, 178.

47. Garland edition, p. 9. References in the text are to this edition.

48. W.H. McBurney sees Mary Davys as Fielding to Haywood's Richardson and traces a number of interesting similarities between her novels and Fielding's. He praises her humor and her restraint, contrasting her with the "typical woman novelist of her day who sought rather to rouse the reader's mind 'to (till then) unknown Pleasures or generous Pity.' " McBurney concludes that Fielding probably never read her works but that she "is interesting as one of the few writers before 1740 to formulate a conscious theory of the novel, to show how realistic comedy might be adapted to the new genre, to place emphasis upon characterization and setting rather than upon simple variety of action, and to bring sturdy commonsense and humor to a literary form which had been dominated by the extravagant, the scandalous, and the sensational" ("Mrs. Mary Davys, Forerunner of Fielding," *PMLA* 74 [1959], 351, 355).

49. Garland edition, p. 10. References in the text are to this edition.

50. Perry, *Women, Letters, and the Novel*, 137.

# Paula R. Backscheider

## Defoe and the Geography of the Mind

Defoe's immortality will always rest on *Robinson Crusoe*, that immensely subtle, complex book with its simple plot. Defoe gives us a character of compelling reality who appears in one archetypal incident after another. Crusoe is, of course, living one of the most common fantasies of humankind: what if I were stranded in a foreign place? alone on an island? completely unable to escape? what if I had almost nothing with me on the island? Crusoe is both *isolated* and *imprisoned* in an unfamiliar place. His questions are entirely predictable: is survival possible? how can the most basic needs for food, water, warmth, safety be met? Once these questions come to mind, we could construct the next equally obvious set: why did this happen? why to him? what does it mean? what will the experience do to him? As we follow Crusoe, we will watch physical, experiential, and mental resources brought to bear upon this common "what if" fantasy.

No one who conjures up this fantasy imagines himself deteriorating into a ragged savage, howling and eating raw scavenger flesh. And Crusoe fully embodies this other element in the fantasy: he is successful. He will not starve; he will not rave, babble, and throw himself in the sea; he will not even fail to bake bread. He will survive; more than that, he will triumph. And to triumph, whether it be in our imaginations or in Crusoe's story, is to achieve an admirable standard of living and a heroic state of mind in the most elemental and moving way. Crusoe will master himself and his environment; he will create a civilized and satisfying life.

*Robinson Crusoe* is far more than a good story, however, or we would not instantly assent to Charles Dickens's description of it as "Next to the Bible, the Arabian Nights Entertainments, and Æsop's Fables, perhaps the best-known book in the world."[1] The book holds us because it absorbs and integrates so many of the most significant strains in Western thought. Here are the ambivalences and ambitions that continue to occupy the mind. Cast into improbable and extraordinary circumstances time after time, Crusoe reacts in recognizably human and ordinary ways even as his thoughts reveal the diverse threads that lead to our opinions and decisions. Time after time, we are struck by the fullness of the mind Defoe has given his hero. Crusoe is truly what his critics have found him to be: adventurous, economic, political, religious, and yet ordinary.

Almost any paragraph selected will show the rich blending of ideas: ". . . I made abundance of things, even without Tools, and some with no more Tools than an Adze and a Hatchet, which perhaps were never made that way before, and that with infinite Labour. . . . But my Time or Labour was little worth, and so it was as well employ'd one way as another" (I:77).[2] Here Crusoe notes his accomplishment with pride ("perhaps were never made that way before") and considers what we call "cost effectiveness" even as he tells us how he built his table and chairs and how it felt to build them that way. His society has taught him to compare the value of the time and effort with the worth of the product.

> . . . I came to an Opening . . . and the Country appear'd so fresh, so green, so flourishing . . . that it looked like a Planted Garden.
> I descended a little on the Side of that delicious Vale, surveying it with a secret Kind of Pleasure, (tho' mixt with my other afflicting Thoughts) to think that this was all my own, that I was King and Lord of all this Country indefeasibly, and had a Right of Possession; and if I could convey it, I might have it in Inheritance. . . . (I:114)

Again we have the consciousness of the immediate, the physical experience joined inextricably to the feelings the experience awakened. Defoe was writing at a time when beautiful English formal gardens were highly valued, and he himself had helped his Scots friends design gardens. The beauty and order of the scene remind Crusoe of England; he feels again his exile but, more strongly, his ownership. His words, "King . . . indefeasibly" call to mind the political controversies of his age. For three generations Englishmen had quarreled over what constituted an "indefeasible" —inalterable and uncancellable—right to rule; here Crusoe finds it. Men of Defoe's time believed in the consent if not the design of Providence in the determination of kings, and Crusoe's "King and Lord" rings with biblical echoes. Finally, he remembers that this land could be an "inheritance," the day-to-day legal embodiment of the right to rule, the most ordinary "right" a man had with his possessions.

> I might have rais'd Ship Loadings of Corn. . . . I had Timber enough to have built a Fleet of Ships. I had Grapes enough to have

made Wine, or to have cur'd into Raisins, to have loaded that
Fleet, when they had been built.   (I:148)

> With these Reflections I work'd my Mind up, not only to the
> Will of God in the present Disposition of my Circumstances; but
> even to a sincere Thankfulness for my Condition. . . .   (I:152)

Here Crusoe is master of his environment; he can produce far more than
he can eat or use, and he muses about products that England valued highly.
For example, writers separated as widely in time as Sir William Temple
and Alexander Pope wrote about the patriotic duty English landowners
had to raise trees for the Navy, and tracts such as *Mr.
Williamson's Memoirs* (1717) explained how to make the Royal Navy's shipyards more
productive and profitable. The detail of Defoe's economic thought is
present in the idea of building a fleet and then loading the ships. Immediately after he surveys his island's wealth, Crusoe turns to religious
"reflections" as mixed and predictable as his secular thoughts.

In the pages that follow, he can be the seventeenth-century preacher
who draws a moral: "all the good Things of this World, are no farther good
to us, than they are for our Use." He can be superstitious enough to note
the coincidence of significant dates in his life. He can be melodramatic
enough to compare himself with Elijah fed by the ravens. He can be
practical enough to see that he had every reason to expect more suffering
on the island and spiritual enough to find the hand of "Providence" in the
good fortune that brought the ship to the island. He can borrow from the
language and aspirations of his religious upbringing to long for a "Mind
entirely composed by resignation to the Will of God" and to be aware that
he has led a "dreadful" life "perfectly destitute of the Knowledge and Fear
of God."

In these passages, we can see the elements of a wide variety of literary
and subliterary forms such as travel literature, spiritual autobiography,
adventure story, pirate story, and memoir. Criticism in the last twenty
years has relentlessly chipped away at the idea that Defoe was accidentally
great, that he was the master of verisimilitude, impersonation, and episode and not much more than that. We now recognize his complex blend of
genres, his sophisticated and broad interests, the ways he absorbed and
transformed a large number of intellectual debates; and we are beginning
to understand his fictional structures and techniques. Although we still
see Defoe as a moralist and an economic theorist, we understand many of
the ways he knits his opinions and arguments into his themes and charac-

44

ters so that they are not encrusted comment but integrated into the novels.

---

I

Defoe transformed basically mono-referential forms into vehicles that satisfied readers' desires for adventure and for emotional exploration.[3] In *Robinson Crusoe*, for example, we have the thrill of exciting adventures, views of foreign lands, exotic animals and people, and stirring natural sights and disasters combined with the presentation of a reflective character who can explain his reasons for making the laws he does for his island and also agonize over the most profound religious questions. A glance at the literary forms scholars have associated with this novel reveals Defoe's greater complexity and broader concerns.

Travel literature offered a way to cater to the century's lively interest in geography and natural history even as it provided a convenient vehicle for adventure stories. Readers valued what Defoe called "infinite Variety" and exciting incident more than unity; the number of anthologies of voyage tales, such as the very popular *Navigantium atque Itinerantium Bibliotheca* by John Harris (1705), testifies to their fascination with places and events as opposed to, for example, character development. *Robinson Crusoe* and *Farther Adventures* (which were invariably sold together until 1750) take the reader to Newfoundland, South America, western Europe, and northwest Africa; around the continent of Africa to Madagascar; to India, the islands of the East Indies, and China; across the continent of Asia and through European Russia to Archangel; and around the Scandinavian countries by sea. In the course of these travels, Crusoe fights strange animals and peoples, considers various religions, and compares political and social customs with English ones. His adventures are truly "strange and surprising" and endlessly varied. Even a superficial look at the books identified as the most important influences upon *Robinson Crusoe* (such as Robert Knox's *An Historical Relation of Ceylon* and William Dampier's *Voyages*)[4] or entirely fictional contemporary works (such as *A Voyage to the New Island of Fonseca*, 1708) indicates the great differences between them and *Robinson Crusoe*. Defoe may be concerned with geographical accuracy, but he subordinates descriptions of the unfamiliar customs and clothing to the function these places and people serve in motivating adventures and affecting the opinions of his hero. Furthermore, Defoe is simply uninterested in giving the kind of detail about fish, insects, and plants on the individual islands that we find in, for example, William Chetwood's *The Voyages . . . of Captain Falconer* (1720).

In the West, travel literature has almost always had symbolic or even allegorical meanings. Most commonly, the voyage stands for man's journey through life; it involves a quest for understanding in the world, and often for God's relationship to man and man's place in the universe. Extended voyages have been understood as punishments or exile, as was the Israelites' wandering in the wilderness. John Richetti has pointed out that the "diversity of scene and event" so common to travel books is balanced in English literature by a narrative voice that continually looks for the workings of Providence.[5] The integration of the religious themes, then, in *Robinson Crusoe* is no radical innovation, and it is hard for us today to imagine the corrective that G.A. Starr's *Defoe and Spiritual Autobiography* and J. Paul Hunter's *Reluctant Pilgrim* were to earlier Defoe criticism.[6] Both pointed out *Robinson Crusoe*'s relationships to conduct books, collections of "remarkable providences," and spiritual autobiographies such as John Bunyan's *Grace Abounding to the Chief of Sinners*. They traced the Protestant pattern of salvation in the island episode: awareness of sin, sense of divine wrath and obligation to God, humiliation before God, confession, hatred of sin, and "accepting, receiving, and resting upon Christ alone for justification, sanctification, and eternal life, by virtue of the covenant of grace" ("Of Repentance" in the 1646 Westminster Confession).

Again, comparison with these precursors reveals Defoe's greater complexity. Robinson Crusoe is a modern man, a secular man who asks whether things happen in the world—specifically to him—by accident or design. He is a capitalist working out his relationship to God in a setting rich in typological possibilities. Defoe begins by establishing how ordinary Crusoe is, a middle-class third son with the ambitions that young men usually have—to find adventure and prosperity. His discussions with his father, who opposes his plan to go to sea; his appeal to his mother to take his side, and her refusal; his attempt to conform before he rebels; and his successful time as a Brazilian planter all set the stage for our involvement with the intense spiritual conflict on the island. Were Crusoe not so ordinary and so worldly, the religious themes would have made *Robinson Crusoe* strike the reader as fable or sermon. Instead, they become part of a human being's desperate attempt to remain sane and make sense of an experience harrowing almost beyond our imagination.

We never forget that the work of salvation is not Crusoe's only business, and once he has worked out his relationship to God, his religion is no more intrusive than most men's. For the Protestant of Defoe's time, experienc-

ing religion was much like marriage. During courtship (the stage equivalent to Crusoe's attempt to come to terms with God) the couple is
obsessed with itself, and work and leisure activities are somewhat subordinated; once a good marriage is established, the couple becomes secure
and turns back to former concerns, always keeping in mind the obligations
and pleasures of the marriage. It is one of Defoe's most notable achievements that he integrates Crusoe's religion into his character in the last
part of *Robinson Crusoe* and in *Farther Adventures*. Unlike Chetwood's
Falconer, who continues to remark in a quite didactic and digressive way
on the actions of Providence, Crusoe draws upon his religious beliefs as
one, but only one, of several determinants of action as he does when he
refuses to join the other sailors in their slaughter of the Indians on
Madagascar.

So it is in *Moll Flanders*. The "rogue biography," by then ubiquitous
because of its popularity in ballads, newspapers, pamphlets, and the Newgate ordinary's accounts, becomes a full-scale novel based upon yet another universal fantasy.[7] For more than 250 years, Moll has represented the
uncrushable human spirit and the idea that "unwearied Industry" will
finally be richly rewarded. The genius of this novel is that Moll's "Diligence and Application" are so often devoted to immoral or criminal cheats
and yet stand in intimate relation to her desire "to be able to get my Bread
by my own work" and to the overarching, moral world that promised
discovery and punishment of sins.

The technical skill evidenced in the first fifty pages assures the effect of
the rest of the novel. Defoe establishes important elements of Moll's
character and the nature of the world before she becomes a criminal. In
most narrative fiction, the reader joins the initiated, experienced characters in looking at the naive and idealistic with amusement and even scorn.
Not so in *Moll Flanders*, where the experience is reversed. Moll's ambitions in her youth in Colchester are naive to the point of irony, yet they are
simple. She wants to be able to get her own bread, and later she wants a
lasting, faithful love. That the townspeople, regardless of their affection
for her, can laugh at her desire to earn a living and see the irony in the very
vocabulary of her aspirations is a comment on the opportunities for
women in the society[8] and on the vocabulary developed to obscure hard
truth and responsibility. Moll does manage to earn her living with her
needle, but anyone familiar with the hours, hardships, and uncertainties
of her occupation would regard it as temporary as well as unusual and
admirable.[9]

Her seduction by the older brother in the house where she is servant-
companion was formulaic by the time Defoe wrote his novel. Again the

reader knows what the outcome will be. Servant women could not expect justice even if raped, let alone seduced,[10] and Moll makes every mistake from giving up her maidenhead to accepting money. Nevertheless, her feelings are deeply human. She believes herself worthy of the brother's love, and if she is vain, she is also aware that she has worked hard to improve her natural advantages. She believes his promises and grieves over the loss of his companionship as well as her hopes for marriage. Defoe uses the pattern of such episodes to set Moll Flanders apart. The end of the affair is as expected, and the dialogue is trite: she asks if "this [is] your Faith and Honour," he promises to "love as Friends all our Days," and every time they meet they "fell into the same Arguments all over again." But the end is even worse than anticipated, for Moll is coerced into a marriage to her lover's brother and articulates the full emotional pain of her position. She asks, "Can you Transfer my Affection? . . . is it in my Power . . . to make such a Change at Demand?" She becomes ill and "a thousand Times wish'd" to die rather than recover. Faced with being turned out of the house as a "cast off Whore," she marries Robin and spends five years aching for his brother.[11] Moll emerges stripped of illusions about occupation and marriage, but behind the predatory woman lives the girl who wanted independence, respect, and a constant love.

Although Moll becomes first like Rufina in *La Picara* and then like the anatomies of cheats,[12] hints of the idealistic girl survive. She can rejoice in the peace of her few years of happy marriage, can be vulnerable enough to suffer when she and Jemmy must separate, and can imagine the situations of people she robs to be like her own. As short and even ironic as these moments are, they remind us of a woman forced into a lifestyle not of her own choosing. Rufina, for example, in *La Picara*, makes no effort to marry her victims and wants unlimited wealth; Moll accepts the economic nature of marriage and tries to get the best, most stable man she can. Her choices are usually admirable men, and that they turn out to be short-lived, close kin, or destitute Irishmen is not her fault.

The story of Moll's career as thief is even closer to the familiar rogue's tale. Prefaces to these stories explained their benefits for three groups of readers: those inclined to crime might be deterred; criminals might be frightened into reform; and the virtuous might learn to avoid the cheats. In fact, the delight in these books came from the trickster's dexterity and ingenuity, the fantasy of breaking the law and going beyond limits, and the suspense built into each attempt. The reader knew that the trickster would be caught; he might be pumped or thrashed, sent to prison or hanged, but he would be caught and punished. This expectation worked not only to create suspense but to diminish the evil in each criminal act. In

the ultimate scheme of things, the bundle stolen was insignificant because the stakes were actually the physical and eternal life of the criminal.
Whether or not we see *Moll Flanders* in the form of the spiritual autobiography, as G.A. Starr does, the moral universe of such pamphlets as *Strange
and Wonderful news from Lincolnshire* (1679) and the ordinary's *Accounts* frames Moll's career and promises its end. As in *Robinson Crusoe*,
the complex blend of genres supports traditionally inharmonious themes
and world views.

## II

Until the 1970s, much of the scholarly work on Defoe's novels concentrated upon the sources of his ideas and material, and explained the ways
the novels embodied "the world of Defoe."[13] The more we know about his
age, the more we realize how fully he participated in the intellectual life of
his time and how attuned he was to politics and religion, the two factors
that determined so many men's fortunes between 1660 and 1731. Every
novel he wrote draws upon an intimidating knowledge of immediate
situations, profound issues, and published works of history, economics,
philosophy, literature, science, and even theosophy; and he puts this
knowledge to work in small as well as large ways.

The most significant constitutional achievement of Defoe's lifetime
was the establishment of parliamentary rather than hereditary succession
to the English throne. As W.A. Speck has said, the problem plagued
"British politics until the final defeat of the Jacobite rebels in 1746."[14] The
Accession of King George I, a Hanoverian cousin but distantly related to
Queen Anne, provoked widespread riots and even invasions by the Jac-
obites, supporters of Catholic James, "the Pretender." Defoe wrote some
fifty-five individual works in support of the Protestant Settlement, and
the conflict and his opinions about it find their way into his fiction. In fact,
it is the subject of three of his "lives"; *Memoirs of John Duke of Melfort*
(1714), *An Account of the . . . Actions of James Butler* [1715], and *The
Memoirs of Majr. Alexander Ramkins* (1719) all describe how Jacobitism
ruined the lives and fortunes of promising men and, together with many of
Defoe's shorter fictionalized journals and minutes written in the cause,
show his skill with dialogue and exemplary fable. For example, Butler's
distinguished service under King William is negated by his Jacobite activities, and Ramkins slowly falls into poverty, prison, and even periods of
mental illness, dramatized by rambling and often funny speeches.

The novels, written in a lull in Jacobite activity, occasionally illustrate how much a part of ordinary life the issue was and how it could suddenly and unexpectedly affect men's lives. Colonel Jack, for a number of small but understandable reasons, is a Jacobite sympathizer.[15] He is no zealot and feels no need to deny the fact; when the Preston rebels are near his home, he joins them more out of curiosity and whim than commitment. The result, however, is devastating. Suddenly he is a traitor, himself subject to execution and his estate to seizure. Fearing discovery even back in Virginia and obsessed by thoughts of "being discover'd, betray'd, carried to England, hang'd, quarter'd, and all that was terrible," he goes on a trading voyage to the West Indies, where he is unknown, and sends his wife to England to sue for his pardon. The terror and inconvenience he suffers for his impulsive gesture end with George I's general pardon, but not before he has feared enslavement in the Spanish mines and has been held against his will on the islands. An even briefer episode occurs in *The Four Years Voyages of Captain Roberts* (1726), when Roberts avoids a potentially disastrous quarrel with the pirates because their toast to the Pretender is worded so that Roberts can interpret it as suited to "the man on the throne."

The eighteenth was the century in which England built her empire, and the Peace of Utrecht's most advantageous clause gave England supremacy in the "three-corner" trade, the slave trade. Again, Defoe wrote extensively about these closely related issues, and *Colonel Jack* includes an enthusiastic endorsement of the colonies and a carefully developed model for controlling slaves on a North American plantation. Robinson Crusoe describes himself as a colonial governor, and through him Defoe comments upon the responsibilities, rights, and methods of many governors being sent from England to various parts of the world. When he shows Crusoe arranging elaborate settlement contracts, enhancing the power of the office by delayed appearance and a show of weapons, behaving paternalistically in such matters as arranging marriages, and finally leaving the colony without developing its full potential, he reflects the behavior of far too many English governors.[16]

Peter Earle reminds us that at no other time have there been "so many ships at sea whose sole function was to seize or destroy other ships."[17] *The Farther Adventures of Robinson Crusoe, Captain Singleton, Col. Jack, Captain Roberts,* and dozens of Defoe's pirate lives mirror the viciously competitive and predatory climate that led to the War of Jenkins' Ear shortly after Defoe's death. Some of his characters are victims and some are victimizers, but all understand the nature of the trade and the elements of national politics. Defoe is specific about where the ships go, what they pick up at various ports, and what will sell in specific places. These novels are redolent with the coffee, cocoa, saffron, cinnamon, rum, and tobacco of the New World; glittering with the diamonds, emeralds, jade, rubies, and semiprecious stones of the Mediterranean trade; and full of the textures of European wools, bays, serges, linens, and calicoes. Singleton's experiences illustrate the truths of the trade; for instance, he takes a ship of rebellious slaves, and cargoes useful to him on the African coast are useless to him in the West Indies. Some pirates avoid the ships of certain nations out of patriotism, and all, like Singleton, can sketch the character of a country's ships. The Spaniards "generally had Money on board," Singleton tells us, but the English were to be avoided because "we were sure of more Resistance from them" and they carried less "Booty." The Spaniards believe the English have "greater Presence of Mind in their Distress" than others; they "outsail" other boats in pursuit of Crusoe in *Farther Adventures*, and even the natives believe the English superior to the other nations in navigation.[18] Fortunes are made and lost in these novels, and the men who trade are the daring risk-takers, the unemployed, and the desperate men described by Crusoe's father in the opening pages of that novel.

Robinson Crusoe is very much a part of this world. Drawn to an active, enterprising, acquisitive life in spite of his desire to obey his parents and an understanding of the blessings of the "middle station," he builds a fortune on a Brazilian plantation and is on a slaving trip when he is shipwrecked. He is a castaway in the midst of the most active, most optimistic, and most opportunity-rich part of his life, and to endure that state of isolation for twenty-eight years while other men living ordinary lives become rich and successful could drive the strongest man mad. Here we can see the enormous complexity of Defoe's novel as he unites the economic ambitions, the psychological strains, and the most controversial religious tenets.

First of all, Crusoe is a realistic psychological being whose efforts to maintain his sanity are heroic, in both his large and small actions. To notice the number and variety of those efforts is to see the degree of Defoe's artistry. In some ways, the small touches are the most impressive: the way Crusoe plans the day's work, the stick on which he records his passing days, the triumph he feels when he can predict rainfall and seasonal changes in order to produce better crops. He tells us, for example, "That I was very seldom idle; but having regularly divided my Time, according to several daily Employments. . . ." His struggle against despair recurs and changes in intensity, waxing and waning in spite of his efforts to moderate his emotions along with his life. Very late in his time on the island, he can fall into the despair of the early weeks; he exclaims, "O that there had been but one or two; nay, or but one Soul sav'd out of this Ship, to have escap'd to me, that I might but have had one Companion, one Fellow-Creature to have spoken to me. . . . I believe I repeated the Words, *O that it had been but One!* a thousand Times. . . ." and this thought drives him to desperation.[19]

Within this context and running parallel to Crusoe's efforts to find ways to occupy, order, and give meaning to the hours of his days, Crusoe's spiritual quest assumes thematic centrality, coherence, and credibility. Crusoe's initial questions to God are the questions of Job: why do I *suffer*? why do *I* suffer? He asks why a good God would "ruin" a "poor creature" and repeatedly describes himself as "singl'd out." At one point he says specifically, "I am singl'd out and separated, as it were, from all the World to be miserable" (I:75). Soon he develops a shallow faith that allows him some comfort and peace. It is at this time that he nearly dies of a fever and has the terrifying dream of a man descending from a black cloud to threaten him with a sword. In the reflections that follow his illness and dream, Crusoe takes the first step toward salvation: an awareness of his sin which becomes remorse. He soon finds true comfort and joy in religion and concludes, "[God] could fully make up to me, the Deficiencies of my Solitary State, and the want of Humane Society by his Presence, and the Communications of his Grace to my Soul, supporting, comforting, and encouraging me to depend upon his Providence here, and hope for his Eternal Presence hereafter" (I:129). God becomes the companion he has longed for, and he lives in tranquillity for a year.

Crusoe's faith is tested and his religious education continued when he finds the footprint. He tells us, "Thus my Fear banish'd all my religious Hope." Out of the fear and doubt, however, comes submission to God and a correct understanding of His relationship to the world. Crusoe, no longer substituting his judgment for God's, finds God a dependable ally rather than an adversary and reinterprets experience in the light of his new understanding. The footprint and the subsequent knowledge of the cannibals' visits to his island lead him to reflect upon how often man asks for things that will not make him happy; the presence of the cannibals, for example, makes his desire for other men on the island ironic. Crusoe, as retrospective narrator, also looks back on such incidents as his discovery of the barley growing on the island—his first reaction that it was a miracle performed by God for Him, his disillusionment and rejection of God when he discovers the way the barley seed came to be on the island, and his final understanding that the barley was an example of God's care for his creatures. Crusoe, like Job, determines that some of the ways of God are unknowable and that omniscience would bring misery and fear rather than wisdom and happiness. "How infinitely good that Providence is" that hides events and dangers which would "distract his Mind, and sink his Spirits," Crusoe says (I:227–28).

In *Farther Adventures,* he elaborates specifically on the relationship between second causes and God's care when he notes that the native woman who believes God sent the Bible when her husband prayed for it was not entirely mistaken: "It is true, that providentially it was so, and might be taken so in a consequent Sense [and] . . . that God may be very properly said to answer our Petitions . . . but we do not expect Returns from Heaven, in a miraculous and particular Manner, and that it is our Mercy that it is not so."[20]

Crusoe's religious questions not only are universal but gain intensity because of the seriousness with which his contemporaries discussed them. His pressing need to know whether things happen to him by accident or design summarizes questions about the existence and nature of God as well as about God's actions in the world. His distress at not being able to determine whether events, dreams, and even thoughts are signs or messages from God raises the same issues. His questions and his answers are in many ways trite; for example, philosophers and psychologists have long said that man would create God if there were none, and we can see this novel in the context of the age that constantly struggled against its own deep skepticism. When Addison admonishes his readers to remember the moment in which they felt faith and cling to that memory (*Spectator* No. 465), he speaks for a nation that wanted to believe in God as they thought their fathers had and yet could not "prove" God's existence or rest on the assumptions of an earlier generation.

Crusoe's resolution is satisfyingly modern and different from the explanations of a Richard Baxter or a John Bunyan. He does find more design than accident in the world; he does find God acting directly and benignly toward his creatures; he does find religious faith to be strengthening and cheering. But he also finds that God acts through natural law and that there are vast areas of permanent uncertainty. He concludes that the business of life is to serve God when the opportunity arises (as he does when he teaches Friday or the island settlers), but primarily he takes up his time and thoughts with secular pursuits. He has to work out his relationship with God not only for salvation but also for temporal peace of mind. Once he has done so, he becomes no meditating hermit or pious propagandist.

The preface of *Robinson Crusoe* echoes *Paradise Lost* by stating that one intention of the narrative is "to justify and honour the Wisdom of Providence," and the reader is therefore somewhat prepared for the centrality of the examination of God's relationship to humankind. To some extent this theme, with the related exploration of accident and design, exists in all of Defoe's fiction. The same question drives "H.F." in *A Journal of the Plague Year* and operates at crucial turning points in *Moll Flanders* and *Colonel Jack.*

Natural disasters and interpretation of signs were among the most vexed religious questions of the time.[21] Each new threat of plague intensified debates over the causes and responses to it. *A Journal of the Plague Year* (1722) dramatizes them all, from the nationalization of the health profession to the flourishing of mountebanks. H.F. records the progress of the plague and the waxing and waning of fads in prevention; he takes a stand on the actions of magistrates, shutting up houses, and reciting charms. In many aspects, his own decision to flee or stay is a microcopy of the national problem of interpretation. He searches for a sign and endlessly vacillates; he alternately walks the streets and locks himself away. He survives, and the city rises and even grows, but the meaning remains hidden. The blind faith of *Due Preparations for the Plague* (1722), with devout provision for death and pious thanks for deliverance, seems as good as anything else. Because Defoe recreates the experience of the plague so vividly, makes so many characters generous and even heroic, and traces the effects on trade convincingly, *A Journal* does not become frustrating because of its lack of resolution. Instead, the very lack of a certain answer reflects the experience of Defoe's contemporaries; to see God's directing hand would have seemed superstitious to many of them and to have a scientific explanation would have been equally unconvincing. As Maximillian E. Novak has said, the novel becomes a celebration of the endurance of London and its people;[22] out of the fire and the plague will come the nation of shopkeepers grown prosperous in the rebuilding and refurnishing of London.

In a world they believe governed by a benign God, people often ascribe the unpleasant events they cannot explain to Fate or Fortune. Defoe's characters use this habit of thought and occasionally take it beyond figure of speech to refer to outgrowths of early eighteenth-century writings on accident and design. For example, no reader of criminal literature or collections of cases of supernatural occurrences would be surprised to find Moll Flanders blaming the devil for some of her crimes. Many still held the opinion that the world was an active battleground between God and Satan and that Satan could act directly in the world. The theory followed that some crimes were so heinous or out of character that only Satan could give people the idea of committing them. All of the collections of manifestations of spirits in the world including Defoe's own *The Political History of the Devil* (1726) and *An Essay on the History and Reality of Apparitions* (1727) recorded "promptings." Just as Moll hears an irresistible voice urging her to take the bundle that is her first theft, so others heard voices telling them to cut their throats or strangle a rival. Whether these experiences were supernatural or not is never answered, but their vividness and frequency could not be dismissed in Defoe's time. That he includes them and allows them to have a powerful effect on his characters is but another example of the way he integrates the ideas of his time and uses them to extend possibilities.

Almost any intellectual issue we select can be found in Defoe's novels. With the erosion of support for hereditary monarchies came unprecedented consideration of theories of government, and the great works of Hobbes, Harrington, Locke, and others were familiar to all Englishmen. Thinkers from Rousseau on have seen the paradigmatic function of Crusoe's island and praised Defoe's dramatization of complex political and social philosophies. Invigorating these abstract ideas are what writers have seen as some specifically English values. James Joyce, for example, called Crusoe the "true symbol" of the British, far more accurate than John Bull. Crusoe for James carries the "whole Anglo-Saxon spirit": "the manly independence, . . . the persistence; . . . the practical, well-balanced religiousness" and can become "an architect, a carpenter, a knife-grinder, an astronomer, a baker, a shipwright, a potter, a saddler, a farmer, a tailor, an umbrella-maker, and a clergyman."[23] So, of course, can Captain Singleton and John, the biscuit-baker in *A Journal of the Plague Year,* and both are legislators and kings as well. They are the enterprising, energetic Englishmen who were transforming England into the world's market, as Defoe called it, and into a nation of factories and merchants; they would make it the industrial innovator for generations. They are master tinkerers, improvisers, jacks-of-all-trades. How English this conception is can still be seen today. After a demonstration of American professional football in the summer of 1983, the *London Times* compared "American specialization" to the (superior) amateurism and the need for a variety of skills in the English games of rugby, soccer, and cricket. The civilization that Crusoe creates is distinctly English, from its most domestic details to its largest political contracts and assumptions. Crusoe builds himself a summer house in the cooler part of the island, and he stratifies his government as the British saw the world's class system.

Time after time, Defoe absorbed his culture into a familiar, intriguing human fantasy, drew upon narrative forms that satisfied people's desires for adventure and for emotional exploration, and encompassed the intellectual and physical worlds of the early eighteenth century. By doing so, he ensured that the reader would assent to the truths in his novels, to the characters' reactions and reasoning, and to the ways experience and education shape the mind. Because he saw the dynamic relationships of issues in his time, he could create such gripping fictions as a capitalist working out his relationship to God in a typological setting.

---

### III

In recent years, much attention has been given to the ways in which Defoe's works are fictional, partaking of the mainstream techniques and themes of the English novel. As imposing as the task is, critics have attempted to work with increasingly large numbers of Defoe's nonfiction writings; the result is that the development of his art through such works as *The Consolidator*, *The Storm*, and even the Bangorian controversy tracts, and through such subliterary forms as journalism and propaganda, has been clarified.[24] More and more critics have gone beyond the study of single ideas to argue Defoe's place in "the House of Fiction" and to elucidate his engagement with the major themes and narrative problems of English fiction.[25]

It is a cliché that the great subject of the English novel is money-and-marriage, and Defoe's *Moll Flanders*, *Col. Jack*, and *Roxana* take the relationship between the two as rich material.[26] All three of these characters share Jack's desire: "a settled family Life was the thing I Lov'd, had made two pushes at it . . . yet the Miscarriage of what was pass'd did not discourage me at all but I resolv'd to marry . . ." (II, 61). Whom the characters marry depends upon their wealth, and they and their lovers are full of tricks to exaggerate their values. All have exceptionally bad luck in their spouses, whose deaths, drink, folly, profligacy, and even incest cast them repeatedly back into the "market." Within each novel, Defoe unites money and marriage in a variety of ways. We are most conscious of the theme in *Moll Flanders*, where one of the Colchester daughters states bluntly, ". . . *Betty* wants but one Thing, but she had as good want every Thing, for the Market is against our Sex just now . . . if she have not Money, she's no Body." The truth of that statement is dramatized repeatedly until Moll leaves the market for her career as a thief and finds deft, imaginative expression in, for example, the way she tallies up her assets at the end of each marriage to determine if she has gained or lost and titillates her husband/brother with a kind of monetary striptease, revealing day by day a little more money. Roxana watches her first husband's assets drain away until she is left destitute and later fears to mix her "tainted" money with the Dutchman's legitimately earned funds. Jack debates the advantages of marrying poor women and finds the trappings of prosperity in women especially deceptive.

Many of the opinions found in Defoe's conduct books such as *The Family Instructor* (1715), *Religious Courtship* (1722), *Conjugal Lewdness* (1727), and even *The Complete English Tradesman* (1726) find their way into the novels.[27] Although these opinions are often used in *exempla*, they are completely thematically functional. For instance, Defoe believed that young men should be financially secure before marriage, and Singleton, Crusoe, and Jack all follow this pattern. After a life of adventure and hardship, they see marriage as an important part of a prosperous, happy life. Defoe cautions young women about marriage and writes lists of questions for them to ask their suitors, for "the danger is principally" on the woman's side, and Moll and Roxana often exemplify his points. Defoe's conduct books are also full of family problems and family arguments, and Jack struggles with a drunk, a spendthrift, and a rebellious wife. Defoe may have been the first to bring marital bickering to life in English fiction, and some of that bickering is about money.

A second commonplace about the English novel is that it profoundly recognizes the power of the past. Characters are shaped by their country's history as well as by their own. The "English character," the recalcitrant individualist, and the rather phlegmatic intelligence are still recognized in books with titles such as *An Ungovernable People* (1980). Old prejudices, old triumphs, and old rivalries seem to flicker into life just when events seem beyond memory. In many of Defoe's characters, we find commercial acumen in the Dutch and the Quakers, cruelty in the Portuguese and Spaniards, sneakiness and frivolity in the French, and ingenuity, diligence, and piety in the English. More open-minded than most, he nevertheless gives us three lascivious Italians for every sympathetic Catholic priest. Part of a nationalistic generation, he obviously revels in the opportunities, diversities, and wealth of England.

"Puritan" and "Victorian"—the two terms used most frequently to identify English attitudes—both have predominantly moral overtones, and that is no coincidence. The religious past invades every aspect of English life, and Defoe wrote at a moment when religion and politics intertwined and affected almost everyone. *Memoirs of a Cavalier, A Journal of the Plague Year,* and *Robinson Crusoe* explicitly draw upon the Puritan past as it intersected the secularism and skepticism of the Restoration. That he finds the faith of the Cromwellians and of the most conservative of the plague victims ultimately unsatisfactory deepens his books, for he sees pathos, loss, disillusionment, and uncertainty more often than liberation. The Cavalier makes lists of evils and reflects upon the distance between the ideals of the Parliamentarians and the result. Crusoe's island, a structure perfect for the kind of meditation and reflection designed into the seventeenth-century prison, gives way to the city, a structure representing the chaos, diversity, competition, and crowding found in the eighteenth-century prison. The competition of the need to retire and reach deep into the self with the call to engage and find a place in a modern economy bring the past and present into powerful tension. The enmity between country and court, Whig and Tory, comes into Defoe's novels through his awareness of historical forces.

The greatest of Defoe's characters vibrate deeply to their own personal histories as well as to their country's. Crusoe's and Roxana's tormenting guilt comes from the mingling of religious symbolism assimilated into the fiber of their minds with the consciousness of mistakes. The Puritan mind has given Crusoe images of himself as Jonah and the prodigal son, of recalcitrant, petulant rebel. It has given Roxana the conception of the "Blast of Heaven."[28] Singleton, Jack, Moll—each character looks back on a "dreadful life" and finds the sum nearly unbearable. The very list of sins that Moll enumerates to the minister seems to be nearly too long for the telling, numerous beyond the time available for the minister to hear her, and Singleton's despair is one of the most extended treatments of suicidal impulses in eighteenth-century literature. The personal past shaped in part by a cultural past is the most consistent source of psychological stress in Defoe's characters.

A third preoccupation is the sense of conflict between the individual and society.[29] The English novel has consistently developed great characters who feel limited, confined, and even alienated from their society. Rather than finding their ideals reflected in or their aspirations aided by social institutions, they find hypocrisy, corruption, and obstructionism. Perhaps no writer besides Dickens explores this idea in as many thematic and stylistic ways as does Defoe. Because of this conflict, the very act of defining the self becomes problematic in English society. If the character does not feel that society's place for him or her is correct, then who is he? After all, "place" was definition, determinant of education, occupation, recreations, and aspirations. What happens to the Betty's who cannot bear the thought of a lifetime of bedmaking and hearth scrubbing? to the Crusoe's who feel that a good trade would be as constricting as an out-of-the-way corner of a rural cottage? Educated beyond their stations, with ambitions beyond their expectations, they fear they may be rebelling not simply against their stratified society but against the order of God's world denoted by their births. Without birth, money, education, religion, or the other tokens of society, many of Defoe's characters are nearly without identity, for "beggars" and "rabble" and "charity children" are amorphous terms reducing those so classified to indistinguishable parts of a dispensable group. In defining themselves, they must come not only to understand but also to redefine society's tokens of value until, in the words of Timothy J. Reiss, they are reconciled with society and society with them.[30] Later writers simplified the task by building in the fortunate discovery of a titled parent that elevated one character to the level of the beloved (as Fielding and Burney do) or by substituting a clear, superior moral value for a social value (as Richardson does in *Pamela*). Defoe takes a more difficult route; he attempts to make his readers accept ability, courage, leadership, or some combination of such qualities as equalizers and definers, and then complicates his task by refusing to obscure the fact that money is often the middle term in the act of reconciliation. The result is a harsh vision of human nature, unpleasantly unlike the satisfaction of finding "virtue rewarded" in the good-hearted, the ebullient, and the pious.

Defoe's clear apprehension of the complex relationship between the individual and society often finds expression in the dissonance of appearance and reality. The space between the longing, thinking interior of a character and the blank social being is often huge. Moll's disguises can make her all but invisible in the crowds with which she mingles in order to steal. Signs of the life within, such as Jack's tears during the plantation master's speech, always surprise the other characters. The constant misperceptions that lead to such an outcome as Jack's first marriage or Jemmy and Moll's, the desperate drama played out by Moll and her seducer in the midst of the Colchester family, and the horrors of the interior lives led by Moll while married to her brother and Roxana to the Dutchman are but a few of the ways Defoe works with perception and interiority. The loneliness characters feel in such situations is part of the "new subject" Ian Watt sees in Defoe's work. Singleton can describe his adult experience in England in terms that make his hurt grueling: ". . . I speak *English*; but I came out of *England* a child, and never was in it but once since I was a Man, and then I was cheated and imposed upon. . . ." For most of Moll's and Jack's lives no one cares where they are and no one would miss them if they died. Slashed horribly by a French swordsman, Jack seeks help from strangers; faceless plague victims die alone.

The failures and hypocrisies of social institutions throw the characters back on their own resources and even into the hands of criminals. The provisions for the care and education of Moll, Jack, and Singleton; the character of the Newgate ordinary in *Moll Flanders*; the inadequacies of marriage and divorce laws; and the treatment of pregnant women as

illustrated by the harsh, inhospitable behavior the pregnant Moll encounters in several parishes systematically undercut the pious admonitions of
professional men and respectable people. Because Defoe finds ideal and
practice in society out of harmony and human beings hard to read, he
presents the ambiguity of life without apology.

The great problem for the early English novel was form. Because the age
imposed a number of moralistic demands upon its literature, the early
novel self-consciously mimicked those forms which had respectability.
Defoe, for example, wrote *The Memoirs of a Cavalier, A Journal of the
Plague Year*, the *life* of Singleton, and the *histories* of Jack and Roxana.[31]
Like so many of the earliest fiction writers, he used the first-person point
of view for all his novels, insisting upon the credibility that personal,
eyewitness accounts bear. His novels, then, become pseudo-autobiograph-
ical and, in order to maintain the pretense, take on the characteristics of
immediacy, familiarity, subjectivity, and structural untidiness. They do,
however, gain the means to explore the character's inner life in great depth
even as they can present adventures and experiences in the physical world.

Rather than "writing to the moment," Defoe uses the retrospective
narrator. His characters can identify "critical moments," construct sequences and patterns, assign meaning to events, emphasize and subordinate with some self-consciousness, and reflect upon the memories of
experiences. Crusoe, one of the most self-conscious narrators, does all
these things. He assigns the significance leaving home has, labels his early
shipwrecks as warnings, interprets his dreams, and finally calls his life, as
Jack does his, a "Chain of Causes." By giving us an account, his journal,
and his reflections on his early days on the island, Crusoe juxtaposes three
kinds of thinking about an experience and can offer a variety of interpretations. The reader joins the narrator in the process of attempting to make
sense of a life and to draw lessons from it. Just as the narrator analyzes
economic, political, and social structures and pressures, so does the reader; and as the narrator finally judges his own life, so does the reader decide
whether the protagonist is saved or damned, repentant, deluded, or insincere.

For those of us who see Defoe's fiction as shaped both by his own
imagination and by the lively publishing world in which he worked, his
novels seem to be deliberate experiments drawing with increasing self-
consciousness upon fictional structures and strategies. For example, he
seems to rely more confidently upon incident, metaphor, and symbol in
his later books than in *Robinson Crusoe*. The language of *Crusoe* is more
traditionally biblical, more repetitious, and more expository than that of
*Roxana*. Defoe increasingly creates private "emblems" and symbols as he

does with Newgate Prison in *Moll Flanders* and the Turkish costume in *Roxana*. With growing daring, he begins to exploit secular themes as he does in *Col. Jack* and to use fiction to collapse time in order to bring history to bear on human psychology and current events as he does in *The Memoirs of a Cavalier*. He begins to play social, legal, and religious transgressions off against each other until he creates Roxana, a character who, if she breaks the law at all, is a "white collar" criminal, sins rather than commits crimes and feels more pursued than either of the "notorious" criminals, Moll and Singleton. He probes deeper and deeper into the ways people think and respond to situations; *Crusoe*, after all, does embody the *form* of the spiritual autobiography which was recognized as mimicking *the* path to salvation; H.F. puzzles and reasons; Roxana moves farther and farther into her own private, inner world; and Moll sometimes seems to be an unreliable reporter of external events. Relationships become increasingly complex and psychological; William Walters and Singleton, Amy and Roxana, and the characters who have lived Moll's and Jack's own stories as her mother and his tutor have become vehicles for the development of character and theme.

Defoe, of course, was a great formal realist.[32] He does give us the streets, the objects, and the common events of his society, and he does seem to be *reporting* on human experience with a fullness and a lack of manipulation (or "art") that carry their own credibility. His years as a journalist and writer of lives designed to be published in periodicals or pamphlets, his unequaled familiarity with the histories and travel literature (biographical and geographical) of his time gave him knowledge and writing experience simply unavailable to any other writer before Melville. It made little difference whether he drew upon the pattern of crime literature, pirate biography, voyages to Ceylon or the Caribbean islands, or accounts of the Great Northern War; all focused on event, relying upon an economical presentation of an exciting event in the present time and upon a variety of "strange and surprizing" incidents rather than upon the unity of plot and effect common to most drama and poetry. And all reported not only upon events but upon setting: readers knew that a crime was committed with a knife on White Horse Lane, that a pirate took his first ship at a particular reading of latitude and longitude, that a ship coming from the New World was carrying rice, sugar, rum, and tobacco when it sank, that penguins and natives in feathered loincloths populated a specific island, and that the King of Sweden had 65,000 men at his command for the first battle of the year.

Such particularity contributes in unexpected ways to the very subjectivity and structural disorder of the novel. For example, the details recorded depend on the narrator, even though travel literature had established a list of points to be covered including topography, location of ports, major city, natural products, customs, and so on. Crusoe tells us several times in *Farther Adventures* that he is omitting things that would be useful only to those who intend to travel; Singleton is most interested in animals and in natural things that can be used to build and caulk a boat. Such selectivity reinforces the idea that Crusoe is an experienced, elderly traveler, and that Singleton is alert to means to reduce labor and alive to the beauty and strangeness of elephants, cats, birds, and other creatures.

A second contribution of such particularity is that the reportorial nature of the forms Defoe mimicked inclined him toward chronological presentation rather than toward the kind of artistic, thematic emphasis and studied composition that leads to the subordination of some topics in favor of others. Although each form met well-defined reader expectations and even had formulaic elements, all rejected the careful formal patterns and aesthetically pleasing structures that we find in the novels we admire so much by Eliot, Hardy, and James. Even a retrospective narrator could not order his life and recognize climax as well as Fielding's grand conductor or Austen's wry observer. Genuine autobiography is often admired for revealing more than the writer intends or even understands; in order to reproduce the pleasure of biographical and autobiographical forms, Defoe must leave some of the disorder of those forms.

That Defoe is a great formal realist and a master at reproducing the physical world of his characters does not necessarily mean that he must sacrifice the kind of imaginative representations of the world that novelists use to reach deeper insights about experience and the nature of the world. In fact, the very lack of introspection in the young Singleton helps us see the callousness and immorality in the world, and the absence in Moll of Crusoe's emotional agonizing reinforces our sense of her fortitude and the world's indifference. Time after time, Defoe isolates his characters and has them invent civilization all over as he does most obviously with Crusoe and Singleton; he has them meet basic needs, form governments, and stratify society. Crusoe's island is not Lilliput, of course, but it does represent and comment upon English government and the nature of man. Moll Flanders is not Bigger Thomas, but she shows the destructive distance between the rich and the poor, and her "life" criticizes her society; her trial is as prejudiced and predetermined, even as political, as his.

Because Defoe so often creates a structure that seems to reproduce the shape of the life it describes, we fail to recognize how easily he moves between his character's thoughts and experiences and how effectively he communicates the psychic being of even the least reflective characters.

The realistic sounds made by the African animals become the symbols of Singleton's fear and his awareness that he is in a strange, alien land that is vast and unknown beyond imagination. The screams and cries in *A Journal of the Plague Year* seem both disembodied and massed, representing H.F.'s fear and the way London has become a foreign land to him. Singleton stands near the center of the wide part of the continent of Africa, looks ahead at a "horrour," realizes that he has just passed through a "horrour" and that he has only four days' supplies with him. This realization takes but a few lines, yet it gives us a detailed description of the landscape as well as immediate understanding of his awe, weariness, and, finally, determination. Paul Alkon has demonstrated Defoe's control of pace, tempo, duration, simultaneity and space and the ways Defoe uses these experienced natural phenomena in thematic and structural techniques. Defoe's use of repetition, foreshadowing, and cross-referencing develop our expectations about characters and help develop our sense of their moral nature.[33]

As certainly as Richardson and Sterne, Defoe shaped the course of the English novel. When we define the novel, we often think in terms of its formal realism, of its concentration upon the life of an individual, of its generically mixed nature, of its reportorial qualities, and of its probing of the individual's psychological interaction with the empirical world. Certainly a very large number of novels deal with the self in society, with the outcast or rebel, with the alienated and the guilty, with the self-made or self-destructive, and with direction-changing events in the history of a nation. Experiments with illusions of truth, point of view, perception, narrative time, and form continue. As Ortega y Gasset said, the novel still does not want to look like a literary form but like "a bundle of letters, a journal, like life itself."

Finally, those who would begin the history of the novel after Defoe might consider the number of "Robinsonades" published since 1719 and reflect upon the words of some of the greatest novelists in our culture:

> Sir Walter Scott: [The popularity of *Robinson Crusoe*] has equalled that of any author who ever wrote. . . . even had he not been the author of *Robinson Crusoe*, De Foe would have deserved immortality for the genius which he has displayed in [*A Journal of the Plague Year*], as well as in the *Memoirs of a Cavalier*.[34]

> James Joyce: The first English author to write without imitating or adapting foreign works . . . and to infuse into the creatures of his pen a truly national spirit, to devise for himself an artistic form which is perhaps without precedent, except for the brief

monographs of Sallust and Plutarch, is Daniel Defoe, father of the English novel.[35]

It was Defoe's style which Thomas Hardy imitated and which impressed the publisher Alexander Macmillan, his friend John Morley, and George Meredith enough for them to encourage Hardy's career as a novelist. In his earliest fiction, they saw the writing to be "admirable," "strong and fresh," and having an "affected simplicity" and recognized the "power and insight" and "realism of circumstantial detail" even as they remarked that "the thing hangs too loosely together" and that some of the scenes "read like some clever lad's dream." Out of Hardy's study of Defoe came his vigorous, flexible, efficient prose[36] and his ways of expressing the charged relationship between man and society, perception and experience. The pilloried Dissenter who created the solitary castaway, the thief, and the haunted courtesan lives in the work of countless writers.

### Notes

1. "A Gentleman of the Press," *All the Year Round* 2 (1869), 132.

2. Page numbers for Defoe's novels refer to the Shakespeare Head Edition (1927; rpt. Oxford: Blackwell, 1974).

3. The term is Mas'ud Zavarzadeh's from *The Mythopoeic Reality* (Urbana: Univ. of Illinois Press, 1976).

4. A.W. Secord's *Studies in the Narrative Method of Defoe* is still the best work on sources (Urbana: Univ. of Illinois Press, 1924).

5. John Richetti, *Popular Fiction before Richardson* (Oxford: Clarendon Press, 1969), 62.

6. G.A. Starr, *Defoe and Spiritual Autobiography* (Princeton, N.J.: Princeton Univ. Press, 1965); J. Paul Hunter, *Reluctant Pilgrim* (Baltimore, Md.: Johns Hopkins Univ. Press, 1966).

7. For discussion of crime literature in England, see Peter Linebaugh, "The Ordinary of Newgate and His *Account*," in *Crime in England 1550–1800*, ed. J.S. Cockburn (London: Methuen, 1977), 298; Frank W. Chandler, *The Literature of Roguery* (Boston: Houghton Mifflin, 1907).

8. In her childhood, Moll makes a number of people laugh when she tells them she wants to be a "gentlewoman," and cannot understand why they call her "madam." Moll's ambitious dreams have been discussed in numbers of books and articles; see, for example, Michael Shinagel, *Daniel Defoe and Middle-Class Gentility* (Cambridge, Mass.: Harvard Univ. Press, 1968), 144–46.

9. Wages were low, and social historians have documented the rigors of the work; for example, a fairly high number of milliners and seamstresses were blind or nearly so by middle age because of the poor light in which they labored. See M. Dorothy George, *London Life in the Eighteenth Century* (New York: Capricorn, 1965), 164–73, 234ff.

10. Even when men were convicted of raping servants, they were often pardoned. See Peter Wagner, "The Pornographer in the Courtroom: Trial Reports

about Cases of Sexual Crimes . . .," in *Sexuality in Eighteenth-Century Britain,* ed. Paul-Gabriel Boucé (Totowa, N.J.: Barnes & Noble, 1982), 126–27.

11. Moll tells us, "I was never in Bed with my Husband, but I wish'd my self in the Arms of his Brother . . ." (I:58).

12. [Alonso de Castillo Solorzano], *La Picara, or the Triumphs of Female Subtilty,* translated with "alterations and additions" by John Davies (London, 1665); a representative "anatomy," or collection, of cheats is Charles Cotton's *Compleat Gamester* (London, 1674).

13. The phrase is Peter Earle's; see *The World of Defoe* (New York: Atheneum, 1977). One of the most important of these books is Maximillian E. Novak's *Defoe and the Nature of Man* (London: Oxford Univ. Press, 1963); Starr's *Defoe and Spiritual Autobiography* and Hunter's *Reluctant Pilgrim* also fall into this category.

14. W.A. Speck, *Stability and Strife* (Cambridge, Mass.: Harvard Univ. Press, 1979), 152.

15. A recent discussion is David Blewett, "Jacobite and Gentleman: Defoe's Use of Jacobitism in *Colonel Jack,*" *English Studies in Canada* 4 (1978), 15–24.

16. See, for example, Leonard W. Labaree, *Royal Government in America* (New Haven, Conn.: Yale Univ. Press, 1930), esp. 102–18, 131–49, 374, 383, 393, 401.

17. Earle, *World of Defoe,* 59.

18. *Farther Adventures,* III:2, 119; *Four Years Voyages of Captain Roberts* (London, 1726), 160 respectively. The natives also say that the English are superior in "Physick, Conjuration, and Arithemetick."

19. *Robinson Crusoe,* I:217–18.

20. *Adventures,* III:62–63; see Keith Thomas, *Religion and the Decline of Magic* (New York: Scribner, 1971), 108ff., for a discussion of the growth of this opinion.

21. Thomas, *Decline of Magic,* 79–91 and passim.

22. Maximillian Novak, "Defoe and the Disordered City," *PMLA* 92 (1977), 241–52. See also Everett Zimmerman's fine discussion in his *Defoe and the Novel* (Berkeley: Univ. of California Press, 1975).

23. "Daniel Defoe," trans. Joseph Prescott, in *Buffalo Studies* 1 (1964), 24–25.

24. Paul Alkon's phenomenological reading of Defoe's novels in *Defoe and Fictional Time* (Athens: Univ. of Georgia Press, 1979), Geoffrey Sill's *Defoe and the Idea of Fiction* (New Brunswick, N.J.: Rutgers Univ. Press, 1983), and Lennard J. Davis, *Factual Fictions: The Origins of the English Novel* (New York: Columbia Univ. Press, 1983) are among the books that discuss the relationships between Defoe's earlier works and his novels. See also Maximillian Novak's forthcoming essay, "Sincerity, Delusion and Character in the Fiction of Defoe and the 'Sincerity Crisis' of His Time."

25. The phrase is Henry James's and is used by David Blewett in the introduction of his own critical study, *Defoe's Art of Fiction* (Toronto: Univ. of Toronto Press, 1979).

26. One of the most studied themes in Defoe's work, marriage/money, is discussed by Arnold Kettle, "In Defence of Moll Flanders," in *Of Books and Humankind,* ed. John Butt (London: Routledge & Kegan Paul, 1964), 55–67; Spiro T. Peterson, "The Matrimonial Theme of Defoe's *Roxana,*" *PMLA* 70 (1955), 166–91; William H. McBurney, "Colonel Jacque: Defoe's Definition of the

Complete Gentleman," *SEL* 2 (1962), 321–36; and Samuel Rogal, "The Profit and Loss of Moll Flanders," *SNNTS* 5 (1973), 98–103.

27. See McBurney's *"Colonel Jacque"*; see also my "Defoe's Women: Snares and Prey" in *Studies in Eighteenth-Century Culture*, ed. Ronald C. Rosbottom (Madison: Univ. of Wisconsin Press, 1976), V:103–20, and "Defoe's Prodigal Sons," *SLI* 15 (1982), 3–18.

28. Detailed studies of Roxana's personality and conscience have proliferated in recent years. See, e.g., Steven Cohan, "Other Bodies: Roxana's Confession of Guilt," *SNNTS* 8 (1976), 406–18; Terry Castle, " 'Amy, Who Knew My Disease'/ A Psychosexual Pattern in Defoe's *Roxana*," *ELN* 46 (1979), 81–96; Maximillian Novak, "Crime and Punishment in Defoe's *Roxana*," *JEGP* 55 (1966), 445–65. See also the *Roxana* chapters in Zimmerman, *Defoe and the Novel*, and Novak's *Realism, Myth, and History in Defoe's Fiction* (Lincoln: Univ. of Nebraska Press, 1983).

29. Again, this is a theme commonly discussed, especially by the Marxist critics. See, for example, Kettle, "In Defence of Moll Flanders," and Ian Watt's chapter on *Moll Flanders* in *The Rise of the Novel* (Berkeley: Univ. of California Press, 1957).

30. T.J. Reiss, *The Discourse of Modernism* (Ithaca: Cornell Univ. Press, 1982), 294–327.

31. The age would have agreed with Bacon that a history "either representeth a time, or a person, or an action. The first we call chronicles, the second lives, and the third narrations or relations" (Francis Bacon, *The Advancement of Learning*, ed. Arthur Johnston [Oxford: Clarendon Press, 1974], 72).

32. Watt, *Rise of the Novel*.

33. Alkon's *Defoe and Fictional Time* is a sophisticated study of these techniques.

34. "Defoe" in Scott's *Miscellaneous Prose Works* (Edinburgh, 1827).

35. Joyce, 7.

36. Florence Emily Hardy, *The Early Life of Thomas Hardy 1840–1891* (New York: Macmillan, 1928), 76–81. Hardy never forgot the power of Defoe's novels, especially *Robinson Crusoe*, which he mentions in *Far from the Madding Crowd*, *Jude the Obscure*, *The Woodlanders*, *The Laodiceans*, and other works.

# Margaret A. Doody

## Saying 'No,' Saying 'Yes': The Novels of Samuel Richardson

Here I sit down to form characters. One I intend to be all goodness; All goodness he is. Another I intend to be all gravity; All gravity he is. Another *Lady G*—ish; All *Lady G*—ish is she. I am all the while absorbed in the character. It is not fair to say—I, identically I, am any-where, while I keep within the character.[1]

Samuel Richardson's statement (although it refers specifically to his last novel, *Sir Charles Grandison*) may be taken as a description of his method of writing in all his novels. It is an interesting and puzzling remark—even self-contradictory. The novelist starts by speaking of "forming" his characters, emphasizing his own intention, speaking of qualities ("goodness," "gravity") as if they were distinct entities with which he could endow his personages—or rather, as if the personages were made out of a quality, as out of a substance: "All gravity he is." There is a deal of comedy in the formulation, which soon radically alters: the name of a character (*Lady G____*) becomes the quality and the quality the character; she is an entity in herself, with unique attributes only to be described by naming her. The novelist is no longer forming a personage by representing one dominant quality; the character herself is a full-blown, complex creature existing, as it were, outside the novelist's powers of creation as much as "goodness" or "gravity." His only responsibility is to maintain her being with fidelity. The godlike, forming novelist ("Here I sit down to form characters") now becomes fragmentary and diffused. From a parallel of God the Father he becomes more like the Holy Ghost, moving everywhere, centered no-where. The "I" is not to be found; self unselves to make the selving of the characters. The novelist is definable as that which becomes the characters; he has a responsibility to "keep within" his character, rather than to form—he is "absorbed" by what he has made.

No other novelist of the eighteenth century made any statement like this. Richardson's view of the novel was, like that of all his contemporaries such as Fielding and Smollett, fundamentally moral. But it was also fundamentally aesthetic, and aesthetic in ways both romantic and mod-ern. In his letters we have, in scattered but cumulative remarks, the nearest thing to a novelist's personal discourse on the Art of Fiction that we were to get until Scott; in manner and substance Richardson's com-ments can remind us of Henry James. His sense of the art of the novelist differs from that of Fielding—more specifically, the Fielding of *Tom Jones*. Richardson's kind of novel gives authority to the character or characters—gives it to them in the strictest sense, for it is the characters who are the authors, and the novelist lives and moves and has his being only in them, and they in him. The author's moral intention must be fulfilled by the workings of the characters; the author cannot step in and tell us what to think and how to read.[2] What Richardson is describing to Lady Bradshaigh is something very like the *"Negative Capability"* that Keats was to praise in Shakespeare. The author should have freedom to withdraw, should not exert authority to impose. He must be delighted with all energies, not only those of which he officially approves. What displeases the moralist must delight the chameleon poet[3]—or novelist. Certainly in Richardson's novels the central characters are never morally or ethically simple; they are always complex, and hence capable of being variously interpreted both inside and outside the text. They are energies rather than static qualities, and they are always in a process of dynamic change. The modern, or nineteenth-century, idea that a character should *develop*, should grow and change and not just display different sides of the same standard self—this idea is found in Richardson, who anticipates in so many ways the nature of the novel to come. His letter-writing characters develop, change, change their minds; they may even be observed altering their opinions or rethinking an issue during the process of writing a sentence.

Richardson has been seen as the first great exemplar of what was in the twentieth century to be called "stream-of-consciousness"—though that phrase is unsatisfactory: the writing of a letter is a conscious act of communication rather than reverie. But Richardson stresses "writing to the moment,"[4] so that we catch a character's thoughts in an unformed state. Everything is progress and process, nothing seems finished; this quality is congenial to readers of Joyce and Woolf, authors who may themselves have learned something from Richardson. The characters do the intense living, thinking, reevaluating; the reader, without overt guid-ance or commentary from the novelist, understands what is going on as plot and story, and perpetually reinterprets what the characters say and do. The novel in letters was not in itself a new form in the mid-eighteenth century; indeed, by then it was fairly well established in domestic English fiction, as research by McBurney and Richetti has shown us.[5] But Richardson was the first novelist truly to exploit the possibilities of this mode hitherto presented in minor fictions. He raised the novel in letters to a great form with philosophical implications. Indeed, he is a novelist of philosophic depth; later authors of the Enlightenment, such as Rousseau and Diderot and Mme de Staël, were acute appreciators of what he had wrought.

Richardson's kind of novel in letters sets human life in the context of both the unknowable and the knowable; for Richardson, God is real and knowable, but His ways may not be knowable at every step. More puzzling still, other human beings are not easily knowable but must be perpetually read by clues and hints and changing signs. The society in which we live, though it declares itself a knowable structure manifest in both law and daily institutions, is a large, complex, and obscure creation that the lonely self may touch at every turn and yet cannot ever fully know or control. Time is the unknowable element in which we think and through which we live. Human beings always guess at the future and make scenarios for it, but these rarely come to pass (one source of Richardsonian irony). Even the past is not necessarily safely tucked away, perfectly known and static, but is always subject to interpretation again. The writers of Richardson's letters are in each letter in a little island of time, stuck in "now," here on Wednesday and remembering Tuesday but not in control of Thursday— though the reader may command the events of Thursday by turning over the pages. Richardson's characters are not narrators of a known past who have come to the end of a full sequence, like first-person narrators such as Roderick Random or David Copperfield or Jane Eyre. Rather, they are always uttering in the middle of events, forced to judge and act before all the facts are in; they cannot look back on their past selves with a smile of superiority, for they are involved in doing something right now. They have to decide; they feel responsible for what comes next. It is they, not the author, who must be anxious, and the whole that each is trying to create is nothing less than a life.

Richardson's characters thus mirror the state of each one of us during the process of living, and it is this that makes them all most sympathetic. It is in this that the central philosophical realism of the novels consists, if we take "realism" to mean what is like life in the way we know it. Other kinds of realism have perhaps been overemphasized in discussions of the novel in general; realism is an element that an author can use, and he may put in as many references to tea-pots and trains and slum landlords and so on as are useful to his aesthetic design and his purpose of showing us something about our lives. His duty to appeal to us so that we must say

"Yes, this is how life is, how it feels" is a standard that must in any novelist take precedence over a fidelity to irrelevant facts (though he must be strict in his aesthetic feel for what is relevant and what is not). The great realism may legitimately take precedence over the verisimilar; it has been objected that Lovelace and Clarissa write more than anybody could do in the couple of hours they are supposed to spend, but that is the sort of instance in which heightened reality of effect may take precedence over verisimilitude.[6]

The Richardsonian novel written by characters who are also readers—characters engaged in reading signs and clues and changeable hints in the world exterior to themselves and in themselves—is a kind of novel congenial to very modern forms of reading and of criticism. It seems no accident that Richardson is the first eighteenth-century author to attract the new-style critics of modern persuasions, structuralist or deconstructionist, such as Castle and Warner.[7] Richardson's novels invite that sort of treatment, even anticipate it, because they call attention to their own structure, to the *bricolage* of their putting together, and because the characters themselves, especially in *Clarissa*, move in on each other's interpretations of life and events in order to break down or blow up an antipathetic construction.

Richardson's own narrative art is so finely tuned that few critics have been able to avoid becoming involved with the characters. It is the kind of involvement the novels demand and Richardson the man delighted in, as can be seen in his tendency both to defend any character of his who is attacked by a reader and to question the perfection of one praised too warmly or too easily.[8] William Beatty Warner's attack on Clarissa, the heroine, and warm defense of Lovelace shows him to be just as deeply engaged with those characters as Richardson could have wished; Warner believes in them as warmly as any reader ever has done, and deconstructionism cannot save him.

It is difficult to remain coolly detached from an author who has made his central themes the groundwork of our being. All Richardson's stories are about sex and sexual relationships,[9] and his central conflict is always the conflict of heterosexual love in a society that has arbitrarily assigned certain roles and attitudes to both men and women and is itself arbitrary. Social arrangements and preconditions impose false selves on both sexes, but it is particularly the woman who most obviously suffers from what she is supposed to be. Richardson's men and women are busily engaging each other's interest and as busily engaged in resisting each other. They all "know their place" as defined by both gender and class, and they all try to move from that place.

It seems natural that Richardson's novels have attracted the attention of Marxist and feminist critics.[10] However much society may seem to have changed since Richardson's time, there is not one single sexual issue raised in Richardson's works that is now outmoded. The very permanence and intimacy of these issues have given Richardson criticism (for or against) in every period a certain edge. One's attitude to him identifies not necessarily one's gender but one's attitudes to sexual roles and appropriate behavior.

There has been a feeling on the part of some that to sympathize too much with Richardson's heroines puts one in danger of taking a "feminine" attitude to sexuality, attacks gentlemanliness.[11] Pamela makes too much fuss over her virginity; a woman should not care too much about giving a man the satisfaction he needs. Why make so much fuss about rape when there are serious issues in the world? The kind of anger that such an approach can inspire in someone who takes Richardson seriously, who feels that female sexuality has been terribly abused in much fiction as well as in life, can be felt in my own sentences here. It is true that there is never any "solution" to "the problem of the sexes." A solution suggested in a work of fiction may seem quite satisfactory in one light, unsatisfactory in others. A picture of the right relationship between a man and a woman can come to seem like the imposition of another falsehood. None of us is capable of imagining a mode of union between members of the two sexes not related to the way we already live. Richardson's own consciousness of the difficulty of resolving the relations between the sexes can be seen in the very different relations between men and women he proposes in each of his major novels and the different sorts of endings he brings about. Does one say "Yes," does one say "No"? Richardson was a restless innovator and experimenter in fiction, but we shall never be able to discuss his artistic imagination separately from the sexual substance of his stories. Perhaps that is why Richardsonn could be so aesthetically innovative, so creatively sophisticated; the intensity of our own sexual feelings and anxieties will ensure the reader's doing the work of examining the characters, putting their stories together, decoding, reconstructing, and comparing. The characters absorb our energies as they did their author's.

I

In 1739 Richardson was requested by two booksellers, Osborn and Rivington, to produce a little volume of model letters "in a common Style, on such subjects as might be of Use to those Country Readers who were unable to indite for themselves." Compilations of model epistles had been common since the late Renaissance, and it was not unusual for such "letter-writers" to offer entertainment in characters and situations. The letter-writer, a cross between instruction and fiction, provided the spur Richardson needed to become at last a writer of fiction. He explained his genesis as a novelist in his most complete autobiographical work, the long letter of 2 June 1753 to his Dutch translator, Johannes Stinstra. By that time, as a master novelist with three great works to his credit, Richardson could openly recognize the importance of his life work as a writer, and he himself was curious to speculate about the origins or at least original signs of this "kind of Talent":

> I recollect, that I was early noted for having Invention. I was not fond of Play, as other Boys: My Schoolfellows used to call me *Serious* and *Gravity:* And five of them particularly delighted to single me out, either for a Walk, or at their Father's Houses or at mine, to tell them Stories, as they phrased it. Some I told them from my Reading as true; others from my Head, as mere Invention; of which they would be most fond: & often were affected by them.[12]

The storytelling impulse had to be suppressed for a time; the young boy, apprenticed to a printer at age seventeen, had to work extremely hard and knew he had no one to rely on but himself. His family was poor; his father, by trade a "Joiner" (i.e., a carpenter and furniture-maker), at one point evidently hoped to educate young Samuel for the clergy, but this scheme had to be abandoned. A University education was an impossibility, and by the standards of the time a true "education" was denied him. Richardson may have learned the rudiments of Latin at his school, but no more than that, and in the eighteenth century the educated person, the "gentleman," was to be distinguished from the "low" and "illiterate" by his knowledge of Latin literature. Women, even of the upper class, were not supposed to know Latin and could be ridiculed if they tried to learn it; at the same time, their ignorance was often cast up to them as a failing and a sign of their weakness.

Richardson was thus involuntarily on the side of the female sex in being disabled from participating in the life and work of the ruling class, the true gentlemen who became judges, bishops, members of Parliament, administrators—the leaders who governed others and made public policy. Richardson was, however, not only a member of the new middle class that is always rising, but an entrepreneur, a man who set up his own business and made it succeed. Moreover, as a printer and member of the Stationers'

Company, he belonged to a profession that had a proud tradition from the early Renaissance of participating in the dissemination of learning. Printers (who were often in effect what we would term "publishers," too) had taken a leading role for nearly three centuries in spreading ideas and changing opinions.[13] Richardson built up a business that rested on the power of words. It does not seem coincidental that his novels are apparently written by authorial characters who are, like their author, very conscious of the power of words. Like the novelist, they propose to change others' opinions through the exercises of writing and reading.

Not until he was fifty, well established in his business and profession, could Samuel Richardson, Master Printer, afford—psychologically afford—to spend his energies in creative work. Writing those first mildly fictional sample letters apparently kindled the creative flame. He told Stinstra that Pamela's story "had some slight Foundation in Truth"—he had heard years before the story of a master and maidservant from a gentleman who had it from the landlord of an inn; the story thus grew from oral tradition of a sort—but the novelist did not know the persons concerned. He had not expected to write the story when he began what was to become *Familiar Letters,* though in carrying out that assignment he was interested in creating characters rather than flat *personae* writing eighteenth-century requests for loans or thank-you notes.

> Will it be any Harm said I, in a Piece you want to be written so low, if we should instruct them how they should think & act in common Cases, as well as indite? They were the more urgent with me to begin the little Volume, for this Hint. I set about it, & in the Progress of it, writing two or three Letters to instruct handsome Girls, who were obliged to go out to Service, as we phrase it, how to avoid the Snares that might be laid against their Virtue; the above Story recurred to my Thought: And hence sprung Pamela.[14]

*Pamela* "sprung" very rapidly into full two-volume, novelistic identity; Richardson temporarily laid aside the letter-writer to pursue his new story. As he told Aaron Hill, "I began it Nov. 10, 1739, and finished it Jan. 10, 1739–40."[15] After completing a draft, he returned to *Familiar Letters* and also revised his novel, which did not appear in print until November 1740. (Even so, it came ahead of the "letter-writer," which appeared the following January).

The model letters were supposed to be "written low," in a low style, in the voice of common people. *Pamela* is a tour de force of the low style, an example of strange decorum, for almost the whole narrative consists of

Pamela's own letters in a style suited to a teenaged servant girl. In his first novel, then, Richardson chooses as his central character, and as the central voice, one of the "low," one of the disadvantaged. Pamela is triply disadvantaged. She is young, a minor under law (she is fifteen when the story opens, sixteen in the main action). She comes from a poor family without resources, financial or social, to deploy in sheltering their daughter, let alone in taking on persons of wealth and influence; the Andrewses, though respectable, are near the bottom of the social pyramid, belonging to the classes without the vote. And Pamela is of course a female, a member of the sex which is never, at any level of society, given the vote and which is not expected to cause trouble by rioting or rebellion; women are supposed to do what men tell them.

Mr. B____, the villain-hero, is a parallel and complement. He is Pamela's superior in every public respect, the "Master"; to her, he represents public life, wealth, government. He is in his mid-twenties and, as a member of the country gentry, not only votes but belongs to the class that sends members into Parliament. He is a Justice of the Peace: that is, as one of the area's central landholders he is one of the rural administrators of justice, the very judge before whom Pamela would have had to plead her case had she sought legal redress for her injuries. There are no police to protect her, and there is no national body to which she can appeal. There is, as Pamela comes to realize pretty clearly, no law of use to her, for the law is arranged for the convenience of the wealthy and powerful gentlemen who make it. At one point she realizes with some fear that Mr. B____ could causelessly accuse her of having stolen from him; if he did, he would be believed. There is no public machinery to protect her when he engages in a serious campaign of sexual harrassment rising to abduction and threatened rape.

Mr. B____ takes outrageous liberties, of course, even given the liberties of his position—partly because he cannot believe that Pamela will not give in pretty easily. He has known her for some years; she was his mother's little maid, and after his mother's death he relieved her fears about losing her job by promising that she would be kept on. Pamela's first letter is very definitely a servant's letter, expressing as it does, amid genuine grief for the loss of "my good Lady," the servant's relief at finding she is not unemployed:

> Well, but God's Will must be done!—and so comes the Comfort, that I shall not be oblig'd to return back to be a Clog upon my dear Parents! For my Master said, I will take care of you all, my Lasses; and for you, *Pamela* (and took me by the Hand; yes, he took me by the Hand before them all) for my dear Mother's sake, I

will be a Friend to you, and you shall take care of my Linen. God bless him! and pray with me, my dear Father and Mother, for God to bless him: For he has given Mourning and a Year's Wages to all my Lady's Servants.[16]

Richardson shows from the very first paragraphs his tendency to confuse or question set hierarchies, including the moral and aesthetic. Because Pamela is "vulgar" and "low," in a traditional representation her concern for money and job would be an indication that her grief for her lady's death is mere hypocrisy—she would illustrate the callous and greedy nature of the servant class. Richardson, however, makes us feel for the servant, the working person to whom survival is important and work necessary. Here it is not a question of *either* genuine grief *or* practical concern but both/and. Characters and qualities are mixed. Pamela does have a real interest in money; she is not a romance heroine. Yet there are things she values more, and her resistance of financial temptation is the more credible and creditable once we have seen that to her and her poor parents money really does matter.

Mr. B___ waits a year after his mother's death before making his attempts on Pamela. She has become used to living in his household and takes some while to recognize the true necessity of leaving. Mr. B___ seemed up to this point to have been behaving properly—i.e., appropriately—in the master-servant relation. Employers of servants had a responsibility for them, and servants were part of the large "family." In saying he would be a "Friend" to Pamela, Mr. B___ is using in public speech an old sense of the word that we have practically lost: a person's natural "friends" were his or her natural family and immediate superiors—the village squire would be a "friend" to his tenants or servants in that sense. It is "friend" as we use it in "befriend," for to befriend someone is to be benevolent from a superior position, not to take up an intimacy founded on similar tastes and equal relations; in modern usage we do not *befriend* our real friends.

The use of the word "Friend" in that first letter is an interesting form of novelistic pun. There is a triple meaning in the word. A second sense is a sexual one, referring to a paramour as in Iago's "Or to be naked with her friend a-bed"—a sexual sense that colors the modern words "boyfriend," "girlfriend." The third meaning is the primary one, and the only modern sense: "one joined to another in mutual benevolence and intimacy," as Johnson has it. "Friend" in this sense demands an equality and reciprocity and loving respect that cancel out the notions of superior/inferior. Mr. B___ takes the lofty post of superior "Friend" and misuses it, trying to make Pamela into his sexual "friend" and thus denigrate her to the position of prostitute. Ultimately, he acknowledges her as real to him, and they begin a friendship (starting with their long argument by the pond at the end of Volume I) that leads to marriage, the only available relationship (however hierarchical it may seem to us and at times even to Pamela) that can provide for sexual love in mutuality. By marrying Pamela, Mr. B____ signifies that he acknowledges her as valuable, not as a thing to be used but as a person—as a "friend." In the unfolding of the latent meanings of the word "Friend" in the first letter lies the development of the novel.

The hint in "you shall take care of my Linen" is not to be lost upon the reader: "linen" means shirts but also underclothing. We can recognize the secret significance of which Mr. B____ is not perhaps fully conscious at that moment; certainly the point is not lost upon the Andrews parents, who at once begin to interpret Pamela's first letter and spy out sinister meanings: "And Oh! that fatal Word, that he would be kind to you, if you would do as *you should do*, almost kills us with Fears" (I, 27). As Nancy Miller says, "The Andrewses are good hermeneuts (if Pamela isn't) and know how to interpret."[17] They immediately (in the second letter of the novel) write a whole scenario of Pamela's fall and shame, which causes her to come up with an indignant and dramatic alternative (see the third letter). But she will have to make her melodramatic choice of "Rags and Poverty, and Bread and Water" into a real moral choice amid ambiguities to which the simple-minded parents are strangers. Pamela's father's first letter alerts both Pamela and the reader to the mental as well as moral duty to consider what things may mean, not to take words at face value. Pamela and Mr. B____ spend time and energy, each trying to read what the other means by words and actions, though neither is always fully conscious of what he or she really feels or is really giving away. Pamela must leave the childhood Eden of simplicity and enter the world of multiple meanings and necessary interpretation. Once there, she soon leaves her parents far behind; they seem stuck in moral fables and simplicities, while her life, both inner and outer, becomes more complex than they can allow for.

Mr. B____, failing in his purpose, is chagrined when he allows Pamela to go home—or rather, dismisses her like a boss who is displeased with an employee—because he patently thinks he is calling her bluff, and Pamela annoys and hurts him by not begging for mercy at that point, not pleading for her job back. Instead, she goes—thinking she is really departing and that this is her last glimpse of Mr. B____, "at the Window, in his Gown" (I, 97), gazing haughtily down and deigning at last to nod to her. By the time she narrates her departure, Pamela knows this was all a sham and that he was tricking her; the reader also sees he is sulking. Pamela is not allowed to go home to her parents and country labor but is instead abducted, shut up as a prisoner in Mr. B____'s house in Lincolnshire, under the guardianship of ugly Mrs. Jewkes.

Like most novels, this is a "comical romance" (to borrow the indicative title of Paul Scarron's early novel); Pamela is a romance heroine in unromantic circumstances—instead of being in a tower by the sea, she is imprisoned in a prosaic farmhouse, surrounded not by mountainous crags but by cows and fields, cucumbers and sunflowers. Instead of a haughty jailor in armor, or a hideous dwarf and numbers of mastiffs, she is guarded by a fat, lewd, time-serving housekeeper:

> She is a broad, squat, pursy, fat Thing, quite ugly . . . about forty
> Years old. She has a huge Hand, and an Arm as thick as my Waist,
> I believe. Her Nose is flat and crooked, and her Brows grow over
> her Eyes; a dead, spiteful, grey, goggling Eye, to be sure she has.
> And her Face is flat and broad; and as to Colour, looks like as if it
> had been pickled a Month in Salt-petre: I dare say she drinks! She
> has a hoarse man-like Voice, and is as thick as she's long; and yet
> looks so deadly strong, that I am afraid she would dash me at her
> Foot in an Instant, if I was to vex her.—So that with a Heart more
> ugly than her Face, she frightens me sadly; and I am undone, to be
> sure if God does not protect me; for she is very, very wicked—
> indeed she is.
>
> This is but poor helpless Spite in me!—But the Picture is too
> near the Truth notwithstanding. She sends me a Message just
> now, that I shall have my Shoes again, if I will accept of her
> Company to walk with me in the Garden—To *waddle* with me,
> rather, thought I. (I, 107)

Pamela's "poor helpless Spite" is both childish and sympathetic; Richardson shows us that the ways of heroism may not be elegant. The psychic processes by which we assure ourselves of continued resistance to external pressures may not be dignified. The housekeeper is frightening to Pamela in her strength and her sexual ambiguity; she is "man-like" and has already oppressed the girl by physical caresses:

> But I said, I don't like this sort of Carriage, Mrs. *Jewkes*; it is not
> like two Persons of one Sex.
>
> She fell a laughing very confidently, and said, That's prettily
> said, I vow; then thou hadst rather be kiss'd by the other Sex? I
> f'ackins, I command thee for that! (I, 102)

The environment of Mrs. Jewkes is an environment of sexual knowingness; her company alone represents a loss of the innocence of ignorance, a sort of sexual initiation. In the middle of the novel she is a comic surrogate for the absent Mr. B____ and, as Pamela's vulgar and unromantic antagonist, voices very clearly the attitudes—sexual and social—that Pamela must fight. Mrs. Jewkes has given up having any conscience of her own, choosing a soft berth and wages while persuading herself that she has no moral choice: "Look-ye, said she, he is my Master, and if he bids me do a Thing that I can do, I think I ought to do it, and let him, who has Power, to command me, look to the Lawfulness of it" (I, 104).

The housekeeper represents in a comic nightmarish manner the fate that can befall someone of Pamela's rank and sex. Mrs. Jewkes is in ugly middle age, past being an object of sexual pleasure (Restoration and eighteenth-century writers almost inevitably treat forty as a menopausal age, past childbearing and past sexual desirability.) Having evidently gained favor while young by offering sexual favors to men, Mrs. Jewkes, now undesired, must be willing to act as a female pander if she is to enjoy gentlemen's patronage. A woman's sexual power is short-lived, and it is never real power. A woman of low rank who survives her bloom may be used, but contemptuously used. Mrs. Jewkes calls the imprisoned Pamela in her charge "Madam" with ostentatious and semisatirical respect, for teenaged Pamela, if she becomes Mr. B____'s mistress (as Mrs. Jewkes believes she must), will be set above the middle-aged housekeeper as a lady, as mistress of the house—at least for a while. Even in her imprisonment, she is to be treated as a lady, while Mrs. Jewkes is still a servant. Mrs. Jewkes has accepted the position of her servitude, cynically internalizing it, just as she has accepted the rules of the sex game and the triple standard it entails. She believes, like the world around her, that there is one law for gentlemen, who must be allowed to be sexually free and have their way, and another for real ladies, who may (indeed must) keep their virgin purity until marriage; but for a servant girl, a low-class Pamela, to regard her own sexual status and her identity as if she were a lady is ridiculous. Mrs. Jewkes will serve the stronger party. Let Mr. B____ be responsible for the morality of their actions, even for their lawfulness (whether Christian law or law of the land). Her cynical abrogation of her own conscience is her worst act. Such a betrayal of self threatens women and the poor, who have so little power or encouragement to do otherwise than acquiesce in the given situation. Mrs. Jewkes has acquiesced. Pamela refuses to acquiesce. She maintains her right to say "No."

Mrs. Jewkes is the third most important character in the novel and performs a number of valuable functions, both structural and thematic. In the narrative she stands in for that reader (or one side of many readers) who wishes to hurry Mr. B____ on, who wants seduction and even rape to happen in the story. Once such attitudes are voiced clearly (as they are) by Mrs. Jewkes, in all their crude vulgarity, the reader is forced to recognize that such desires are ugly and her "common sense" view untenable. She has reduced sex to a series of clichés, though they are the clichés of her (and even our) world. She hopes to see the rape of Pamela by her Master and utters loud encouragement: "What you do Sir, do; don't stand dilly-dallying. She cannot exclaim worse than she has done. And she'll be quieter when she knows the worst" (I, 176).

Voyeurism has disturbed her vision. She misapprehends not only the nature and rights of Woman, which she has debased within herself, but the nature of Man, even though she herself imitates the masculine. She thinks male sexuality a much simpler thing than it is, that is, she has accepted the eighteenth-century equivalent of locker-room lore and believes that Mr. B____ wants only Pamela's subjugated body, that he would be happy with a rape. (She also thinks that Pamela herself would be femininely submissive once her sexual initiation had been so brutally fulfilled.)

Mr. B____ himself believes such clichés but cannot act on them. He can create dramatic (and comic) scenarios of sexual violence, such as when he comes into the bed disguised as Nan the drunken maid. He can threaten rape, but when Pamela does not take her anticipated part in the scenario, when she is earnest in resistance, he knows that is not what he wants. If he were truly a rapist, all Pamela's fainting would certainly not save her; it saves her precisely because her unconsciousness dramatically and definitely thwarts his real objective. Mr. B____ is not a monster; he is just acting out the beliefs of his time and class. Once they receive a check, he has to reconsider. The Mr. B____ whom the reader sees is not quite the Mr. B____ Pamela sees, though she presents him to us. We can see the spoiled youth, affected by his mother's death, trying to get back at his mother and prove himself a man by having her maid—and at the same time missing the unquestioning love that his mother was once there to give. He is looking for love but must be willing to jettison the clichés and some of his privilege as male, landowner, Justice of the Peace, governor in order to achieve it. Behind his posturing as tyrant there is a wavering, uncertain, vulnerable, and rather loveable human being whom it is Pamela's job to rescue. The story of Mr. B____ is also developing, and Pamela has to learn to understand that story and to read his inwardness as well as her own.

When she is imprisoned in Lincolnshire, Pamela is also pent up with her own emotions, forced to observe herself as never before. She very truly (and deeply) gives, as we say, an account of herself—that account is largely the novel—even as her power to communicate receives a severe check. Mr. B____ commits various crimes against Pamela's utterance: he forges a letter from her, dictates a letter she must write, and then has her letters intercepted. The threat of censorship is arguably the most terrible threat that any Richardson character has to face. Since Pamela cannot write letters home in the confidence that they will be received, or depend on getting advice in return, her letters become a Journal. This is an important change.

In her Journal Pamela insensibly begins to express more of herself, taking more time to think and apprehending subtleties that would not be possible within her parents' frame of thought. Indeed, her parents show themselves very imperceptive in advising her to marry Parson Williams, not only a cynical and unloving act but useless as a protection against the poor curate's employer and patron (the Andrewses show their naiveté in thinking that it would be). Very properly, in this instance, Pamela does not take her parents' mistaken advice. She thinks for herself and begins to read both herself and Mr. B____ attentively. She notices anomalies in her own self that puzzle her: "What is the Matter, with all his ill Usage of me, that I cannot hate him? To be sure, I am not like other People!" (I, 157). There is a secret she has to keep from herself, and the Journal writing shows her guarding against this knowledge as well as searching for knowledge. To admit that she loves Mr. B____ would weaken her capacity for survival; to admit the feeling would be to will it into existence. We see her rationalizing her own emotions, interpreting and then hastily readjusting.

Pamela thinks in emblems and signs; in the fishing scene she makes a connection between herself and the hapless fish. Yet in a world of signs and interpretation, there is also reinterpretation. The reader is encouraged to enter into the ambiguity and uncertainty, to apply an interpretation to, for instance, Pamela's being frightened from her first escape attempt by a cow that she mistakes for the dangerous bull (I, 136-37). Pamela herself interprets her mis-visions and mis-takes here as the effects of fear—an indication of her disabled, distraught inner state. We may carry on where she leaves off in deciding what the scene means. We do not, however, lose respect for Pamela (we may laugh at her sometimes, but that is a different thing). She remains the primary voice, the major interpreter to us of everything in the tale. Indeed—and this is a crowning point—the story is *hers*. She writes it. Particularly in the uninterrupted Journal sequences, she is undistractedly and definitely the Author—the source of the story, of the narrative, of the first interpretation.

As Author, Pamela—helpless female teenager without money or power to back her up—has *authority*. It is her novel, and she is the teller. Mrs. Jewkes is known to us because Pamela tells us about her; she has the power to set her jailer down in memorably spiteful words. Writing about events and people gives Pamela her sense of control—a control lacking in the outside world, in which a girl is supposed to have no control at all. A female work, subversive and illicit, her Journal account of the world is subject to suppression and threatened with destruction. At one point she buries it under a rose tree—the site in legends and ballads of dead lovers. But the manuscript is resurrected, dug up again. To keep her work safe, Pamela goes about with it secreted between her garments and her skin, stitched into her clothing—an anthology of herself, a body of text, momentarily independent of interpretation and identical to herself. The manuscript is taken by Mr. B____, but savingly—to be read, not destroyed; the papers lose their emblematic closed nature and become a communication, as they should. Mr. B____ reads them at last; he is a long while in catching up with us, and we have read the accounts in the proper order, which he at first cannot. Nevertheless, from being sundered, scattered, and threatened pages, Pamela's work becomes a whole.

At one point early in her imprisonment, trying to write both to her parents and to Parson Williams, Pamela thinks of a stratagem to deceive Mrs. Jewkes, who does not wish the girl to communicate with the world outside. To make her believe the writing is harmless, Pamela shows Mrs. Jewkes "a Parcel of broken Scraps of Verses, which I had try'd to recollect . . . that she might see, and think me usually employ'd to such idle Purposes." And in Mrs. Jewkes's presence she writes, instead of speaking, her side of their conversation: "Thus I fooled on, to shew her my Fondness for scribbling" (I, 113). Pamela pretends to write what is broken, fragmentary, meaningless. The figure of her "broken Scraps" alerts us to the good irony of her narrative. Pamela is engaged in making a whole. The character's drive towards narrative wholeness is, of course, a reflection of the drive of her author, who wrote the first draft of *Pamela* at a white heat in two months. But we believe in Pamela as speaker—she makes a coherent Journal, a coherent story, and at last forms herself and Mr. B____ into coherent wholes, too. She was always a maker. The story begins with a gap and a death, with the figure of speech—employed at the beginning of most novels and romances—of breaking and sundering ("and so broke off a little," I,25). Pamela is "expert at her Needle"; she sews, makes things— even embroiders things, we must admit, if we think of her *flowering* the waistcoat. She is the novel's maker, the one who puts things together to contrive a whole; she brings about union where Mr. B____ had thought of rape. We see her literally with a needle and thread, like her own cheerful Fate. She is the character who meets the novel's breaking motif (*rexis*) with her power of bringing together (*enosis*).[18] Power is given into her hands—to this "rebel," this low-class girl with the vulgar and hearty turns of phrase.

82

The novel is one of the century's great democratic statements. Recognizing Pamela as Author and authority, we can see why Mr. B⸺ is so named. The dash or blank signifies real life: in newspapers and magazines, real people of consequence were referred to thus to evade the laws of libel; the blank in Mr. B⸺'s name is therefore a sign of his position. But it is also a sign of this "master's" blank-ness, his helplessness, his own need (femininely) to be filled in. But why *B* of all letters of the alphabet? Because Pamela Andrews is *A*, Author, alpha, primacy.

## II

Between Richardson's first novel and the novel generally referred to as his greatest, there is the sequel to *Pamela* (published December 1741), which shows Pamela married. Other writers, most of them hacks, had taken over Richardson's highly popular story and were writing uncanonical sequels; it is no wonder Richardson wanted to reclaim his characters and their fate. The story of Pamela married (given no separate title and referred to as volumes three and four of *Pamela*, or as *Pamela II*) suffers from a lack of the kind of tension that Richardson most prefers. Not until the middle of it do we come upon its central and challenging situation: when Pamela is wrapped up in her first baby, Mr. B⸺ nearly has an affair with "the Countess"—in fact, Pamela thinks he is in love with the woman, and her jealousy is awakened. She takes at first the advice offered by the conduct books and the magazines of her time—not to notice—and the marriage is nearly wrecked. Mr. B⸺ wants her to notice, and it is only by turning to honesty and defying the rule books for womanly behavior that Pamela is able to rescue their marriage.

This defiance of common rules is in keeping with the honesty of the girl we knew in *Pamela I*. Once set free by Mr. B⸺, *that* Pamela was able to meet the challenge of the truth by acknowledging to herself the hard fact of her love for Mr. B⸺, despite her self-rebukes and attempts to check that feeling: "Thus foolishly dialogu'd I with my Heart, yet all the time, this Heart is *Pamela*!" (II, 217). Once Mr. B⸺ professes his love and asks her to return, Pamela takes the gamble and goes back (rushes back indeed), even though she knows that if she is wrong about his good intentions she will be blamed by everyone, including herself. Like an Ibsen heroine, Richardson's characters need to be allowed freedom in which to act. Small rules and the common sense of worldly clichés make them nervous and depressed.

The Pamela of *Pamela II* is hampered by knowing that she is already a known character. Everyone in her world (as in the real London of 1741) has read *Pamela*, is curious to meet the heroine, and expects certain responses from her. She is looked upon as a model. To her new friends her past is literally an open book, and she suffers from this publicity. Florian Stuber has pointed out the relation of this narrative to *Don Quixote*, Part II, and the similarity of Pamela's situation to that of the hapless Don, who has read the book in which he appears and knows that others have read it too.[19] *Pamela II* is thus another of England's many Quixote narratives, but if Pamela is the first Female Quixote, she is not divinely foolish and cannot fail. Her story, unlike that of the Spanish knight, is a success story, and the less interesting as there seem to be so few challenges to her success. That she is herself not perfectly serene is seen in the letter she writes in case she dies in childbirth, expressing great anxiety about her relation to herself as model: perhaps she had not met B____'s expectations; perhaps he was bored with her after all. Her suspicions are essentially unfounded and her fears mistaken (it is her lively friend Polly Danford who is to die in childbirth). Despite vicissitudes, Pamela's married life is a success. Her domestic conduct and her interest in the education of her children (with her comments on Locke's views on education) were to influence Jean-Jacques Rousseau; Richardson led the philosopher to see not only the possibilities in a fictional account of education, as in *Émile*, but also the potential of a philosophical novel, as in his *Julie ou la Nouvelle Héloïse*. Julie may be a counterpart to Clarissa, but in her ordering of her home and children she is a Pamela.

*Pamela II* opens up its narrative to a number of correspondents and offers us of a group of characters, rather than—as does *Pamela I*—concentrating on two, with one dominant point of view. The use of several correspondents was good practice for the next novel, *Clarissa*, in which a number of writers share the work of narration. The higher social sphere, too, anticipates the settings of the next two novels. The multiplying of characters and of their diverse but related interests in *Pamela II* is often thought to prefigure *Grandison*, and one can see in the pert but amiable Polly a personage prefiguring Charlotte Grandison more closely than she does her immediate successor, Anna Howe. That the *Pamela* sequel is often, and understandably, treated by critics as a sketch or preliminary exercise on the way to the other works means that the novel's own real merits may be utterly overlooked. Yet in presenting a heroine who is trying to say "Yes," trying to fit into society as it is without radically rude questions, Richardson loses much of the rebelliousness that is his special strength. And in presenting Pamela as what woman ought to be, not the defiant or independent virgin but the settled obedient wife and attentive mother, Richardson seems to have forced his heroine into a mold a size too small.

## III

In his next novel, *Clarissa; or, The History of a Young Lady*, Richardson again chooses as his central character a young woman who is in conflict with the world around her and with the hero and the hero's view of herself. Again the heroine is threatened with rape. This young woman is not, however, a simple country girl, but a "Young Lady"; she is not only beautiful but well educated and talented, and she belongs to a class that counts for something in the world.

Indeed, class is very much at the center of the novel. The Harlowes, Clarissa's family, are members of the rising gentry, the families that had developed through the new capitalism as entrepreneurs and shrewd improvers of their landholdings. Clarissa's uncles have made profits during their lives, the more energetic Anthony as a sea captain, the more passive and amiable John merely by having coal mines discovered on his estates. They have kept single, settling on Clarissa's father, James Harlowe, to marry and have the children. The three brothers plan to pool all their resources and push the heir upward on the social ladder. The heir is Clarissa's brother, James, the only male in the third generation; he is to marry well, to go into Parliament. The Harlowes are moving from a world in which they lived as quiet rustic landholders into the new world of Walpole's England, and into power. In the game they play, estates are the pieces that matter, and persons are to be invested in estate-getting.

Clarissa apparently belongs to this modern world of improving; she has a dairy set up on her grandfather's land, which she tends and which she is able to make profitable. Her grandfather renames his estate; *The Grove* becomes *The Dairy-house* (I,6). Clarissa indeed has proved herself so well equipped to manage an estate that the grandfather horrifies all the family by willing *The Dairy-house* to her. In her teens, she is mistress of an estate—casting a gloom over the vexed male members of the family, who took for granted their right to all their progenitor's lands. Clarissa is a girl—the wrong sort of inheritor. One can see why Richardson thought of calling the novel "The Lady's Legacy," for the inheritance is the original cause of all that follows: an ironic blessing that, given the social world in which Clarissa has to live, becomes a curse.

Young James's suspicions are further aroused when a handsome young aristocrat, the nephew of an earl, courts Clarissa. The plain elder sister, Arabella, is secretly jealous; Lovelace was mistakenly introduced to the wrong "Miss Harlowe" at the outset but contrived to make Bella refuse him, an action that Bella always inwardly regrets, though pride prevents her explaining to her family how she feels. Delighted at the prospect of the accession of one of their members to a noble family and (very probably) a title, the Harlowe elders think of, as it were, investing in Clarissa—leaving her much of the Harlowe wealth so she and her husband Lovelace will be able to support a revived title. Young James has already seen that senior males in his family can and do bequeath real property to Clarissa. Furious, he attacks Lovelace, making him fight; when James is (slightly) wounded in an encounter Lovelace never provoked, the cunning brother has gained his point. The Harlowes drive Lovelace from their doors, and James loses no time in trying to force his beautiful younger sister into a humiliating marriage with a wealthy old miser.

Most of what has been described above is background to the novel; we enter the narrative when events are underway and read Clarissa's summary, in which there are some puzzled gaps. Almost as soon as we meet her, she is in conflict with her family, and she is very soon fighting for survival against their plan to marry her to Roger Solmes. Her siblings have their own axes to grind, while the elders are moved by the fact that Solmes's estates lie next to the Dairy House; they can hope all this land will revert to the Harlowes—though their hopes are based on a foolish gamble.

Clarissa has to learn that the other members of her family are governed by motives and beliefs quite different from her own, and they are surprised by what they term her "violence" and "stubbornness." Surely she must oblige her family—and in any case, what can she do? Apparently all she can do is say "No." But forced marriages have been committed, and the Harlowes become moved to the point where they would consider even such a brutality, such a legal rape. As far as James Jr. is concerned, either the Solmes marriage or an elopement with Lovelace would do; either as a settled woman (miserably subjected and rightly punished) or as a disgrace to the family and a wanton, his sister would no longer be his rival.

Clarissa has moral and spiritual resources to draw upon; her refusal goes very deep, for she will not swear before God a promise that she cannot keep—to love, honor, and obey—though she sees very clearly that the marriage service is man-made, not in itself necessarily divine. Yet her strong religious sense and her moral fastidiousness do not mean being a "good girl," as the family wishes its pretty daughter to be. She is no plaster saint—as can be seen in her remarks about the provoking Bella's "plump high-fed face," or in her retort pointing to her sister's lack of suitors: "It is not my fault, Bella, the *opportune* gentleman don't come!" (I, 290; Ev. I, 214).[20]

Clarissa does not have the narrative to herself as Pamela did. For one thing, her correspondent and confidante, her best friend Anna Howe, takes a lively part. Unlike the Andrewses through much of *Pamela*, Anna is not waiting in some shadowy wings; she is an urgent presence. And Anna subjects Clarissa's narrative and her language to teasing scrutiny. For instance, pressed as to whether she is in love with Lovelace, Clarissa says that "one might be driven by violent measures, step by step, as it were, into something that might be called—I don't know what to call it—A *conditional kind of liking*, or so" (I, 183; Ev. I, 135). Anna picks up the phrase and makes fun of her friend "when you affect reserve; when you give new words for common things; when you come with your *curiosities*, with your *conditional likings*, and with your PRUDE-encies (Mind how I spell the word)" (I,255; Ev. I, 188).

Clarissa is sensitive about her phrase, defends it, and anticipates Anna's objections and commentary:

> I said . . . that I would not be in Love with this man for the world: And it was going further than prudence would warrant, when I was for compounding with you, by the words *conditional liking*; which you so humorously rally.
>
> Well, but, methinks you say, what is all this to the purpose? This is still but reasoning: But if you *are* in Love, you *are*. (I, 275–76; Ev. I, 203)

Clarissa herself truly does not know whether she is "in Love" and wishes for her own safety and independence not to be. What exactly are her feelings for Lovelace, he himself often speculates upon; this mystery is one of the questions pursued in the story.

Lovelace is Clarissa's counterpart in looks and intelligence; and he is her antagonist, her lover, and ultimately her destroyer. He is also the second major narrator, the opposing viewpoint. Not only does the heroine not have the text to herself; she shares her story, unknown to herself, with another set of statements. The epistolary method is used in *Clarissa* with a degree of sophistication not met with before; Richardson gives us various views of the same situation and even of the same scenes. Lovelace represents a different set of assumptions, a different ideology. He believes in the male ethos in its most extreme version. A rake and libertine, he has a low opinion of women and resents falling in love. He desires Clarissa and wants to prove that she is no better than the other women he has known, that she is at the core a daughter of Eve (another "Lady's Legacy"): weak, inviting seduction, at heart a harlot.

Lovelace's extreme version of male supremacy is closely related to his position as an aristocrat. He comes of a noble family (far above the level of Mr. B___ as well as of the Harlowes), and he is the last of his line. His family wishes him to marry and produce an heir; Lovelace does court Clarissa originally intending marriage, but the insult given him by the Harlowes seems to him to justify any course he might take. He prowls around the grounds of Harlowe Place, which he refers to as "sprung up from a dunghill" (I, 231; Ev. I, 170), like a wily Satan around an already fallen Eden. Wooing Clarissa in disguise is part of a mock-romance that he arranges. Lovelace, as an aristocrat in the world of the rising (and unattractive) Harlowes, is both an object of desire and something of an anachronism. Eighteenth-century aristocrats were conforming or had conformed to the ways of the new gentry and the new capitalists. Power rested on trade and land deals, and (as Lovelace, who has an acute sense of history, really knows) his position and the future title are shadows. Like Don Juan, he wants real power, and the last arena in which it can be found is the sexual arena. There he can conquer and subdue. He has already "ruined" a number of girls. Two of them, Sally and Polly, he has set up as partners in Mrs. Sinclair's brothel, a thriving concern, which is accustomed to offer him "the first fruits of their garden" (III, 285; Ev. II, 190). He prefers taking virgins, subduing territory not conquered before.

Lovelace clings with a witty, perverse heroism to the notion that women are only objects of desire and that the desire must fulfill certain patterns. When Clarissa (partly by a trick) is induced to run away with him, the idea of testing this daughter of the Harlowes comes to fruition in his mind. What may be called Lovelace's Test is only a complete formulation of the prevailing idea of woman, of her place and nature. It is axiomatic that the wife of a man of good family must be unimpeachably pure; otherwise the property may suffer by being bequeathed to heirs not of their father's getting and "the old Patriarchal system" (Lovelace's phrase; VI, 99) be set at naught. If a woman of family must be pure, she should go warranted a virgin to her bridal; any man who sleeps with a woman under promise of marriage finds out thus that she is a whore and not worthy to marry him. Lovelace suspects (more deeply than he knows) that all women are whores. In order to preserve his family, he argues, and assure himself of acquiring what he must deserve, a wife above suspicion, ought he not to test his future bride?

88

> To the Test then—And I will bring this charming creature to the *strictest* Test, "that all the Sex . . . may see what they *ought to be;* what is *expected* from them . . . and how careful they ought to be . . . not to give him cause to think lightly of them for favours granted, which may be interpreted into *natural weakness.* For is not a Wife the keeper of a man's honour? . . . "
>
> It is not for nothing, Jack, that I have disliked the Life of Shackles. (III, 81; Ev. II, 36)

The game that Lovelace sets up is one that Clarissa cannot win—that no woman could win according to the rules of social and sexual conduct. If a woman exhibits no feeling, she is a prude, affected, or frigidly incapable of love; but if she betrays any sexual feeling, she degrades herself by "natural weakness" and excuses a man from giving any of his honor into her care or treating her honorably. The articulation of his test does not mean that Lovelace does not complain vigorously of Clarissa's coldness; indeed, the more careful she is, the more determined he is to humiliate her. She is not meant to win—she cannot, since she is a woman. He will seduce her by fair means or foul. He lodges her in a brothel, giving the brothel-keeper (whom we know only by Lovelace's name for her, "Mrs. Sinclair") and her partners instructions as to how to behave like virtuous women letting lodgings. Clarissa Harlowe lodged in a brothel is Clarissa Harlot—as women are, in Lovelace's view. "Clarissa" means most fair, most shining—is she most glorious, or simply most glorious of harlots?

Lovelace tests her through various devices, involving her in a world of deception where the appearances she believes in are not the realities. But when he has a false fire set in the middle of the night in order to pretend to rescue her and make love to her, she sees his design and runs away. Excited by this determined opposition, Lovelace gets her back into the brothel by another set of stratagems, and there has her drugged and rapes her. Her passing the test meant simply that stronger methods had to be used to make her realize she is only woman, a sexual object, and his. By penetrating her unwilling and unconscious body, Lovelace is sure he has set his brand upon her. She belongs to him.

Up to this point, Lovelace has seemed the central protagonist, the active plotter who sets events working. He rejects with hauteur what he is told by Belford and by Clarissa, that he has been "*James Harlowe's* implement" (VI, 35; Ev. III, 268); yet it is quite true. In running off with Clarissa and raping her, he has done exactly what James wished, trampling James's too-bright sister into the dust and ridding him of an envied sibling, a young woman who had got above herself. The Harlowes have all, in a sense, conspired to create the rape of Clarissa.

The events leading up to the central act are narrated by Lovelace, who is in control, apparently, of the narrative as well as the action in the story. He involves the escaped Clarissa in another drama of deception, this time coaching some elegant prostitutes to impersonate his own relations; the "ladies" visit Clarissa at Hampstead and are to take her home with them, stopping off at the house in Dover Street (which Clarissa still does not know is a brothel) to pick up her things. The instruction and rehearsal of characters who are to personate people in his plot always delights Lovelace. He is not only an actor himself but the director and constant author of a drama in which he is to star. He is sure of himself as a brilliant comic hero:

> I believe, generally speaking, that all the men of our cast are of my mind—They love not any Tragedies but those in which they themselves act the parts of tyrants and executioners; and, afraid to trust themselves with serious and solemn reflections, run to Comedies, in order to laugh away compunction on the distresses they have occasioned, and to find examples of men as immoral as themselves. . . .
>
> Sally answered for Polly, who was absent; Mrs. Sinclair for herself . . . in preferring the comic to the tragic scenes.—And I believe they are right; for the devil's in it, if a confided-in Rake does not give a girl enough of Tragedy in his Comedy. (IV, 143; Ev. II, 270)

Rakes are comic heroes; a rake may make "Tragedy" for the woman, but what is tragic for her is comic to him. His comedy must take precedence over her tragedy. This belief Lovelace illustrates in his zestful plotting in the last stages before what he sees as the complete overthrow of Clarissa. The event is itself dealt with in the laconic letter, dramatic but un-dramatizing, sent to his confidant, Jack Belford: "And now, Belford, I can go no farther. The affair is over. Clarissa lives" (V, 291; Ev. III, 196).

After the rape, Lovelace can indeed "go no farther." The center of the action is now Clarissa. It is she who takes action and makes the decisions, overthrowing Lovelace's plans and assumptions. Once undeluded, even at the cost of the assumptions that had made day-to-day living possible, she is unexpectedly strong.

Clarissa's strength does not, however, come easily. She must rise from great dereliction into a new identity; she is in fragments before she can be whole again. Her desperate and incoherent sense of herself and her life is

signified in the series of ten deranged writings, neither letters nor medita-
tions, which she pens and throws away. Clarissa's mad papers make a kind
of sense (and a poetic sense: they were admired by Blake),[21] but they do not
make the rational sense we have been used to in the heroine. Richardson
uses the resources of typography to display on the page the disorder of
Clarissa's mind, in the slantwise and irregular arrangement of the scraps
of pottery she remembers and evidently applies to her own case—scraps
that cry out for identification and application by the reader, who may thus
have a clue to the movements of Clarissa's mind. Clarissa thus does really
(in the reality of fiction) what Pamela pretended to do when she scribbled
"a Parcel of broken Scraps of Verses" in order to deceive Mrs. Jewkes.

The work of creating a whole—a whole self, a whole identity—is infinitely more difficult for Clarissa; she rises into creativity and makes her
completeness out of a great depth of madness and sorrow. But her first and
vital action (an act that must be constantly repeated) is saying "No." She
surprises Lovelace in the strength of her refusal to marry him: "I now tell
you—*That the man who has been the villain to me you have been, shall
never make me his wife*" (V, 325; Ev. III, 222).

Hers is a fortifying "No," and it amazes Lovelace, who had always
assumed "I can marry her when I will" (IV, 22; Ev. II, 252). Clarissa is not
acting according to his understanding of the female type: women want
marriage; that is what they beg for; it is the best prize he has to offer. And a
woman once sexually taken must be humble: "Of all the Sex I have
hitherto known, or heard, or read of, it was *once subdued, and always
subdued*. The *first* struggle was generally the *last*; or, at least, the subsequent struggles were so much fainter and fainter, that a man would rather
have them than be without them" (V, 330; Ev. III, 225).

He does realize that Clarissa cannot justly be said to have been "subdued" when she was drugged and raped, but he believes a repetition of the
rape must establish the true sexual relation and force the compliance he
failed to obtain. Clarissa, however, is not so easily deluded as before; once
the scales have fallen from her eyes, once she knows she is in a brothel and
what he is, Lovelace cannot trick her with false scenarios. In the "Penknife
Scene" she triumphs over him by stating that she sees through his decep-
tions and by threatening to kill herself if he should approach. Awed,
Lovelace gives up the struggle for the time being, leaving Clarissa imprisoned in the brothel in the care of the women, who think they may be
able to manage her. Clarissa escapes. Lovelace does not know he has seen
her for the last time, and his speculations, thoughts, plans become as
pointless as they are remote from what is really taking place in Clarissa's
life and mind.

Clarissa endures a full knowledge of what Lovelace has done and all the lies he has told as she gathers evidence; she endures an imprisonment for debt in the coarse spunging-house with its cracked walls and barred windows. She reinterprets her own life and her relations to her family, to Lovelace, to herself, and to God. In her last days she succeeds at last in living as an independent person, arranging her own life and her own dying. Right after the rape she had been unable to sign her name as other than a complete blank; later she exclaims, "My name . . . is now *Wretchedness!*" (VI, 250; Ev. III, 427). More resignedly, she recognizes that "I am Nobody's"—a statement of abandonment that is also a statement of freedom. Ultimately she accepts the fact that her parents have still not forgiven her and that she will not see them again: "Easy as my departure seems to promise to be, it would have been still easier, had I had that pleasure. BUT GOD ALMIGHTY WOULD NOT LET ME DEPEND FOR COMFORT UPON ANY BUT HIMSELF" (VIII, 84; Ev. IV, 339).

The calm process of Clarissa's dying is presented through her letters and through the accounts of Jack Belford, Lovelace's friend who has now changed his allegiance to become an invaluable and genuine friend to Clarissa in her last weeks. She also shows her own independence and strength of will, as well as a capacity to grow in affection and to change responses; for in making Belford a friend, she not only rescinds her first impressions of him but also defies the proprieties that would make her a more acceptably penitent daughter if she were not seeing a known rake. She is paying heed to essentials, not externals.

The force with which Clarissa goes toward death renders the agitations of others faintly absurd. And Lovelace, with his meaningless dashes to and fro, his menaces, prayers, and jokes, really does become absurd. Clarissa plays one great trick on him, so that he will leave her in peace. She sends him a letter: "Sir, I have good news to tell you. I am setting out with all diligence for my Father's House" (VII, 215; Ev. IV, 157).

Lovelace, taking her allegory literally, believes for some time that she is going home to Harlowe Place and that he will be able to follow and renew his addresses. Unaccustomed to having to penetrate the wit of others, he becomes a bad interpreter—himself the deluded instead of the grand deluder. Recognizing at last that she is dying and that he is forbidden to go near her, he experiences real pain; yet all he can do is to ride back and forth in Knightsbridge, blaming his mother for the way he has turned out, blaming Belford and everyone else as well as himself. Her death sends him mad for a short while—thus he is shown as repeating the experience of Clarissa's own suffering and dereliction. Narrative and dramatic control has eluded him; Clarissa's Tragedy has broken down his Comedy. The story becomes his tragedy also, and he has brought about his own death.

When Richardson was writing the novel (which appeared in installments), he was besieged with many requests—by James Thomson and Henry Fielding, among others—to create a happy ending; those close to him who knew how the story turned out begged him to change his mind. Given an era in which *King Lear* was played with a happy ending, the request is understandable, but Richardson, on offering Aaron Hill volumes five and six of the first edition, said, "These will shew you . . . that I intend more than a Novel or Romance by this Piece; and that it is of the Tragic Kind."[22] The author was aware that *Pamela: or, Virtue Rewarded* had been criticized for the apparent material and social rewards attending Pamela's virtue; perhaps he had not expected to be so strongly opposed in creating a picture of Virtue not rewarded at all in this world. Clarissa loses all those things Pamela gains—reputation, social position, rank, money, house, and lands. The house that she, the legal mistress of an estate, buys in the end is her last "house," a coffin.

Some later critics have also been displeased with the ending of the story. Dorothy Van Ghent sees in Clarissa's death and her going to her Father's house only an allegory of bourgeois life and a Freudian father-fixation[23]—a position all the more remarkable because Richardson's novel provides such a devastating analysis of what Shaw was to call middle-class morality, as well as a critique of the values of the expanding gentry. Clarissa, it should be noted, defies her father, a nominal potentate with a "Prerogative" like that of a monarch, which still cannot and should not hold sway over the child. Some feminist critics have seen in Clarissa's end only the desire of the male author to penalize even the most nominal unchastity with death: Clarissa is another Lucretia (a case cited in the novel) forced to die to vindicate her sexual virtue.[24] There is some merit in this case, but it leaves out too much of the tone and feel of the novel.

The question arises—what other ending would be possible? Lovelace anticipates and parodies other closures, as when he imagines a sadder and wiser girl going penitently to her estate and living like an old maid ("everything will be old and penitential about her" [V, 265; Ev. III, 177])—or when he fantasizes about a seduced and abandoned Clarissa with a baby, living on her estate with an Anna Howe likewise seduced, abandoned and fruitful—and the friends' two children, both Lovelace's offspring, incestuously marrying (VI, 13; Ev. III, 251). Putting aside Lovelace's imagined closures of the heroine's story (of which he ever desires to be the author), it is true that the heroine's survival would reduce the rape to a mere incident and thus tend to support Lovelace's overt public claim of its unimportance.

(Though of course to Lovelace at the depths it is not at all unimportant.) To have Clarissa live and marry another man would cast immense doubt on the seriousness of her experience, the meaning of her violation and the depth of her reaction. She might indeed seem to her contemporaries, as to Lovelace, a "harlot." It should be noted, however, that the choice is offered her in the novel, not without some emotional appeal: Mr. Wyerley, who courted Clarissa and was rejected by her before she met Lovelace, proposes marriage after the rape in full knowledge of what has occurred, and makes his offer out of a generous love. Richardson offers us that possibility so we can imagine and reject it, while feeling that this solution—in some respects the sensational one—would be dull and evasive.

The "happy ending" most readers longed for—the union of Lovelace and Clarissa—would have been a denial and trivialization of everything the book says about human relations and the deep discord between sexes and classes. Richardson's own ending is the inevitable one. As Florian Stuber has pointed out, we are not even required to assume that Clarissa's death is the strict result of what she has undergone. No one's life is certain. If the Harlowes had known that their daughter was to die at nineteen, they would not have persecuted her.[25] All human morality must apply under the great shadow of mortality. Our moral actions, the requirements of our behaviour to one another, must always take death into consideration to have worth and meaning.

Richardson insisted that his last two novels were based on his own "Invention," not, like *Pamela*, on a story he had heard.[26] His claim to originality is not lessened because *Clarissa* has a strong connection to earlier fiction by women, and to the heroic drama of the Restoration.[27] Like all great novels, Clarissa also is related to myth, fairy-tale, and romance—a point raised by Carol Houlihan Flynn.[28] Indeed, more might be made of the relation of Richardson's novel to the oldest surviving romances of Western literature, for instance to the *Aethiopica* of Heliodorus (2nd or 3rd century A.D.) To believe that the motif of the threatened virgin is a product of Richardson's own sexual imagination is to rest on ignorance of literary history. Reading the adventures of the beautiful and threatened Chariclea in Heliodorus' Greek romance, one may well be struck with this heroine's resemblance to Clarissa. The righteous virgin is a product not of the Christian imagination—or of that only—but of the Hellenic world. Richardson's analysis of sexuality goes very deep into the patterns, and what Jung called "archetypes," of our civilization.

Nevertheless, V.S. Pritchett says disapprovingly that Richardson was "possessed with sex." Walter Allen, though an admirer of the heroine and (with reservations) of the novel, thought it contained "an element of inescapable pornography," doubting "whether it is possible for the critic who comes to *Clarissa* after reading Freud to deny that the novel must have been written by a man who was, even though unconsciously, a sadist in the technical sense."[29] It *is* possible to deny it; anybody can be called "unconsciously" anything whatever, in "the technical sense" or the Pickwickian sense, and the pleasures of armchair psychology are easily obtained. Morris Golden took up the suggestion in his vivacious *Richardson's Characters*, a short book based on and illustrating the premise that Richardson was a sadist. Golden explores, as the jacket's blurb says, "a dark world where manly significance is measured by the urge to dominate and by acts of sadism."[30] By centering the source of disturbance within the psyche of the novelist, such critics get rid of the more disturbing implications that the "dark world" of dominance and aggression Richardson shows us is the real one, and that the customary male view of women has indeed the implications that his novels illustrate. It seems roughly a parallel with the older critical attempt to locate the meaning of that other disturbing work, *Gulliver's Travels*, within the madness of Jonathan Swift; the world escapes scatheless.

Freudianism of the older kind is less and less in fashion, particularly as some disturbing facts have been aired regarding Freud's life and writings. Richardson could have written quite a gripping novel about Freud's treatment of "Dora." It is noticeable that the discomfort at Richardson's "prurience," pornography, and sadism has been felt more by male than by female critics. For a woman there can often be a sense of liberation in reading Richardson, as if a distressing truth (or one side of it, at least) gets told—whereas the real chauvinist cruelty and complacent authoritarianism of Fielding's "Battle in the Churchyard" in *Tom Jones* may drive a woman reader into a fit of powerless fury for which she will find no patriarchal authorization in the work of male critics. Fielding's class sense limited him terribly in telling anything like the truth about sex, and in a pinch he always opts for the status quo. Richardson in a pinch tends to question (or make his characters question) received notions. The world of *Clarissa* is for the reader very unstable; a multitude of flickering views and interpretations illuminate a violent and dark social and psychic landscape.

No short summary is able to do justice to the breadth and depth of the novel, to its subtleties and the coloring wherewith it presents its characters' minds. It is a very dramatic novel. Kinkead-Weekes believes that Richardson presages Beckett and Pinter.[31] Its dramatic scenes are also almost all perverse, taking subtle shifts, exhibiting games of force and power with one character trying to take control of another. This is so not

only between hero and heroine; the scenes between Clarissa and her
mother are also a good example, as the mother loves and betrays and tries
to blackmail her daughter. There are instances of expressive (one might
say expressionistic) dialogue reminiscent of Jacobean drama, as in Arabella's taunts while she brings out patterns of fabrics, and mockingly
designs wedding garments for the sister who is to be the old miser's bride:

> Dear Heart!—how gorgeously will you be array'd!—What! silent,
> my dear! . . . silent still?—But, Clary, won't you have a Velvet
> Suit? It would cut a great figure in a country church, you know:
> And the weather may bear it for a month yet to come. Crimson
> Velvet, suppose? Such a fine complexion as yours, how would it
> be set off by it! What an agreeable blush would it give you!—High
> ho! . . . And do you sigh, Love?—Well then, as it will be a solemn
> wedding, what think you of *black* Velvet, child?—Silent still,
> Clary!—Black Velvet, so fair as you are, with those charming eyes,
> gleaming thro' a wintry cloud, like April Sun!—Does not Lovelace
> tell you they are charming eyes!   (I, 319–20; Ev. I, 335–36)

Crimson or black velvet—Clarissa is to choose between being a whore and
a corpse.

The novel presents not only the imagery of speech and the conflict of
dialogue but also the movements of mind and the images and associations
made by the mind. The letter mode, the "writing to the moment," is used
for full psychological purpose. We know not only what the characters do
and say but what they think, and we see even the gaps in their own
perception of themselves. We also know their dreams, half-suppressed
notions, and fantasies. Lovelace's mental powers are particularly striking;
even when he is at his most absurd, he has the faculty of expressing
himself through brilliant images and allusions, as in his analogy of the
Fair:

> But here in the present case . . . is a pretty little Miss just come
> out of her hanging-sleeve-coat, brought to buy a pretty little
> Fairing; for the world, Jack, is but a great Fair, thou knowest, and
> . . . all its Joys but tinselled hobby-horses, gilt gingerbread,
> squeaking trumpets, painted drums, and so forth.
>
>   Now behold this pretty little Miss skimming from booth to
> booth, in a very pretty manner. . . . Till at the last taken with the
> invitation of the *laced-hat orator*, and seeing several pretty little
> bib-wearers stuck together in the flying-coaches, cutting safely
> the yielding air, in the One-go-up the Other go down-picture-of

the world-vehicle, and all with as little fear as wit, is tempted to ride next.

In then suppose she slily pops, when *none of her friends are near her:* And if, after two or three ups and downs, her pretty head turns giddy, and she throws herself out of the coach when at its elevation, and so dashes out her pretty little brains, who can help it?—And would you hang the poor fellow, whose *professed trade* it was to set the pretty little creatures a flying?   (VI, 100–101; Ev. III, 316-17)

In this satirical analogy, which parodies Bunyan (and hence Clarissa's seriousness) in its elaborate description of the world as "a great Fair," Lovelace insistently diminishes Clarissa (to a "pretty little" thing) and himself. If she is the childish rider on the primitive ferris wheel, he is the tinselled showman, repetitively calling, *"Who rides next! Who rides next!"*—a tradesman in charge of a machine. Richardson dares to allow Lovelace an extensive and lively parody of the story of the whole novel, a mock version whose challenge the novel itself must meet and overcome. In the nervous energy of Lovelace's mind as he pursues his own quick thoughts, we can detect the function of imagination in making the psyche comfortable with the unspeakable; the fancy carries out the fantastic work of rationalization. But the attempt betrays itself. In Lovelace's effort to create contempt, we can hear the pulses of fear; violence bursts out in what he hopes is an exaggeration of what is in store: if he speaks of Clarissa as "dashing out her pretty little brains," she will not be seriously ill. The wheel of fortune, of which the flying-coach vehicle is an emblem, cannot hold anything as bad as that. His mock-moral resort to common sense (everyone must have some ups and downs) is later turned against him, when he has the fearsome dream that ends with his falling, falling . . . (VII, 187–88; Ev. IV, 135). Lovelace attempts to interpret that dream (VII, 216–18; Ev. IV, 158–59) and in doing so—and in misinterpreting what his fears and conscience are saying—reveals himself as hermeneutically poor, though rich in images. No other novel of the period, and few novels of any, have invited us so far into the interior world. Save for Proust and Joyce, Richardson has no rivals in giving us the intensity of inner experience and its deep processes combined with a full and credible world of things and places and people, social institutions and social forces.

## IV

This day I was kept at North End, to receive a breakfast-visit from two very worthy ladies . . . both very intimate with one Clarissa

Harlowe: and both extremely earnest with me to give them a
*good man*. Can you help me to such a one as is demanded of me?
He must be wonderfully polite; but no Hickman! How can we
hope that ladies will not think a good man a tame man?[32]

This letter of 4 June 1750 justifies Richardson's claim in the Preface to *The
History of Sir Charles Grandison* that his new novel was demanded,
"insisted on by several of his Friends who were well assured he had the
Materials in his Power, that he should produce into public View the
Character and Actions of a Man of TRUE HONOUR." In his final novel
Richardson gave the title role to a male character, a change paralleling
Fielding's change from male names to a woman's name as the title of *his*
last work of fiction. *Amelia* (1751) represents Fielding's response to *Clarissa* (which he admired); it gives a new place to feminine influence and the
domestic life. But his heroine is not a furious virgin who dies in a garret;
she is the image of what woman should be, the wife and mother. In equal
and opposite reaction, Richardson asserts his right to the world of masculine power, to the creation of a gentleman landowner who travels about
the world and is universally beloved. His hero is not a slapdash scapegrace
like Tom Jones, however, but a man of principle. In their last novels, Henry
Fielding and Samuel Richardson both initiated the central enterprise of
the English novel to follow, the effort to combine Fielding and Richardson.
Both produced new sorts of novels; apparently, too, they initiated new
phases of their own work that neither could live to complete.

The central official project of *Sir Charles Grandison* was the creation of
a good man, and Richardson recognized the problems involved. The Good
Man must have his distresses and must fall in love, but his distresses and
his love must be caused by good women, and the whole should end happily.
Moreover, Sir Charles was to present "the Example of a Man acting uniformly well thro' a Variety of trying Scenes," as the author announced in
the preface. He could not sin and repent, or grow from imperfect to better.
As a man, a gentleman, Sir Charles must not be in danger of seeming weak,
his goodness the effect of incapacity or fear. A heroine could be admired in
distress, for women were not in control of their lives, but a gentleman, a
young patriarch, must be in control. Richardson saw that he must give
Grandison a few faults, lest he become a *"faultless monster,"*[33] but he
gives him no weaknesses. Sir Charles is perfect as a son, a brother, a
guardian, a legatee, a friend. He orders the lives of everyone around him,
and they learn (pretty smartly) to bless his name. The faults he does have,
principally pride, are worse perhaps than Richardson intended. It is not
that Sir Charles is a stick, or incredible; as critics from Lady Bradshaigh to

Morris Golden have recognized, he is strongly related to Lovelace in his strength and masculine assurance. With a little imagination one can tilt him into real history and see him as an ancestor of America's Founding Fathers—so articulate, so assured, so decisive about government, so fit to be a patriarch of a new order of the ages, *Novus Ordo Seclorum*. Ruskin once said that Sir Charles was his favorite literary character, along with Don Quixote. No one else has agreed with him, yet he was certainly right in recognizing a kinship. Sir Charles is a Quixote who succeeds in his knight-errantry and does reform the world.

*Grandison* itself is a quixotic departure for Richardson in many ways. Having imagined his *"good man,"* he creates a world the opposite or the obverse of that in *Clarissa,* a place in which male sexual and aggressive power is to be used solely for good; it is thus an optimistic world from which the dangers that afflict the heart can truly be exorcised. There is nothing cold or dark about the novel; amazingly, for a work by a man in his sixties, it has a light and springlike feeling. The setting is the estates of eighteenth-century gentry; and instead of being mocking prisons like Harlowe Place, they are comfortable, spacious, Jamesean good places, harmonious environments for the development of the heart and refinement of the senses.

If the official project was the creation of a "good man," the other and related quixotic project in *Grandison* was the creation of a woman who may (and must) say "Yes" to love. The world of *Grandison* is not the world of *Clarissa,* which exists here as a novel the characters have read (I, II, 229),[34] not as contiguous and continuous territory. In *Tom Jones* we come upon a character known to us in *Joseph Andrews,* and in *Ferdinand Count Fathom* we meet characters from *Roderick Random,* but there is philosophically no possibility of the characters of *Clarissa* and of *Grandison* occupying the same moral space; the two novels' views of the world are fundamentally different. In *Clarissa* there is a streak of depravity and cruelty existing throughout fallen nature; in *Grandison* everything is salvageable—everything grows towards the light.

A woman who may safely love can be imagined as existing only in an undepraved world where male mankind have been redeemed (as they are in Grandison) from perversity. In a sense, Sir Charles is merely a necessary logical proposition to be postulated before Harriet and Clementina can be created; he is antecedent to them logically, rather than transcending them in importance. The dramatic attention is focused on the two young women, one English, one Italian, who fall in love with the same man (Sir Charles). The Englishwoman (and true heroine), Harriet Byron, falls in love with Sir Charles almost at once, with a promptness that distresses her, when he rescues her from the clutches of Sir Hargrave Pollexfen, who is trying to abduct and marry her forcibly. Sir Hargrave, another Richardsonian rake-villain, wants not rape but marriage—the ceremony to be magically pronounced over the resisting Harriet. Lovelace once (mistakenly) dreaded Clarissa's acceptance during his proposal after the rape: "I had instantly popt in upon me, in imagination, an old spectacled Parson, with a White Surplice thrown over a Black Habit [A fit emblem of the halcyon office, which, under a benign appearance, often introduces a life of storms and tempests] whining and snuffling through his nose the irrevocable Ceremony" (VI, 33–34; Ev. III, 266). What Lovelace once feared in imagination (and he thought men dreaded marriage while women desired it) is the realized object of Harriet's fear and loathing:

> A vast tall, big-boned, splay-footed man. A shabby gown; as shabby a wig; an huge red pimply face; and a nose that hid half of it, when he look'd on one side. . . . He had a dog's ear'd common-prayer book in his hand, which once had been gilt; open'd, horrid sight! at the page of matrimony! . . .
> The man snuffled his answer thro' his nose. When he opened his pouched mouth, the tobacco hung about his great yellow teeth. . . .
> *Dearly beloved,* began to read the snuffling monster. (I, I, 154–55)

Harriet in a frenzy "dashed the book out of the minister's hand." Sir Hargrave holds her by force:

> Virago as she is, I will own her for my wife—Are *you* the *gentle,* the *civil* Miss Byron, madam? looking sneeringly in my face. . . .
> *Dearly beloved,* again snuffled the wretch. . . .
> I stamp'd, and threw myself to the length of my arm, as he held my hand. No *dearly beloved*'s, said I. (I, I, 154–55)

Though she dashes the book down, in the rest of the novel Harriet will desire to have "the page of matrimony" read, though over a different groom. Moreover, "the page of matrimony" is what is to be studied throughout the novel, in which a variety of marriages and kinds of marriages are put on view. Most of the people Harriet will come to know do become "dearly beloved's." This parody wedding, this non–marriage ceremony, is a sort of initiation through which she must pass in order to enter the Grandisonian world—and aside from Harriet we have not met the central characters yet. Sir Hargrave is not of the importance he believes himself to be, in his life or in our novel. The heroine's struggle with a ravisher occurs early in the story; only at this point is Harriet a Pamela or a Clarissa. She says "No" and is at last taken at her word, but she does not have to keep on saying "No." Having passed through the mock-wedding, the threat, she progresses to her real wedding by the way of love.

Harriet's problem is the reverse of Pamela's or Clarissa's. She is in love—and at last knows herself to be heartily so—with a man who, she fears, does not love her. Far from being besieged, she seems unsought by the lover she desires. Her strength is her capacity to recognize her own feelings and try to face up to the consequences. Under the friendly but persistent questioning of Sir Charles's sisters, who adjure her to speak out and forsake reserve, Harriet makes her avowal: "I will own, that the man, who by so signal an instance of his bravery and goodness engaged my gratitude, has possession of my whole heart" (I, II, 422). She is only too aware of the difficulties in her position. Sir Charles has said "that he would not marry the greatest princess on earth, if he were not assured, that she loved him above all the men in it." But Harriet knows that men are put off by an easy love and make fun of a forward woman: "I fancy . . . that we women, when we love, and are doubtful, suffer a great deal in the apprehension, at one time, of disgusting the object of our passion, by too forward a Love, and, at another, of disobliging him by too great a reserve" (I, II, 423).

Harriet is, incidentally, a contradiction of all that is advocated in Richardson's *Rambler* 97 (19 February 1751), which advocates modesty, diffidence, and reserve, and expresses distaste for women who have not "patience and decency to stay till they were sought." "That a young lady should be in love, and the love of the young gentleman undeclared, is an heterodoxy which prudence, and even policy, must not allow."[35] Harriet is heterodox; she forsakes prudent reserve for honesty (and some readers were startled and displeased at her frankness). Nevertheless, Harriet is in the courtship snare that has so many other young ladies of fiction in its toils, from Jane Barker's Galesia to Austen's Jane Bennet: a man will not marry a woman save when he is assured of her love, and will hardly ask until he is certain, but how can a woman let him know, before he has "spoken," without losing that maidenliness he admires and seeming too easy to be interesting? No sooner has Harriet admitted her love, said her first big "Yes," than she finds out that Sir Charles is (apparently) involved in a previous commitment to a woman in Italy. Harriet is in a most unorthodox, not to say dismal, position for a heroine of a novel, caught off balance in an unromantic—an unheroine-like—posture in her unrequited love. Harriet's story is certainly a change from Richardson's allegories of resistance. She is openly desiring, and her fear is that her desire may not be met.

The secondary heroine, Clementina, is another example of intense female desire, though in her case the "Yes" of desire is mingled with resistance and subterfuge. Locked into an aristocratic Italian family of which she is the youngest member, and sharing their strong Catholicism (one brother is a bishop), Clementina has been taught to be passive, not to have a will of her own. Her own budding desire she tries to suppress and deny; suppression causes psychic convulsion. She herself quotes *Twelfth Night*. "With the accent of her country she very prettily repeated those lines: *She never told her love*" (II, III, 153). But Clementina immediately denies that Shakespeare's lines have any application to her. Harriet sympathetically makes the application, admiring the Italian lady's silence (a dignity she herself has lost) and yet seeing its dangers.

Clementina gives herself a moral holiday in her madness—it is the only way she can make her family hear her, and she quite patently if unconsciously wants to punish them. But her feelings and desires still have to go in psychological masquerade, not admitted by herself, particularly since she believes that to love and to marry a "heretic" would be a sin. Her desires find expression in unconscious emblems, as in the scene where she runs away from the doctors who are trying to bleed her and displays "her lovely arm, a little bloody." Her mother, her brother, and Sir Charles try to persuade her to endure the operation; she turns to Grandison: "Will it, will it, comfort *you* to see me bleed?—Come then, *be* comforted, I *will* bleed. But you shall not leave me" (I, III, 193). Clementina's censored sexuality is visible in this travesty of erotic consent, mingled with a propitiating masochism and fear of destruction. If she really wishes to bleed sexually, to be pierced by Sir Charles, Clementina is also deeply aware that to prevent this sin, her family is trying to bleed her of energy, of the lifeblood of personality.

The della Porrettas, well meaning and crushing in their affections, are a different kind of "family of love" from the Grandisons. The Grandisons as Harriet knows them (now freed of a tyrannical rake of a father who had made his daughters' lives a misery) represent a human attempt to capture wholeness without forsaking diversity. The diversity in union is symbolized by the constant references to music (Richardson is the first novelist to supply a story with a musical motif). Harriet Byron, an orphan, has never suffered from the kind of family oppression or paternal prerogative known to Clarissa, or to Charlotte and Caroline Grandison. Harriet's grandmother is important to her; her uncle, aunt, and cousins have supplied her with family love and care; but the questions of prerogatives and power have not cropped up. The Grandisons enlarge their new extended family by seeking out kin. In the course of the story we also see them beginning marriages and founding friendships. Relationships extend and extend (the reverse of the Harlowe tendency to draw together in a close phalanx). Within the family, latitude is to be allowed for individuality.

Especially is this seen in the vivacious Charlotte Grandison, with her lively wit and decided opinions. The favorite character of many admirers of the novel, she is also very visibly the sort of woman an old-style family like the della Porrettas could never produce. Though perhaps there is no social or narrative arrangement quite ready for her, in some sections of the novel Charlotte is at the center, capturing most of the reader's attention and sympathy—in *Grandison*, narrative centrality is shared, not monopolized. Charlotte's marriage to Lord G. can start a controversy among readers today: should such a woman have married such a dull if well-meaning man? Sir Charles's anxiety to get his twenty-five-year-old sister married is understandable, as is his belief that Charlotte could not marry a man who wanted to dominate her, and would have a very hard time with a man who was her equal in intelligence. (Charlotte is a character with a psychological history visible to the reader; her stormy relation with her own father makes her critical of men and very likely to fight when domination is attempted.) There is, however, a certain pathos to Charlotte's position as she is benignly browbeaten into an immediate marriage: "Unprepared in mind, in cloaths, I am resolved to oblige the best of brothers" (II, IV, 317).

Charlotte's marriage, which occurs in mid-novel, is a proleptic parody of the wedding of Sir Charles and Harriet. This comic wedding takes place, significantly on Tuesday, April 11; Clarissa's fatal elopement was on April 10. Somewhere Richardson is following the same novelistic calendar. It is as if *Grandison* is trying to go back and mend the damage afflicting the characters of *Clarissa*; if Clarissa had been married on April 11th, the rest of her story would not have happened. Charlotte's wedding is a parody of Clarissa's absent marriage, as well as of that between the hero and heroine of this novel; it also picks up and plays with the travesty wedding Sir Hargrave tried to bring about:

> I overheard the naughty one say, as Lord G. led her up to the altar. You don't know what you are about, man. I expect to have all my way: Remember that's one of my articles before marriage.
>
> He returned her an answer of fond assent to her conditions. . . .
>
> The good doctor began the office. *No dearly beloveds*, Harriet! whispered she, as I had said, on a really terrible occasion. (II, IV, 340–41)

We again read "the page of matrimony," and in this case we behold assent—grudging, comic, but real (and the groom's "fond assent" is the one that rests in the narrative).

Emotions and life continue after marriage; personalities do not die after the wedding ceremony, as we see in the marital spats between Lord and Lady G. No assent is really simple; before her own marriage Harriet has a long and troublous dream that reveals reluctance and anxiety on her part, a fear of marriage to "the best of men" as well as desire. Emotions do not exist unmixed. The novel does not end with Harriet's wedding but flows past it into the territory of marriage and pregnancy, the consequences of saying "Yes." The story cannot end until Clementina has been redeemed into full responsibility for herself through a visit to Grandison Hall, an abode of happy affirmatives resting on the right to consciousness.

It is no wonder that Jane Austen, as her nephew asserted, had the minute familiarity with *Grandison* that comes from full enjoyment and repeated reading.

> Her knowledge of Richardson's works was such as no one is likely again to acquire. . . . Every circumstance narrated in Sir Charles Grandison, all that was ever said or done in the cedar-parlour, was familiar to her; and the wedding days of Lady L. and Lady G. were as well remembered as if they had been living friends.[36]

It is *Grandison* rather than *Clarissa* that James Austen-Leigh singles out, and the number of references to Richardson's last novel in Austen's works bear him out. In *Sir Charles Grandison*, Richardson really founded the new type of novel, the comic novel of domestic (often provincial) life of families, of personalities in conflict and in tune. The novels of Burney, Austen, even George Eliot and Trollope and Henry James spring from the *Grandison* tradition. *Clarissa* was an important influence on Rousseau, Diderot, Laclos, and Goethe and has been admired by novelists from Fielding to Angus Wilson, but it did not found a new kind of English novel in the way that *Grandison* did. The allegories of acceptance were more in tune with the British frame of mind than the allegories of resistance, and tragedy was folded back into comedy once more.

## Notes

1. Richardson to Lady Bradshaigh, 14 February 1754, *Selected Letters of Samuel Richardson*, ed., John Carroll (Oxford: Clarendon Press, 1964), p. 286.

2. It is generally agreed nowadays that the increased number of footnotes in *Clarissa*, commenting on a character or pointing out matters the reader should

have picked up, are a break in the design and an aesthetic error. Richardson was, however, tempted to this course by the careless misreading of which he found some of his public guilty.

3. "Negative Capability," Keats to George and Thomas Keats, 21 December 1817, *The Selected Letters of John Keats*, ed. Lionel Trilling (New York: Farrar, 1951), p. 92.

4. "I love to write to the *moment*," says Richardson's Robert Lovelace, and in this he is typical of Richardson's central characters (IV, 362; Ev. II, 498—see n. 20 below). Richardson draws attention to this technique in his Preface to *Clarissa:* "All the Letters are written while the hearts of the writers must be supposed to be wholly engaged in their subjects (The events at the time generally dubious): so that they abound not only with critical Situations, but with what may be called *instantaneous* Descriptions and Reflections" (I, ix; Ev. I, xiv).

5. See William H. McBurney, *A Check List of English Prose Fiction, 1700–1739* (Cambridge, Mass.: Harvard Univ. Press, 1960), and *Four before Richardson: Selected English Novels, 1720–1727* (Lincoln: Univ. of Nebraska Press, 1963). See John J. Richetti, *Popular Fiction before Richardson: Narrative Patterns, 1700–1739* (Oxford: Clarendon Press, 1969).

6. Richardson himself expressed some unease about this: "I am afraid I make the Writers do too much in the Time" (*Selected Letters*, p. 63). George Sherburn says that Lovelace on June 10 "is supposed to write something like 14,000 words." But Sherburn is defending his indefensible abridgment, the grossest insult of censorship that could be perpetrated upon a great novel and a shame to the schools who teach it. To defend such a travesty as this abridgment (Riverside edition; Boston: Houghton Mifflin, 1962) by any appeal, however oblique, to verisimilitude is to mistake the nature of literature.

7. E.g., Terry Castle, *Clarissa's Ciphers: Meaning and Disruption in Richardson's Clarissa* (Ithaca: Cornell Univ. Press, 1982), a hermeneutic-structuralist account of the novel; William Beatty Warner, *Reading Clarissa: The Struggle of Interpretation* (New Haven, Conn.: Yale Univ. Press, 1979), a structuralist-deconstructionist (and "masculinist") reading of the novel. These works were preceded by Leo Braudy's "Penetration and Impenetrability in *Clarissa,*" in *New Aspects of the Eighteenth Century,* ed., Phillip Harth, Essays from the English Institute (New York: Columbia Univ. Press, 1974).

8. E.g., "Let me ask—Have you read Lovelace's Bad, and not his Good?—Or, does the abhorrence which you have for that Bad, make you forget, that he has any Good?" (letter to Edward Moore, 3 October 1748, *Selected Letters*, p. 89). "Don't you think too highly of Miss Howe's Character? Surely, it has great Blemishes, as well as Beauties" (letter to Sarah Chapone, 2 March 1752, *Selected Letters*, p. 203).

9. Cf. Ian Watt: "But the supreme reason for Richardson's dependence on the novel's mode of performance is, of course, his concern with that most private aspect of experience, the sexual life. The stage, in Western Europe at least, has never been able to go very far in the description of sexual behaviour, whereas in his novels Richardson was able to present much that in any other form would have been quite unacceptable to an audience whose public demeanour, at least, was very severely controlled by the intensified taboos of a Puritan morality" (*The Rise of the Novel: Studies in Defoe, Richardson and Fielding* [1957; rpt. Berkeley: Univ. of California Press, 1974], 199).

10. Ian Watt reawakened the academic (and reading) public to the strengths of the eighteenth-century novel, and the place of major novelists and novels in a real historic world. Christopher Hill, the Marxist historian, published a most interesting essay, "Clarissa Harlowe and Her Times," in *Essays in Criticism* 5 (1955), 315–41; the essay is marred only by Hill's derivative notion that Richardson had no idea what he was doing and hit on all his insights utterly unawares. Richardson gets more credit in the recent study by the Marxist critic Terry Eagleton, *The Rape of Clarissa: Writing, Sexuality and Class Struggle in Samuel Richardson* (Oxford: Basil Blackwell, 1982). Recent feminist studies include chapters in Nancy K. Miller, *The Heroine's Text: Readings in the French and English Novel, 1722–1782* (New York: Columbia Univ. Press, 1980); Janet Todd, *Women's Friendship in Literature* (New York: Columbia Univ. Press, 1980); and Rachel Mayer Brownstein, *Becoming a Heroine: Reading about Women in Novels* (New York: Viking, 1984). Terry Castle's work (*Clarissa's Ciphers*) has its feminist elements. Not all feminist critiques are favorable to Richardson, many seizing on *Clarissa* as an endorsement of feminine masochism, self-silencing, and angelic weakness. I regard myself as a feminist but do not agree with that view.

11. The first great exponent of that view is Fielding in his *Shamela;* modern Fieldingites, like Martin Battestin introducing and praising that parody novel, endorse it. See Martin C. Battestin, "Introduction" to *Joseph Andrews* and *Shamela,* ed. Martin C. Battestin, Riverside ed. (Boston: Houghton Mifflin, 1961), v-xi.

12. Richardson to Johannes Stinstra, 2 June 1753, in *Selected Letters,* p. 232; p. 231.

13. For a most interesting and full discussion of this matter, see Elizabeth Eisenstein, *The Printing Press as an Agent of Change,* 2 vols. (London: Cambridge Univ. Press, 1979); also her "Print Culture and Enlightenment Thought" (paper given at Stanford, May, 1983).

14. Richardson to Stinstra, *Selected Letters,* p. 232. His "letter-writer" was published in January 1741, under the title *Letters Written to and for Particular Friends, on the Most Important Occasions. Directing Not Only the Requisite Style and Forms to be Observed in Writing Familiar Letters; But How to Think and Act Justly and Prudently, in the Common Concerns of Human Life;* the relevant letters are numbers 138 and 139, from a daughter to her father.

15. Richardson to Aaron Hill, 1741, *Selected Letters,* p. 41.

16. All quotations from the novel are taken from the Riverside edition, ed. T.C. Duncan Eaves and Ben D. Kimpel (Boston: Houghton Mifflin, 1971) and cited by volume and page. This edition is based on the first edition, but it should be noted that Richardson altered his novels throughout his lifetime, rather as contemporary poets did their poems. The last state of *Pamela* can be found in the Penguin edition, edited by Peter Sabor with an Introduction by Margaret A. Doody (Harmondsworth, Eng.: Penguin, 1980).

17. Miller, *Heroine's Text,* 39.

18. I have developed the idea of the breaking trope (to which I have given the fancy Greek name *rexis*) and of its counterpart figure of mending, knitting up, making (*enosis*) in novels and romances in "Romance and the Novel," paper given at the MLA Convention, New York, Dec. 1981.

19. Florian Stuber, "*Pamela II:* 'Written in the Manner of Cervantes' " (paper read at NEASECS conference, Syracuse, New York, October 1983). Stuber points out the importance of Pamela's "posthumous" letter in revealing a very anxious relation to her model self.

20. All quotations from *Clarissa* in this essay are taken from a late edition in my possession: *Clarissa; or, the History of a Young Lady: Comprehending the Most Important Concerns of Private Life: And particularly Shewing the Distresses that May Attend the Misconduct, both of Parents and Children, in Relation to Marriage,* 8 vols. (London: J.F. and C. Rivington, T. Davies, H. Law, T. Cadell *et al.,* 1785). Ideally, quotations should be taken from the third edition of the novel, which is, alas, not readily accessible. The 1785 edition is based on those published by Richardson at the end of his life; it supplies his title and his emphases in punctuation, capitals, italics, etc. References in my text are made to volume and page of this edition, immediately after a quotation. But following each of these, a reference is also given to the Everyman edition, *Clarissa, or the History of a Young Lady,* with an Introduction by John Butt, 4 vols. (London: Dent; New York: Dutton, 1932, rpt. 1962). The Everyman edition is the only complete version now in print, though we may soon expect a Penguin *Clarissa,* presumably complete, edited by Angus Ross.

21. See Mark Kinkead-Weeks, *Samuel Richardson: Dramatic Novelist* (London: Methuen, 1973), 237, for the relation of Clarissa's Paper VII to Blake's "O Rose, thou art sick"; for a detailed commentary on the mad papers, see Kinkead-Weekes, pp. 233–42. It should be stressed that Clarissa's mad papers show a painful process of self-knowledge. She looks at herself as at another person, from the outside, referring to herself in third or second person, as when she accuses: "Thou . . . couldst put off every-thing but thy Vanity!" (Paper IV: V, 305; Ev. III, 206).

22. Richardson to Hill, 7 November 1748, *Selected Letters,* p. 99.

23. See Dorothy Van Ghent's chapter on Clarissa in *The English Novel: Form and Function* (New York: Holt, Rinehart & Winston, 1953).

24. See, e.g., Castle, *Clarissa's Ciphers,* 173: "It does not occur to [Richardson], obviously, that a female reader—even a moderately pious one—might not necessarily take an unalloyed pleasure in seeing one of her sex made over into a decomposing emblem of martyred Christian womanhood, or respond wholly favorably to that equation between sexual violation and death which he seems unconsciously to have accepted as a given." For similar and related objections, see also Miller's chapter on *Clarissa* in *Heroine's Text,* and Brownstein's "An Exemplar to Her Sex," in *Becoming a Heroine.* For a history of the use of Lucretia in literature, see Ian Donaldson, *The Rapes of Lucretia: A Myth and Its Transformations* (London: Oxford Univ. Press, 1982).

25. Florian Stuber, "*Clarissa and Her World*" (MS).

26. "Clarissa is a Piece from first to last, that owes its Being to Invention. The History of my Good Man is also wholly so" (Richardson to Stinstra, 2 June 1753, *Selected Letters,* p. 233).

27. The sources of Richardson's many quotations from Restoration plays and their significance were first touched upon by Alan Dugald McKillop in his important pioneering study, *Samuel Richardson, Printer and Novelist* (Chapel Hill: North Carolina Univ. Press, 1936), a work to which all subsequent studies must, directly or indirectly, be indebted. My own book, *A Natural Passion: A*

*Study of the Novels of Samuel Richardson* (Oxford: Clarendon Press, 1974), deals with the relation of the novel to contemporary English domestic fiction and to the drama. Mark Kinkead-Weekes (*Samuel Richardson*) has stressed Richardson's own dramatic method.

28. See Carol Houlihan Flynn, "Horrid Romancing: Richardson's Use of the Fairy Tale," ch. 4 of her *Samuel Richardson, A Man of Letters* (Princeton, N.J.: Princeton Univ. Press, 1982).

29. Walter Allen, *The English Novel: A Short Critical History* (New York: Dutton, 1954), 39.

30. Morris Golden explicitly rejects the social issues raised by Watt (in *The Rise of the Novel*) and McKillop (in *Samuel Richardson*), as also by David Daiches, in "The Novel from Richardson to Jane Austen," part of his *Critical History of English Literature*, 2 vols. (New York: Ronald Press, 1960), II, 700-65, and by Leslie Fiedler in *Love and Death in the American Novel* (New York: Criterion Books, 1960). Golden insists that "the make-up of Richardson's mind is far more important in determining these positions on the basis of a fantasy of dominance than is some scheme of symbolism involving the relations between the aristocracy and the bourgeoisie" (*Richardson's Characters* [Ann Arbor: Univ. of Michigan Press, 1963], 12). Oddly enough, Golden is at present working on a book exploring the historical and journalistic world of the eighteenth-century novelists; set against this background of litigation, sensational crime, and crime reporting, Richardson (among others) appears realistic and indeed outward-looking.

31. Mark Kinkead-Weekes has a very fine passage on some of Richardson's best dramatic effects: "In reading these scenes one entirely forgets that they are technically 'past.' They happen while we read, and they cry out (as several of the book's first readers exclaimed) for the stage. In the equally sustained dialogue with Sally and Polly in the prison [VI, 251ff; Ev. III, 432ff.] even the dash disappears, and Richardson captures an even harder effect; the pressure of the voice on silence. The dialogue is extraordinarily monosyllabic, and as far as Clarissa is concerned apparently expressionless; but it holds our attention precisely because of the silences: the suffering, aggression, or despair that lie between the words. It is a very long road from Richardson to Beckett and Pinter, but the eighteenth-century novelist is further along it than any eighteenth- or nineteenth-century playwright" (*Samuel Richardson*, 403).

32. Richardson to Susannah Highmore, 4 June 1750, *Selected Letters*, p. 161.

33. Richardson to Hester Mulso, 11 July 1751, *Selected Letters*, p. 185: "Well, but, after all, I shall want a few unpremeditated faults, were I to proceed, to sprinkle into this man's character, lest I should draw a *faultless monster.*"

34. Harriet Byron draws a comparison between Anna Howe, who teased her awkward well-meaning suitor so mercilessly, and Charlotte; the latter at once understands the allusion: "Upon my word, Lucy, she makes very free with him. I whisper'd her, that she did—A very Miss Howe, said I. To a very Mr. Hickman, re-whispered she.—But here's the difference: I am not determined to have Lord G. Miss Howe yielded to her Mother's recommendation, and intended to marry Mr. Hickman, even when she used him worst" (I, ii, 229).

All quotations from the novel are taken from the Oxford Novels edition.

3 vols., ed. Jocelyn Harris (London: Oxford, Univ. Press, 1972). The first Roman numeral refers to the Oxford Novels volume; the second, to the relevant number of Richardson's seven original volumes.

35. [Samuel Richardson], *Rambler* 97, 19 February 1751, quoted from *The Rambler* in *The Works of Samuel Johnson, LL.D.*, ed. Arthur Murphy, 12 vols. (London: Thomas Tegg, 1824), V:164–71.

36. J.E. Austen-Leigh, *Memoir of Jane Austen*, ed., R.W. Chapman (Oxford: Oxford Univ. Press, 1926), 89. Austen's nephew himself does not have quite so clear a memory; the wedding day of Caroline Grandison, Lady L., is not dramatized, and he must surely be thinking of the wedding day of Harriet Byron. Jocelyn Harris promises us a book on Richardson and Austen.

# Sheridan Baker

# Fielding:
# The Comic Reality of Fiction

Fielding's achievement in his four novels is immense. *Joseph Andrews* (1742) is not only the first English comic novel but the Declaration of Independence for all fiction. *Jonathan Wild* (1743), though imperfectly, turns Augustan satire into a novel. *Tom Jones* (1749) supersedes and absorbs the drama as the dominant form and, more significantly, culminates the Augustan world of poetry and Pope in the new poetics of prose. *Amelia* (1751) signals the eighteenth century's sombre midday equinox as its undercurrent of sentiment and uncertainty wells up through the cool neoclassic crust. *Amelia* is the first novel of marriage, and it explores a new and modern indeterminacy of character. Notwithstanding Defoe's and Richardson's achievement in fictionalizing the lonely struggle of modernity, Fielding proclaimed the truth of fiction as he gave the novel form. He also gave it mystery with the romantic, and psychic, discovery of identity, acceptance, and success. He gave it its omniscient narrator and comprehensive scope.

Fielding is not of Defoe's and Richardson's rising middle class, where the individual makes himself and the future, where the underdog's struggles are no longer comic. Fielding is a young aristocrat down on his uppers.[1] His is the Augustan perspective, a sophisticated detachment that staves off evils and passionate dogmas through satire and irony, seeking a rational balance between violent extremes. His allegiance is to hierarchy in orderly rank. Like Swift, he prefers Ancients to Moderns. Like Pope, he perceives God's providential creation with calm optimism, and amusement.

He elects himself a Scriblerian. His first major effort, his anonymous *The Masquerade* (1728), a satire in Swiftian tetrameters, is "By LEMUEL GULLIVER, Poet Laureate to the King of *Lilliput.*" Soon, with his eminent cousin, Lady Mary Wortley Montagu, he is writing a burlesque of Pope's recent *Dunciad* (1728). His first stage satire and ballad opera, *The Author's Farce* (1730), is "Written by *Scriblerus Secundus,*" emulating the *Dunciad* in a trip to the underworld of the Goddess of Nonsense. *Tom Thumb*

(1730), which imitates Swift's Lilliputian-Brobdingnagian contrasts and, in its final form, Pope's mock-scholarly preface and footnotes, is also by *Scriblerus Secundus*, who becomes *H. Scriblerus Secundus*, with Fielding's initial, in the expanded *Tragedy of Tragedies* (1730). The *Grub-Street Opera* (1731) is by *Scriblerus Secundus* in all three versions. In short, Fielding set out to emulate the three Augustan masterpieces, all deriving from the brief heyday of the Scriblerus Club (February to June 1714): Swift's *Gulliver's Travels* (1726), Gay's *Beggar's Opera* (1728), Pope's *Dunciad* (in three books, 1728). As Sherburn suggests ("*Dunciad*"), Pope confirmed the alliance by borrowing back from Fielding's farces the kaleidoscopic court of Dulness in his fourth book (1742, 1743).

The theater was Fielding's apprenticeship.[2] It gave him stock characters and situations, repeated until they became universal types. It gave him a knack for scene and dialogue, the balanced structural arch of *Tom Jones*, and the long, downward comic slant of fortune that thrusts suddenly upward like a reversed check mark. It gave him social satire and comedy of manners aimed at a serious point.

Fielding's first play, *Love in Several Masques* (1728), written at twenty-one, forecasts *Tom Jones* in surprising detail. It is intricately plotted. Its hero is Tom Merital, a meritorious rake, a preliminary Tom Jones. Tom's wealthy lady love is an orphan guarded by an aunt and uncle—a stock preliminary Sophia, to be married against her will to save her from the rake. The heroines speak up for the hero, and the aunts respond.

> *Lady Trap:* I have wondered how a creature of such principles could spring up in a family so noted for the purity of its women. (II.vi)
>
> *Mrs. Western:* You are the first—yes, Miss *Western*, you are the first of your Name who ever entertained so groveling a Thought. A Family so noted for the Prudence of its Women. . . . (VI.v)

Lady Trap is also an Amorous Matron—the first Lady Booby, Mrs. Slipslop, Mrs. Waters, and especially Lady Bellaston, who, like Lady Trap, has bad breath: "Brandy and Assafoetida, by Jupiter," cries kissing Tom.

Here, at the play's mathematical center, the heroine catches Tom just as Sophia will discover her Tom and Mrs. Waters at central Upton. We also have the stock comic maid, saucy and ingenious, who will become Mrs. Honour. Finally, we have Wisemore, a junior and sourer Allworthy, a virtuous young country squire who introduces Fielding's perpetual contrast with the wicked city and represents the play's moral center, a book-read idealist whom his mistress twice calls Don Quixote. Wisemore will also transform comically into Parson Adams.

In his six rehearsal-farces—no one else wrote more than one—Fielding discovered himself as parodic satirist. In *The Author's Farce* (1730), he also discovered his autobiographical authorship of comic romances, a comic double self-portraiture in hero and author alike. Harry Luckless, the "author," is young playwright Harry Fielding, luckless with Mr. Colley Cibber of Drury Lane, who appears in no less than two comic versions and two more allusive thrusts. Harry loves Harriot, in the twinnish way of romance, whom his nonentity denies him—courtly love in a London roominghouse. Then Harry stages his show in the Popean realm of Nonsense and becomes Fielding commenting on his work as it goes. In the giddy finale, a pawned jewel proves Luckless a farcical foundling, lost heir of a fabulous kingdom, who may now marry and live happily ever after as Henry I. Fielding's blithe comedy distances his wish for recognition, the universal yearning typical of romance, as we simultaneously fulfill and recognize our fancies in the way of *Joseph Andrews* and *Tom Jones*.

Fielding eventually put nine commenting authors on the stage—seven in the rehearsal-farces (two in *Pasquin*) plus two authorial inductors like Gay's in *The Beggar's Opera*—breaking the bonds of drama to reach for narration. Many of their comments Fielding will repeat less facetiously in his novels. Medly, in *The Historical Register* (1737), Fielding's last, comes particularly close:

> Why, sir, my design is to ridicule the vicious and foolish customs of the age . . . I hope to expose the reigning follies in such a manner, that men shall laugh themselves out of them before they feel that they are touched.

Fielding says of *Tom Jones* (in the Dedication):

> I have employed all the Wit and Humour of which I am Master in the following History; wherein I have endeavoured to laugh Mankind out of their Favourite Follies and Vices.

But *The Historical Register* brought down Sir Robert Walpole's wrath, and the Licensing Act (1737) shut Fielding from the stage. He made himself a lawyer and followed the circuits along the roads of his future novels. He turned to journalism with the *Champion*, the opposition newspaper backed by Lord Chesterfield and Lord Lyttelton, Fielding's Eton school-friend. He is now "Capt. Hercules Vinegar, of Hockley in the Hole," slaying the Hydras of political corruption like the popular cudgel player and boxing promoter of that name. Like Pope, who had declared himself "TO VIRTUE ONLY AND HER FRIENDS, A FRIEND" in his first *Imitation of Horace* (1733), Fielding is the champion of England against Walpole's government, the future essayist as novelist who will dedicate *Tom Jones* to Lyttelton, believing that it will serve as "a Kind of Picture, in which Virtue becomes as it were an Object of Sight."

Fielding's religious concern deepens in the *Champion*. We can almost see *Shamela* and *Joseph Andrews* accumulating. In the spring of 1740, Fielding pauses in his political championship to write four thoughtful essays about the materialism and vanity of the clergy and the necessity of humble charity. The first (March 29) is untitled. Then in the next issue (April Fool's Day, by luck or design), he satirizes Walpole, along with a new book by "the most inimitable Laureat," none other than *An Apology for the Life of Mr. Colley Cibber, Comedian, Written by Himself.* Cibber had been a standing joke as political sycophant and bad writer ever since Walpole had made him poet laureate in 1730. Moreover, Cibber, from his side of the political fence, had in his *Apology* called Fielding a mudslinger and failed writer. So Fielding interrupts his religious meditation here and returns in several papers to ridicule the vanity and grammar of his old personal and political opponent, whom he will enthrone as an egotistical fraud in *Shamela* and *Joseph Andrews,* as Pope would also in the *Dunciad.* Fielding then continues with his religious essays under the ironic title "THE APOLOGY FOR THE CLERGY,—*continued.*"

As Cibber and the clergy mix in Fielding's mind, another new book appears: *A Short Account of God's Dealings with the Reverend Mr. George Whitefield* (1740), written by himself in what would seem Cibberian conceit at God's personal attention. It stirred a controversy between the new Methodist (and old Calvinist) belief that only faith and God's grace warranted Heaven as against the doctrine that "Faith without works is dead" (Battestin, *Moral Basis,* 18), which Fielding had asserted in the *Champion.* Whitefield's *Dealings* would become Shamela's favorite reading, as Fielding mocks Pamela's egotistical piety, and Parson Williams espouses spiritual grace to release the body for pleasure.[3] Fielding turns these negatives positive when he transforms Williams into Adams, who, with Methodist John Wesley, prefers a virtuous Turk to a tepid Christian (Woods, "Fielding," 264). Adams is a lovingly comic portrait of a Whitefieldian enthusiast, who shames the fatness of orthodoxy and nevertheless condemns Whitefield's enthusiastic grace:

> "Sir," answered *Adams,* "if Mr. *Whitfield* had carried his Doctrine no farther . . . I should have remained, as I once was, his Well-

> Wisher. I am myself as great an Enemy to the Luxury and
> Splendour of the Clergy as he can be." (I.xvii)

But selfless charity was the center of Fielding's religion, and Whitefield stood ready with Cibber to coalesce with pious Pamela, when she arrived in the fall, as symbols of meretricious vanity and hypocrisy.

*Pamela: Or, Virtue Rewarded*, the "real" letters of a serving girl, prefaced by twenty-eight pages of letters praising its moral excellence, is really *An Apology for the Life of Mrs. Shamela Andrews* (1741)—so proclaims Fielding's title page in the typography of Cibber's *Apology*, with "Conny Keyber" as author: *Keyber* being the standard political slur at Cibber's Danish ancestry. Parson Tickletext, who can dream of nothing but Pamela undressed, sends a copy of the new best seller to Parson Oliver so that he too can preach it from the pulpit (as had actually been done in London). Oliver tells Tickletext the book is a sham, doctored by a clergyman who can make black white. The girl is really Shamela, a calculating guttersnippet from London working in a neighboring parish. Richardson's Mr. B. is really Squire Booby; his busybody Parson Williams is really an adulterous poacher of Booby's hares and wife. He sends Tickletext the real letters—Fielding's breezy parodies of Richardson's, which concentrate on his two bedroom scenes, now lifted to peaks of hilarity as Fielding brilliantly condenses two volumes to some fifty pages.

Fielding's title page tells us immediately that something has happened to fiction, now allusively declaring and enjoying in the Augustan way the fictive pretense Defoe and Richardson had pretended real. English fiction has become literate. Here, suddenly, is a book that—like Joyce's *Ulysses*, let us say—generates its being, and its meaning, from other literature as it gets its hold on life. By declaring his letters true to tell us ironically they are not—precisely the comic pose Cervantes shares with his readers—Fielding asserts both the validity and power of fiction, which he will proclaim in *Joseph Andrews*. *Shamela* is probably the best parody anywhere, but it is also a broadly Augustan burlesque of social ills—moral, political, religious, philosophical—in the true Scriblerian mode (Rothstein, 389).

In naming "Conny Keyber" the author, Fielding concentrates his inclusive satire in a bawdy sexual symbol. "Conny" merges Cibber's first name with that of the Rev. Mr. Conyers Middleton, whose dedication to his *Life of Cicero* (February 1741, less than two months before *Shamela*) Fielding closely parodies as a dedication by Conny Keyber to "Miss Fanny, & c." Middleton had dedicated his *Cicero* to John, Lord Hervey, Walpole's propagandist; and Hervey, an effeminate bisexual, had acquired the epithet "Fanny" from Pope's first *Imitation of Horace* (1733), where Pope had saucily Anglicized Horace's Fannius, a bad poet and a homosexual. Now, as Rothstein notes (387), *Conny, coney,* and *cony* (for "rabbit") were all pronounced "cunny"—a version of the still-prevailing obscenity for the female pudendum, and *Fanny* and *et cetera* were both slang terms for the same (382).

In parodying one of Richardson's introductory letters praising Pamela, Fielding writes, "it will do more good than the C——y have done harm in the World," wherein one may read both the *clergy* and the *cunny* of Fielding's satirical attack. Later, Shamela reports that her husband gave her a toast so wicked she can't write it and that Mrs. Jewkes then "drank the dear *Monysyllable;* I don't understand that Word, but I believe it is baudy." Williams and Booby likewise drink to and joke about her "*et cetera.*" In short, Cibber, Hervey, Middleton, Richardson, and Pamela, "that young Politician" named on the title page, are all moneysyllabic prostitutes in their various ways. Fielding's slyest touch is in quoting directly another introductory letter telling Richardson he had "stretched out this diminutive mere Grain of Mustard-seed (a poor Girl's little, innocent, Story) into a resemblance of Heaven, which the best of good Books has compared it to." Fielding alters only the parenthesis of this extravagant Biblical allusion (Matt. 13:31): "has stretched out this diminutive mere Grain of Mustard-seed (a poor Girl's little, *&c.*) into a Resemblance of Heaven."

*Shamela* sharpened Fielding's belief, to be formulated in *Joseph Andrews,* that comedy can be both realistic and morally instructive. No serving maid was ever named Pamela, after the romantic princess in Sidney's recently republished *Arcadia,* nor wrote such letters, if she could write at all. The realistic idiom of Shamela and the housekeepers, and even their calculating morality, amusingly point up the falsity in Richardson's idea of virtue. Tearful Pamela, proud of her dead mistress's clothes, becomes Shamela, wanting to set herself up with Parson Williams, since "I have got a good many fine Cloaths of the Old Put my Mistress's, who died a whil ago." Her language rings colloquially true and yet mimics Richardson at every turn. Shamela actually seems more honest, and Mrs. Jewkes more wholesome, than their prototypes. Nothing seems more typical of Fielding's realistic countryside than Booby riding in his coach with Shamela and catching Williams poaching. Yet as Williams rides off in the coach with Booby's bride, we realize that this is all a mime of an episode in *Pamela* where we find Williams walking, book in hand, at the meadowside; he is met, reconciled, and finally taken into the coach by Mr. B. with his Pamela.

The close parody of Richardson's bedroom scenes taught Fielding the high comedy of sex. The amorous scenes in his plays are heavy. The ladies know what's what. But *Shamela* shimmers with the comic hypocrisies of civilized sex. Pamela wants—not simply for prestige—to submit to her master, but everything she believes in prevents her desire from even breaking surface. Richardson, simply to keep his story going, has her stay when she wants to go, writing into his tale this elemental sexual hypocrisy that gives it the mystic dimension of Beauty and the Beast. In burlesquing it, Fielding learned what it was. His stage ladies wish to appear proper only in the eyes of others; Lady Booby and Mrs. Slipslop of *Joseph Andrews* wish to appear proper in their own eyes as well. A great deal of the comedy in Fielding's novels comes from the universal struggle of hidden passion against propriety or, on the masculine side, of passion against the best of intentions. *Shamela*, more than anything before, brought this to the center of Fielding's comic vision.

Parson Oliver, another step toward Fielding's commenting author, decrying Richardson's lascivious images and meretricious rewards, spells out the moral. He declares the future lesson of *Tom Jones*: Prudence must rule. *Pamela*, he says, encourages young men to impetuous matches that will "sacrifice all the solid Comforts of their Lives, to a very transient Satisfaction of a Passion." In *Tom Jones*, Fielding will seek "to make good Men wise" by instilling in them "that solid inward Comfort of Mind, which is the sure Companion of Innocence and Virtue." Oliver writes of "the secure Satisfaction of a good Conscience, the Approbation of the Wise and Good . . . and the extatick Pleasure of contemplating, that their Ways are acceptable to the Great Creator of the Universe." "But for Worldly Honours," Oliver continues, "they are often the Purchase of Force and Fraud." Tom Jones cries out concerning Blifil, who has defrauded him:

> What is the poor Pride arising from a magnificent House, a numerous Equipage, a splendid Table, and from all the other Advantages or Appearances of Fortune, compared to the warm, solid Content, the swelling Satisfaction, the thrilling Transports, and the exulting Triumphs, which a good Mind enjoys, in the Contemplation of a generous, virtuous, noble, benevolent Action? (XII.x)

*Shamela*'s success made Fielding a novelist; he gives *Pamela* another parodic turn in *Joseph Andrews* (1742) and also finally brings Cervantes to English life. At last, Fielding finds his authorial voice in the playful ironies of Cervantes and Scarron:

116

> Now the Rake *Hesperus* had called for his Breeches. . . . In
> vulgar Language, it was Evening when *Joseph* attended his Lady's
> Orders.  (I.viii)

> And now, Reader, taking these Hints along with you, you may, if
> you please, proceed to the Sequel of this our true History.  (III.i)

He now ironically holds up Pamela and Cibber as consummate models for
the kind of biography he is writing. He extends the joke of *Shamela* in its
next inevitable mutation, transposing the sexes for the more ludicrous
effect. Pamela Andrews, who had become Shamela Andrews, will now
become Pamela's equally virtuous, and hence more comically prudish,
brother: a footman named Joseph, after the biblical hero who resisted
Potiphar's wife. Lady Booby now pursues *her* servant—Squire Booby is her
nephew—as Mr. B. pursued his. Richardson's Mrs. Jewkes, "a broad, squat,
pursy, *fat thing*" who drinks, becomes Mrs. Slipslop, who also reflects
Cervantes's grotesque chambermaid, Maritornes,[4] a libidinous little dwarf
with shoulders somewhat humped and a breath with "a stronger *Hogoe*
than stale Venison" (I.iii.2). Mrs. Jewkes's salacious lesbianism becomes
Slipslop's comic passion for Joseph.[5] Fielding even dares to name his
heroine after the obscene "Miss Fanny" of *Shamela*, rinsing the name
clean without losing all of its comic pubic potential. In fact, Fielding's
Beau Didapper, who attempts to rape the purified Fanny, is none other than
Lord Hervey again (Battestin, "Hervey"), the original "Miss Fanny," as if
everything of *Shamela* must be converted to new uses. Finally, Mr. B.'s
curate Williams becomes, through the wringer of *Shamela*, Lady Booby's
curate Adams.

Adams is Fielding's triumph. At twenty-one, as a student at Leyden,
Fielding had tried to naturalize Cervantes in his *Don Quixote in England*—eventually a ballad opera (1734). Now, in *Joseph Andrews* ("Written
in Imitation of the Manner of Cervantes") he finally creates a thoroughly
English Quixote, a country parson drawn from the very life—from Fielding's friend from childhood, the absentminded parson William Young.
Like Cervantes, Fielding comically confronts the ideal quest of romance
with the satiric picaresque tour of society. Adams is his comic knight, a
quixotic Christian benevolist embodying the virtues outlined in the
*Champion*. Like Quixote, he is book-blinded, but by the New Testament
and classics alike. His tattered cassock replaces Quixote's patchwork
armor. His borrowed horse, soon abandoned, a Christian Rosinante, frequently stumbles to its knees. He rescues "Damsels" (Fanny) and stands
up for the innocent with his crabstick against the selfish world's wind-

mills. Andrews travels the English roads and inns as realistic squire to the daft idealist and, like Sancho Panza, grows in wisdom.

Fielding's parody becomes *paradiorthosis,* as the Greeks would say, an emulative borrowing and bending of a master's words, well loved by Augustans, except that Fielding finds creative joy in allusively reapplying whole characterizations, episodes, and dramatic arrangements. Richardson furnishes his major structure—two wild bedroom episodes at beginning and end, followed by the discovered truth of identity and social elevation of romance, which Pamela had also enacted. It is almost as if Fielding had cut *Shamela* down the middle and pulled the halves apart to accommodate his Cervantic roadway. The first bedroom scenes (I.v- vi), in which first Lady Booby and then Mrs. Slipslop try to possess Joseph— "Madam," says Joseph, "that Boy is the Brother of *Pamela*"—are probably the most hilarious chapters in the English novel. The second and concluding bedroom episode (IV. xiv) is more broadly comic, a reworking of the old picaresque fabliau about a wrong turn into bed that simultaneously parallels two versions from Cervantes and three from Scarron, as critics from Cross to Goldberg have detected, and primarily into the bed of Mrs. Slipslop, that caricature of Mrs. Jewkes, in whose bed Richardson's second scene of attempted rape is laid, if one may use the term. Even Lady Booby must laugh at the universal selfish scrambling of sex to which intrinsic virtue is impervious (Spilka, 403).

Fielding's central Cervantic journey is linear and episodic, as Joseph becomes both romantic hero and practical companion to idealistic Christianity. When Lady Booby dismisses him, he heads not for home (as Pamela longs to do) or for "his beloved Sister *Pamela*," but to Lady Booby's country parish to see the girl he loves. Fielding's genius is nowhere more blithely evident than in his ability to change his lighting and reveal the young man within the parodic abstraction—this very funny male Pamela—without losing his hero, or his readers. Joseph matures, as Taylor notes, and clearly becomes the romantic hero at an inn, very near the center of the novel (II.xii), which reunites the major characters (except Lady Booby) in much the way the inn at Upton will do at the central climax of *Tom Jones.*

Fielding is reworking an episode from Cervantes he had already used for the whole of *Don Quixote in England,* where the lovers, as Tom and Sophia will be at Upton, are under the same roof unbeknownst to each other. Adams has brought the rescued Fanny, who, like Dorothea in the play and Sophia in *Tom Jones,* has set out across country in search of her lover. Mrs. Slipslop in her coach has picked up Joseph along the road and brought him in "Hopes of something which might have been accomplished at an Ale-house as well as a Palace" (II.xiii). As in Cervantes, our heroine hears a beautiful voice singing. But realism renders romance comic. Joseph's pastoral song ends in sexual climax, with Chloe "expiring." Fanny, only recognizing the voice, cries "O Jesus!" and faints. Adams, to the rescue, throws his beloved Aeschylus into the fire, where it "lay expiring," and enraged Slipslop rides off in disappointment.

Balancing this comic juxtaposition of ideal and sexual love is another structuring episode Fielding will also elaborate in *Tom Jones*. This is Mr. Wilson's story, just on the other side of the central divide between Books II and III, which is, as Paulson ("Models," 1202) and Maresca (199) have noted, Fielding's realistic version of the *descensus Averno* (*Aeneid* VI.126), the trip to the underworld for truth.[6] Our travelers descend a hill in spooky darkness, cross a river, and find Elysium in the country Eden of Wilson, who tells them the truth about the wicked world of London. Wilson's straightforward account fills out Fielding's social panorama, and Wilson, in the end, neatly fits into Fielding's comic romance as the long-lost father of cradle-switched Joseph, whose white skin (which, as with Tom Jones to come, a lady discovers in succoring the wounded hero) has already disclosed to the reader of romances his unknown nobility.

Fielding comically fulfills the romantic dream of Harry Luckless. He opens his preface by assuming that his readers will have "a different Idea of Romance" from his, never before attempted in English, which will be "a comic Romance." He takes his term from Paul Scarron's *Romant Comique* (1651), the *Comical Romance* in Tom Brown's translation (1700), recently read, which augments Cervantes's authorial facetiousness and claims of "this true History,"[7] and sends its lovers chastely down the picaresque road disguised as brother and sister, in the amusingly incestuous twinship of romance that Fielding will exploit with Joseph and Fanny, the almost identical foundlings of romance from *Daphnis and Chloe* onward. His identical portraits gently parody those typical of Scudéry's romances (Shesgreen, 33–34; Maresca, 200–201), especially in their noses "inclining to the Roman" (I.viii; II.xii). In Joseph's nose and brawny physique, Fielding has again pictured himself both accurately and comically as romantic hero.

"Now a comic Romance," he writes, "is a comic Epic-Poem in Prose." From his bows toward the epic, the twentieth century has largely ignored his, and his readers', context: the vast French romances—which he names, and which had virtually shaped the fancies, manners, and idiom of English elegance—and the new romance of princess Pamela, the serving maid. He is not writing the high life of epic, which can live among modern realities only in mock heroics: "Indeed, no two Species of Writing can differ more widely than the Comic and the Burlesque," touches of which he has indulged here and there to amuse his classical readers. In his conclusion, he insists again on distinguishing his realistic comedy from "the Productions of Romance Writers on the one hand, and Burlesque Writers on the other." His new "Species of writing . . . hitherto unattempted in our Language" avoids both the impossibilities of "the grave Romance" and the absurdities of the comic mock-epic. His comic romance will draw from the realities of ordinary life, as his friend Hogarth has done pictorially, to illustrate the vanity and hypocrisy everywhere and eternally evident.[8]

This comic realism he outlines in III.i, which, most likely written before his preface, stands as his Declaration of Independence for fiction. Unlike actual historians, he says, Cervantes has written "the History of the World in general," as have Scarron, Le Sage, Marivaux, and other authors of "true Histories," including the *Arabian Nights*. Fiction is truer than history. It illustrates the typical, the perennially true in human nature in all time and every country: "I describe not Men, but Manners; not an Individual, but a Species." One might add only that typicality is the very stuff of comedy, along with the celebration of life (which Wright and Langer point to)—that central romantic thread on which the comic typicalities are strung, and which *Pamela* seriously exploits: the unknown nobody's becoming somebody in happy marriage. Fielding keeps the wish fulfillment of all us Harry Lucklesses playfully comic, letting us know in his affectionate irony that our deep-seated yearning is real enough, but with no Richardsonian guarantee. Romance encapsulates the central psyche: one's secretly noble self, whom no one appreciates, crying for recognition and riches, especially in the classless world emerging as Fielding wrote, and surely representing his own déclassé impulse. His comic-romantic perspective acknowledges the comic impossibility of the ideal and romantic glories of life, yet affirms their existence and value.

Adams, like Quixote, comically embodies the romantic struggle of the ideal against the cruel realities. As with Quixote, we begin in laughter and end in admiration. For the Duke and Duchess who amuse themselves at Quixote's expense, Fielding gives us an actual practical-joking country squire—son-in-law of the Duchess of Marlborough, indeed (Wesleyan ed., xxiv)—who cruelly abuses Adams for a laugh, and we uncomfortably discover ourselves in company with the laughers at the noble in spirit. In fact, Fielding goes beyond Cervantes, first with Adams and then even with Slipslop, as true nobility rises within the comic bubble without bursting it. When Lady Booby threatens Adams with losing his livelihood if he proceeds to marry Joseph and Fanny, he answers: "I am in the Service of a Master who will never discard me for doing my Duty. And if the Doctor (for indeed I have never been able to pay for a Licence) thinks proper to turn me out of my Cure, G—— will provide me, I hope, another." If necessary, he and his numerous family will work with their hands. "Whilst my Conscience is pure, I shall never fear what Man can do unto me" (IV.ii). Adams's comically honest parenthesis deepens the effect as it sustains the amusing characterization, and the scene returns to amusement as Adams awkwardly bows out, mistakenly thinking Lady Booby will understand.

Fielding never again equals this. Neither Quixote, his model, nor Jones to come must stand up for others against tyranny with all they have. And Fielding repeats this feat, in which comedy contains the feeling that would destroy it, when funny old never-to-be-loved Slipslop, the image of the selfish world, turns selfless in Joseph's defense—"I wish I was a great Lady for his sake"—and a chastened Lady Booby mildly bids her good-night as "a comical Creature" (IV.vi). Evans well illustrates how in *Joseph Andrews* and *Tom Jones* comedy necessarily absorbs the tragic in its broader rendering of the "whole truth" ("World," "Comedy"). *Tom Jones* is the masterwork, of course—bigger, richer, wiser, more Olympian—but because of Adams and his comic depth here achieved, along with the very neatness of the parody, its enduring comic realism, and its joyous energy, *Joseph Andrews* achieves a perfection of its own.

In *Jonathan Wild* (1743), Fielding turns from comic romance for an uneven experiment in sardonic satire. As Digeon suggests, he patched it together for his *Miscellanies* (1743), during a time of sickness and trouble, from previous satirical attempts perhaps beginning as early as 1737, the bitter year when Walpole drove him from the stage. Indeed, a dialogue between Wild and his wife, little suiting them, carries a stage direction: *"These Words to be spoken with a very great Air, and Toss of the Head"* (III.viii).[9] Fielding takes his tone from Lucian, as he had in the dreary *Journey from This World to the Next*, also published in the *Miscellanies*. Although Fielding's Booth calls Lucian "the greatest in the Humorous Way, that ever the World produced" (*Amelia*, VIII,v), and although Fielding claims to have "formed his Stile upon that very Author" (*Covent-Garden Journal*, 52), his Lucianic writings are among his least attractive, uncongenial in a way he could not see.[10]

In *Jonathan Wild*, Fielding tries in a Lucianic-Swiftian way to emulate Gay's *Beggar's Opera* without the Scriblerian verve. Gay had already animated the standing Opposition parallel between Walpole, the "Great Man" of public power, and Wild (executed 24 May 1725), the "Great Man" of London's underworld. As Fielding says in his Preface, "the splendid Palaces of the Great are often no other than *Newgate* with the Mask on."

Defoe's pamphlet on Wild (1725), one of Fielding's sources (Irwin, 19), indicates the difficulty. Defoe "does not indeed make a jest of his story . . . which is indeed a tragedy of itself, in a style of mockery and ridicule, but in a method agreeable to fact." Life down here is tragic, not to be viewed from Fielding's comic heights.[11] The vicious life of Newgate is too real for comedy, too dark for Fielding's satire on human foibles. It rises again in *Amelia*, after Fielding's exposure as magistrate, again to cloud his comic optimism.

Nevertheless, *Jonathan Wild* constantly reflects Fielding's characteristic situations, turns of style and thought, as it exposes his uncertainty. His real hero is Wild's victim, Thomas Heartfree, an older merchant-class Thomas Jones, innocently trusting hypocritical avarice; a Booth, married, with children, jailed for debt by the mighty to seduce his wife. Like Adams, Heartfree believes that "*a sincere* Turk *would be saved*" (IV.i). Like Jones, he extols a good conscience, "a Blessing which he who possesses can never be thoroughly unhappy" (III.v). Not harming others brings him "the Comfort I myself enjoy: For what a ravishing Thought! how replete with Extasy must the Consideration be, that the Goodness of God is engaged to reward me!" (III.x).[12] Fielding has idealized Heartfree from his honest friend, the jeweler and playwright George Lillo (Digeon, 121). But this is the serious middle-class world of Defoe and Richardson, essentially alien to Fielding, in spite of his generous condescension.

Fielding distinguishes "Greatness" from "Goodness" in his preface and opening chapter. The "*true Sublime* in Human Nature" combines greatness with goodness, but the world associates greatness only with the powerful rascal, the "Great Man." Fielding hopes to tell the world that greatness is not goodness (cf. Hatfield, "Puffs," 264–65). But as Dyson remarks (22), no one can believe Wild's great roguery generally typical enough to be of much interest, and Heartfree's goodness is both unconvincing and sentimental.

Of course, Fielding manages some genuine comedy here and there, especially in Mrs. Heartfree's disclaimer of pleasure in repeating compliments to herself (IV.xi). But all in all, *Jonathan Wild* strains at ideas already overworked—Walpole had fallen from power the previous year. Fielding, in ill health and with his wife desperately ill, has tried to clear his desk for his *Miscellanies*, make some badly needed money, and end his career as writer:

> And now, my good-natured Reader, recommending my Works to your Candour, I bid you heartily farewell; and take this with you, that you may never be interrupted in the reading these

122

> Miscellanies, with that Degree of Heart-ach which hath often
> discomposed me in the writing them.   (Preface, *Miscellanies*)

A year later, in his preface to his sister's *David Simple* (July 1744), Fielding reiterated his farewell. But before long (Wesleyan ed., xxxviii), Lyttelton prompted *Tom Jones*, with financial support. "It was by your Desire that I first thought of such a Composition," writes Fielding in his Dedication. Lyttelton evidently had proposed something new, a novel recommending "Goodness and Innocence" and the "Beauty of Virtue." Fielding adds its rewards: "that solid inward Comfort of Mind," the loss of which "no Acquisitions of Guilt can compensate." He also adds the lesson most likely to succeed, the one taught Tom Heartfree, "that Virtue and Innocence can scarce ever be injured but by Indiscretion." Prudence is the theme, because "it is much easier to make good Men wise, than to make bad Men good."

Again Fielding's hero, handsome, impetuous, generous, is comically romantic self-portraiture, amusing but now admonitory, played opposite an affectionate version of his dead wife. Again, a Cervantic idealist and realist, now reversed as young Jones and old Partridge, travel English roads in picaresque satire. The story is again the essence of romance: the mysterious unknown foundling, with the qualities and white skin of noble knighthood, discovers identity, paternity, riches, and marriage. Fielding called his new book *The History of a Foundling* as late as six months before publication, and others continued to call it *The Foundling* after it appeared (Wesleyan ed., xliii–xlvi). Indeed his title, usually foreshortened, is actually *The History of Tom Jones, a Foundling*. To keep the comic-romantic expectation before us, across the tops of its pages marches not "The History of Tom Jones," but "The History of a Foundling." But Fielding nevertheless seems to find this generally different from *Joseph Andrews*, with its comically positive Christian championship. *Tom Jones*, though philosophically positive, is morally cautionary. Be wary, or your goodness comes to naught. The old Adam should grow wise before he is old. In this cautionary balance and wiser view, Fielding culminated the Augustan perspective.

Martin Price epitomizes (3) the neoclassic period in the concepts of *balance* and *the detached individual*. Irony and satire stake out for the individual the ground on which he dare not dogmatize. Any stand is extreme, smacking of Commonwealth enthusiasm and bloody fanaticism. With orthodoxy shattered, the emerging individuals of either the middle-class Defoes or the shaken aristocrats must regain their footing, the Defoes in engagement, the aristocrats in detachment. *Tom Jones* embodies the detached Augustan's vision. As Pope in his *Essay on Man* (1733–34) surveyed the cosmic maze in gentlemanly ironic detachment, balancing deism and orthodoxy in a synthesis of divine immanence and contemporary psychology, so Fielding works out the ways of Providence in this conflicting world.

Battestin well makes "The Argument of Design."[13] This evidently unjust and accidental world has really a Providential order. The mighty maze has a plan, comically and affectionately fulfilled. Fielding had declared Pope "*the inimitable Author of the* Essay on Man," who "*taught me a System of Philosophy in* English *Numbers*" (Fielding's preface to *Plutus, the God of Riches,* 1742). Fielding's literary creation reflects the providential order beyond our limited vision:

> All Nature is but Art, unknown to thee;
> All Chance, Direction, which thou canst not see;
> All Discord, Harmony, not understood;
> All partial Evil, universal Good. . . .    (Pope, *Essay,* I:289–92)

Fielding illustrates this *concordia discors,* the Horatian harmony of discords (*Ep.* I.xii.19) that one finds repeatedly echoed in Pope and other Augustans, with a superbly comic "as if," which reflects both the ultimate resolution and its daily dissonance. Chance is really direction: a stupid guide misdirects Jones from the sea toward the army and Upton; Sophia chances upon the same guide to change her direction toward Jones; Blifil's betrayal works out Jones's identity and marriage with Sophia, the name of the "wisdom" he is to obtain (Powers, 667; Battestin, "Wisdom," 204–205; Harrison, 112). Fielding's very sentences reflect the balancing of opposites, the ordered containment of discords, of Pope's couplets as well as of his serenely balancing philosophy (Alter, 61; Battestin, "Design," 297).

All the thorny vines of Nature are really God's Art. And art, in its providential ordering, reflects God's universe. Providence orders the macrocosm; Prudence (semantically linked in Latin) orders the microcosm, man (Battestin, "Design," 191). Fielding the novelist plays God to the world of his creation, illustrating God's ways to man. Fielding sums this in a crucial passage, pausing with ironic detachment in the architectural middle of his comic confusion. He warns the reader not to criticize incidents as "foreign to our main Design" until he or she sees how they fit the whole, for "This Work may, indeed, be considered as a great Creation of our own," of which any fault-finder is a "Reptile" (X.i), a proud and imperceptive Satan in the creator's garden. The analogy, he says in ironic humility, may be too great, "but there is, indeed, no other." The artist brings order out of chaos and reflects God's providential order. Form symbolizes meaning (Battestin, "Design," 301).

Fielding's remarkable ironic balancing of opposites, first comically coupled for him in Cervantes, illustrates both the universal harmonizing of discords and the Augustan sense that opposites mark the norm without defining it: the principle "of Contrast," says Fielding, "runs through all the Works of Creation" (V.i). Everyone notices the contrasting pairing: Tom and Blifil, Allworthy and Western, each with a comically learned spinster sister; Sophia and Mrs. Fitzpatrick, as well as Sophia contrasted successively with her worse and worse opposites, Molly, Mrs. Waters, Lady Bellaston; Thwackum and Square; even the two brothers Blifil and Nightingale. Everything balances as formal artifice ironically orders daily chaos: six books for the country, six for the road, six for the city, as Digeon first noted (175, n.2). Hilles diagrams the remarkable structural balances on the scheme of a Palladian mansion, of which Ralph Allen's at Bath furnished one of the models for Allworthy's—a wing of six rooms angled up to the central six, a wing of six rooms angled down.[14]

For his architectural reflection of providential order, Fielding has heightened the linear episodic structure of *Joseph Andrews* into the arch of formal comedy. The episodic scene from *Don Quixote in England* now becomes the centerpiece. The high hurly-burly of sex and fisticuffs in the inn at Upton spans Books IX and X at the novel's mathematical center. As in the play, our heroine, running off in pursuit of her lover on the eve of forced marriage, arrives at the inn where he is, both lovers unaware of the other's presence. Fielding again comically contrasts sex and love, as Mrs. Slipslop's purpose with Joseph climaxes with Mrs. Waters and Tom, and bedrooms are scrambled as wildly as those concluding *Joseph Andrews*. As in the play, a foxhunting squire with his hounds rides up in pursuit, now converted from the unwanted suitor into Western, the heroine's father. The actual name *Upton* coincides with Fielding's peak of comic complexity (Wright, 89–90). It even seems the top of a geographical arch, as Sophia pursues Tom northward and then Tom pursues Sophia southward.

Fielding combines his favorite dramatic plot of the worthy rake and the heiress with the basic romantic story of the foundling, both in hopeless courtly love. *Love in Several Masques* has proliferated into a novel, complete with the country lover pursuing his mistress into the wicked city, an element repeated in three other plays (*The Temple Beau*, 1730; *The Lottery*, 1732; *The Universal Gallant*, 1735). In fact, four plays from Fielding's burgeoning year of 1730 awaken in *Tom Jones* nineteen years later. Here again is the wicked brother bearing false witness to defraud the hero of his birthright (*The Temple Beau*), the threat of inadvertent incest through unknown identity (*The Coffee-House Politician, The Wedding Day,* written c. 1730), and especially the comic pattern of discovered identity already borrowed from romance for *The Author's Farce.*

As readers have frequently noticed, Fielding balances two retrospective stories precisely on either side of his central theatrical peak: a lesson for Tom, a lesson for Sophia. The first is another *descensus Averno,* as if Fielding had lifted Wilson's account of wasted youth from the middle of *Joseph Andrews,* put it before his Cervantic inn, and also put it on Mazard Hill to suggest the greater peak to come. In *Joseph Andrews,* our travelers descend "a very steep Hill"; now Jones and Partridge, their quixotic counterparts, ascend "a very steep Hill" because Jones wants to cultivate his romantic "melancholy Ideas" by the "Solemn Gloom which the Moon casts on all Objects" (VIII.x). Partridge fears ghosts. They see a light and come to a cottage. Jones knocks without initial response, and Partridge cries that "the People must be all dead." Like Wilson, the Man of the Hill has retired from the world of debauchery and betrayal, which he describes for Jones and the reader. But Wilson, with wife and children, lives like people "in the Golden Age," as Adams remarks (III.iv); the Man of the Hill is an embittered recluse. Young Jones rejects his misanthropy and urges Fielding's lesson of prudence—the old man would have continued his faith in humanity had he not been "incautious in the placing your Affection" (VIII.xv). In his *descensus,* Jones has learned the truth. On the other side of Upton, Sophia hears from her cousin Mrs. Fitzpatrick a tale of elopement and amours that illustrates what she should not do with Jones.

Upton emphasizes the balanced theatrical architecture of *Tom Jones.* And many have noticed the theatricality of the city section (Cross, II:202; Haage, 152). Two scenes—with Lady Bellaston behind the bed, then Honour, then both—are pure theater (XIV.ii, XV.vii). Moreover, Lady Bellaston descends directly from Fielding's versions of Congreve's Lady Wishfort, beginning with Lady Trap in his first play. Tom Jones courts her to get at her ward, just as Mrs. Fitzpatrick urges him to court Mrs. Western (XVI.ix), the very ruse of her own ruin (XI.iv), as Fielding thrice deploys Tom Merital's strategem, acquired from Congreve. But Fielding shapes the whole novel in the abstract pattern of five-act comedy: Act I, exposition; Act II, intrigue; Act III, climactic complications; Act IV, unraveling toward disaster; Act V, depression shooting upward into triumph—the playlike ending already traced in Joseph's reprieve from Platonic celibacy and Heartfree's from the gallows.

If we treat the central six books as Act III, dividing the first and the last six books in halves, we find startling references to the theater at each break, except the invocation to Fame that begins the London section, or

"Act IV." At "Act V," where the stage expects the final darkness before dawn, Fielding talks, first about the playwright's problem of prologues (XVI.i) and then, in the next Book, most facetiously about the playwright's problem of concluding a comedy or tragedy, and about his own in extricating "this Rogue, whom we have unfortunately made our Heroe," whom he may have to leave to the hangman, though he will do what he can, since "the worst of his Fortune" still lies ahead (XVII.i). "Tragedy is the image of Fate, as comedy is of Fortune," says Susanne Langer (p.333). Indeed, the formal structure of comedy, superimposed on the novel's more realistic vagaries, comments more quizzically on Fortune than a simple affirmation. It sustains with an ironic detachment Fielding's demonstration that the partial evils, the accidents that happen (in his frequent phrase), interweave fortunately in "universal Good." As "we may frequently observe in Life," says Fielding, "the greatest Events are produced by a nice Train of little Circumstances" (XVIII.ii). The author, like the Craftsman of Creation, is shaping our nearsighted joys and blunders, the realities of life.

Life does have odd coincidences. Apparent evils do often prove blessings as life flows on. For Fielding, as Stevick shows, history has meaning, just as his comic "true History" reflects a meaningful actuality. There are people, who, like Jones, have in fact accidentally taken the right road. Possessions, like Sophia's little book with a £100 bill in its leaves, have in fact been lost and luckily recovered—perhaps have even changed a course of life, as when Jones turns from the army to find Sophia. Acquaintances do turn up in restaurants and airports, like Partridge, Mrs. Waters, or Dowling, who seems to dowl his way through apparently random events to conclude the mystery. Accident, bad and good, which Ehrenpreis finds a weakness (22ff.), is actually the very stuff in life from which comedy creates its mimesis.

Fielding's third-person detachment, on which comedy also depends, may seem to deny the inner life that Defoe and Richardson opened for the novel with first-person narration (Watt, *Rise*). But actually, we are perceiving psychic complexities exactly as we do in life—from the outside, from what people do and say. Dowling, apparently only a comically busy lawyer, proves a complex rascal in blackmailing Blifil and keeping Tom from his birthright, yet he is affable and even sympathetic. Bridget, the sour old maid, actually attracts all eligible males. Her secret passions, simmering toward forty, not only beget the illegitimate Tom but thwart her plans for him (Crane, 119) as, again pregnant, she rushes to marry Blifil, whom she has evidently trapped—with his calculated concurrence. She takes a sly pleasure in having Thwackum whip her love-child, when Allworthy is away, for the psychic strain he has caused her, but never her legitimate son, whom she hates, as Fielding tells us directly. She later attracts not only Thwackum but Square, with whom (now that she is past the threat of pregnancy) she has an affair—from which Fielding turns our eyes even as he ironically confirms it, attributing it to malicious gossip with which he will not blot his page (III.vi). Before Tom is eighteen, he has openly replaced Square in her affections, with a hint of the incest that plays comically through Tom's affairs (Hutchens, 40), incurring Square's hatred and his own expulsion from Paradise.[15] Fielding's psychological realism abounds in little self-deceptions: Sophia's about Jones is neatly symbolized in her muff, which appears when love blooms, turns up in Jones's empty bed at Upton, and accompanies him to London, an amusingly impudent visual pun in pubic slang (Johnson, 129–38). Jones has put his hands into it, as Honour reports: "La, says I, Mr. *Jones*, you will stretch my Lady's Muff and spoil it" (IV.xiv).

But Fielding's implied psychology fails with Allworthy. From the first, readers have found him bland if not unreal: the ideal benevolist and ultimate judge, taken in by duplicity, throwing out the good. Fielding seems to have intended a more dignified comic Adams. Allworthy talks "a little whimsically" about his dead wife, for which his neighbors roundly arraign him (I.ii). And we first meet him indeed in a bedroom, absentmindedly in his nightshirt, contemplating "the Beauty of Innocence"—the foundling sleeping in his bed—while Fielding wonderfully suggests that Mrs. Wilkins, "who, tho' in the 52d Year of her Age, vowed she had never beheld a Man without his Coat," believes she was summoned for another purpose (I.iii). Had Fielding sustained this comic view of the imperceptive idealist—he must make him imperceptive at any rate—his book would have fulfilled the perfection it very nearly achieves. But except for some touches about Thwackum's piety and Square's "Philosophical Temper" on his misperceived deathbed (V.viii), Allworthy fades from comic view.

As Hutchens says, Fielding takes an ironic and "lawyer-like delight in making facts add up to something unexpected" (30), and he does the same with the facts that convey personality. Mrs. Western, the comic six-foot chaperone, proud of her little learning and political misinformation, is also the superannuated coquette. Fitzpatrick has fooled her; she treasures in her memory a highwayman who took her money and earrings "at the same Time d——ning her, and saying, 'such handsome B——s as you, don't want Jewels to set them off, and be d——nd to you' " (VII.ix). To avoid forced marriage with Lord Fellamar, Sophia slyly flatters her with the many proposals she claims to have refused. "You are now but a young Woman," Sophia says, one who would surely not yield to the first title offered. Yes, says Mrs. Western, "I was called the cruel *Parthenissa*," and she runs on about "her Conquests and her Cruelty" for "near half an Hour" (XVII.iv). And Western, with his vigor, his Jacobite convictions, his Somerset dialect, his views as narrow as the space between his horse's ears, who has cruelly driven his wife to the grave, yet stirs our compassion as Fielding reveals the feeling that threatens and heightens the comic surface in a Falstaff or Quixote, as he had done with Adams and Slipslop. Western's comic limitations reveal their pathos in London, where—lonely, beaten by Egglane, bewildered—he pleads with Sophia:

> 'Why wout ask, *Sophy?*' cries he, 'when dost know I had rather hear thy Voice, than the Music of the best Pack of Dogs in *England.*—Hear thee, my dear little Girl! I hope I shall hear thee as long as I live; for if I was ever to lose that Pleasure, I would not gee a Brass Varden to live a Moment longer. Indeed, *Sophy,* you do not know how I love you, indeed you don't, or you never could have run away, and left your poor Father, who hath no other Joy, no other Comfort upon Earth but his little *Sophy.*' At these Words the Tears stood in his Eyes; and *Sophia,* (with the Tears streaming from hers) answered, 'Indeed, my dear Papa, I know you have loved me tenderly'. . . . (XVI.ii)

And the scene soon returns to full comedy as Western leaves in his usual thunder of misunderstanding.

This is the comic irony of character, the comedy of limited view, of the *idée fixe,* which plays against our wider perception and the narrator's omniscience, and in turn makes us part of the human comedy as we think we see all but learn that we do not.[16] Fielding's omniscience guides and misguides us constantly; in his lawyerlike way, he presents the evidence and conceals the mystery, tempting our misunderstandings along with those of his characters, whom we believe less percipient than ourselves, or pretending ironically not to understand motives to guide our understanding: "Whether moved by Compassion, or by Shame, or by whatever other Motive, I cannot tell," he will write of a landlady who has changed her hostile tune when Jones appears like an Adonis and a gentleman (VIII.iv). This is Cervantes's mock-historian elevated to mock-psychological ignorance in the ironic service of psychology. This is Fielding's Cervantic omniscience, which delights us by showing in comic fiction life as it is, comic in selfish imperception, comic in providential blessing.

Fielding's commenting authorship has reached its full ironic power and elegance, and much more pervasively than in *Joseph Andrews.* The earlier twentieth century scorned this kind of "intrusive author." But McKillop (123) and, especially, Booth have well certified the central impact and necessity of Fielding's authorial presence. He has become his own most worthy character, amiable, wise, benevolent, literate, balanced between extremes, engaging us constantly through a long and pleasant journey until "we find, lying beneath our amusement at his playful mode of farewell, something of the same feeling we have when we lose a close friend, a friend who has given us a gift which we can never repay" (Booth, 218). He has shown us the world of Sophias and Toms, Blifils and pettifoggers, but he has also shown us that it contains a wonderfully ironic and compassionate intelligence we have come to know, which is something very like the wisdom of a benevolent God surveying our selfish vices and romantic yearnings.

Booth, of course, insists on the "implied author," a fictive creation clear of biographical irrelevancies. When the author refers to himself as infirm, Booth says that it "matters not in the least" whether Fielding was infirm when he wrote that sentence: "It is not Fielding we care about, but the narrator created to speak in his name" (218). But I dare say readers do care about Fielding as Fielding—Keats as Keats, Whitman as Whitman, Joyce as Joyce—else why our innumerable researches? Booth also oddly implies that Fielding's introductory chapters, which we can read straight through "leaving out the story of Tom," comprise all the narrator's "seemingly gratuitous appearances" (216). But Fielding actually "intrudes" on every page as the authorial voice ironically displaying life's ironies or commenting earnestly, with or without the "I."[17]

Fielding clearly considers that he himself addresses his readers, however much he may pretend, in the Cervantic way, that his history is true, that Allworthy may still live in Somerset for all he knows, or that he has given us "the Fruits of a very painful Enquiry, which for thy Satisfaction we have made into this Matter" (IX.vii). He is playful or straight, facetiously elevated or skeptically glum, exactly as he would be in conversation or anecdote, writing as if he were actually present—as indeed he was when he read his book aloud to Lyttelton and others before publication. He hopes that some girl in ages hence will, "under the fictitious name of *Sophia*," read "the real Worth which once existed in my *Charlotte*," and that he will be read "when the little Parlour in which I sit this Instant, shall be reduced to a worse furnished Box," and all this in a wonderfully mock-heroic invocation conveying his actual aims and beliefs as a writer (XIII.i). As Miller says ("Style," 265), "he is Henry Fielding all right." As with Pope—who characteristically begins by addressing a friend, who refers to his garden, his grotto, his ills, his aims, and concludes again in autobiography—the "implied author" seems unnecessary, or irrelevant. Fielding is projecting himself, playing the kind of role we all must play in whatever we do, as teacher, citizen, neighbor, fellow trying to write a scholarly essay, or whatnot. He dramatizes himself, of course, but in a way quite different from those partial versions of himself he comically (or guiltily) dramatized in Harry Luckless, Andrews, Jones, and Billy Booth.

As Miller well says, Fielding in his comic romance gives us a seamless weave of the real and ideal with life inhering "down to the smallest particle" ("Rhetoric," 235). Many have admired these verbal particles that reflect the universe. Take his "solid comfort." Here is the common reality of life, verbally and emotionally. *Shamela's* Oliver upholds "all the solid Comforts of their Lives." In his preface to the *Miscellanies*, Fielding says that his wife, dangerously ill, gives him "all the solid Comfort of my Life." In *Tom Jones*, he writes to Lyttelton of the "solid inward Comfort of Mind" that will reward benevolence and that Tom will aver as "solid Content" (XII.x). Yet Fielding acknowledges the universal ambiguity even in sincere belief, playing ironically with his favorite term in an extended passage revealing the motives of Bridget and Captain Blifil, who—bearded to the eyes, built like a plowman—bristles virility: Bridget expects a solid phallic comfort; Blifil, the comfort of hard cash.

> She imagined, and perhaps very wisely, that she should enjoy more agreeable Minutes with the Captain, than with a much prettier Fellow; and forewent the Consideration of pleasing her Eyes, in order to procure herself much more solid Satisfaction. . . .
> The Captain likewise very wisely preferred the more solid Enjoyments he expected with his Lady, to the fleeting Charms of Person. (I.xi)

That "Minutes" speaks sexual volumes.[18]

With *Amelia* (1751), the realities darken beyond comic affirmation.[19] The Augustan certainties, earned in irony, have faded into the doubts and sentimentalities of the century's second half. Free will now enters the providential scheme (Knight, 389), infinitely more chancey than the happy accidents of comedy. Individual responsibility replaces comic Fortune, now only an "imaginary Being." Each must shape his own luck in an "Art of Life" that resembles the cagey and protective maneuvering of chess. What we blame on Fortune we should blame on "quitting the Directions of Prudence," now active as well as cautionary, for "the blind Guidance of a predominant Passion" (I.i). The world of *Tom Jones*, which had darkened from country to city, reversing the progress of *Joseph Andrews*, now opens in the Newgate of *Jonathan Wild*, with a diseased and vicious Mrs. Slip-slop, no longer funny, as Blear-eyed Moll. The subject is the "various

Accidents which befel a very worthy Couple," as the husband redeems "foolish Conduct" by "struggling manfully with Distress," which is "one of the noblest Efforts of Wisdom and Virtue"—a struggle and virtue the hero hardly exhibits. In his Dedication, Fielding says that he also wants to expose "the most glaring Evils," public and private, that "infest this Country," and here, at least, he succeeds.

Fielding has attempted another new species of writing. For the first time, he adopts an epic, the *Aeneid,* for his "noble model" as he tells us in the *Covent-Garden Journal* (Jensen, ed., I.186). His serious subject can now sustain the epic parallel his comic romance had prohibited as burlesque mock-heroics. In his Court of Censorial Inquiry, "a grave Man" stands up to defend "poor Amelia" from "the Rancour with which she hath been treated by the Public." He avows "that of all my Offspring she is my favourite Child," on whom he has "bestowed a more than ordinary Pains" (186). Fielding's strange favoritism doubtless owes to his loving fictionalization of his dead wife, complete with scarred nose, whom he elevates to his title and make the virtuous lodestone (Wendt, "Virtue"):

> H. Fielding [writes Lady Mary Wortley Montagu] has given a true picture of himself and his first wife, in the characters of Mr. and Mrs. Booth, some compliments to his own figure excepted; and, I am persuaded, several of the incidents he mentions are real matters of fact. (Cross, II.328)

Fielding is clearly working out some remorse, perhaps for the same infidelities both religious and sexual through which Booth suffers.

Powers demonstrates how closely Fielding parallels the *Aeneid.* Like Virgil, Fielding begins *in medias res* with the long, retrospective first-person accounts of the central action that are typical of epic and new in Fielding.[20] Powers matches characters and actions throughout the book, beginning with Miss Matthews (Dido), who seduces Booth (like Aeneas, separated from his wife with a new order to establish), though Powers omits remarking how starkly the chamber in Newgate reflects Virgil's sylvan cave. Fielding's masquerade at Ranelagh matches Aeneas's *descensus,* though moved from *Aeneid* VI to *Amelia* X, where Aeneas meets the resentful shade of Dido and Booth the resentful Miss Matthews. The masquerader's conventional "Do you know me?" in "squeaking Voice" (*Tom Jones,* XIII.vii; *The Masquerade,* 190) now becomes Miss Matthews's caustic "Do'st thou not yet know me?" (X.ii). In the end, Fielding replaces the pious Aeneas's defeat of violent Turnus with Booth's escaping a duel and affirming a new order in his Christian conversion.

As Cross notes, however (II.325), Fielding also characteristically re-works his plot from three of his plays. From *The Temple Beau* (1730), he had already taken the evil brother defrauding the good of his inheritance, with an accomplice, as models for Blifil and Dowling. He feminizes this for *Amelia*. In the play, a father dies and disinherits his heir, abroad in Paris. His brother, through a false witness, had blackened the heir's charac-ter "and covered his own notorious vices under the appearance of inno-cence" (*Works*, VIII.115). Amelia's older sister likewise vilifies her while abroad. She learns in Paris of her mother's death and her disinheritance. But now sister Betty and her accomplices forge a new will reversing the mother's decree to leave her and not Amelia penniless, as Fielding adds a touch from actuality. Four years after the play, Fielding eloped to marry against a mother's wishes, as does Booth. Similarly, his wife's mother died soon after, but nevertheless left her estate to his wife, cutting off her elder sister with a shilling (Cross, II.330).

In *The Coffee-House Politician* (1730), Fielding also foresketches his and Booth's elopement, and introduces the good magistrate who untangles things in *Jonathan Wild* and becomes another self-portrait in *Amelia* (Cross, II.322): the unnamed justice who, about to dine, hears the evidence and resolves, "Tho' it was then very late, and he had been fatigued all the Morning with public Business, to postpone all Refreshment 'till he had discharged his Duty" (XII.vi). Fielding concludes his play with his justice: "Come, gentlemen, I desire you would celebrate this day at my house." Similarly, the justice in *Amelia*:

> Whether *Amelia*'s Beauty, or the Reflexion on the remarkable Act of Justice he had performed, or whatever Motive filled the Magistrate with extraordinary good Humour, and opened his Heart and Cellars, I will not determine; but he gave them . . . hearty Welcome . . . nor did the Company rise from Table till the Clock struck eleven. (XII.vii)

*The Coffee-House Politician* indeed frames *Amelia*'s plot, with the instrumental justice at the end, and at the beginning a half-pay army captain, on his way through London streets at night to a rendezvous for elopement who aids a person attacked and is jailed as attacker by a venal judge through false witness—exactly as Booth lands in Newgate at the outset.

*The Modern Husband* (1732) furnishes Fielding's central matter, already worked in *Jonathan Wild*: two influential men, one a lord, ruin and jail a husband in order to seduce his virtuous wife. The husband has an affair and suffers a painful conscience. His extravagance becomes Booth's addictive gambling. His wife's fear of a duel, which keeps the lord's advances secret, becomes the actual challenge Amelia keeps secret. In play and novel, the wife's constancy inspires contrition, confession, and reform. The play's contrasting "modern" couple, who collude in adultery for extortion, become the Trents of *Amelia.*[21]

Except at beginning and end, Fielding's sustained epic parallel has no force, as it would have in the comic contrasts of a mock-epic or a *Ulysses.* It passes unnoticed into Fielding's romance motifs, now similarly forsaken by comedy and indeed more prevalent. Booth has himself smuggled into his lady's hostile household in a basket straight from the flowery thirteenth-century romance of *Floris and Blancheflour.*[22] As Maurice Johnson commented to me in a letter (26 April 1965), this smuggled entry midway in Book II matches precisely the Grecian warriors' entry into the enemy's citadel inside the Trojan horse, midway in *Aeneid* II. But implausible romance obliterates the epic.

Indeed, in spite of the book's seamy realism (Sherburn, "*Amelia,*" 2; Butt, 27), Fielding's first instance of comic self-portraiture, *The Author's Farce,* now lends surprising and uneasy touches of romance to this more extended autobiographical fiction, no longer comic. Lady Mary, noting the autobiography, complained of *Amelia,* along with *Tom Jones:* "All these sort of books . . . place a merit in extravagant passions, and encourage young people to hope for impossible events . . . as much out of nature as fairy treasures" (*Letters,* III.93, quoted in Blanchard, 102). The burlesque of wonderful endings, which Fielding initiated in his *Farce* and continued playfully in *Joseph Andrews* and *Tom Jones,* now indeed becomes the fairytale strained by realism. In the play, Harry Luckless has pawned a jewel. His servant's return to the pawnshop enables a bystander to find him and disclose his identity and his kingdom far from London's unjust indifference.

In *Amelia,* this hero's jewel has multiplied. Fielding modifies an episode from Ariosto's *Orlando Furioso*—the story of Giocondo (Canto 28), the same that gives Spenser his Squire of Dames—in which the hero, departing reluctantly from his wife, forgets a little jeweled cross, a farewell gift. Booth, on his departure for war, forgets a little casket, similarly given, which should have contained a jeweled picture of Amelia, lost a month before. Her foster brother and silent courtly adorer—in the submerged incestuous way of romance, which is no longer comic as with Joseph and Fanny—has stolen it. Nothing so clearly illustrates Fielding's fall from comedy as the contrast between this scene and that with Lady Booby in bed and Joseph Andrews beside it. Now, the new noble servant Joseph Atkinson is abed, visited by Mrs. Booth. Fielding's instinctive self-revision—the Josephs, the As, the Bs—here turns romance lugubrious. Atkinson, tears gushing, returns the picture to his lady, who has come to her poor lovesick knight, with words widely adapted—in fiction and actuality both, one suspects—from that famous and monstrous romance so prominent on Fielding's early blacklist, La Calprenède's *Cassandra*: "that Face which, if I had been the Emperor of the World . . ." (XI.vi.)[23] Later, Amelia pawns the picture; a second visit to the pawnshop discloses that a bystander has identified her by it, and his information leads to her long-lost inheritance and an estate far from London's unjust indifference.

Harry Luckless's ancient dream of the disinherited and the happy accidents of comedy dissolve into pathos and implausibility in the tragic world of *Amelia*. As Rawson says (70), Amelia's despairs carry the novel's conviction: "There are more bad People in the World, and they will hate you for your Goodness," wails Amelia to her "poor little Infants"; "There is an End of all Goodness in the World"; "We have no Comfort, no Hope, no Friend left" (IV.iii, VII.x, VIII.ix). This is the modern existential woe of Clarissa:

> What a world is this! What is there in it desirable? The good we
> hope for, so strangely mix'd, that one knows not what to wish for:
> And one half of Mankind tormenting the other, and being
> tormented themselves in Tormenting!   (Richardson's *Clarissa* II,
> Letter vii)

Augustan detachment becomes sentimental involvement. The ironic providential overseer has departed, leaving a less frequent sociologist:

> . . . I myself (remember, Critic, it was in my Youth) had a few
> Mornings before seen that very identical Picture of all those
> ingaging Qualities in Bed with a Rake at a Bagnio, smoking
> Tobacco, drinking Punch, talking Obscenity, and swearing and
> cursing with all the Impudence and Impiety of the lowest and
> most abandoned Trull of a Soldier.   (I.vi)

The reader, as Coley notes (249–50), has likewise diminished from the "ingenious" to the "good-natured" who enjoys a "tender Sensation." Goodness must demonstrate its sensitivity in faintings and tears (Ribble). Parson Harrison, a realistic Adams, replaces the author as evaluative intelligence, and yet in his uncomic blindness, which drives Amelia to despair, he becomes one of Fielding's most plausible characters in this new indeterminacy of characterization (Coolidge). The quixotic Adams, upholding virtue, now also becomes Colonel Bath, the swordsman upholding only the passé code of honor—pistols were to be the weapons of James's duel.[24] The type no longer represents the comic universals in humanity. The limited view is no longer comically typical but painfully characteristic of human imperfection.

Indeterminacy replaces comic truth in typicality. The psychological complexities authorially implied in a Bridget now become the unreliable testimony of a Mrs. Bennet. Booth agonizes and develops, as against the characteristic comic changelessness of Andrews and Jones (Coley, 251). This is a new age; subjective consciousness breaks through Augustan order and objectivity. Human nature is no longer everywhere the same. Hume's solipsistic feeling has overturned reason, and Hume is clearly Fielding's unmentioned antagonist as he attempts to adjust the new philosophy to the providential Christianity it so profoundly unsettled (Battestin, "Problem").

Booth's Epicurean fatalism wavers toward atheism. Chance is no longer providential direction nor a "blind Impulse or Direction of Fate." Man acts as his uppermost passion dictates and can "do no otherwise" (I.iii; cf. Thomas). Booth is a prisoner, psychically and physically, throughout the book—limited at best to the Verge of Court (Lepage; Wendt, "Virtue," 146; Battestin, "Problem," 631). In the end, Barrow's sermons free Booth from his passional fatalism, as Harrison frees him from custody for his providential reward. But Fielding's demonstration contradicts his theory that the will can shape the passions and one's fate. Hume's emotive philosophy has persuaded him more than he recognizes. Dr. Harrison bases his strongest argument for religion on Hume's passional doctrine, which Fielding had set out to refute (Battestin, "Problem," 632–33). Harrison asserts that men act from their passions, and that "the strongest of these Passions; Hope and Fear," support the truth of religion (XII.v). Booth converts, and Providence fulfills the dream of escape to Eden with the affluent lady, in the line of Luckless's Harriot, Wilson's Harriet Hearty, Heartfree's Mrs. Heartfree, and Jones's Sophia.

From the first play to last novel, Fielding repeats himself perhaps more than any major writer, working and reworking literary conventions as living paradigms. Even amid the sentimentalities in *Amelia*, his fictive truth persuades us that life is like this: selfish, conceited, agonized, wishful, looking for philosophical certainty. The primordial foundling of romance lives in our dreaming self-pity. The noble Quixote lives in our ideals. When Fielding insulated aspiration in comedy, ironically acknowledging both its truth and probable unfulfillment, he achieved the incomparable *Joseph Andrews* and *Tom Jones*.

## Notes

1. Genealogists deny his family's connection to the royal Hapsburgs (Cross, I.2–3), but Fielding and his contemporaries assumed it. "Most members of the family . . . have uniformly added the quartering of Hapsburg and displayed their arms upon the double headed eagle of the Holy Roman Empire" (Henley, ed., XVI.xlvi). Fielding used the double eagle as his seal on at least one letter. Oddly, Hogarth's portrait of Fielding shows an unmistakable Hapsburg lower lip. Battestin has recently identified another probable portrait ("Pictures").

2. I borrow extensively throughout from my essays listed in "Works Cited." Historical details and many other points originate in Cross. Texts are Henley for plays; Wesleyan for *Joseph Andrews* and *Tom Jones*; first editions for *Shamela*, *Jonathan Wild*, and *Amelia*.

3. See Evans on the *Whole Duty of Man*, a book central to Fielding's charitable Christianity since childhood. Shamela, like Pamela, approves it but with the major duty of charity missing, and Whitefield condemned it as useless for the Grace of being born again.

4. Paulson, *Satire*, 103–04; Brooks, 161; my "Irony," 142–43; Goldberg, 146–47, 232–33.

5. Golden sees in Fielding's older women assaulting the heroes "the same stuff as the witches of child lore"; the aggressive males are ogres, "grotesques of adults in the child's fantasy" (145). But this wholly ignores the comic, adult perspective.

6. Originating in the *Odyssey* and taken over by Lucian and the romances as well—Ariosto sends Rinaldo to the moon; Cervantes sends Quixote down the cave of Montesinos and both Sancho and his ass down another cavern—the *descensus* became an Augustan favorite: Swift's Glubbdubdrib, Pope's Cave of Spleen (*Rape*) and Elysian shade (*Dunciad*), Fielding's *Author's Farce* and *Journey from This World to the Next*. For the long prevalence of the *descensus*, see Boyce.

7. Lucian also wrote a satiric *Vera historia*, a "true history," and, like Fielding, claimed a new way of writing (Coley, 241). But Fielding's phrase and manner comes directly from Cervantes, underlined by Scarron's more frequent reiteration; see my "Comic Romances."

8. The twentieth century takes "comic epic in prose" as Fielding's generic category, ignoring his defining term, "comic romance," as it also overlooks his romantic plot and Cervantic perspective. Neither he nor his contemporaries thought of his novels as epics, or even as "comic epics" like the *Dunciad*, from which he borrows his remarks on Homer's mock-heroic *Margites*, now "entirely lost." Pope's "Martinus Scriblerus of the Poem" in turn borrows, tongue in cheek, from Aristotle (*Poetics*, IV.12). But Aristotle does not mention loss. Pope says "tho' now unhappily lost." Fielding's similar reference in his preface to *David Simple* has "tho' it be unhappily lost," indicating Pope as his source. As Goldberg (7) and Miller (*Romance*, 8, 16) indicate, *epic* for Fielding means simply "extended narrative." This, for the eighteenth century, was indeed the primary meaning. Johnson's primary definition of *epic* in his *Dictionary* (1755) is: "Narrative; comprising narrations, not acted, but rehearsed." In fact, Fielding has taken "comic epic in prose" from Cervantes's defense of romances (I.iv.20): "Epicks may be well writ in Prose as Verse." Cervantes's discussion clearly indicates that he takes *epic* to mean "any significant narrative," whether history,

classical epic, or romance. Fielding also borrows his reference to the *Telemachus* from the Ozell-Motteux translator's footnote to this passage: "The *Adventures of Telemachus* is a Proof of this." J. Paul Hunter errs particularly in a fanciful derivation of *Tom Jones* from the *Télémaque*. See my two articles on this head, esp. "Fielding's Comic."

9. In 1754, Fielding revised this to "*These Words were spoken. . . ,*" along with changing "Prime Minister" (Walpole) to the innocuous "Statesman" (Digeon, 120). Miller sees this passage as imitating Lucian's dialogues (*Essays,* 367n).

10. Saintsbury claims that "Fielding has written no greater book . . . compact of almost pure irony" (vii-viii). Digeon finds it "profound and rich in various lessons" (127); Shea, "a highly complex satire" (73). Wendt argues that Fielding deliberately made Heartfree "imperfect" ("Allegory," 317); Hopkins (passim), that the sentimentality is really comic irony; Rawson rightly disagrees with both (234ff., 253–54), and extends his perceptive analysis through the latter half of his book (101–259). Miller observes that Fielding's confident and skeptical perspectives simply reflect different moods, with the usual human inconsistency (*Essays,* 75).

11. Hopkins (225–27) points out that Fielding satirizes Defoe's *The King of Pirates* in Mrs. Heartfree's travels and (less convincingly) Defoe's matrimonial dialogue in his *Family Instructor.*

12. Fielding changed this to read (1754) "that Almighty Goodness is by its own Nature engaged. . . ." Hopkins takes this passage as rendered intentionally ridiculous by *ravishing,* already punned upon sexually in Wild's addresses to Laetitia, and in *ecstasy.* But this is exactly the serious language of Parson Oliver and Tom Jones; see the foregoing discussion of *Shamela.*

13. Battestin, "Design," 290; see also Work and Williams. Preston, Knight, Poovy, Vopat, Braudy, and Guthrie resist the providential reading in various ways. Snow finds Battestin's providential equation "intriguing but ultimately a misreading of the teasing, obfuscating narrator and his story" (50). But she herself misreads Fielding's reference to secrets that "I will not be guilty of discovering" till the muse of History "shall give me leave" (II.vi). Snow believes that Battestin posits "Fielding's belief in a benevolent deity who, in effect, works like a detective in a murder mystery, perceiving the pattern of cause and effect, discovering the innocent and guilty, and distributing the rewards and punishments" (40). She takes *discover* to mean "find out" (39–40). But this is not Fielding's (or Battestin's) conception of an omniscient deity who eventually *reveals* ("discovers" in the eighteenth-century sense) the benevolent design behind apparently haphazard events.

14. Hilles elaborates Van Ghent's architectural suggestion ("Art," 81). Battestin quotes Palladio himself (pref., bk. IV) on how "these little Temples we raise, ought to bear a resemblance to the immense one of [God's] infinite goodness," in which all "parts . . . should have the exactest symmetry and proportion" ("Design," 300).

15. Knight well notices the imperfections in this country Paradise Hall, which Tom's restoration redeems. E. Taiwo Palmer and Combs work out the implication of Fielding's Miltonic expulsion, though this, like Fielding's naming of Allworthy's estate, seems a happy afterthought to authenticate his grand providential design.

16. Stephanson well describes this process in *Joseph Andrews*. See also McKenzie and McNamara.

17. See my "Narration"; Stevick: "Every word is 'told,' nothing is impersonally rendered" ("Talking," 119).

18. Alter also analyzes this passage (42). See also my "Cliché," 358. Hutchens demonstrates the similar ironic shadings in *prudence*, Fielding's central word and concept (101–18). Also see Hatfield (*Irony*).

19. From the first, readers have found *Amelia* a "failure" (Cross, II:328ff.; Sherburn, "*Amelia*," 1). See Wolff, Eustace Palmer, Hassall, Osland, Donovan, among others cited passim.

20. Cross, II:326; Digeon, 195–96; Sherburn, "*Amelia*," 4.

21. Fielding had introduced to the stage a situation aired in two contemporary lawsuits (Cross, I:121; Woods, "Notes," 364).

22. Only this romance, and Boccaccio's version, *Filocopo*, where Fielding probably read it, have the lover carried past hostile guardians in a basket. Dudden calls it a device from the comic stage (811), probably thinking of Falstaff's basket: a means of escape, not of entrance. The chest in *Decameron* II.ix and in *Cymbeline*, and the jars in *Ali Baba*, all serve hostile intentions.

23. Miss Matthews responds to Booth's "*Scene of the tender Kind*" (III.ii), describing his emotional departing from Amelia, with a sigh (nicely leading to his seduction): "There are Moments in Life worth purchasing with Worlds." In *Cassandra*, Statira, widow of Alexander, "emperor of the world," says that she prefers death to "the Empire of the whole World with any other Man" (V.106; also IV.109, IV.204). Lady Orrery classed "the works of the inimitable Fielding" with "*Cassandra, Cleopatra*, Haywood's novels" and "a thousand more romantick books of the same kind" (quoted in Foster, 102). Watt points out that "Amelia" and "Sophia" were the most popular romance names ("Naming," 327).

24. Atkinson's nocturnal "wineskin" battle with his wife, a poor attempt at the bedroom fisticuffs in *Joseph Andrews*, is another remnant from Cervantes, which he had derived from Apuleius (Becker, 146–47; Putnam, I:483n).

**Works Cited**

Alter, Robert. *Fielding and the Nature of the Novel*. Cambridge, Mass.: Harvard Univ. Press, 1968.

Baker, Sheridan. "Bridget Allworthy: The Creative Pressures of Fielding's Plot." *Papers of the Michigan Academy of Science, Arts, and Letters* 52 (1967), 345–56.

———. "Fielding and the Irony of Form." *Eighteenth-Century Studies* 2 (1968), 138–54.

———. "Fielding's *Amelia* and the Materials of Romance." *PQ* 41 (1962), 437–49.

———. "Fielding's Comic Epic-in-Prose Romances Again." *PQ* 58 (1979), 63–81.

———. "Henry Fielding and the Cliché." *Criticism* 1 (1959), 354–61.

———. "Henry Fielding's Comic Romances." *Papers of the Michigan Academy of Science, Arts, and Letters* 45 (1960), 411–19.

———. "The Idea of Romance in the Eighteenth-Century Novel." *Papers of the Michigan Academy of Science, Arts, and Letters* 49 (1964), 507–22.

_____. Introduction to *An Apology for the Life of Mrs. Shamela Andrews*. Berkeley: Univ. of California Press, 1953.

_____. Introduction to *Joseph Andrews and Shamela*. New York: Crowell, 1972.

_____. "Narration: the Writer's Essential Mimesis." *Journal of Narrative Technique* 11 (1981), 155–65.

Battestin, Martin C. "Fielding's Definition of Wisdom: Some Functions of Ambiguity and Emblem in *Tom Jones*." *ELH* 35 (1968), 188–217.

_____. "Lord Hervey's Role in *Joseph Andrews*." *PQ* 42 (1963), 226–41.

_____. *The Moral Basis of Fielding's Art: A Study of Joseph Andrews*. Middletown: Wesleyan University Press, 1959.

_____. "Pictures of Fielding." *Eighteenth-Century Studies* 17 (1983), 1–13.

_____. "The Problem of Amelia: Hume, Barrow, and the Conversion of Captain Booth." *ELH* 41 (1974), 613–48.

_____. " 'Tom Jones': The Argument of Design." In Miller, Rothstein, and Rosseau, 289–319. Reprinted as "Fielding: The Argument of Design," ch. 5, in Battestin's *The Providence of Wit: Aspects of Form in Augustan Literature and the Arts*. Oxford: Clarendon Press, 1974.

Becker, Gustav. "Die Aufnahme des Don Quijote in die englische Literatur." *Palaestra* 13 (1906), 122–57.

Blanchard, Frederic T. *Fielding the Novelist: A Study in Historical Criticism*. New Haven, Conn.: Yale Univ. Press, 1927.

Booth, Wayne C. *The Rhetoric of Fiction*. Chicago: Univ. of Chicago Press, 1961.

Boyce, Benjamin. "News from Hell: Satiric Communications with the Nether World in English Writing of the Seventeenth and Eighteenth Centuries." *PMLA* 58 (1943), 402–37.

Braudy, Leo. *Narrative Form in History and Fiction: Hume, Fielding, and Gibbon*. Princeton, N.J.: Princeton Univ. Press, 1970.

Brooks, Douglas. "Richardson's *Pamela* and Fielding's *Joseph Andrews*." *Essays in Criticism* 17 (1967), 158–68.

Butt, John. *Fielding*. Writers and Their Work, no. 57. London: Longmans, Green, 1954.

Coley, William B. "The Background of Fielding's Laughter." *ELH* 26 (1959), 229–52.

Combs, William W. "The Return to Paradise Hall: An Essay on *Tom Jones*." *South Atlantic Quarterly* 67 (1968), 419–36.

Coolidge, John S. "Fielding and 'Conservation of Character.' " *Modern Philology* 57 (1960), 245–59.

Crane, R.S. "The Plot of *Tom Jones*." *The Journal of General Education* 4 (1950), 112–30.

Cross, Wilbur L. *The History of Henry Fielding*. 3 vols. New Haven: Yale Univ. Press, 1918.

Digeon, Aurélien. *The Novels of Fielding*. London: Routledge, 1925.

Donovan, Robert Alan. *The Shaping Vision: Imagination in the English Novel from Defoe to Dickens*. Ithaca: Cornell Univ. Press, 1966.

Dudden, F. Homes. *Henry Fielding, His Life, Works, and Times*. London: Oxford Univ. Press, 1952.

Dyson, A.E. *The Crazy Fabric: Essays in Irony*. London: Macmillan; New York: St. Martin's Press, 1966.

Ehrenpreis, Irvin. *Fielding: Tom Jones*. London: Arnold, 1964.

Evans, James E. "Comedy and the 'Tragic Complexion' of *Tom Jones.*" *South Atlantic Quarterly* 83 (1984), 384–95.

———. "Fielding, *The Whole Duty of Man, Shamela,* and *Joseph Andrews.*" *PQ* 61 (1982), 212–19.

———. "The World According to Paul: Comedy and Theology in 'Joseph Andrews.' " *Ariel* 15 (1984), 45–56.

Fielding, Henry. *Amelia.* London: A. Millar, 1752.

———. *An Apology for the Life of Mrs. Shamela Andrews.* London: A. Dodd, 1741.

———. *The Complete Works of Henry Fielding, Esq.* Ed. William Ernest Henley. 16 vols. New York: Croscup & Sterling, 1902.

———. *The Covent-Garden Journal.* Ed. Gerard Edward Jensen. 2 vols. New Haven, Conn.: Yale Univ. Press; London: Oxford Univ. Press, 1915.

———. *The History of the Adventures of Joseph Andrews.* Wesleyan ed. Ed. Martin C. Battestin. Oxford: Clarendon Press, 1967.

———. *The History of Tom Jones, a Foundling.* Wesleyan ed. Ed. Martin C. Battestin and Fredson Bowers. [Middletown, Conn.]: Wesleyan Univ. Press, 1975.

———. *The Life of Mr. Jonathan Wild the Great.* In *Miscellanies,* Vol. III.

———. *Miscellanies.* 3 vols. London: A. Millar, 1743.

Foster, James R. *History of the Pre-Romantic Novel in England.* New York: Modern Language Association, 1949.

Goldberg, Homer. *The Art of Joseph Andrews.* Chicago: Univ. of Chicago Press, 1969.

Golden, Morris. *Fielding's Moral Psychology.* Amherst: Univ. of Massachusetts Press, 1966.

Guthrie, William B. "The Comic Celebrant of Life in *Tom Jones.*" *Tennessee Studies in Literature* 19 (1974), 91–106.

Haage, Richard. "Charakterzeichnung und Komposition in Fieldings *Tom Jones* in ihrer Beziehung zum Drama." *Britannica* 13 (1936), 119–70.

Harrison, Bernard. *Henry Fielding's* Tom Jones: *The Novelist as Moral Philosopher.* London: Sussex Univ. Press, 1975.

Hassall, Anthony J. "Fielding's *Amelia:* Dramatic and Authorial Narration." *Novel* 5 (1972), 225–33.

Hatfield, Glenn W. *Fielding and the Language of Irony.* Chicago: Univ. of Chicago Press, 1968.

———. "Puffs ánd Politricks: *Jonathan Wild* and the Political Corruption of Language." *PQ* 46 (1967), 248–67.

Hilles, Frederick W. *The Age of Johnson: Essays Presented to Chauncey Brewster Tinker.* New Haven, Conn.: Yale Univ. Press, 1949.

———. "Art and Artifice in *Tom Jones.*" In Mack and Gregor, 91–110.

Hopkins, Robert H. "Language and Comic Play in *Jonathan Wild.*" *Criticism* 8 (1966), 213–28.

Hunter, J. Paul. *Occasional Form: Henry Fielding and the Chains of Circumstance.* Baltimore: Johns Hopkins Univ. Press, 1975.

Hutchens, Eleanor. *Irony in Tom Jones.* University: Univ. of Alabama Press, 1965.

Irwin, William Robert. *The Making of Jonathan Wild.* New York: Columbia Univ. Press, 1941.

Johnson, Maurice. *Fielding's Art of Fiction*. Philadelphia: Univ. of Pennsylvania Press, 1961.

Knight, Charles A. "*Tom Jones*: The Meaning of the 'Main Design.' " *Genre* 12 (1979), 379–99.

La Calprenède, Gaultier. . . . *The Famous History of Cassandra*, tr. abridged. London: Cleave et al., 1703.

Langer, Susanne K. *Feeling and Form: A Theory of Art*, New York: Scribner, 1953.

Le Page, Peter V. "The Prison and the Dark Beauty of 'Amelia.' " *Criticism* 9 (1967), 337–54.

Mack, Maynard, and Ian Gregor, eds. *Imagined Worlds: Essays on Some English Novelists in Honour of John Butt*. London: Methuen, 1968.

McKenzie, Alan T. "The Process of Discovery in *Tom Jones*." *Dalhousie Review* 54 (1974), 720–40.

McKillop, A.D. *Early Masters of English Fiction*. Lawrence: Univ. of Kansas Press, 1956.

McNamara, Susan P. "Mirrors of Fiction within *Tom Jones*: The Paradox of Self-Reliance." *ECS* 12 (1979), 372–90.

Maresca, Thomas. *Epic to Novel*. Columbus: Ohio State Univ. Press, 1974.

Miller, Henry Knight. *Essays on Fielding's Miscellanies: A Commentary on Volume One*. Princeton, N.J.: Princeton Univ. Press, 1961.

———. *Henry Fielding's Tom Jones and the Romance Tradition*. ELS Monograph Series, no. 6. Victoria: *English Literary Studies*, 1976.

———. "Some Functions of Rhetoric in *Tom Jones*." *PQ* 45 (1966), 209–35.

———. "The Voices of Henry Fielding: Style in *Tom Jones*." In Miller, Rothstein, and Rousseau, 262–88.

Miller, Henry Knight; Eric Rothstein; and G.S. Rousseau, eds. *The Augustan Milieu: Essays Presented to Louis A. Landa*. Oxford: Clarendon Press, 1970.

Montagu, Lady Mary Wortley. *Letters and Works,* 2d ed., ed. Wharncliffe. London: Tentley, 1837.

Osland, Dianne. "Fielding's *Amelia*: Problem Child or Problem Reader?" *Journal of Narrative Technique* 10 (1980), 56–67.

Palmer, E. Taiwo. "Fielding's Tom Jones Reconsidered." *English* 20 (1972), 45–50.

Palmer, Eustace. "*Amelia*—The Decline of Fielding's Art." *Essays in Criticism* 21 (1971), 135–51.

Paulson, Ronald. "Models and Paradigms: *Joseph Andrews*, Hogarth's *Good Samaritan*, and Fénelon's *Télémaque*." *Modern Language Notes* 91 (1976), 1186–1207.

———. *Satire and the Novel in Eighteenth-Century England*. New Haven, Conn.: Yale Univ. Press, 1967.

Poovy, Mary. "Journies from This World to the Next: Providential Promise in *Clarissa* and *Tom Jones*." *ELH* 43 (1976), 300–315.

Powers, Lyall H. "The Influence of the *Aeneid* on Fielding's *Amelia*." *Modern Language Notes* 71 (1956), 330–36.

Preston, John. *The Created Self: The Reader's Role in Eighteenth-Century Fiction*. London: Heinemann, 1970.

Price, Martin. *The Restoration and the Eighteenth Century*. New York: Oxford Univ. Press, 1973.

Putnam, Samuel. *The Ingenious Gentleman Don Quijote de la Mancha.* New York: Viking, 1949.

Rawson, C.J. *Henry Fielding and the Augustan Ideal Under Stress.* London and Boston: Routledge & Kegan Paul, 1972.

Ribble, Frederick G. "The Constitution of Mind and the Concept of Emotion in Fielding's *Amelia.*" *PQ* 56 (1977), 104–22.

Rothstein, Eric. "The Framework of *Shamela.*" *ELH* 35 (1968), 381–402.

Saintsbury, George. Introduction to *Jonathan Wild,* Everyman ed. New York: Dutton, 1932.

Shea, Bernard. "Machiavelli and Fielding's *Jonathan Wild.*" *PMLA* 72 (1957), 55–73.

Sherburn, George. "The *Dunciad,* Book I." *University of Texas Studies in English* 24 (1944), 174–90.

——. "Fielding's *Amelia*: An Interpretation." *ELH* 3 (1936), 1–14.

Shesgreen, Sean. *Literary Portraits in the Novels of Henry Fielding.* DeKalb: Northern Illinois Univ. Press, 1972.

Snow, Malinda. "The Judgment of Evidence in *Tom Jones.*" *South Atlantic Review* 8 (1983), 37–51.

Spilka, Mark. "Comic Resolution in Fielding's *Joseph Andrews.*" *College English* 15 (1953), 11–19.

Stephanson, Raymond. "The Education of the Reader in Fielding's *Joseph Andrews.*" *PQ* 61 (1982), 243–58.

Stevick, Philip. "Fielding and the Meaning of History." *PMLA* 79 (1964), 561–68.

——. "On Fielding Talking." *College Literature* 1 (1974), 119–33.

Taylor, Dick, Jr. "Joseph as Hero in *Joseph Andrews.*" *Tulane Studies in English* 7 (1957), 91–109.

Thomas, D.S. "Fortune and the Passions in Fielding's *Amelia.*" *MLR* 60 (1965), 176–87.

Van Ghent, Dorothy. *The English Novel: Form and Function.* New York: Rinehart, 1953.

Vopat, James B. "Narrative Techniques in *Tom Jones*: The Balance of Art and Nature." *Journal of Narrative Technique* 4 (1974), 144–54.

Watt, Ian. "The Naming of Characters in Defoe, Richardson, and Fielding." *RES* 25 (1949), 322–38.

——. *The Rise of the Novel.* Berkeley: Univ. of California Press, 1957.

Wendt, Allan. "The Moral Allegory of *Jonathan Wild.*" *ELH* 24 (1957), 306–20.

——. "The Naked Virtue of Amelia." *ELH* 27 (1960), 131–48.

Williams, Aubrey. "Interpositions of Providence and Design in Fielding's Novels." *South Atlantic Quarterly* 70 (1971), 265–86.

Wolff, Cynthia. "Fielding's *Amelia*: Private Virtue and Public Good." *TSLL* 10 (1968), 37–55.

Woods, Charles. "Fielding and the Authorship of *Shamela.*" *PQ* 25 (1946), 248–72.

——. "Notes on Three of Fielding's Plays." *PMLA* 52 (1937), 359–73.

Work, James A. "Henry Fielding, Christian Censor." In Hilles, *Age of Johnson,* 137–48.

Wright, Andrew. *Henry Fielding, Mask and Feast.* Berkeley: Univ. of California Press, 1965.

# Jerry C. Beasley

## Smollett's Art:
## The Novel As "Picture"

"A Novel," remarked Tobias Smollett in the mock-dedication (to himself) introducing *The Adventures of Ferdinand Count Fathom* (1753), is "a large diffused picture, comprehending the characters of life, disposed in different groupes, and exhibited in various attitudes, for the purposes of an uniform plan."[1] These comments represent, in part, the only extended statement Smollett ever made concerning a theory of fiction, and they have usually been dismissed by critics as conventional and trite or as irrelevant to any meaningful understanding of his work. But actually they are quite crucial, for they exactly describe the intentions with which their author approached each of his five novels, different as they all are from one another.

The brief analogy to painting was, in other words, no mere exercise in metaphor. Smollett's conception of his novelistic art may in fact be best illustrated by reference, not to the works of a writer like his contemporary Henry Fielding, whose *Tom Jones* has been so justly praised for the beauties of its organic design, but to such famous series of dramatic paintings as William Hogarth's *Industrious Apprentice* and *Rake's Progress*.[2] In any case, Smollett was a deliberately experimental storyteller whose imagination apprehended experience directly in the scattered fragments by which it presented itself to his observing eye. In composing his narratives he sought always for meaningful forms, but he cared little for the conventional laws of causality and process. Instead, he turned his fertile genius enthusiastically to the creation of self-contained episodes occurring in hurried succession, each rendered as a separate dramatic picture of assorted and often wonderfully eccentric character types engaged in abrasive interaction with a fast-moving central personage or (in *Humphry Clinker*) group of personages.[3]

One of the chief pleasures in reading Smollett's stories arises from the continual surprises made possible by the fragmentation of their structures. The individual parts of a seemingly erratic Smollett plot, like the scenes in a Hogarth series, do eventually add up to a whole, but by a method more cumulative than linear. There is always resolution at the end, the fulfillment of a "uniform plan." Roderick Random gets his beloved Narcissa; Matt Bramble goes home happy and healthy to Wales. Resolution occurs, however, only after passage through the entire gallery of pictorial episodes has been completed, when what has been observed and powerfully felt is at long last made fully intelligible to reader and protagonist alike. With understanding comes redemption and, finally, the reward of happiness and repose. The endings of Smollett's novels are always providentially contrived and thus fanciful in some degree, though never quite gratuitously so. They identify him as a comic writer who subscribed to, and reflected, a generally optimistic Christian interpretation of history, despite an abiding consciousness of human meanness and moral deformity that often drove him to the riotous cynicism of bitter Juvenalian satire.[4]

Smollett began writing novels when he was still young (*Roderick Random* came out just two months before his twenty-seventh birthday), though not as the result of some early ambition. He seems to have dabbled in poetry as a boy in Scotland, but his first and fondest hope was for fame as a playwright. When he left home for London in 1739, he had folded away in his pocket a quite inferior tragedy, *The Regicide,* with which he expected to dazzle the great city. He also carried with him letters of introduction from the two Glasgow surgeons he had served as apprentice, William Stirling and John Gordon. Smollett may have dreamed of literary celebrity, but he needed a livelihood, and surgery was to provide it. Though descended from an old and respected Dumbartonshire family, he was poor. His father, Archibald Smollett, had defied his parents by marrying a penniless woman and had been disinherited. When Archibald died shortly after Tobias's birth in March 1721, he left his wife and children to depend for their livelihood upon the small and uncertain kindnesses of relatives. The future novelist was lucky enough to study at the local grammar school for five or six years and then to attend lectures at Glasgow University. He entered upon his appreticeship in 1737, but a persistent cough determined him to seek a warmer climate, and so he set off for London to pursue a medical career there. And indeed for most of the following decade he did so with some vigor, although with only modest success.

Smollett met with nothing but frustration in his efforts to have *The Regicide* produced upon the stage. The bitterness of this early failure never entirely left him, partly because he kept renewing it over the next several years with periodic fresh assaults upon the good will and judgment of theatrical managers. Finally, after the success of *Roderick Random* had earned him a certain recognition, he simply published the play by subscription in 1749 and thereafter gave up hope of ever seeing it acted. His unhappy adventure with *The Regicide* did, however, furnish him with materials for the story of the poet Melopoyn that occupies Chapters 61–63 of his first novel, where Smollett damned those who (so he believed) had mistreated him. *Roderick Random* draws heavily upon other early experiences of its author, including the vividly remembered misfortunes of his family at the hands of a stingy and hardhearted grandfather. His years with Stirling and Gordon gave Smollett abundant opportunities to observe firsthand the quackery and charlatanism of eighteenth-century medical practice. Stirling and Gordon were themselves gifted and devoted physicians, but many of their colleagues were not. The situation was even worse in London, and Smollett made the deception, hypocrisy, and incompetence of doctors and apothecaries an important subject for satiric treatment in *Roderick Random* and indeed in all of his novels.

In April 1740, probably out of a desperate need for money, Smollett completed the required examinations and shipped as a surgeon's mate on board the *Chichester*, an eighty-gun man-of-war registered with the fleet sent out to prosecute the new war against Spain. He was present at Carthagena, where the British navy suffered a bloody and humiliating defeat, and this experience was the obvious source for Roderick Random's adventures as one of the crew of the *Thunder*. Smollett devoted a substantial portion of his story (Chapters 24–37) to his hero's shipboard days, and his account of the horrors of eighteenth-century sailing life is still considered one of the most graphic and authentic we possess. By 1744, Smollett was back in London, newly married to the daughter of a Jamaican plantation owner and ready to take up once more his vocation as a surgeon and his avocation as a writer. The latter, it appears, occupied his attention in a share disproportionate to the rewards it brought him, at least during the several years preceding *Roderick Random*. He made no further progress with the fortunes of *The Regicide*, and the four poems he managed to publish earned him little recognition and less money. Two of these poems, *Advice* (September 1746) and *Reproof* (January 1747), are satires in imitation of Alexander Pope. They are negligible things of their kind, but in composing them, Smollett may have gotten the idea for his first novel, which he conceived—as he explained in a letter to his Scottish friend Alexander Carlyle—as a "Satire on Mankind."[95]

This new work was written hurriedly—"begun and finished," Smollett wrote to Carlyle, "in the Compass of Eight months, during which time several Intervals happened of one, two, three and four Weeks, wherein I did not set pen to paper."[6] At the close of all this frenzied activity, *The Adventures of Roderick Random* was published in two duodecimo volumes on 21 January 1748; and it proved an immediate and enduring favorite with the public. Three editions totaling 6,500 copies (a very large number in those days) had appeared by November 1749; thereafter the novel was translated into German (1754) and French (1761), while it continued to be reprinted and read in a dozen English editions throughout the remaining years of the eighteenth century. The most resplendent of these, issued in London in 1792, was adorned by the illustrations of Thomas Rowlandson. Eventually, the fame of Smollett's book spread all over Europe, and indeed only a very few other English novels of its early period (one of them was Smollett's own *Humphry Clinker*) managed to equal or exceed *Roderick Random* in general popularity.

No doubt the extraordinary appeal of Smollett's novel derived in part from his ability to join in a fresh combination the attractions of several different kinds of familiar narrative: rogue or picaresque "biography," the imaginary voyage, the sentimental novel of love and intrigue, the romance of disinheritance and discovery. In its eclecticism, *Roderick Random* closely resembles the work of its author's nearest rivals, Samuel Richardson and Henry Fielding. It is important to remember that in the mid-eighteenth century the modern novel was still in its formative stages, and every major writer of fiction (and some not so major) was engaged in experiments involving the re-creation of conventional materials into what Richardson called a "new species of writing."[7] Like Fielding, Smollett was deeply influenced by Cervantes, whose immensely popular *Don Quixote* he signed on to translate sometime during the year 1748.[8] His most immediate model for the story of *Roderick Random*, however, was the celebrated *History and Adventures of Gil Blas of Santillane*, by Alain René LeSage, an episodic picaresque tale of roguish escapades that had for several decades enjoyed an enthusiastic following in translation from the French. As it happens, Smollett was preparing a brand-new English version of *Gil Blas* while *Roderick Random* was regaling its first readers, and he may actually have begun this task before sending his own book to the printer.[9] We may be sure that LeSage's lively story was in Smollett's mind, along with his own recently published verse satires, during those "Eight months" of furiously sporadic writing in 1747 when he happened upon his real talent as a novelist.

Despite his acknowledged admiration for *Gil Blas*, Smollett makes it plain in the preface to *Roderick Random* that he means to depart significantly from the example of LeSage. Gil Blas, he observes, is hardly credible as a moral agent: the fictional environment through which he travels is projected as too neutral, and there is little in his character to command anyone's sympathetic identification. Or, as Smollett himself puts it, the "conduct" of LeSage's picaro "prevents that generous indignation, which ought to animate the reader, against the sordid and vicious disposition of the world."[10] Roderick struggles through life in a pattern of fits and starts, ups and downs, and seemingly aimless wandering that superficially resembles the course of Gil Blas's adventures, and the two characters are much alike in their raw instincts for survival, their resourcefulness, and their function as outsiders who become instruments of satire. Both Smollett and LeSage seem deeply conscious of the long tradition of picaresque narrative, extending back to the Spanish prototype in *The Life of Lazarillo de Tormes* (1554), as a species of satiric writing against the chaos and destruction with which a corrupt society threatens the individual. Smollett, however, introducs a dimension of moral idealism into his version of the picaresque, which is typically so limited by cynicism as to preclude all possibility of such idealism. Roderick, a "friendless orphan" beset by "his own want of experience" as well as the "selfishness, envy, malice, and base indifference of mankind,"[11] is not only a vehicle of satire but also the object of Smollett's severe judgment for his understandable yet punishable failure to recognize the world's dark "apparitions" for what they are and for his consequent near-descent into self-destruction.[12]

*Roderick Random* is actually built upon a foundation of paradox, and in its tentative way it anticipates the later *Bildungsroman,* or "education" novel. Experience beleaguers one so violently and mercilessly, it appears, that pain and continual hardship inevitably seem to constitute the only reality that matters, just as a response in indignation and cynicism seems the only alternative to passive submission and thus absorption. Chance governs the world, which is without hope. The episodic structure of *Roderick Random,* with its long pauses over unpredictably disparate incidents and the characters who play them out dramatically with the hero, enforces this sense of things. But unrestrained indignation negates moral identity, for it is the surest means to helpless identification with what is being scourged.[13] Nothing less than reliance on the ideals of love, Roderick must learn, can redeem the self and ensure release from the threat of ensnarement.

The pattern of providential interventions in *Roderick Random* and the final, complete transformation of its fictional world affirm Smollett's belief in the ultimate precedence of a moral reality that provides the only meaningful framework for human happiness, indeed for the preservation of personal integrity. Smollett was no fool; he knew that even the most determinedly pious do not always thrive in real life. There is a strong element of the Christian fable in *Roderick Random,* as there is to one extent or another in all of Smollett's novels—and in many others of his day besides (*Robinson Crusoe,* for example, and *Pamela,* and *The Vicar of Wakefield*). Smollett's story, we may say, is an intricately detailed metaphor defining the very meaning of human redemption from the thralldom of worldly evil. In this respect, *Roderick Random* bears strong resemblances to Fielding's more famous *Tom Jones.*[14] Fielding's world is potentially as dark and perverse as Smollett's, and his wayward hero, like Roderick, must rise into self-knowledge from a nadir of misfortunes and personal failure before he can enjoy the reward of marriage to his beauteous heroine. But there the resemblances end. Fielding provides a buffer against villainy in the voice of his playful ironic narrator, and he never permits the reader to forget that his "history" is a work of careful artifice, a deliberate "Creation" that proclaims in its every device the ordering power of comic and providential vision. Smollett, in effect, turns the imaginary world of a Fielding upside down and inside out. His angle of vision is very different; it does not allow for much protection of his characters or his reader against irruptions of stupidity or meanness or violence in the fictional environment.

Even in *Peregrine Pickle, Ferdinand Count Fathom,* and *Sir Launcelot Greaves*—all of which (like Fielding's novels) employ third-person narrators to relay their respective stories of roguery, villainy, and comic quixotism—the representation of experience focuses on the way it is registered by the consciousness of the character who must live it and eventually arrive at some interpretation of it. Smollett is by no means a psychological novelist in the twentieth-century sense of the term, but he proves much more interested than Fielding in capturing the sometimes crazily textured immediacy of life's felt hardships, perplexities, and rewards. In *Roderick Random* and *Humphry Clinker,* two novels in which he relies on the carefully particularized voices of imagined characters as the instruments of transmission, the effects of immediacy are uncommonly powerful. *Roderick Random,* because it projects so convincingly the illusion of an angry "autobiographical" account of personal suffering and misjudgments, has actually fooled many readers (among them several modern critics) into believing that Roderick is a self-portrait of his author, whose performance in the work (some say) so lacks detachment and so confuses the relationship between narrator and audience that it must be judged at least a partial failure.[15]

There can be no doubt of Smollett's emotional identification with his hero, whose experience does in numerous details exactly coincide with his own; and it is likely that the strength of that identification influenced the course of his narrative, even promoted the improvisational qualities of certain richly textured and extended episodes. But it might be argued from a strictly technical standpoint that in *Roderick Random,* as in Defoe's novels or the epistolary narratives of Richardson, the author has retreated to a position of near-invisibility behind the completed product of his creative energy, whatever its sources, leaving his readers to a difficult process of participation and discovery as the principal means toward understanding the story and their own responses. If Smollett had chosen to preserve the anonymity under which he originally published his first work of fiction, or if we knew even less than we do about the facts of his troubled childhood and youth, then the issue of authorial distance might never have arisen to deflect criticism away from a proper consideration of what the text of *Roderick Random* actually means and what it achieves as an innovative and enduring early example of novelistic art.

In any event, the moral ambiguity and the complications of reader response that Smollett attempted in *Roderick Random* go far beyond anything to be found in picaresque tales like *Gil Blas* and *Lazarillo,* not to mention the hundreds of popular rogue and criminal biographies that also form part of the background for the novel.[16] One generally knows how to take LeSage's rather transparent first-person narrator, or the eponymous Lazarillo, but there is much less certainty with Roderick. His character as a modestly virtuous young fellow of respectable birth and education predisposes the reader in his behalf (or so Smollett hoped, as he said in his preface), but the increasing violence with which he avenges himself upon a world that viciously attacks his idealism and good nature simultaneously promotes a vicarious pleasure and compels judgment. In Chapter 20, when Roderick so brutally flogs and strips the wretched villain Captain O'Donnell, he does so out of a combination of mischief and uncontrollable fury, and his actions at least verge upon the criminal. What reader, however, does not share in the satisfaction Roderick feels? Yet what reader does not also recognize that by returning O'Donnell's meanness in kind, Smollett's young hero has sunk to his base level and must therefore be righteously repudiated? Righteousness is not always so easy to sustain as it is here, however. Often—during the episodes on board the *Thunder,* for example— Smollett deliberately endangers the members of his audience by trapping them into a unity of feeling with the increasingly cynical Roderick, causing a loss of distance that threatens to implicate the reader in the hero's failings, his desperation, his self-destructive rage. This novel does not make it easy for us to keep our balance.

Much of the dramatic and moral point of *Roderick Random* is to show how perversely seductive the wicked world can be and how awesome its power over the individual will. The price of the modern ideal of individualism, as Smollett and so many of his contemporaries were already beginning to understand, is a condition of lonely insignificance in the midst of a disordered, bewildering, and sometimes terrifying unknown. "I am old enough," Smollett wrote to David Garrick at the age of forty, "to have seen and observed that we are all playthings of fortune."[17] Roderick is a kind of modern Everyman figure, as his generalized last name suggests. But Smollett particularizes his hero's experience and intensifies our sense of his frightened loneliness by making him a Scotsman (like his author, of course) who, deprived early of the stability of a loving family, becomes the victim of ridicule and abuse in the deeply hostile environment of England. London and, later, the scenes of Roderick's naval adventures serve as almost overwhelming images of modern life in all its bustling inhumanity, grotesqueness, and uncertainty. The people in Roderick's world often seem not quite human. They are monstrosities of avarice, pride, and hypocrisy with names like Lavement, Gawky, Quiverwit, Whiffle, Wagtail, Badger, and Straddle; or, just as often, they are bestial figures with grasshopper legs or canine fangs.[18] Small wonder, then, that reality as Roderick encounters it seems not whole and safe but fragmented, portentous and threatening, void of compassion and love, disfigured.

For all his close attentiveness to the real "facts" of eighteenth-century English life, Smollett was no literary "realist." Roderick's experience of the world partakes of nightmare. Smollett projects this quality of his vision on the very first page of the story with a description of the horrid dream that came to the hero's mother just before her son's birth and her own melancholy death. In the dream Mrs. Random was "delivered of a tennis-ball," which the devil (her midwife) instantly knocked into oblivion, leaving her "inconsolable" until suddenly she beheld it return "with equal violence, and earth itself beneath her feet, whence immediately sprung up a goodly tree covered with blossoms."[19] The old sage who interprets the dream sees in it—rightly as it turns out—a happy conclusion, but also predicts the mercurial pattern of "dangers and difficulties" the child will have to live through. The dream is an involuntary act of prophecy on the part of the mother, and its image of the devil slamming her "offspring" so violently about exactly foreshadows not only the subsequent buffetings of the hero in a darkly evil world but also the nightmarish qualities of that world as he will learn to see it.

By this same device of the dream, Smollett establishes the identity of Roderick as a traveler whose motion is to be perpetual until at last it ceases, as the wise sage said it would, with a resolution in "great reputation and happiness." Percy G. Adams has shown, more convincingly than anyone, how the journey was adopted as a paradigm—a powerful metaphor, really—by Smollett and many other eighteenth-century novelists, who used it to organize their own understanding of experience and to shape their imaginative representations of its meaning.[20] Roderick's path of life is to take him through a succession of encounters with nightmarish "apparitions" in a progress that is partly willed but in the main profoundly directionless, simply because circumstance possesses the power to deflect individual volition. If the end of his journey signifies the perfection of understanding and thus of moral will, then the passage toward that conclusion must inevitably be a tortuous one.

Roderick's lack of real direction ensures great diversity in his adventures. It is of course his persistent presence—manifested in his intensive language, in his role as moral agent, in his restless movement toward decline and finally reward—that provides the unifying center of Smollett's novel. We may trace Roderick's movement, and at the same time exemplify the complex and vividly represented disarray of his world, by simply looking at three or four episodes spaced through his story. Roderick's miseries begin in earnest when he is only a boy, as do his outraged reactions to them. Orphaned, he is sent to school by the mean-spirited patriarch of his family in a condition of ragged wretchedness; there he is flogged when not ignored, and provoked into pranks and mischief, but he advances in his studies anyway—and is punished for it. To prevent him from writing letters begging relief from his grandfather, the schoolmaster "caused a board to be made with five holes in it," and, as Roderick tells us out of painful memory, through it "he thrust the fingers and thumb of my right hand, and fastened it by a whipcord to my wrist."[21] Roderick breaks free of this cruel restraint only by using it against the head of a schoolmate who insults his poverty. Daily brutalized at school, he fares no better on play days at home, where his cousin (now, instead of Roderick, the grandfather's heir) delights in setting his hunting dogs upon him.

With the sudden appearance of the blustering, good-hearted Tom Bowling, one of this novel's more memorable examples of the eccentric sailing man, Smollett inaugurates a pattern that will include several providential interventions in behalf of his hero. The effects of Bowling's rescue and his beneficence are not long felt, however. Roderick thrives for a time at the university where his uncle installs him, but a reversal of fortune casts him upon his own devices. Now comes the first of Smollett's many pictures of grotesque subhumanity in the person of Mr. Launcelot Crab, the corrupt, drunken, and incompetent surgeon who—almost in a parody of Bowling's earlier gesture of avuncular kindness—extricates Roderick from the horrors of approaching want and despair by taking him on as an assistant. The figure of this man, as Roderick describes it, redoubles the suggestiveness of his surname (we may note also the irony carried by his Christian name) and provides an exact definition of his character. He is "about five foot high, and ten around the belly"; his face is fat and round "as a full moon, and much of the complexion of a mulberry," and it is adorned by an enormous nose "resembling a powder-horn" and "studded all over with carbuncles." This remarkable countenance is completed by a pair of "little grey eyes" that reflect the light of day in such an oblique way that when Mr. Crab looks straight ahead, he appears to be "admiring the buckle of his shoe."[22]

The portrait of Crab is a caricature, of course; as such, it succeeds by a strategy of distortion and reduction. What Crab represents, real enough to be sure, is made less dangerous by being thus formed into a ridiculous picture of itself, and Roderick is as able as the reader to laugh at and dismiss him. But as the smug lad is about to find out, nearly the whole world is populated by such grotesques, and they will gradually multiply and surround him. During his progress to London, Roderick meets a sizable collection of misshapen or perverse oddities aboard the wagon on which he hops a ride. His fellow passengers include a "brisk airy girl," obviously a prostitute, oddly dressed and brandishing a whip; a limping, hollow-eyed, wrinkled, toothless old usurer whose long nose and peaked chin approach one another like "a pair of nut-crackers" when he speaks; a thin, small, baboonlike "lady's woman" named Mrs. Weazel; and the amazing captain, her husband, whose bombast masks his cowardice and whose ludicrous appearance Smollett captures in one of the funniest descriptions in the entire novel. Weazel, as Roderick remembers him, was "about five foot and three inches high, sixteen inches of which went to his face and long scraggy neck; his thighs were about six inches in length, his legs resembling spindles or drum-sticks, two feet and an half, and his body, which put me in mind of extension without substance, engrossed the remainder;—so that on the whole, he appeared like a spider or grasshopper erect."[23]

In this cluster of ridiculous and affected characters, Smollett develops a composite portrait of mankind, occasioned by an adaptation from one of the oldest conventions of storytelling and travel narrative, the journey by coach—here, comically, a wagon; and the portrait is presently elaborated by means of the equally ancient convention of riotous misadventures at an inn.[24] For now, Roderick remains capable of amused detachment in his responses, as does the reader; his language is graphic and his vision distorting, but there is no rage because he has not yet entered fully into the utter darkness of the world's troubling reality. The sign that he is approaching it comes during a comic interlude in Chapter 13, when he and his loyal companion Strap lie trembling in their bed as the "terrible apparition" of a tame raven wanders aimlessly through deepest night and into their room at a wayside inn. "I verily believed we were haunted," Roderick recalls; the "violent fright" left him "petrified with fear" and tormented his sleep.[25]

Thus the nightmare begins, and it gathers intensity as Roderick arrives in London, where he encounters meanness and often physical deformity in the face of nearly everyone he meets. The story reaches an early climax during the scenes laid on board the *Thunder*, following Roderick's maddening attempts to fathom the twisted image of the bureaucratic naval establishment. The world of the ship, with its assortment of sick, mutilated, filthy, idiosyncratic, splenetic, depraved, and malicious humanity, is a microcosm, vividly pictured in a hellish version of the convention already employed in the earlier episode of the wagon, its grimness relieved only by the presence of Thomson and Morgan, the latter another of Smollett's unforgettable sailing men. Here the darkness concentrates itself, as do the heartlessness and violence of this world. When Roderick descends below deck to the sick berth, he adjusts his eyes and looks in horrified astonishment upon the putridness, the vileness, the manifestations of unimaginable cruelty and unspeakable indifference he finds there. "Here," he cries out in an almost audible burst of anger,

> I saw about fifty miserable distempered wretches, suspended in rows, so huddled one upon another, that not more than fourteen inches of space was allotted for each with his bed and bedding; and deprived of the light of the day, as well as of fresh air; breathing nothing but a noisome atmosphere of the morbid steams exhaling from their own excrements and diseased bodies, devoured with vermin hatched in the filth that surrounded them, and destitute of every convenience necessary for people in that helpless condition.[26]

This description throbs with energy and feeling, just as the verbal picture startlingly projects its sensual details. Words like *distempered wretches, suspended, huddled, noisome, morbid steams, devoured,* and *vermin* call direct attention to themselves, and convey for Roderick an emotional response as violent as the scene itself.

Language is for Smollett a tricky but trustworthy, if not always fully conscious, signifier of the inner self. Sometimes its effects are comical or even farcical, as in the case of the inadvertent sexual malapropisms of Tabitha Bramble, the man-hungry but outwardly prudish old spinster of *Humphry Clinker*. Roderick's language, from the beginning of his story, steadily increases the frenzy of its response to multiplying absurdities, outrages, and dangers; it actually registers the process by which the world threatens to re-create him in the image of its own dark, fragmented, scarifying madness. There is a paradox here. Roderick's language makes real, in sometimes painfully detailed pictures, the chaotic nightmare of his life; but it also serves—much more reliably than his actions alone could do—as an index of the progressive disintegration of his moral self, of the gradual and almost total loss of his moral identity.[27]

The shipboard scenes display with ghastly clarity the world's great power to destroy. The officers of the *Thunder*, in collusion with the surgeon Mackshane, have created the scene witnessed in the sick berth; they are moral if not physical grotesques, and they soon make Roderick a victim of their mindless cruelty. On a trumped-up charge of mutiny, they chain him to the poop deck, where he lies in a condition of utter isolation and helplessness during a ferocious bombardment. Bespattered by the brains and entrails of his mates, he loses all discretion, bursts into hysterics, and bellows forth an almost elemental cry of "oaths and execrations."[28] From this point forward, Roderick is no longer capable of detachment. His loneliness grows upon him when he is left beaten and naked upon the shore and at first can find no one to relieve his almost unbearable distress. At last (significantly, it is at the very midpoint of his story) he encounters Mrs. Sagely and then the exemplary Narcissa, but he is by then so broken and embittered that he cannot find the path that would unite him with the ideals of benevolence and beauteous virtue they represent.

The restorative image of Narcissa, "amiable apparition" that she seems when Roderick first looks upon her,[29] does remain with him, and its hold upon his imagination tightens continuously. But his journey into self-absorbing and self-destructive cynicism takes him further and further away from his heroine, until despair finally leaves him prostrate in prison. Meanwhile, Smollett continues to throw his hero into adventures that portray human nature in its progressively more sordid variety. Better acquainted with the "selfishness and roguery of mankind" as a result of his painful experiences at sea, Roderick considers himself no longer very liable to "disappointment and imposition."[30] Yet when he travels to France, he is immediately duped by a lusty, hard-drinking, foul-smelling Capuchin friar—a "thick brawny young man, with red eye-brows, a hook nose, a face covered with freckles; and his name was Frere Balthazar"[31]— who takes all his cash. After spending a few weeks as a soldier in the French army, Roderick luckily runs into Strap, from whom he has been long separated, and accepts his old friend's offer of money to set up as a gentleman; the two companions then return to England in quest of a fortune. In a round of balls and assemblies and excursions to the theater, Roderick is deceived by courtesans, sneered at by dandies, and finally seduced into the company of a set of wild young coffeehouse riffraff—Bragwell, Banter, Chatter, Slyboot, and Ranter.

As he sinks ever deeper into riotous iniquities, Roderick grows more susceptible to the world's false appearances and more desperate in his responses to them. His pursuit of the vapid Melinda Goosetrap and her fortune of £10,000 drives him to the gaming tables to support its costs, nearly involves him in a duel with a crazy rival named Rourk Oregan, and at last leaves him defeated, humiliated, and vengeful. He almost rushes into marriage with a mysterious inamorata—a "wrinkled hag turned of seventy!" whose "tygeress"-like advances when at last they meet set his bowels in a convulsion and his feet in speedy motion.[32] The "lewd and indecent" seductions of the sodomite Earl Strutwell, even more hideously than the garlicky pantings of the lusty spinster, define the world as a place going entirely and everywhere mad in its perversity, in the process (it seems) canceling all possibility of fertile, fulfilling love. At "this day," says the leering Strutwell most alarmingly to Roderick, the practice of pedtrasty "prevails not only over all the east, but in most parts of Europe; in our own country it gains ground apace, and in all probability will become in a short time a more fashionable vice than simple fornication."[33]

In the midst of such precisely vivified moral darkness, the image of Narcissa increases in its brightness, even while Roderick's desperate course veers from it at a widening distance. His attempt upon the fortune and the person of one Miss Snapper, the sickly, misshapen, conniving daughter of a rich Turkey merchant, almost brings him to permanent misery. Like the grizzled septuagenarian from whom Roderick has very recently fled in revulsion, Miss Snapper is obviously a foil to Narcissa; should he unite with her in marriage, he would symbolically become one with all that she stands for in her physical and spiritual deformity. Roderick meets this remarkable creature during one of his author's finely executed coaching episodes, this time along the road to Bath. The collection of humanity in whose company he finds himself represents yet another close pictorial grouping of varied character types, among them a blustering soldier, a grave matron, and a shifty lawyer. Miss Snapper herself is drawn with great exactness, and her obsessed suitor does not find her entirely displeasing, though her head bears a certain resemblance "to a hatchet, the edge being represented by her face," and though she is both large-breasted and humpbacked.[34] Roderick abandons his schemes against this fair lady only after he accidentally meets Narcissa once again in the assembly rooms at Bath. This is another providential occurrence, but not the reversal a lesser novelist might have made of it. When the two lovers are separated by Narcissa's brother, Roderick dashes headlong into the last extremities of self-destructive despair. Back in London, he casts his lot with Fortune, turns gambler, swindles a tailor to finance his reckless play, and is arrested and flung into prison.

Throughout these long episodes, as Roderick tries repeatedly and always unsuccessfully to create riches from nothing so as to secure a meaningless future, he becomes more and more not only the helpless wanderer but a foolish and guilty one. His actions shift from the physical riotousness of his earliest days to concentrated deviousness; his language, far from losing its energy and intensity, adds density and subtlety as it reflects his increasing entanglement in the cobwebby sordidness of a darkening world. His crony Banter suggests the scheme that ends in his arrest, and the rationalization by which Roderick leads himself to undertake it is couched in the words and rhythms of subdued frenzy. The language here lacks the overt violence that pulses through the passages describing the horrors of life on board the *Thunder*, but in its fitful twistings it reveals an even more troubled and troubling kind of inner conflict. Banter's wickedly clever proposal, Roderick recalls,

> savoured a little of fraud; but he rendered it palatable, by
> observing, that in a few months, I might be in a condition to do
> every body justice; and in the mean time, I was acquitted by the
> honesty of my intention—I suffered myself to be persuaded by his
> salvo, by which my necessity, rather than my judgment, was
> convinced; and. . . actually put the scheme in practice.[35]

The blatant criminality of this enterprise, only half acknowledged if at all, is hinted at in Roderick's reversals upon the words *justice, acquitted*, and *honesty*, while his use of the military term *salvo* suggests the brutality of this culminating assault of the world's artillery of evil against him. Conquered at last, he submits.

The prison where Roderick finds himself next, like the city and the microcosm of the ship, is closely particularized as a revealingly bleak image of the world at large, and it completely encloses him along with his fellow criminals—and victims. His energy gone, and his resilience with it, Roderick no longer possesses even the language to express his grief, despair, and loss. The failed and suffering poet, Melopoyn, furnishes the expression he needs by reading aloud one of his elegies in imitation of Tibullus, but the experience leaves Roderick so weakened and distraught that he takes to his bottle, sleeps, and then wakes "in the horrors," his imagination haunted with "dismal apparitions."[36] Later, the interpolated tale of Melopoyn's terrible misfortunes, in an echo of the earlier history of Nancy Williams (Chapters 22–23), calls forth from Roderick a response in generosity and sympathy by reminding him that the troubles of others may be greater than his own. This long interlude, despite its obvious references to Smollett's disappointments with *The Regicide*, is thus not a merely gratuitous intrusion of personal vindictiveness. Roderick's response to Melopoyn helps to justify the redemption that is to follow, though it does not precipitate it. Still hopeless, Roderick grows altogether "negligent of life," loses his appetite, and degenerates into "such a sloven" that by the morning of his deliverance he has been for two months "neither washed, shifted nor shaved."[37] The punishment inflicted upon Roderick for his failings is severe, but it is at last enough. When his uncle reappears miraculously to renew his faith in the power of human affections, he is "transported" at the sight; his relief is as complete as it is sudden, and happy resolution—a new journey toward discovery of his father in the New World, marriage to the constant Narcissa, joyous retirement to idyllic Scotland—follows swiftly. In the end, by an "amazing stroke of providence,"[38] the chaotic, dark, hideously evil world of *Roderick Random* is re-created into an ordered, serene paradise of love, light, and beauty. Roderick proceeds from a language of indignation and self-negating despair to a language of ecstasy, and the reader becomes fully conscious—perhaps for the first time—that this retrospective story, told in the past tense, has achieved its often astonishing effects of immediacy by the contrastive visual faculties of Roderick's memory. The "dismal apparitions" of his nightmare existence, their power to control him dissolved, are like the airy figures of dreams, now receded from the center of his consciousness, which has recovered them in such striking pictures. They are as illusory as the rule of Fortune, or Chance, while the "amiable apparition" Narcissa, emblem of the providential love Roderick had once denied at his peril, represents all that is real and enduring. "Heaven," this faithful girl had knowingly written to Roderick at the crucial moment just prior to his arrest, will surely contrive some "unforeseen event in our behalf,"[39] and she was right.

Smollett's readers have sometimes complained that the providential maneuverings with which he concluded *Roderick Random* weaken the work, wreck its consistency of texture, surprise too much, and finally are just too trivially conventional to be convincing or effective.[40] There is some merit in the objection to the suddenness of the novel's ending, and Smollett may actually have rushed the composition of his last chapters, bestowing upon them less care than he had given to earlier portions of the narrative. Nevertheless, the resolution he provided is vital to his overall design, and it is deliberately anticipated from his very first page, which records the mother's dream. The bright presence of Bowling, Strap, Thomson, Mrs. Sagely, and Narcissa contributes importantly to the preparations for the eventual triumph of all that they represent. Without the comic and providential ending, Roderick's experience would (from Smollett's point of view at least) lack all relevance to the human problem of sustaining moral identity in a worldly context of intensifying and confusing secularity—a context without a center, so to speak. Roderick's autobiographical narrative, taken as a whole, expresses his clear-eyed, full, secure understanding of the accumulated facts of entropic reality and their deeply felt, scarifying threats—now past—to his survival; and the reader knows that his redemption, more suffered for than earned, came in part as a consequence of his fixation upon the transcendent image of the matchless Narcissa. The "picture" of this "lovely creature," Roderick remarks during the account of his prison experiences, "was the constant companion of my solitude."[41] The necessarily radical transformation of Smollett's fictional world and of his Everyman hero proclaims with dramatic urgency the vast distance dividing most of society from restorative idealism, while it also imaginatively adumbrates—in the manner of the Christian fable—the much greater wrenching of the whole creation by which, Smollett believed, Providence would at last redeem the miserable failures of mankind and restore the perfections of Eden.[42]

*Roderick Random* achieves its striking rhetorical effects precisely because its structure provides so purposefully diffuse a picture of the rampant disorder of life, wrought into order by benevolent authorial interposition. Despite its comic resolution and its echoes of Christian orthodoxy, however, Smollett's novel develops a deep and unmistakable ambiguity in its approach to the nostalgic ideals of faith. By a rapid-fire sequence of scattered episodes portraying the world's harshness, its indifference to moral life, and most of all its shattering uncertainty, *Roderick Random* verges on a vision of existential absurdity and is thus in some ways very modern. Its portrait of a hero who is in important respects an *anti*-hero likewise anticipates conceptions of character made familiar in the works of such recent writers as James Joyce, William Faulkner, Saul Bellow, Joseph Heller, and John Barth.[43] Surely these are among the reasons why Smollett's first novel continues to be read and why it is currently attracting more admiring attention than at any time since the days immediately following its original publication.

Unlike *Roderick Random* and the masterly *Humphry Clinker*, the three novels of Smollett's middle years—*Peregrine Pickle, Ferdinand Count*

*Fathom*, and *Sir Launcelot Greaves*—have been all but forgotten in the twentieth century, except among a small circle of academic specialists. For that matter, they were hardly popular favorites in their author's own time. Still, they are worthy of our interest as lively and sometimes bold new experiments in the art of fiction-writing. Smollett was surprisingly slow to take advantage of his initial success with the novel-reading audience. He allowed three years to elapse between *Roderick Random* and *Peregrine Pickle*. In the interim he published his translation of *Gil Blas* and, at last, *The Regicide*. Meanwhile he collaborated with Handel in an aborted effort for the musical theater, spent several months on the Continent, and, just as he was about to turn away from his disappointing surgical practice for a permanent career as professional man of letters, purchased a medical degree from Aberdeen University.[44] *Peregrine Pickle*, much of which is set in Europe, seems to have resulted in large part from its author's travels, and the bulk and scope of this sprawling novel suggest that Smollett conceived it as a comprehensive satiric study of all of contemporary English and European life.[45] The remarkable range of the book comprises scores of episodes, a dozen or more carefully pictured major settings, and a vast exhibition of clever character portraits, many of them obviously improvised as Smollett's vigorous imagination followed Peregrine in his restlessly energetic wanderings. Readers have frequently observed, and rightly so, that Smollett's second novel lacks the concentration of effect that distinguishes his first. The difficulty may have begun with his decision to employ a third-person narrator, thus preventing the kind of intensity he achieved by allowing Roderick Random to speak in his own voice. Whatever the reason, in writing *Peregrine Pickle* Smollett did not entirely solve the problem of how to keep its multiple ingredients and purposes under control and in sharp focus.[46] But he may in fact have been less interested in that problem than in capitalizing upon the gratifyingly steady popularity of *Roderick Random* with another story that would allow his still evolving talent free rein in an uninhibited exploration of its possibilities.

*The Adventures of Peregrine Pickle* certainly reveals to us in rawest and truest form the essential qualities of Smollett the young novelist. Only a month away from his thirtieth birthday when his new work was published in four volumes on 25 February 1751, he had not yet grown beyond his almost obsessive interest in the character of the resourceful rebel, nor had he mellowed in his bitterness against enemies who, he believed, had so unjustly disappointed his ambitions as a playwright and scorned his abilities. *Peregrine Pickle* revels in, though it finally chastens and punishes, the roguery of its eponymous hero, while it sprinkles through its pages a

160

quantity of savage references to antagonists old and new: the actors David Garrick and James Quin, the ungenerous patrons Lyttelton and Chesterfield, the novelist Henry Fielding. As a literary performance, Smollett's second novel subordinatres art to exuberance, the principles of organic design to the unrestrained flow of imaginative energy, stylistic decorum to the thrill of the intensive word or phrase. The novel's almost antiformalistic qualities, despite the disordering effects of their impact upon its compositional texture, are the sources of *Peregrine Pickle's* greatest attractions, as anyone who has looked closely at the shortened, softened, more polished, but less interesting second edition of the work (1758) already knows.[47]

Peregrine resembles his forebear Roderick in many respects, though he is an Englishman by birth and thus no outsider, at least in London and environs. He is less a victim of circumstance than Roderick, whose difficult beginnings his own hard childhood experiences nevertheless replicate, and his roguery springs not from the rage of disappointed idealism but from native impulse. An initiator by nature, Perry is an incorrigibly mischievous prankster, a sometimes vicious predator upon innocence, a picaro of sorts who delights in impishness for its own sake and knows no joy equal to that of exposing hypocrisy and affectation—as, for example, during the long Continental episodes (Chapters 46–70) when he engages in repeated and merciless humiliation of a nameless posturing physician and a ridiculously talentless painter, Mr. Pallet.[48] As roguish character and as instrument of satire, Peregrine is much closer to the model of LeSage's Gil Blas than is Roderick, and he is an even less sympathetic figure. Consequently, the attempt to impose a providential resolution upon the end of his story rings false in a way that Smollett's similar manipulations in *Roderick Random* do not.

The record of Perry's life rushes headlong from first page to last, taking him from his boyhood home to the university, to London, to the Continent, to Bath, to the corridors of power in contemporary politics, to the garrets of Grub Street. In the course of these pell-mell adventures, he breaks numerous heads and as many female hearts, ruins a quantity of reputations, and dupes, swindles, abuses, or mocks everyone he can. No doubt Perry's feats of ingenuity at the expense of fools and weaklings momentarily satisfy the reader's dreams of superiority as well as his own, but he leaves himself liable to harsh judgment and chatisement, which his author duly inflicts upon him in prison episodes (Chapters 105–112) that echo similar scenes in *Roderick Random*. Perry's eventual redemption is justified in part—if at all—by his almost indomitable high spirits; in part by the continued affection of the lovely Emilia, whom he has failed to seduce in all his many artful attempts upon her perfect virtue; and most of all by the undying loyalty of his companion Tom Pipes, his old friend Jack Hatchway, and his remarkable uncle Commodore Trunnion.

Pipes, Hatchway, and Trunnion, former sailors all, are among Smollett's greatest triumphs in comic portraiture; no reader who encounters them in the pages of *Peregrine Pickle* can forget their amazing eccentricities of behavior and language. There are other portraits nearly as fine: Perry's henpecked father Gamaliel Pickle, for example; his aptly named spinster aunt, Grizzle; and in later episodes the curmudgeonly misanthrope Cadwallader Crabtree. The great care taken with these delightful characterizations is set off by the reckless abandon of Smollett's decision to introduce two lengthy interpolated histories, the racy "Memoirs of a Lady of Quality" (Chapter 88) and an account of the "unfortunate" James Annesley (Chapter 106), who fought a long and widely publicized legal battle to reclaim the noble birthright allegedly stolen from him by a wicked uncle. The presumably authentic "Memoirs" of Lady Frances Vane, puffed up in the press in advance of the publication of *Peregrine Pickle*, were no doubt incorporated as a way of fanning popular interest in the new work by the author of *Roderick Random*, and the extended allusion to the Annesley affair served a similar topical purpose.[49] Both interpolations seem gratuitous, though interesting in their own right, and there is no denying their awkward intrusion upon the integrity of the narrative as a whole. In Smollett's defense it ought to be said that extraneous "histories" and "memoirs" were commonplace in the fiction of his day, their primary sanction residing in the example of *Don Quixote*, a work known to everyone in some translation or other and widely imitated by many. We may mention also that the adventures of Lady Vane, who is something of a female picaro, parallel those of the rambunctious Peregrine and thus provide an illuminating analogue to them, while the misfortunes of the brave Annesley indict a corrupt aristocracy as one major source of the disorder and moral rottenness Smollett exposes elsewhere in his story.

*Peregrine Pickle* is indeed a "large diffused picture" of life, the largest and most diffuse of any of its author's novels, and an important experiment in the development of his conception of an art of fiction.[50] The book failed with its audience, however, for reasons that are not entirely clear and probably never will be. Certainly readers of the day were a heterogeneous lot, not always discriminating in their tastes, and lesser performances than *Peregrine Pickle* enjoyed the kind of enthusiastic reception denied to it. No new edition of the novel appeared until the emasculated version of 1758, which was prepared in answer to no particular call from the public. Smollett believed, possibly with some justification, that his enemies had conspired to suppress his book by preventing reviews and discouraging reprintings. In any case, he decided to try a different, more restrained, and less brashly topical approach in his next novel, *The Adventures of Ferdinand Count Fathom*, which appeared in a pair of small volumes almost exactly two years after the disappointment of *Peregrine Pickle*. *Ferdinand Count Fathom* is a much shorter work, though the range of its scenery is hardly less broad and varied, and it deliberately develops an unhesitating portrait of a thoroughgoing, unregenerate rogue.

Smollett portrays Fathom as an outsider like Roderick Random, a rascally picaro like Peregrine Pickle, and an instrument of satire like them both. Literally a nobody of no particular country, Fathom learns the tricks of thievery and deception at the knee of his gin-soaked camp-following mother, and then perfects them into the confidence man's art by practicing upon the naive good nature of his foster family, the Melvils, who kindly took him in when he was orphaned as a child. Never sympathetic but always fascinating in his resourcefulness and his capacity to assume convincing disguises, Fathom moves relentlessly through a world whose stupidities and ridiculous affectations make it ripe for his schemes of plunder and seduction. From the salons of Paris to the taverns and coffeehouses of London to the fashionable watering places at Bath and Tunbridge Wells, Smollett's bogus count proves himself a triumphant genius of evil. His portrait is, in fact, a study in the truly criminal character; his adventures in roguery carry him beyond the exploits of the picaro and into a close identification with the hero-villains of popular criminal biography. Fathom represents a new kind of experiment for his author, and in his day only Fielding and Richardson, in their figures of Jonathan Wild and the dazzling Lovelace, exceeded his success in capturing both the attractions and the dark perversions of the criminal intelligence in action.

Smollett's talented crook is sometimes duped, but never defeated, by sharpers whose abilities approach his own. When the authenticity of his aristocratic title is challenged, he quickly shifts his vocation to music and then to medical quackery in order to continue his predatory assaults upon the pockets of gullible gentlemen and the virtue of innocent maidens. Twice thrown into prison following momentary lapses of concentration, he is twice rescued by his boyhood companion, Renaldo Melvil, who continues to love him until at last he is simply forced to see Fathom for what he really is. The fortuitous reappearances of Renaldo, in both instances after long absences from the story, represent a pattern of reversals upon the conventions of providential manipulation, and they serve to keep the example of young Melvil's perfect virtue before the reader's eye. On the second such occasion, Renaldo returns in the belief that his beloved Monimia, from whom Fathom (who desired her succulent flesh for himself) had succeeded in separating him, is dead.[51] His discovery that she lives brings the story to a crisis, leads to the exposure of Fathom's true nature, and lays the groundwork for the final triumph of virtue over villainy. In the end, Renaldo and Monimia are happy, while Fathom is undone, made miserable, brought to repentance, and then simply displaced—only to surface again as the benevolent apothecary Grieve, whom the travelers in *Humphry Clinker* meet unexpectedly along the road.

Smollett's story makes it appear that only perfected goodness and charity have the power to overthrow what Fathom represents. Renaldo and Monimia prove less interesting as characters than their counterpart in perfected wickedness, but as the central figures in the novel's carefully maintained and finally predominant subplot, they are critically important to its rhetorical strategy and to the definition of its moral center. Smollett purposely "raised up" the portraits of virtue, as he says in the dedication to the work, "with a view to amuse the fancy" of the reader, "engage the affection, and form a striking contrast which might heighten the expression, and give a *Relief* to the moral of the whole."[52] This statement makes clear the multiple functions of Smollett's double plot and underscores the terms of his definition of the novel as dramatic "picture" given only a few paragraphs earlier (the word *relief*, of course, is drawn from the vocabulary of the painter). In some ways, *Ferdinand Count Fathom* is Smollett's most deliberate and most interesting experiment with this formal conception. As in his other novels, he proceeds from episode to episode in a pattern of apparent randomness, introducing again and again clusters of carefully sketched imaginary people embodying the varied types of human character and conduct. Along the way he provides some splendid individual portraits: Sir Stentor Stile, the bumpkin squire; Sir Mungo Barebones and the other eccentrics in whose midst Fathom finds himself during his first stay in prison; the kindly Jewish moneylender, Joshua Manasseh.

*Ferdinand Count Fathom* is also a topical work, filled with references to real people and real events both recent and current. Among these are allusions to a pair of brilliant generals, the Duke of Marlborough and Prince Eugene of Savoy; to Prince Charles Edward Stuart, leader of the Jacobite Rebellion of 1745–46; and to the bloody eighteenth-century wars fought over the Spanish succession (1702–13) and the Austrian succession (1740–48). But in this third novel Smollett largely avoids the savage personal satire of *Roderick Random* and *Peregrine Pickle*; when he is topical, it is almost always for a generalized purpose. His glances at the real world are not in every instance pictorial, but they contribute to the development of his novel as a picture designed to capture the permanent as well as the immediate truth about human nature.

This point requires some elaboration. In the years following the publication of *Ferdinand Count Fathom*, Smollett proved himself a gifted historian of public affairs, able and determined to record with scrupulous accuracy the steady march of events through time. But as a novelist interested in the "facts" of private experience, he knew that the progress of life as lived by individual men and women was not steady at all but forever erratic and uncertain, in all times and in all places. We have already seen how, in *Roderick Random*, it is the intensity of scattered individual experiences that gives existence its real texture, which can be made finally intelligible only by a process of accumulation. Smollett's first novel actually conflates and reorders certain facts of recent history, merging them with the author's personal recollections to create a new and inventive configuration. The portion of Roderick's story beginning with his entanglements in the bureaucracy of the naval administration and leading to his encounter with Melopoyn in the Marshalsea Prison encompasses the years from 1739 to about 1747 and occasions many references to the great European war of that same period, to the 'Forty-Five, and to Smollett's efforts in behalf of *The Regicide*. But the novel compresses this span of time into months, disregarding the laws of chronology and suggesting that, when appropriating historical or biographical fact for fictional purposes, Smollett found his way to understanding by focusing upon the particular moment and its power to reveal the truth that lies beneath the orderly surface of things as dutifully recorded by historians. The imaginative, or poetic, interpretation of human history places its epitomizing events side by side, though not necessarily in their proper temporal sequence, and thus displays their timeless commonality. Considered in this way, history itself becomes—like one of Smollett's novels—a "large diffused picture" of life.

Smollett's fictional uses of history represent a significant departure from the practice of other storytellers of his generation, almost all of whom were as insistently topical but much more synchronic. In *Ferdinand Count Fathom*, Smollett was at his most innovative as a novelistic "historian." Fathom is born in 1711, as the War of the Spanish Succession nears its end, and his youthful rogueries must be partly interpreted against the background defined by the heroic genius of Marlborough and Prince Eugene, whose inspired military leadership saved European civilization from destruction. From the beginning it appears that Smollett will coordinate the career of his villain precisely with the progress of recent events still known to everyone. But he disrupts the expectation he has raised. In

Chapter 29, when Fathom arrives in England at the age of twenty-four or twenty-five, he is immediately confused with that other talented and ambitious adventurer, the glamorous Prince Charles Edward Stuart. Here the fictional date is 1735 or 1736, but the "real" date is 1746 or 1747. A number of the people Fathom encounters in prison only a short fictional time later (in Chapters 39–42) would have been known to Smollett's earliest readers for their part in events and controversies occurring during the half-dozen years immediately preceding the publication of his novel. Fathom borrows from his fellow inmate Captain Minikin a library of books most of which did not appear in print until after 1749. The introduction of Joshua Manasseh in Chapter 47 responds to the widespread public interest in a Jewish Naturalization Act being hotly debated in Parliament at the very moment when *Ferdinand Count Fathom* went to press.

There are many other such anachronisms as these, and Fathom's character receives much of its definition from his deliberate placement in an appropriate context of abstracted history. Smollett's habit of allusion to historical reality in a manner that releases it from the restrictions of rigid sequentiality coincides with, and becomes a meaningful part of, the episodic and only superficially linear structure of his diffuse pictorial narrative. The anachronisms of *Ferdinand Count Fathom*, in other words, are neither the mere products of careless writing nor simply the results of a crass opportunism eager to exploit whatever is at the forefront of the public consciousness. Instead, they represent Smollett's attempts to develop important and unusually subtle relationships between the essentially timeless imaginary world of his creation and certain enduringly relevant facts of the real world it is intended to reflect.[53] As a further sign of Smollett's deliberate testing of the boundaries of fictional possibility in his third novel we may mention the somewhat tentative but still strikingly original gothic episodes found in Chapters 20–21 and 62–64. They are the first things of their kind in the work of a major English writer, and with them Smollett sought to deepen the emotional content of his story by taking it into the realm of psychic terror. In the process he managed to anticipate the new sensibility that would dominate much of the enterprise of fiction-writing throughout the last quarter of the eighteenth century.

*Ferdinand Count Fathom* does give occasional strong hints of haste or straining in its composition. The execution of domestic scenes and particularly of sentimental dialogue is sometimes awkward and unconvincing, and Smollett never seems completely at ease with the mode of third-person narration. The novel is, it must be said, much more carefully crafted than the mammoth, undisciplined *Peregrine Pickle*, and it probably deserves to be ranked above that more generally admired work as an achievement of its author's novelistic art. But on the whole it must be judged only a partial success.[54] Its comparative failure with the contemporary audience seems to have discouraged Smollett, who wrote no other fiction for more than half a decade. Instead, he turned his hand to different projects, more certain in their rewards. His performances as compiler, translator, editor, journalist, critic, and historian during the remaining years of the 1750s brought him a financial security he had never before enjoyed and earned him a new respectability in the world of literary London.[55] When he took up fiction-writing again he was motivated in part by a desire to promote interest in his *British Magazine*, a monthly miscellany he started up in 1760. *The Adventures of Sir Launcelot Greaves* appeared serially in the *British* from January 1760 to December 1761 and, among its relatively few distinctions, lays claim to recognition as the first novel by an important English writer to be presented to the public in this manner.[56]

Publication by installment, one would think, ought to have proved a most congenial venue for a novelist so episodic in his structures as Smollett, but he did not master the rhythms of it as his admirer Dickens was to do in the next century. And besides, his conception—a comic story in close imitation of *Don Quixote*—was already a stale one, often tried (in some instances with great success), and he had nothing new to add.[57] Still, *Sir Launcelot Greaves* apparently did help the sales of the *British Magazine*, and since it was praised by Oliver Goldsmith and others whose judgment Smollett trusted, he was persuaded to publish the work whole in 1762. It attracted almost no attention in that form, however, possibly because it had already exhausted its rather limited appeal in the course of its original appearance in monthly parts.

Today, *Sir Launcelot Greaves* is interesting chiefly because it marks a new mellowness in the works of Smollett the novelist, a shift in sensibility thought to anticipate the tolerant playfulness of *Humphry Clinker*, published a decade later. Greaves is no rogue at all but a quixotic, sentimental adventurer in the cause of goodness—the direct antithesis of Count Fathom. Disappointed in love, he roams through countryside and city reforming wickedness wherever he finds it, until the gathering effects of his benevolence seem to bring about a complete transformation of the world. In the end, he settles into blissful marriage with his original beloved, a romantic heroine named Aurelia, who actually plays only a smallish part in the story. In most respects the overall compositional method of *Sir Launcelot Greaves* differs little from that of other Smollett novels. The protagonist is still a vehicle of satire. Each episode of his experience forms a different dramatic picture reflecting some part of the texture of the varied human scene, and there is a pattern of references (some of them anachronistic) both oblique and explicit to political events and known public figures. Several fine comic portraits enliven the tale, among them the hero's Sancho-like companion Timothy Crabshaw; the infamous Justice Gobble, who is redeemed by the force of Greaves's example; the misanthropic mountebank Ferret; the crotchety old sailor Captain Crowe.

Prison scenes, which seem to have transfixed Smollett's imagination as sordid emblems of modern life, receive renewed attention in this novel. There are, in addition, some fine sketches of what goes on inside madhouses, where Greaves is horrified by the misery and squalor in which the unfortunate inmates must try to survive. Images of darkness abound, along with examples of personal isolation and suffering. And yet Smollett's vision in the work is decidedly festive and optimistic. No threat to the sturdy good nature of his hero is ever allowed to seem too great, and no barrier in the way of his ultimate predominance and happiness ever appears insurmountable. Greaves is sometimes the object of mild ridicule and as often a source of laughter; but his idealism, never defeated, never collapses into cynicism. He is a kind of gentrified, landlocked Tom Bowling, and Smollett joyously celebrates all that he represents.

Sir Launcelot and his story clearly echo Fielding's similar treatment of Parson Adams in *Joseph Andrews*. Smollett's novel, however, does not impart to its version of the quixotic hero the urgent vitality and throbbing internal energy that make Fielding's character such a triumph and such a delight. Greaves remains throughout an exemplary figure only, while Adams is both exemplary and highly individualized. Possibly the mode of third-person narration presented an unexpected inhibition as Smollett turned for the first time in his career to a full-length portrait of simple human goodness. Possibly this kind of portraiture did not really interest him very much. Smollett was at his best when projecting characters at odds not only with their world but with themselves. Every one of his novels except *Sir Launcelot Greaves* dramatizes a conflict that is as much internal as it is external; that is to say, the public environment with which his other protagonists do battle is at least in some partial way a reflection of that dimension of the fragmented private self demanding to be conquered before redemption can take place and wholeness be achieved. It is this multiplicity of tensions that most engages Smollett's imagination, and his failure to generate it in *Sir Launcelot Greaves* must be counted one of the major reasons why his fourth novel seems so weak by comparison with all the others.

During the decade of the 1760s, Smollett once more veered away from fiction-writing. He had not enjoyed full good health since childhood, and now, plagued as never before by nagging illnesses, he traveled extensively in England, Scotland, and Europe, seeking a climate that would offer comfort to his aching, ailing body. It is a commonplace that the valetudinarian Matt Bramble is a gently ironic self-portrait of his author during this hard period of his life, and it is almost a certainty that Smollett's own journey to his native Scotland in 1766 provided the impetus for *Humphry Clinker*. In the meantime his visit to Europe in 1763 occasioned the fine *Travels through France and Italy* (1766), an epistolary work so artful and so intensely imagined that a good many modern students of eighteenth-century literature have begun to treat it almost as a novel. The *Travels* is by and large a genial narrative, though decidedly blunt in recording its author's sharp-eyed observations. The passionate, relentlessly satiric Smollett surfaces once more in *The History and Adventures of an Atom* (1769), a violent, caustic, penetrating commentary on the social history and partisan politics of the dozen or so years preceding its appearance.[58]

In 1768, exhausted from work and very sick, Smollett settled his affairs at home and left for Italy, never to return. He took up residence near Leghorn and there, in almost daily anguish, wrote *The Expedition of Humphry Clinker*. The three slender volumes of this new novel went to the London bookstalls in mid-June 1771, just three short months before its author's death.[59] It is a sad irony that after so many years of straining to repeat the early success of *Roderick Random*, Smollett was denied all enjoyment of the vigorous applause that greeted *Humphry Clinker*. The critics raved about the novel, and the public loved it; it was many times reprinted and eventually translated into several languages.[60] The reasons for so much enthusiasm are not difficult to guess, for *Humphry Clinker* is a work both cleverly conventional and profoundly original. Its readers had never seen anything quite like it before, and yet its parts must have seemed very familiar. Smollett's work is a comic romance in the epistolary style, it is a lively narrative of travels, it is a "biographical" or "historical" account of ordinary characters, it is a collection of satiric vignettes, it is a spoof of the new cult of sensibility, and it is a fable of passage through the world of experience toward restful retirement in tranquility. In short, it is a stunningly eclectic performance, and one suspects that Smollett, in projecting what he must have known would be his last book, sought to join in a kind of definitive, paradigmatic form the many assorted attractions of the new and developing art of the novel as practiced by his seminal generation of writers.

Its radical eclecticism marks *Humphry Clinker* as the most strikingly literary of Smollett's experiments in fiction, and surely it is no mere coincidence that this same work represents the culminating manifestation of the theory of novelistic composition laid down almost two decades earlier in the dedication to *Ferdinand Count Fathom*. *Humphry Clinker*, so very careful in its design, is most emphatically a "large diffused picture" of the human environment. Life is still a decidedly chaotic business in this novel, whose characters bounce along the highways in a seemingly random pattern that exposes them to an extraordinary range of experience. The ultimate configuration of things is easy to discover. Smollett's confidently hopeful vision, so different from the almost defiant optimism of the early works, is directly conveyed by the circular motion of Matthew Bramble and his traveling party from Wales to England to Scotland and finally back to Wales again—a motion whose shapeliness becomes an emblem of the book's central emphasis upon a progress from fragmentation to wholeness. But the texturing of Smollett's design reveals its full significance very gradually, in an internal structure—like that of his other novels—of accumulating vivid pictures. Bramble, whose developing consciousness is so much at issue in the story, arrives at health and fullness of understanding only after his repeated and deeply felt encounters with the variety of human nature have helped him to affirm the value of his own innate good-heartedness, to balance passion with reason, and to unclog both his bowels and the wheels of his moral and emotional life.

The first and most prominent group of representative characters to be portrayed in *Humphry Clinker* is, obviously, the Bramble entourage itself. As passengers through the fictional world, they are also part of it. In effect, *Humphry Clinker* adapts the familiar convention of the journey by coach, with its rhythm of wayside stops at taverns and inns. What he had previously used only as a means of sketching out the occasional episode in his first four novels, Smollett now expands into the principal device of his entire plot. Matt, his nephew and niece Jery and Lydia Melford, his sister Tabitha, the servant girl Winifred Jenkins, and later Clinker and Lieutenant Lismahago add up to a microcosm of humanity. The intricately drawn fictional macrocosm outside their family circle reflects and thus illuminates their little tensions and conflicts, imbalances and excesses, while luring them into the vortex of its own activity. By this reflexive process Matt, Jery, and Lydia come finally to know who they are, both privately and in relation to all that surrounds them.

In developing a focus upon multiple protagonists instead of a single figure, Smollett departs from his practice in earlier stories—although, with remarkable dexterity and stylistic virtuosity, he does manage in *Humphry Clinker* to catch each of his central characters separately and alone, in definitive poses and gestures, through the words of their individual letters. But because the narrative method systematically combines the self-revelations of carefully particularized language with the more detached commentary of fellow correspondents, the reader is never allowed to forget that all these travelers are bound together in a human community.[61] Matt Bramble is the most lovingly detailed portrait, for the important personal reasons already suggested. Matt is a type of the splenetic hypochondriac, a funny but not terribly subtle conception. Smollett deepens his character by testing it against a world full of riotous noises, foul odors, vexations, and hostilities. To these violent stimuli the sensitive Matt responds with a passion that vents his misanthropy and eventually opens him to the free-flowing life of Edinburgh and the Scottish countryside, where for the first time he discovers the full possibilities of equilibrium and joy. In the meantime, his trials include the persistently exasperating presence of his amazing sister, Tabitha, whose ludicrous social pretensions and affectedly spinsterish sexual prudery are wonderfully exposed in the malapropisms of her letters. The hilarious quirkiness of Tabitha's language coincides with and reinforces the reader's sense of her physical oddities, so that when she is in the end married off to the ridiculously quixotic half-pay soldier Lismahago—a battered, patch-pated, naturally irascible Scottish veteran of an Indian scalping—the match seems perfect for them both. This bride and groom are by any estimation two of the finest of Smollett's comic characterizations in *Humphry Clinker*, and they are only rarely equaled in his other novels.

Lydia Melford, Bramble's niece, directly anticipates the character of Lydia Languish in Richard Brinsley Sheridan's *The Rivals* (1775), though as an object of her uncle's genuine affection, she is rather more than just a parody of the conventional sighing heroine of romance and sentimental novels. Her brother Jery is very subtly developed and is in his way almost as interesting a figure as Bramble. A decidedly smug Oxonian, Jery prides himself on a talent for amused detachment from the world and its inhabitants, and he is often Smollett's most reliable descriptive voice. But his capacity for change, for growth in affections, and for a deepening of understanding gives Jery's character a richness that even he cannot recognize until the spectacle of his uncle's gradual metamorphosis provokes responses in feeling that alert him to it. The original entourage is completed in the person of Win Jenkins, whose innocence makes the unintentional sexual jokes of her semiliterate correspondence even funnier than the comparable malapropisms of her mistress Tabitha—when she marries Clinker, Win says, it is the "grease of God" that joins them.[62]

Win Jenkins is a sympathetic foil to the more imposing Tabitha, while her bridegroom—an heir deprived of his birthright by circumstance—provides Smollett with a means of simultaneously mocking and affirming the idealism of romance. This ragtail titular hero does not even appear until the novel is well underway, and he is in fact no hero at all but a "poor Wiltshire lad" whose torn breeches expose bare posteriors (their skin "fair as alabaster," Win observes) that his tattered shirt is inadequate to cover. Clinker is, in Matt's kindly ironic words, a "notorious offender" against custom and decency who stands "convicted" of "sickness, hunger, wretchedness, and want."[63] A sturdy fellow, he is the very soul of simple, incorruptible, quixotic good nature, and though foolishly inclined to religious enthusiasm (especially Methodism, which his author scorned), he fully deserves the exaltation and happiness that come to him as the result of the late, comically transforming discovery that he is Bramble's son. The bonding of Bramble and Clinker (or Loyd, to use the name of his true lineage) in a family relationship is highly appropriate, for the lowly servant is the most important and most continually visible among the numerous examples of human deprivation whose suffering repeatedly calls Matt's benevolent instincts into action, helping to release him at last from the restraints of his misanthropic irritability.

The obvious joke embedded in its title suggests that *Humphry Clinker* sets out to toy with its reader's expectations, and in fact this novel is more playful (as Fielding's *Tom Jones* is playful) than any of Smollett's others. It is also more artfully festive, as Jery affirms when, in a dramatic analogy at the very beginning of his last letter, he observes that the "comedy is near a close; and the curtain is ready to drop."[64] Smollett's name for the latecomer hero who is not a hero almost winks from his pages. "Humphry," of course, derives from the stockpile of romance, but its tentative grandeur collapses under the comic weight of the surname "Clinker," with its twin allusions to the humble cinder of the blacksmith's forge and to a product of human defecation. The phrase "Humphry Clinker" announces from the beginning that Smollett's story will deal in scatological gags, as in fact it regularly does, and that these will participate in a rhetorical strategy whose purpose is to undermine affectation and reduce life to its elemental levels of common denomination. Through his devices of reduction, Smollett reveals how head and heart, body and spirit, action and feeling may be brought into the positive harmonious relationship that alone can ensure comfort and joy.[65] In this connection we may remember once again the self-revealing scatologies of Tabitha Bramble's language, and the fact that it is only when Matt is able to loosen his bowels *and* his naturally good feelings that he finds satisfaction and pleasure in living.

Smollett's method in his narrative creates a complexity of perspective. Each pause in the progress of the travelers occasions a series of letters in which the several correspondents record their responses to the sights and sounds and, of course, to each other. Here is the source of one's sense that in *Humphry Clinker* Smollett has captured every setting whole. The numerous letters from Bath, for example, seem to circle the place, gazing at it from a variety of vantage points, until finally the picture lacks nothing.

To the astonished Lydia, the fashionable city is "a new world.—All is gayety, good-humour, and diversion. The eye is continually entertained with the splendour of dress and equipage; and the ear with the sound of coaches, chairs, and other carriages."[66] This "earthly paradise," as Lydia characterizes it, looks very different to her uncle. In Matt's reductive view, Bath is a mob scene, "the very centre of racket and dissipation," where all the "noise, tumult, and hurry" of pretentious exhibitionism reveal only "a mass of ignorance, presumption, malice, and brutality." Neither the grand new buildings nor the silly people who mill around in them display "the least idea of propriety and decorum."[67] The waters are foul with seepage from the running sores of diseased bodies, and the Roman baths, where everyone goes, contain "the strainings of rotten bones and carcasses" left over from a burial ground that used to cover the spot.[68]

Jery Melford sees the busy, glistening city with still different eyes. Like his sister, he is struck by its splendors and diversions; like his uncle, he mocks the follies to be witnessed everywhere. But the scenery excites in him laughter instead of sentimental effusions or misanthropic grumblings. Especially at the baths, Jery says,

> a man has daily opportunities of seeing the most remarkable characters of the community. He sees them in their natural attitudes and true colours; descended from their pedestals, and divested of their formal draperies, undisguised by art and affectation—Here we have ministers of state, judges, generals, bishops, projectors, philosophers, wits, poets, players, *chemists, fiddlers,* and *buffoons.*

And in the public rooms, where the ornaments of place and class are put on once more, there is the great entertainment arising from "the general mixture of all degrees" without distinction of "rank or fortune." This "chaos" of social pretension and ridiculous decadence provides Jery with "a source of infinite amusement."[69]

Bath is a specific and familiar setting, its parade of humanity displayed in all its variety by Smollett's correspondents. But the city is also an image of the great world represented in a concentrated picture, its extremes of ridiculous appearance and laughable or contemptible conduct made fully visible by the devices of reductive emphasis. The individual letters also reveal the character of their authors, each engaged in an ongoing process of self-definition. The differences in perspective that divide the members of the Bramble party from one another suggest imbalance and a fragmentation of identity that must be resolved into a unity of vision and spirit before they can achieve the happy stability of a truly communal family. Such multiplicity as we witness in *Humphry Clinker*—the Bath episode is very typical—is extremely difficult for a novelist to manage successfully. Of all the many eighteenth-century writers who attempted it in an epistolary narrative, only Richardson, in his tragic story of *Clarissa*, equalled Smollett in facility and effect. And Smollett, in *Humphry Clinker*, was the first—and last—English novelist to bring the technique of multiple narration through letters to such perfection in a work of comic fiction.

From Bath, Smollett's travelers move on to London, where they find a city astonishingly larger, more grand, more corrupt and chaotic, more bewildering than any they have yet seen. Their arrival brings them to the very heart of English life. Bramble finds that heart throbbing with hideous energy. This capital, he says, almost personifying it, "is become an overgrown monster." It is dark and dangerous, it smells and is filthy, and it confusingly mixes politeness and gentility with the offal of a disgusting rabble. "The hod-carrier, the low mechanic, the tapster, the publican, the shopkeeper, the pettifogger, the citizen, and courtier, *all tread upon the kibes of one another:* actuated by the demons of profligacy and licentiousness, they are seen every where rambling, riding, rolling, rushing, justling, mixing, bouncing, cracking, and crashing in one vile ferment of stupidity and corruption."[70] No doubt Smollett uses Matt's declamatory voice here and elsewhere to express his own great dismay at the alarming breakdown of the comfortable old English class structure and the ensuing cultural disorder of jumbled social distinctions, the excess in all of what Bramble calls "the different departments of life," and the mad questing after luxury.[71] Quite apart from his author's personal investment in such concerns, Matt's graphic descriptions of London are among the most striking in all of *Humphry Clinker*, and they neatly set up the later pictures of the salubrious, tranquil beauties of the environment of Scotland.

Meanwhile the negative intensity of Bramble's aggravated responses to the great city is balanced by alternative views. Lydia finds London a myriad of delights, with its gardens, pleasure parks, and manifestations of cultivated splendor. She observes without wisdom, but because she is not jaded, she is alert to real attractions that escape her uncle's notice. "People of experience and infirmity," she remarks to her friend Miss Willis in a moment of ingenuous but telling insight, "see with very different eyes from those such as you and I make use of."[72] Jery, predictably, writes from the safe distance of an ironic complacency, steering an easy course between the ripples of his sister's undiscriminating raptures and the violent wake of his uncle's riotous vituperations.

It is the abrasive experience of London that sets Matt's final determination to pursue a northern route on the way homeward to his Welsh "solitude and mountains." The exertion of traveling, he admits, "has been of service to my health,"[73] which will improve to perfection with the further motion of his journey to the land beyond the Tweed. Edinburgh, like the English capital, is a place filled with bustling humanity; it is noisy, and its streets are fouled by garbage and dung. What Matt, Jery, and even Win Jenkins find here, however, is a kind of elemental vitality bounded by spectacular natural scenery. Interestingly, their voices and Lydia's unite in acknowledging their joy in the flow of kindness and hospitality that reaches them all from the good hearts of the Scottish people. Only Tabitha and the most recent object of her matrimonial schemes, the incomparable Lismahago, fail to share in the fullness of this new pleasure, but the comic contrast of their continued cantankerous oddity actually underscores the revolutions in sensibility felt by their companions.

Matt, for his part, now begins in earnest to experience the wholesome benefits of exercise. "I eat like a farmer," he says, "sleep from mid-night till eight in the morning without interruption, and enjoy a constant tide of spirits, equally distant from inanities and excess."[74] The landscape of Dumbartonshire leaves him ecstatic in the contemplation of its beauty, calling forth the most lyrical descriptive writing to be found anywhere in his author's novels. This region of Loch Lomond and Leven-Water—the "Arcadia of Scotland," as Matt characterizes it[75]—was of course the site of Smollett's boyhood home, and his nostalgic tribute to it provides a very touching moment in his narrative. It is no accident that Matt here emerges completely from behind the defensive wall of misanthropy he had thrown up between himself and the world. Jery, meanwhile, gives up his protective detachment as he responds with great sensitivity to the magnificence of the Highlands.

Lydia's fulfillment must await the journey homeward; in the meantime, some moments of deep disillusionment in love bring her closer than she has ever been to the former cynicism of her uncle. "I am heartily tired of this itinerant way of life," she writes, and "Nature never intended me for the busy world."[76] Finally, however, she escapes from the limitations of the shallow sentimental illusions that have forced such unhappiness upon her and is rewarded in marriage to her mysterious suitor. By a remarkable and quite providential coincidence, he turns out to be no other than the son of Matt's old friend from Oxford days, Charles Dennison, now a perfect country gentleman. It is worth noting that Smollett indulges in a very clever and very suggestive paradox by persistently undermining the romantic nonsense of Lydia's languishing sentimentality and then at last allowing the substantive satisfaction of her dreams to stand as an affirmation of the feeling heart and the idealism that it generates.

In defining the erratic but still unmistakably circular motion of his characters toward a multiple resolution in the happiness of a unified vision, Smollett imparts to each of his episodes what we might call a dynamic stasis. The Bramble party stops at this place and the other, but the activity of their progress never ceases. Smollett's stylistic virtuosity helps him to achieve this effect of almost frenzied continuity even during the longest periods of delay. No character in *Humphry Clinker* ever rests. We need only recall the energy of Matt's descriptions of London and Bath to be convinced that this is so. The many precise satiric sketches of eccentric human characters met along the way add measurably to the vibrating life reflected in the various episodes, contributing density to the composite pictures drawn from the materials of the scenery with which every setting is broadly furnished. Some of these sketches are likenesses of real people, identified by name or by revealing hints, which suggests that Smollett was continuing to experiment with the relationship between fiction and reality. By way of a final comment on the texturing of his design, it may be useful to look briefly at the details of two or three of his individualized portraits.

The presence of the superannuated actor James Quin, whom Matt encounters in Bath,[77] helps to define the environment of that city as a haven for persons of such dissipated habits. But the portrayal of Quin's oddity is as affectionate as it is precise and satirical. It is also an instance of Smollett's anachronistic habits, less conspicuous and more gracefully followed in *Humphry Clinker* than in *Ferdinand Count Fathom* but still purposeful and important. Quin is one of those leaders of the old London theatrical establishment who were roughed up in *Roderick Random* and *Peregrine Pickle* for their failure to admire and promote *The Regicide*; his representation here as remnant of a fast-declining generation of great performers compresses three decades of stage history into a single moment and simultaneously closes forever the gash this man had left in Smollett's youthful pride. Quin, now descended into old age and harmless jollity steeped in claret, has become a fixture in Bath. The amusing interlude of his appearance lends a personal touch to the novel's general account of the place while suggesting a larger context of familiar public history.

Another such anachronistic portrait occurs during the London section of the story, when Matt and Jery attend upon the King at St. James's Palace. There they are introduced to the ancient Duke of Newcastle, formerly a powerful minister but now a senile old fool. Smollett's satiric strategy of reduction is overt here. This "ridiculous ape, this venal drudge" (as Matt pictures him almost emblematically in a brief review of the Duke's dissolute politics and execrable statesmanship) represents, for Smollett as for Bramble, the worst of what has been wrong for so long in the domain of the English ruling classes, where power has consistently accrued to the unworthy, rotting what souls and minds they have and breeding disruption and decay throughout their sphere of influence.[78] Newcastle is a fact of history, now past but still relevant and worthy of contemplation. As James Quin is a part of the furniture of Bath, so the Duke remains a presence in London, and his visibility imparts specificity to the generalized descriptions with which Smollett's correspondents reveal the dizzying blur of the giant city's frenetic activity.

The visit to the King's levee provokes several additional character portraits and a number of brief allusions to real people and events, so that the reader comes away with a comprehensive impression of what things are really like within the precincts of the powerful. Smollett draws graphically here, and what he makes us see is not lovely. Fine manners and fine words disguise the dark motives of twisted minds and hide the ugliness of a politics of vicious factionalism, as destructive as it is presumptuous on the part of all the ambitious villains who participate in its divisive machinations. Smollett allows Matt to peer behind the disguises and expose the truth. The manner of his doing so is relentless and devastating.

The whimsical scene taking place at what is unmistakably Smollett's own house during one of his Sunday afternoon literary dinners leads to another composite picture, less topical but delightfully entertaining. The people on hand are real, and many of Smollett's first readers doubtless recognized them with a certain glee. In portraying them, the author shares personal perceptions with his audience in a cleverly intimate way, once again affirming the closeness of fiction, as a species of poetic history, to reality. To the modern reader the identities of these characters are much less important than their roles in a microcosm of representative types waiting to be anatomized, described, and understood. The gathering of struggling authors hugely amuses Jery, a guest among them and the vehicle for his author's verbal portrait. "I question," Jery chuckles, "if the whole kingdom could produce such another assemblage of originals."[79] And then, one by one, he proceeds to sketch them in all their silly, pretentious, talentless eccentricity.

Smollett obviously indulges himself in this comic interlude, but its method is typical and thus precisely indicative of his compositional techniques. In every one of his novels, as we have seen, he follows a pattern of bringing his central characters repeatedly into direct contact with such miniaturized collections of humanity as the one on display around his fictionalized table in *Humphry Clinker*, achieving uniformity in disparateness by a process of accumulation, and creating whole dramatic pictures of the community of mankind. If his last novel represents Smollett's most consummate success as an artist, it is because in this work he managed to capture, more sensitively and more completely than in any other, the abundant diversity of human character, human conduct, and human perception—and because he was able to give to his story a form exactly suited both to his own talent and to the vibrating complexity of his extraordinarily ambitious subject.

*Humphry Clinker* is, by any account, a triumphant work of the literary imagination. If Smollett had written nothing more than this book and his first, *Roderick Random*, he would deserve to hold an honored place as one of the great novelists of the English tradition. But in quantity as well as overall quality of performance—five important works of fiction published within a quarter-century—he bears comparison with the best and most prolific storytellers of later generations, not to mention his contemporaries Richardson, Fielding, and Sterne. With these three giants of eighteenth-century fiction, of course, and with Defoe, Smollett helped to popularize the new species of the novel and to establish it as a dominant form of literary expression. If he has been less admired and less widely enjoyed in recent years than the authors of *Robinson Crusoe*, *Clarissa*, *Tom Jones*, and *Tristram Shandy*, it is surely because he has been less well understood. Unorthodox, irregular in his genius, and at times even outrageous in his adaptations from conventional modes of narrative, this novelist requires our close attention to the peculiarities of his very original compositions, his "large" and "diffused" pictures of life and society. If attention is given as it is demanded, the rewards will be many, they will be

178

substantial, and they will last. Smollett, to conclude simply, is well worth reading, and worth reading well.

---

## Notes

1. *The Adventures of Ferdinand Count Fathom*, ed. Damian Grant (London: Oxford Univ. Press, 1971), 2.

2. Space will not permit full development of this point here, but the reader may wish to consult the following for some useful observations concerning Smollett's connections with and interest in the painterly arts: Milton Orowitz, "Smollett and the Art of Caricature," *Spectrum* 2 (1958), 155–67; George M. Kahrl, "Smollett as a Caricaturist," in *Tobias Smollett: Bicentennial Essays Presented to Lewis M. Knapp*, ed. G.S. Rousseau and P.-G. Boucé (New York: Oxford Univ. Press, 1971), 169–200. Hogarth was Smollett's contemporary, and his visual art of caricature was at the time a relatively new thing in England. Smollett and others were keenly interested in appropriating it as a verbal art. Given the striking pictorial qualities of Smollett's novels, it is not surprising that he attracted the enthusiastic attention of great illustrators like Thomas Rowlandson and George Cruikshank, both of whom provided splendid drawings to accompany major editions of his works. In this same general connection, it ought to be mentioned that the dramatic qualities of the pictorial episodes in Smollett's novels, like the many allusions to plays (especially those of Shakespeare) scattered through them, importantly reflect his lifelong interest in the theater. See Lee M. Ellison, "Elizabethan Drama and the Works of Smollett," *PMLA* 44 (1929), 842–62.

3. I have elsewhere discussed at length the importance of Smollett's theoretical statement in *Ferdinand Count Fathom* and its implications for his narrative structures: see "Smollett's Novels: *Ferdinand Count Fathom* for the Defense," *PLL* 20 (1984), 165–84.

4. For contrasting but complementary views of Smollett's episodic structures and comic endings, see Philip Stevick, "Smollett's Picaresque Games," in *Tobias Smollett: Bicentennial Essays*, 111–30; Paul-Gabriel Boucé, *The Novels of Tobias Smollett* (London: Longman, 1976), esp. ch. 8.

5. *The Letters of Tobias Smollett*, ed. Lewis M. Knapp (Oxford: Clarendon Press, 1970), 6. For a full account of Smollett's early years and their importance to the beginnings of his career as a novelist, see Knapp, *Tobias Smollett: Doctor of Men and Manners* (Princeton, N.J.: Princeton Univ. Press, 1949). I have relied on this authoritative biography for many of the details of Smollett's life introduced throughout the present discussion.

6. *Letters*, 8.

7. *Selected Letters of Samuel Richardson*, ed. John Carroll (Oxford: Clarendon Press, 1964), 41.

8. Smollett's Spanish was not fluent, and he was slow to finish this translation, which did not appear in print until 1755.

9. Smollett's translation of *Gil Blas*, published in October 1748, is still considered the best that has ever been done. The four volumes of LeSage's work were published in France between 1715 and 1735, and English versions followed quickly (from 1716 to 1736, with reprints thereafter).

10. *The Adventures of Roderick Random,* ed. Paul-Gabriel Boucé (Oxford: Oxford Univ. Press, 1981), Preface, xxxv. I have used this World's Classics paperback edition of *Roderick Random* because it is both reliable and readily available. For the convenience of any reader who may have another text in hand, I refer in subsequent citations to chapter (or, as here, to the preface) as well as page numbers.

11. Preface, xxxv.

12. For fuller discussion of Smollett's adaptations from the picaresque, see my essay, "*Roderick Random:* The Picaresque Transformed," *College Literature* 6 (1979–80), 211–20. See also Robert Alter, "The Picaroon as Fortune's Plaything," in *Rogue's Progress: Studies in the Picaresque Novel* (Cambridge, Mass.: Harvard Univ. Press, 1964), 58–79; Alice Green Fredman, "The Picaresque in Decline: Smollett's First Novel," in *English Writers of the Eighteenth Century,* ed. John H. Middendorf (New York: Columbia Univ. Press, 1971), 189–207; Richard Bjornson, "The Picaresque Hero as Young Nobleman: Victimization and Vindication in Smollett's *Roderick Random,*" in *The Picaresque Hero in European Fiction* (Madison: Univ. of Wisconsin Press, 1977), 228–45.

13. Smollett knew this firsthand. His mock-dedication to *Ferdinand Count Fathom* alludes directly to his personal tendencies toward uncontrollable rage and cynicism, and acknowledges his anxiety over their potential injury to his character; much of his adult life was devoted to restraining these impulses. It is in its echoes of this private struggle, more than in its specific references to Smollett's actual experience, that *Roderick Random* may be meaningfully understood as an autobiographical work. Roderick, of course, is not his author, as Smollett himself makes plain in a letter to Alexander Carlyle written shortly after the book's publication (*Letters,* 7–9).

14. In Smollett's view, there were other resemblances besides, too striking to be accidental, and they angered him. *Tom Jones* was published in February 1749, just thirteen months after *Roderick Random,* and Smollett believed that Fielding had plagiarized the character of Partridge from his own Strap. Later, he would be equally convinced that Fielding had stolen the idea for the Miss Matthews of *Amelia* (1751) from *Roderick Random's* Nancy Williams. Despite superficial similarities, Fielding's characters differ importantly from Smollett's, and there was no real reason for such suspicions except perhaps the younger writer's insecurity over his newcomer's position in the literary world of London.

15. Ronald Paulson, for example, finds this lack of detachment a source of Smollett's failure to make a successful transition from Augustan satirist to novelist; see *Satire and the Novel in Eighteenth-Century England* (New Haven, Conn.: Yale Univ. Press, 1967), 165–78 and passim.

16. I have traced this background at considerable length in my *Novels of the 1740s* (Athens: Univ. of Georgia Press, 1982), ch. 4.

17. *Letters,* 98.

18. The apologue prefixed to the fourth edition of the novel (1754, dated 1755) is a modified beast fable that emphasizes the subhuman qualities of some of Smollett's characters—and some of his contemporary critics as well.

19. Ch. 1, p. 1.

20. See Percy G. Adams, *Travel Literature and the Evolution of the Novel* (Lexington: Univ. Press of Kentucky, 1983). George M. Kahrl, in *Tobias Smollett: Traveler-Novelist* (Chicago: Univ. of Chicago Press, 1945), has demonstrated at

great length how deeply Smollett's abiding interest in travel and travel literature affected the style and structure of his novels.

21. Ch. 2, p. 5.

22. Ch. 7, p. 26.

23. Ch. 11, pp. 49–50.

24. See Adams, *Travel Literature*, ch. 8, for full discussion of these two important conventions or (to use Adams's own term) "motifs."

25. Ch. 13, p. 61.

26. Ch. 25, p. 149.

27. For varied discussion of the general question of Smollett's style, see Albrecht B. Strauss, "On Smollett's Language: A Paragraph in *Ferdinand Count Fathom,*" in *Style in Prose Fiction: English Institute Essays, 1958*, ed. Harold C. Martin (New York: Columbia Univ. Press, 1959), 25–54; Philip Stevick, "Stylistic Energy in the Early Smollett," *PQ* 64 (1967), 712–19; Damian Grant, *Tobias Smollett: A Study in Style* (Manchester: Manchester Univ. Press, 1977). Strauss finds the failures of Smollett's sentimental language very revealing with respect to his real talent for the language of hyperbole and emotional violence; Stevick and Grant stress Smollett's stylistic exaggerations and virtuosity as chief attractions in his works, though they understate the importance of intensive language as a means of character definition. Grant argues further that in Smollett, style is almost everything; plot, episodes, and characters are in themselves relatively uninteresting.

28. Ch. 29, p. 168.

29. Ch. 39, p. 219.

30. Ch. 41, p. 235.

31. Ch. 42, p. 240.

32. Ch. 50, pp. 303, 305.

33. Ch. 51, p. 310. Earlier, Roderick had described the effeminate Captain Whiffle of the *Thunder* as guilty of a passion "not fit to be named" (ch. 35, p. 199). Robert Adams Day has recently suggested that Smollett's often repeated antagonism to homosexuality, together with his obsessive interest in scatological humor and word play on the subject of bodily functions, gives rise to a suspicion that he himself may have harbored some latent homosexual tendencies; see "Sex, Scatology, Smollett," in *Sexuality in Eighteenth-Century Britain*, ed. Paul-Gabriel Boucé (Manchester: Manchester Univ. Press, 1982), 225–43.

34. Ch. 54, pp. 326–27.

35. Ch. 60, p. 372.

36. Ch. 61, p. 377.

37. Ch. 64, p. 397.

38. Ch. 66, p. 416.

39. Ch. 60, p. 371.

40. Robert Alter, for example ("The Picaroon as Fortune's Plaything," 76), complains that the conventional happy ending, with its obvious contrivances, defeats the novel's development as an exercise in picaresque satire. The problem with this objection is its failure to acknowledge that Smollett deliberately set out to write a variation upon the picaresque.

41. Ch. 64, p. 397.

42. Smollett was no orthodox Christian, or so his writings suggest. Actually, we know very little about his personal theology. Still, it is clear that he shared

with many of his contemporaries a belief in the providential ordering of the world and in the scriptural guarantee of ultimate redemption for the Christian part of mankind; see Thomas R. Preston, *Not in Timon's Manner: Feeling, Misanthropy, and Satire in Eighteenth-Century England* (University: Univ. of Alabama Press, 1975), 2, 69–120. For fuller treatment of the transformation occurring at the end of *Roderick Random*, see my *Novels of the 1740s*, 122–25.

43. Barth, in fact, provided a most interesting (if unscholarly) afterword for an edition of *Roderick Random* issued some years ago in a popular paperback series (New York: New American Library, 1964). This edition is now regrettably out of print.

44. In doing so, Smollett followed what was a fairly common practice in his day; he paid £28 Scots for his M.D. His work with Handel resulted in a combined opera-tragedy-masque called *Alceste*, now lost, which never made it to the stage. Another lost work for the theater, a comedy entitled *The Absent Man*, was likewise never produced. One additional project of the period immediately following *Roderick Random* had a happier fate: in 1750, Smollett published a second translation from LeSage, *The Devil upon Crutches*, which enjoyed a certain popularity.

45. *Peregrine Pickle*, incidentally, is nearly twice the length of *Roderick Random*.

46. Rufus Putney cautioned long ago, however, against the failure to see that Smollett's second novel, for all its apparent lack of discipline, does have a "uniform plan": to expose corruptions in high society while describing Peregrine's growth in knowledge of the world; see "The Plan of *Peregrine Pickle*," *PMLA* 60 (1945), 1051–65.

47. In this edition, published in March 1758, Smollett removed many of the satiric personal references from his novel, smoothed over some of its rougher passages, and reduced its length by some eighty pages.

48. The physician is possibly a portrait of Dr. Mark Akenside, who was actually a man of considerable accomplishment and eminence in the medical profession. He was also a poet of modest talent and importance.

49. See Rufus Putney, "Smollett and Lady Vane's Memoirs," *PQ* 25 (1946), 120–26; Lewis M. Knapp and Lillian de la Torre, "Smollett, MacKercher, and the Annesley Claimant," *ELN* 1 (1963), 28–33.

50. For very general discussion of the nature of this experiment in *Peregrine Pickle*, and in the other novels of Smollett's youth, see William B. Piper, "The Large Diffused Picture of Life in Smollett's Early Novels," *SP* 60 (1963), 45–56.

51. Smollett borrowed Monimia's name from Thomas Otway's verse tragedy, *The Orphan* (1680). She is a type of the melancholy heroine.

52. P. 3. Thomas R. Preston has usefully suggested that Fathom is actually projected as a kind of object lesson to the "man of feeling"—as a warning, that is, against the worldly threat of evil and destruction. The novel thus inverts the usual sentimental formula, appealing not to the allurements of virtue to deter vice, but to fear instead ("Disenchanting the Man of Feeling: Smollett's *Ferdinand Count Fathom*," in *Quick Springs of Sense: Studies in the Eighteenth Century*, ed. Larry S. Champion [Athens: Univ. of Georgia Press, 1974], 223–39).

53. In "Smollett's Novels: *Ferdinand Count Fathom* for the Defense," I have elaborated upon the importance of Smollett's anachronisms to our understanding of his third novel and of his general conception of the novelist's

art and purpose. So far as I know, Smollett's unorthodox uses of historical fact have heretofore gone unnoticed by modern readers. I became aware of them myself only when engaged in editing *Ferdinand Count Fathom* for the forthcoming University of Delaware Press collection of Smollett's works.

54. There was only one edition of *Ferdinand Count Fathom* in Smollett's lifetime, and so it appears that early readers found it no more attractive than later ones have done. Ralph Griffiths (*Monthly Review* 8 [March 1753], 203–14) anticipated the objections of modern critics when he blamed the novel for crudities and incongruities that regrettably obscure its strong marks of Smollett's genius and his admirable proficiency in the study of mankind.

55. Smollett had begun reviewing for Griffiths's *Monthly Review* shortly after the appearance of *Peregrine Pickle,* and in the mid-1750s he established himself as a judge to be reckoned with in his own *Critical Review,* which he edited from 1756 to 1763. Further energetic journalistic work followed, and in the meantime Smollett managed a truly prodigious output in other fields of literary endeavor. Among other things he wrote a two-act farce, *The Reprisal,* which was produced at Drury Lane in 1757—the first and only one of his plays ever to be acted. Probably his most impressive achievement of this period was the four-volume *Complete History of England* (1757–58), which enjoyed a popularity approaching that of David Hume's celebrated *History of Great Britain* (1754–61). For full details of Smollett's enormous activity during these years see Knapp, *Tobias Smollett,* chs. 7–10.

56. For detailed discussion of the serial publication of *Sir Launcelot Greaves,* see Robert D. Mayo, *The English Novel in the Magazines, 1740–1815* (London: Oxford Univ. Press, 1962), 274–88.

57. The most important novelistic adaptation from *Don Quixote* was, of course, Fielding's *Joseph Andrews* (1742). *The Female Quixote* (1752), by Charlotte Lennox, was another such adaptation, very able and very popular.

58. The *Atom* was once only doubtfully attributed to Smollett, but Robert Adams Day has established his authorship beyond question in preparing the text for inclusion in the Delaware edition of Smollett's works. His other writings during the decade of the 1760s, together with the *Atom* and the *Travels,* add up to a huge total production. Among his many undertakings he continued his journalism in several different periodicals, published a *Continuation* (1760–65) of his *Complete History,* and collaborated on a massive edition of the works of Voltaire (1761–65). See Knapp, *Tobias Smollett,* chs. 11–13; see also Louis L. Martz, *The Later Career of Tobias Smollett* (New Haven, Conn.: Yale Univ. Press, 1942).

59. Smollett died 17 September 1771, having suffered for years (it appears) from a form of tuberculosis that finally left him too weak to resist the violent intestinal infection that killed him. He was buried in the English cemetery at Leghorn.

60. Three editions appeared in 1771 and another in 1772. Translations into German (1772), Dutch (1779), and Danish (1796–98) made Smollett's novel famous all over Europe before the end of the eighteenth century.

61. On the idiosyncratic qualities of individual characters and their relationships to one another, see Robert Alan Donovan, "*Humphry Clinker* and the Novelist's Imagination," in *The Shaping Vision: Imagination in the English Novel from Defoe to Dickens* (Ithaca, N.Y.: Cornell Univ. Press, 1966), 118–39.

62. *The Expedition of Humphry Clinker,* ed. Angus Ross (Harmondsworth: Penguin Books, 1967), Winifred Jenkins [Loyd] to Mrs. Mary Jones, Nov. 20, p. 395. I refer to the Penguin edition because it has been for years the most widely available. Just recently, *Humphry Clinker* has been issued in the World's Classics series of paperbacks (Oxford: Oxford Univ. Press, 1984), as edited by Lewis M. Knapp (rev. Paul-Gabriel Boucé). For the convenience of readers who may possess this or some other edition than the Penguin, I include in all citations the correspondents' names, the postmark (if given), and the date, as well as the page numbers.

63. Jery Melford to Sir Watkins Phillips, London, May 24, pp. 112–13.

64. Jery Melford to Sir Watkins Phillips, November 8, p. 388. The best single discussion of *Humphry Clinker* as a comic fiction is Sheridan Baker's "*Humphry Clinker* as Comic Romance," *Papers of the Michigan Academy of Science, Arts, and Letters* 46 (1961), 645–54.

65. For an interesting Lockean approach to the matter of Smollett's many references to bodily functions, see Donald T. Siebert, "The Role of the Senses in *Humphry Clinker,*" *SNNTS* 6 (1974), 17–26.

66. Lydia Melford to Miss Willis, Bath, April 26, p. 68.

67. Matt Bramble to Dr. Lewis, Bath, April 23, pp. 63, 66.

68. Matt Bramble to Dr. Lewis, Bath, April 28, pp. 75–76.

69. Jery Melford to Sir Watkins Phillips, Bath, April 30, p. 78.

70. Matt Bramble to Dr. Lewis, London, May 20, pp. 118–19. *Kibes* is a Welsh word, here used figuratively, for swollen, inflamed, and sometimes ulcerated sores on the feet.

71. Smollett was always deeply concerned about the eighteenth-century vice of luxury, which, as John Sekora has rightly observed, becomes a central theme in his last novel. One might in fact argue, as Sekora comes close to doing, that Smollett's obsessive satire of excess throughout his career derives from his consciousness that the corrupting desire to possess more than one has—of money, material things, position, power, influence—is the most pernicious of all social evils. See Sekora, *Luxury: The Concept in Western Thought, Eden to Smollett* (Baltimore, Md.: The Johns Hopkins University Press, 1977).

72. London, May 31, p. 124.

73. Matt Bramble to Dr. Lewis, London, May 20, p. 121.

74. Matt Bramble to Dr. Lewis, Edinburgh, July 18, pp. 255, 256.

75. Matt Bramble to Dr. Lewis, Cameron, Aug. 28, p. 286.

76. Lydia Melford to Miss Laetitia Willis, Oct. 4, p. 348.

77. Jery Melford to Sir Watkins Phillips, Bath, April 30, pp. 78-83.

78. Jery describes the visit to Court in a long letter to Sir Watkins Phillips from London, June 2, pp. 126–33; the quotation is from p. 130. Byron Gassman has argued at length that in *Humphry Clinker* Smollett actually echoed the hopes for good government that many Englishmen entertained upon the accession of George III, only to have them promptly dashed by the reality of his failed leadership. The episode at St. James's is thus crucial to the novel's pursuit of political as well as social satire. See "*Humphry Clinker* and the Two Kingdoms of George III," *Criticism* 16 (1974), 95–108.

79. Jery Melford to Sir Watkins Phillips, London, June 10, p. 156. Smollett actually held such gatherings regularly at his London home, and they were attended by many a poor scribbler eager to enjoy his generous hospitality.

# Howard Anderson

## Structure, Language, Experience in the Novels of Laurence Sterne

*Tristram Shandy* and *A Sentimental Journey*[1] are surprises waiting for readers. "I wish either my father or my mother, or indeed both of them, as they were in duty both equally bound to it, had minded what they were about when they begot me. . . . " Tristram's first words to us are urgent, without context, unintroduced. Here is Yorick: "They order, said I, this matter better in France." What the matter is, we have no present way of knowing; our route of discovery is to accompany him on his hasty journey across the Channel.

These initial surprises, anticipatory of greater ones, are Sterne's characteristic mode of approach, and not only in the novels. Consider the opening of the sermon which, though he had himself preached it ten years earlier, he ascribes to Parson Yorick when inserting it in the second volume of *Tristram Shandy*: "For we *trust* we have a good conscience" (II.xvii.88). Here Walter Shandy's response is a sort of surrogate for the reader's,[2] no doubt emulating that of many of those assembled to hear the sermon when the Reverend Mr. Sterne addressed the congregation at the cathedral church of York. Tristram's father is critical of the tone in which the text is read: "Certainly, *Trim*, quoth my father, interrupting him, you give that sentence a very improper accent; for you curl up your nose, man, as if the Parson was going to abuse the Apostle." Walter, the cathedral congregation, and perhaps the reader as well all have ideas about how a scriptural text should be read—preconceptions unlikely to jibe with the skeptical tone Trim gives it. To Walter's embarrassment, however, Trim turns out to have been more fully in touch with Yorick's use of the text than any of the listening company. The context provided by what follows invests the scriptural quotation with a new meaning, different from that furnished by the original passage in the Epistle to the Hebrews—not contradicting, but intensifying it.

Though Walter Shandy acknowledges the error of his assumption within a page or two, he does not usually find it so easy to admit when he is wrong. And for the reader beginning one of Sterne's novels, the narrator's opening gambit may be more alienating than inviting. Like Walter (who often serves as stand-in for our own overconfident intellects), we discover that they are intended to be both. Tristram and Yorick present themselves to us as zanies: Yorick only the more specifically as the kind of traveler who plunges into his life story regardless of the preparation, or wishes, of the person sitting beside him. Wherever we come from as we open these books, there is little chance that we will understand what is happening, and just as little that we will be able to avoid condescending to a speaker who approaches us with such a breathless lack of self-awareness. Our attitude is ensured as Tristram plunges on from that first sentence with a rambling speculation upon the animal spirits (apparently) until we lose sight of the initial subject altogether. Far from pausing to remind us what that was, he drops us into a fragment of a conversation: *"Pray, my dear,* quoth my mother, *have you not forgot to wind up the clock?"* And finally, again nonstop, he concludes this initial chapter with a terse exchange between a putative reader and himself: "Pray, what was your father saying? ———— Nothing." That Mr. Shandy was indeed *saying* nothing is the joke. But it is one that we are barely in a position to get the point of. As we move on, then, our initial condescension may be marked by defensiveness attendant on a dull realization that we do not quite understand what we had thought was so simple.

Many readers never recover from this uncomfortable sense of having been played with by Tristram Shandy, or from the comparable feeling that Yorick is forever one step ahead of us, always leaving us to wonder just where we are as he skips across France and Italy. Those who do recover— that is, those who come to like being played with, rather than resenting it—probably find the remedy partly in the self-recognition these narrators teach us to wrench out of our initial defensiveness and bafflement. Tristram, after evoking responses along the lines I have just sketched, startles us within a couple of pages by showing that he is perfectly aware of his unconventionality and has chosen this unorthodox point of departure self-consciously indeed. Ironically acknowledging his reader's right to be "let into the whole secret from first to last, of every thing which concerns you," he asserts that in beginning with his conception he is politely complying with contemporary taste. The irony is enriched by the fact that we have not been ready to appreciate what he has been letting us into. Then his sophisticated self-awareness emerges, not without ambiguity, as he cites a most respected classical critic as authority for his choice of a starting point: "Right glad I am, that I have begun the history of myself in the way I have done; and that I am able to go on tracing every thing in it, as *Horace* says, *ab Ovo"* (I.iv.4).

Should we be inclined at this point once again to try a laugh at Tristram's expense—remembering that in the *Ars Poetica* Horace commended Homer for *not* starting the *Iliad* with Helen's emergence from the egg, but *in medias res* instead—Tristram catches us: "*Horace*, I know, does not recommend this fashion altogether: But that gentleman is speaking only of an epic poem or a tragedy;————(I forget which)————besides, if it was not so, I should beg Mr. *Horace*'s pardon;————for in writing what I have set about, I shall confine myself neither to his rules, nor to any man's rules that ever lived." The reader by now senses that if anyone lacks self-awareness, it is not Tristram. This narrator's grip on the conventions of storytelling is more secure than our own; the assumptions about narrative procedure that we have gleaned (more or less consciously) from our reading of other books are not entirely adequate preparation for reading this one. Specifically, we are led to consider the limitations of conventional beginnings—how few there are, and how arbitrary—and to grant that Tristram's, which at first seemed merely random, is both *ab Ovo* and *in medias res*. More important, it may well be connected with what is to follow in ways we cannot anticipate. His concept of conception, while eccentric, begins to speak to us. In short, questioning Tristram's judgment leads us to question our own. Willingly or not, we start to see the need of accepting guidance from the teller in making out the tale. *Tristram Shandy* exemplifies the impulse and the necessity of unconventional narrative to teach us how to read it as we go along. In the process, we learn a good deal about reading in general and, at the same time, about our relation to experience outside of books.

The opening of *A Sentimental Journey* is equally sudden. Sterne's habit of immersing the reader in a conversation (indeed *in medias res*) has the effect it always has in *Tristram Shandy*, pushing us to flail about for a context, for other words to give meaning to the ones we are hearing. Who is speaking? Is he really saying that he sets off for France merely in order to put himself into a position of authority on what the French "order better"? And what *is* that? What is the purpose of this trip? Again it is hard to imagine a more arbitrary jumping-off point. By conventional narrative standards, this speaker does not exist for us at all; yet who can deny the impression of life and vigor—the presence—of whoever he is? Readers are challenged to resist, but again, whether altogether willingly or not, we are unlikely to escape being carried along by the persuasive power of Yorick's voice. Perhaps most important, it is nearly impossible to avoid the curiosity and questioning that *engage* us in conversation with Yorick as they do with Tristram. In this novel there is much less discussion of narrative method than in the earlier book; Sterne may in fact have depended to a considerable extent on Tristram to teach us how to listen to Yorick. But in both books the process and the purpose of the experience are similar. A reader's expectations (at whatever level of consciousness) are baffled by the lack of contexts usually taken for granted; the bafflement fuels a search for meaning; the search in turn leads to recognition of our dependence on the narrator—or better, our engagement with him—in a journey of discovery.

The desire for meaning, the recognition of context as the provider of meaning and of conversational intercourse as the means to context—this is the pattern of the experience Sterne engages us in and of what he has to teach us. Sterne can never force us to like the experience or the lesson, but his narrators do their best to win our participation by mocking challenges to our self-reliance and, on the other hand, insinuating appeals to our confidence. As early as the sixth chapter of his first volume, Tristram slips from the former to the latter mode in his first open acknowledgement that his aims require our cooperation:

> In the beginning of the last chapter, I inform'd you exactly *when* I was born;———but I did not inform you, *how. No;* that particular was reserved entirely for a chapter by itself;———besides Sir, as you and I are in a manner perfect strangers to each other, it would not have been proper to have let you into too many circumstances relating to myself all at once.———You must have a little patience. I have undertaken, you see, to write not only my life, but my opinions also; hoping and expecting that your knowledge of my character, and of what kind of a mortal I am, by the one, would give you a better relish for the other: As you proceed further with me, the slight acquaintance which is now beginning betwixt us, will terminate in friendship.____*O diem praeclarum!*____then nothing which has touched me will be thought trifling in its nature, or tedious in its telling. Therefore, my dear friend and companion, if you should think me somewhat sparing of my narrative on my first setting out,____bear with me,____and let me go on, and tell my story my own way:____or if I should seem now and then to trifle upon the road,____or should sometimes put on a fool's cap with a bell to it, for a moment or two as we pass along,____don't fly off,____but rather courteously give me credit for a little more wisdom than appears upon my outside;____and as we jogg on, either laugh with me, or at me, or in short do any thing,____only keep your temper.   (I.vi.6-7)

Beginning with ironic modesty (he has already let us into more details about his origins than a "proper" teller would do), the passage emerges from irony in its straightforward statement that the narrative depends on our tolerance and good nature. The development and exercise of those faculties, indeed, turn out to be a prime purpose shaping the experience. We undergo steady pressure to fly off from Tristram's annoyingly erratic narrative. Only "True *Shandeism*" can make us willing to keep reading, as it "opens the heart and lungs, and like all those affections which partake of its nature . . . forces the blood and other vital fluids of the body to run freely thro' its channels, and makes the wheel of life run long and chearfully round" (IV.xxxii.237).

"True Shandeism" is analogous to the "sentiment" through which Yorick appeals and which he attempts to communicate to his reader. Both are grounded in patience, good temper, tolerance, which in turn imply sympathy, consideration, fellow-feeling, capacities for love. In the preface that Yorick pauses to write while seated in a *desobligeant* at Calais, he establishes the premise that "the balance of sentimental commerce is always against the expatriated adventurer" (p. 78). The odds against the exercise of sentiment are not unlike those against Shandean good humor. The foreign world insists on levying inconvenience and petty hardship upon the traveler: "He must buy what he has little occasion for at their own price———his conversation will seldom be taken in exchange for theirs without a large discount———." As in *Tristram Shandy*, obstacles to communication stand at the center of the problem, with selfishness and intolerance the prime causes.

Yorick's attempt to overcome barriers to communication issues from his definition of himself as a "Sentimental Traveller," in contrast to a long list of alternatives, but particularly (and repeatedly), the Splenetic (pp. 81–82). "Spleen and jaundice" are the objects against which he most consistently aims his lance as he makes his quixotic way across the landscape. "Smelfungus" epitomizes the prejudiced and angry traveler whose only response to new experience is resentment that it is different from the old: "The learned **SMELFUNGUS** travelled from Boulogne to Paris____from Paris to Rome____and so on____but he set out with the spleen and jaundice, and every object he pass'd by was discoloured or distorted———He wrote an account of them, but 'twas nothing but the account of his miserable feelings" (p. 116). To nurture the conversation without which there is no communication, Yorick enlists sentiment as Tristram relied on Shandeism: variant forms of the good nature that can connect human beings.

## I

We have begun to see that these narratives constitute tests for the examination and exercise of these capacities in the reader. In *A Sentimental Journey* as in *Tristram Shandy,* these tests of our patience and of our expansive potential appear most regularly in departures from straightforward narrative into digressions (Tristram) and flights of sentiment (Yorick).

The events upon which Tristram's "Life" is based are few and unhappy. His conception, we have observed, is scattered. When he finally emerges from the womb, it is with the dubious aid of a forceps that crushes his nose. His christening, where his father hopes to endow him with a lucky name, results in the opposite: the name he gets means "the sad one."[3] Still a little boy, he is the victim of a falling window sash that (at the very least) circumcises him as he aims to relieve himself one night. At the end of the book, his parents are still debating whether or not it is time to put the child into trousers. These barren facts might be neatly summed up by Hobbes's famous description of life in a state of nature—"nasty, brutish, and short." Tristram himself, just before the chapter begging the reader to "keep your temper," has described the world he was brought forth into as "scurvy and disasterous":

> I wish I had been born in the Moon, or in any of the planets . . .
> for it could not well have fared worse with me in any of them . . .
> than it has in this vile, dirty planet of ours,_____which o' my
> conscience, with reverence be it spoken, I take to be made up of
> the shreds and clippings of the rest . . . for which cause I affirm it
> over again to be one of the vilest worlds that ever was
> made;_____for I can truly say, that from the first hour I drew my
> breath in it, to this, that I can now scarce draw it at all, for an
> asthma I got scating against the wind in *Flanders;*_____I have
> been the continual sport of what the world calls Fortune; and
> though I will not wrong her by saying, She has ever made me feel
> the weight of any great or signal evil;———yet with all the good
> temper in the world, I affirm it of her, That in every stage of my
> life, and at every turn and corner where she could get fairly at me,
> the ungracious Duchess has pelted me with a set of as pitiful
> misadventures and cross accidents as ever small HERO
> sustained.   (I.v. 5–6)

The dismal facts of Tristram's life are interspersed among rambling digressions that interrupt and disconcert the reader in quest of a story much as Mrs. Shandy's question jarred her husband's concentration at the book's (and Tristram's) outset. By the usual criterion of narrative connection—cause and effect—their relevance seems indecipherable. To speak just of the first volume, our expectation that Tristram's conception will lead to his birth is foiled by the story of Yorick and the midwife, by a facsimile of the Shandy's marriage settlement, by the insertion of a pronouncement by the Doctors of the Sorbonne concerning prenatal baptism, and by a long description of Uncle Toby's character as it is elucidated by his response to the story of Aunt Dinah and the coachman. Yet as we look back (which is what Tristram is doing all along), we can see that the material of these digressions does indeed connect with Tristram's life. While all of it centers in other people, all of it affects the conditions of Tristram's birth. This narrator, then, pushes us to contemplate a scheme of cause and effect more esoterically complex than those we have been taught to look for in fiction or in life. When Tristram pauses near the end of Volume I to congratulate himself on what his method has accomplished, we must, perhaps grudgingly, concur that

> in this long digression which I was accidentally led into, as in all
> my digressions (one only excepted) there is a master-stroke of
> digressive skill, the merit of which has all along, I fear, been over-
> looked by my reader,_____not for want of penetration in
> him,_____but because 'tis an excellence seldom looked for, or
> expected indeed, in a digression;_____and it is this: That tho' my
> digressions are all fair, as you observe,_____and that I fly off from
> what I am about, as far and as often too as any writer in *Great
> Britain;* yet I constantly take care to order affairs so, that my
> main business does not stand still in my absence.   (I.xxii.51)

What is to happen to Tristram Shandy has been decided in the lives of other people; to tell of *their* lives and opinions *is* to further the main business of Tristram's book.

At the same time, it is impossible to take Tristram's scheme of cause and effect quite seriously. For instance, we are never fully persuaded that Toby's embarrassed recoil from ideas associated with his aunt's elopement is a more decisive cause of Tristram's troubles than any of a thousand others—all of which remain undiscovered in his past and unrealized in his imagination. Tristram's search for the reasons why he is what he is persuades us instead that it is the search that matters, and what he makes of what he finds. In this way, *Tristram Shandy* comically subverts the solemn foundation of empiricism by disputing the hegemony of factual cause and effect in fiction and in life. First among the rules whose authority he disputes whenever the chance arises—"Is man to follow rules_____or rules to follow him?"—mechanical causation draws Tristram's subversive energy. The epigraph from Epictetus with which the novel sets out points to the importance of this theme: "It is not things that disturb men, but their judgments about things."

But Tristram does not merely put in question the precedence of facts in the causal hierarchy by implying that one will serve as well as another and by burying the conventionally important one under a heap of the esoteric; the effect of such a process is to reduce the unhappy events to the merest framework for an expansive comic structure. Tristram's life in outline is the material of tragedy, at least of domestic tragedy; for if he has not (as he admits) suffered any "great or signal evil," what he has undergone none-theless provides sufficient reason for bitterness. His "pitiful misadven-tures and cross accidents" are of a private nature, but to have his face disfigured by the loss of his nose—not to mention the diminution admin-istered by the falling window—would in itself be enough to sour many men on life.

Instead, like a Shakespeare alternately bringing tragedy and comedy out of parallel material in *Romeo and Juliet* and *A Midsummer Night's Dream*, Tristram chooses to make his misadventures into comedy. He accomplishes the transformation by planting them in the nurturing con-text of the digressions:

> By this contrivance the machinery of my work is of a species by itself; two contrary motions are introduced into it, and reconciled, which were thought to be at variance with each other. In a word, my work is digressive, and it is progressive too,_____and at the same time.
>
> This, Sir, is a very different story from that of the earth's moving round her axis, in her diurnal rotation . . . though I own it suggested the thought,_____as I believe the greatest of our boasted improvements and discoveries have come from some such trifling hints.
>
> Digressions, incontestably, are the sunshine,_____they are the life, the soul of reading;_____take them out of this book for instance,_____you might as well take the book along with them;_____one cold eternal winter would reign in every page of it; restore them to the writer;_____he steps forth like a

bridegroom,_____bids All hail; brings in variety, and forbids the
appetite to fail. (I.xxii.52)

The grandeur of the images Tristram applies to his work is as self-mocking
as it is heroic, but the images are appropriate nonetheless: a man's life may
indeed be pictured by its parallels to a cosmic system that moves in several
orbits at once (despite appearances to the contrary). The image of digressions as the life-giving sunshine is even more compelling: the cold facts of
Tristram's life, as of every life, are simple, and heading deathward (with or
without the aid of "an asthma got scating against the wind in *Flanders*").
So, Tristram shows, what matters is not the facts, but what he makes of
them.

In Volume IV, Tristram denies that his book is intended as an attack on
"predestination, or free will, or taxes," asserting instead that "if 'tis wrote
against any thing,———'tis wrote, an' please your worships, against the
spleen" (IV.xxii.218). I should say that in so directing his book, he does
indeed distinguish the aspects of life where determinism applics from
those in which we have choice. Tristram cannot choose to be undamaged
by forceps or window sash; no act of will or imagination will free him from
his asthma, or from the death that follows on its heels in Volume VII. But
he can and does choose how he will see them—with patience, good
temper, tolerance, and humor. Opting for a vision (and a principle of
narrative selection) that fences against the spleen, he achieves a healthy
and life-giving perspective:

> If 'tis wrote against any thing,_____'tis wrote . . . against the
> spleen; in order, by a more frequent and a more convulsive
> elevation and depression of the diaphragm, and the succussations
> of the intercostal and abdominal muscles in laughter, to drive the
> *gall* and other *bitter juices* from the gall bladder, liver and sweet-
> bread of his majesty's subjects, with all the inimicitious passions
> which belong to them, down into their duodenums. (IV.xxii.218)

So Tristram Shandy's "digressive artistry"[4] is by no means merely
decorative. It is the blood nourishing a *self* created with his art. In this it
parallels the integral function of sentiment in Yorick's *Sentimental Journey* and in his identity. Another way of putting it is to say that sentiment is
to Yorick's journey what opinions are to Tristram's life. And just as that
"life" frequently took perceptible shape against patterns established by
fictional convention, so the "journey" reflects against conventional travel
narratives and guidebooks, popular since before the eighteenth century.
Such works concentrate on the local sights (*videnda*), often with ex-

cruciating circumstantiality—precisely how wide and long is the Piazza San Marco, how tall the Campanile, and so on. Their circumstantiality— feeding the modern passion for facts (compare what we have just seen in *Tristram Shandy*)—had often lent itself to parody and, by extension, to satire excoriating the reduction of the *real* to the brutally material. *Gulliver's Travels* is the preeminent example of this kind of parody and satire. While probably no reader in 1768 came to a work written by the celebrated Laurence Sterne anticipating a conventional travel book— Volume VII of *Tristram Shandy* had already parodied the form—Yorick's unique definition of sentiment exerts its demand in opposition to the simpler visual and muscular capacities required by conventional tours and encouraged by conventional tour books.

Sterne's own "asthma"—in reality the tuberculosis that would cause his death just after the publication of *A Sentimental Journey*—inspired his trips to southern France and Italy between 1762 and 1766. In Volume VII of *Tristram Shandy*, published in 1765, he had already written what he called "a laughing good temperd Satyr against Traveling (as puppies travel)."[5] As Gardner Stout has shown, Sterne's distinctively different treatment of some of the same materials in *A Sentimental Journey* (different in the ways he covers the same ground) was due in part to a shift in popular and critical taste (Introduction, p. 10). Ralph Griffiths, a spokesman for those who had grown "indifferent to the oddities and hostile to the indecencies of Vols. III–VIII," wrote in the *Monthly Review* of February 1765:

> One of our gentlemen once remarked, in *print* Mr. Shandy—that he thought your excellence lay in the PATHETIC. I think so too.
> . . . Give us none but amiable or worthy, or exemplary characters; or, if you will, to enliven the drama, throw in the *innocently humorous*. . . . Paint Nature in her loveliest dress—her native simplicity. Draw natural scenes, and interesting situations—In fine, Mr. Shandy, do, for surely you can, excite our passions to *laudable* purposes—awake our affections, engage our hearts— arouze, transport, refine, improve us. Let morality, let cultivation of virtue be your aim—let wit, humour, elegance and pathos be the means; and the grateful applause of mankind will be your reward.

The sentimental, blending pathos and elegance, is less often pierced by witty ambiguities in Yorick's travels than in Tristram's. And as Griffiths's recommendations indicate, Yorick's excursions into sentiment were un- likely to meet the bafflement, or downright resistance, that Tristram's digressions invited. Nevertheless, Sterne again gives the sentimental elements of the journey their shape by placing them in contrast to the results of more mundane journeys:

> By sending Tristram on a Shandean variation of the Grand Tour governed by the principles of laughter and good humor, rather than by the spleen, Sterne took an important step toward Yorick's *Journey*. And by diverting Tristram from the beaten track of his forerunners in order to demonstrate that such digressions can lead to delightful experiences . . . he indicated the route which Yorick, the Sentimental Traveller, was to take.   (Stout, Introduction, p. 11)

Chief among the predecessors whom Sterne employs as a running foil to his moving scene is Tobias Smollett. Already established as a novelist and as editor of the *Critical Review,* Smollett had published in 1766 his own *Travels through France and Italy.* A physician before he was a writer, Smollett was even more aware than most travelers of the unsanitary conditions he encountered, the daily filth taken for granted by the people he traveled among. It is hardly saying too much to call him obsessed with these sordid facts of life in France and Italy (and *Humphry Clinker,* published in 1771, shows him equally appalled by comparable outrages in Great Britain). Smollett was in bad health when he went abroad, which gave him reason to be especially impatient of inconvenience—but again left him open to contrast with tubercular, humorous Sterne. Even the most universally admired *videnda* arouse only his grudging appreciation; in an infamous passage he reluctantly describes his partial admiration of the Venus de Medici at Florence:

> I believe I ought to be entirely silent, or at least conceal my real sentiments, which will otherwise appear equally absurd and presumptuous. It must be want of taste that prevents my feeling that enthusiastic admiration with which others are inspired at sight of this statue. . . . I cannot help thinking that there is no beauty in the features of Venus. . . . Without all doubt, the limbs . . . are elegantly formed, and accurately designed, according to the nicest rules of symmetry and proportion; and the back parts especially are executed so happily, as to excite the admiration of the most indifferent spectator.[6]

Such a target was too much for Sterne. This is the living figure who lurks behind the allegorical Smelfungus:

> I met Smelfungus in the grand portico of the Pantheon_____he was just coming out of it_____ *'Tis nothing but a huge cock-pit,*

> said he_____I wish you had said nothing worse of the Venus of
> Medicis, replied I_____for in passing through Florence, I had
> heard one had fallen foul upon the goddess, and used her worse
> than a common strumpet, without the least provocation in
> nature.   (pp. 117–18)

Set against such a foil, Yorick's sentimental response to feminine beauty
and spirit is uniquely striking. While the Splenetic Traveller diminishes
the established beauties of the places he visits, the Sentimental one
occupies himself in seeking out those as yet undiscovered.

Unconcerned whether the backsides of statues are "accurately designed" or not, Yorick experiences his most memorable encounters with
living human beings. Most of them are women, of course—Madame de R,
Maria at Moulines, the Fille de Chambre, the Grisset whose pulse he feels:

> I am sure you must have one of the best pulses of any woman in
> the world———Feel it, said she, holding out her arm. So laying
> down my hat, I took hold of her fingers in one hand, and applied
> the two fore-fingers of my other to the artery_____
>
> _____Would to heaven! my dear Eugenius, thou hadst passed
> by, and beheld me sitting in my black coat, and in my lack-a-day-
> sical manner, counting the throbs of it, one by one, with as much
> true devotion as if I had been watching the critical ebb or flow of
> her fever_____How wouldst thou have laugh'd and moralized
> upon my new profession?_____Trust me, my dear Eugenius, I
> should have said, "there are worse occupations in this world than
> feeling a woman's pulse." (pp. 164–65)

This sentimental foray off the beaten track might be open to the charges of
indecency that critics like Griffith had levied against the later volumes of
*Tristram Shandy*—and the charges have been made. But by juxtaposing his
physical-emotional intercourse with women like the Grisset against the
bloodless perverseness of a Smelfungus, Sterne makes Yorick's digressions
into the byways look attractively human.

Furthermore, just as Tristram's digressive artistry manages at the same
time to be progressive, Yorick's sentimental experiences are ends in themselves *and* expand his consciousness toward further ends. The incident
with the Grisset contributes to his discernment of qualities distinguishing the French from the English. When the young woman's husband enters
and complacently observes Yorick's intimacy with his wife, the Sentimental Traveller takes the opportunity to reflect that, while "in London a
shopkeeper and a shopkeeper's wife seem to be one bone and one flesh . . .

in Paris, there are scarce two orders of beings more different: for the legislative and executive powers of the shop not resting in the husband, he seldom comes there———in some dark and dismal room behind, he sits commerceless in his thrum night-cap, the same rough son of Nature that Nature left him" (p. 166).

Yorick's inclination to promote tolerance of foreign mores might be construed here as a stance favorable to his own sexual interests. And in fact it does serve his interests to be uncritical of what might be considered lax or even corrupt by a tougher moralist. But his bemused acceptance, even enjoyment, of foreign ways extends also to behavior which might affront his delicate sensual enjoyment. In a passage that seems first to allude to Shandean hobbyhorses, he remarks:

> It is alike troublesome to both rider and his beast____if the latter goes pricking up his ears, and starting all the way at every object which he never saw before____I have as little torment of this as any creature alive; and yet I honestly confess that many a thing gives me pain, and that I blush'd at many a word the first month____which I found inconsequent and perfectly innocent the second.
>
> Madame de Rambouliet, after an acquaintance of about six weeks with her, had done me the honour to take me in her coach about two leagues out of town____Of all women, Madame de Rambouliet is the most correct; and I never wish to see one of more virtues and purity of heart____In our return back, Madame de Rambouliet desired me to pull the cord____I ask'd her if she wanted any thing____*Rien que pisser*, said Madame de Rambouliet—
>
> Grieve not, gentle traveller, to let Madame de Rambouliet p—ss on____And ye fair mystic nymphs! go each one *pluck your rose*. (pp. 181–83)

In this case, Yorick's digression is superficially *anti*sentimental. Yet while it does not conform to the popular demand for the "elegant" and the "pathetic," Yorick's response embodies his steady insistence that true sentiment be grounded in acceptance and sympathy. And again, these qualities take on definition as characteristic of the Sentimental Traveller when placed against an early letter among those in Smollett's *Travels*, where he fumes (at much greater length than I will quote): "Will custom exempt from the imputation of gross indecency a French lady, who shifts her frowsy smock in presence of a male visitant, and talks to him of her *lavement*, her *medecine*, and her *bidet!*" (p. 35).

Finally, the passage provides another example of the general purpose motivating Yorick's journey: the comparison of foreign manners and customs. While Madame de Rambouliet's manner of expressing her physical need may not "order this matter better" than if she had called it plucking a rose, Yorick's point is that both expressions are equally a matter of linguistic custom. Neither way of speaking is morally superior—though we may suspect that he favors the more direct expression. Beyond that, we may sense that the willingness of a woman of Madame de Rambouliet's character to acknowledge her physicality without blushing circumlocution confirms Yorick in his deepest purpose: the integration of his physical, emotional, and spiritual being.

Smollett, as a model for the Splenetic Traveller, is only the most noted and frequent foil to Yorick. The characterization of the Sentimental Traveller takes shape also in contrast to the Vain or Proud Traveller (among the types listed in the preface written in the *desobligeant*). "Mundungus, with an immense fortune," is a notable example of such a traveler: he "made the whole tour . . . without one generous connection or pleasurable anecdote to tell of; but he had travell'd straight on looking neither to his right hand or his left, lest Love or Pity should seduce him out of his road" (p. 119). Such total insulation from his fellowmen would be hard for Yorick to accomplish even if he wanted to, as necessity requires that he bargain for vehicles and accommodations. But just as the contrast with Smelfungus stresses the moral benefits of tolerant good humor, so placing Yorick against Mundungus defines the value of sympathy and fellow feeling. Mundungus has the attributes of the selfish man whom Sterne had described in a sermon on the Good Samaritan, which he published as one of the *Sermons of Mr. Yorick* in 1760. This "sordid wretch," in contrast to the Samaritan himself,

> goes to the end of his days, in the same selfish track in which he first set out . . . as if afraid to look up, lest peradventure he should see aught which might turn him one moment out of that straight line where interest is carrying him_____or if, by chance, he stumbles upon a hapless object of distress . . . unwilling to hazard the inconveniences which pity might lead him into upon the occasion.[7]

Sterne chose in *A Sentimental Journey* to capitalize upon the fashionable taste for sentiment that he had himself been most instrumental in establishing. But Yorick's essays in the sentimental do not confine themselves merely to the elegant and pathetic qualities which for readers like Griffiths constituted the meaning of the concept. Sympathy, grounded in the good temper and tolerance that make it possible, is the soul of Yorick's sentimental response to the figures he encounters as he crosses the landscapes of France and Italy. The Sentimental Traveller's manners are striking, but it is generous spirit that finally distinguishes him from Smelfungus and Mundungus, even as it allows him to grant them pitying acceptance:

> Peace be to them! if it is to be found; but heaven itself, was it possible to get there with such tempers, would want objects to give it_____every gentle spirit would come flying upon the wings of Love to hail their arrival_____Nothing would the souls of Smelfungus and Mundungus hear of, but fresh anthems of joy, fresh raptures of love, and fresh congratulations of their common felicity_____I heartily pity them: they have brought up no faculties for this work; and was the happiest mansion in heaven to be allotted to Smelfungus and Mundungus, they would be so far from being happy, that the souls of Smelfungus and Mundungus would do penance there to all eternity. (p. 120)

## II

For both Tristram and Yorick, then, "experience is the force that mediates between the human character and its hidden destiny"; Wolfgang Iser's potent description of what happens in *Pilgrim's Progress* applies equally to the relations between Sterne's storytellers and their unique, but communicable, experience.[8] "Character" in this sense constitutes inherited capacities—the modes of seeing and feeling that Tristram receives from his father and uncle and mother; Yorick's innate self-gratifying inclination to spend two livres a bottle for wine and his perverse reluctance to give much to charity.

"Destiny" remains elusive for Tristram and Yorick as for everybody else. But it manifests itself in events like the ones we have seen descend upon Tristram; it is finally embodied in Death, which pursues him across the Channel in Book VII and lies in wait for him and Yorick somewhere beyond the last pages of their narratives. And "experience"? That is even harder to pin down; but so far in this inquiry it has begun to emerge from the narrators' efforts to get beyond their inherited and innate limitations, both physical and spiritual. It takes form as they resist and move beyond the impulse to settle bitterly for the conditions they are born to—an effort that the likes of Smelfungus in both books decidedly do not make.

We have noticed that the abiding purpose of the digressions in the two books is connective. Tristram's carry him toward the men (and occasionally women) who inhabit his past, and simultaneously into conversation with the reader. Both these complementary motions serve to establish and connect him with himself, as well. Yorick's sentimental impulses are similarly communicative and reflexive. I should like to consider now the central part that Sterne's language—more specifically, his conscious *view* of language—plays in the integrative "experience" that Sterne embodies in the digressive progress of his two novels.

Sterne's verbal associationism is the most notorious linguistic feature of *Tristram Shandy*. From Samuel Richardson, who called it "too gross to be inflaming,"⁹ to F.R. Leavis, for whom Sterne's "irresponsible (and nasty) trifling" was reason enough to leave him out of *The Great Tradition*,¹⁰ double-entendre has been the chief target of hostile critics. "Give up your Long Noses . . . your Andoüillets . . . try your strength another way . . . Mr. Shandy," begged Ralph Griffiths in the letter I quoted from earlier. But while to such readers Sterne's irrepressible play on words seems only a tasteless ornament, verbal associationism is in fact vital to what Tristram aims to discover and reveal.

We should begin by recognizing that sexual double-entendre is only one of the forms of associationism that pervade the book; its function, as we shall see, is to connect narrator and reader. Meanwhile, Tristram's father and uncle are engaged in their private obsessions, or hobby-horses, based in associations of ideas that give individual words radically contradictory meanings for each of them. The following exchange is exemplary:

> To understand what *time* is aright [begins Walter Shandy] . . .
> we ought seriously to sit down and consider what idea it is, we
> have of duration. . . . In our computations of *time*, we are so used
> to minutes, hours, weeks, and months,_____and of clocks (I wish
> there was not a clock in the kingdom) to measure out their
> several portions to us . . . that 'twill be well, if in time to come,
> the *succession of our ideas* be of any use or service to us at all.
>
> Now, whether we observe it or no, continued my father, in
> every sound man's head, there is a regular succession of ideas of
> one sort or other, which follow each other in train just like
> _____A train of artillery? said my uncle Toby._____A train of a
> fiddle stick!_____quoth my father.   (III.xviii.138–39)

Uncle Toby, the old soldier entirely preoccupied with warfare and fortification, seizes upon the first word that makes sense to him in his brother's dissertation. Simultaneously, Walter, obsessed with categorizing phenomena and winning arguments, is furious that Toby invests "train" with a meaning dragged in from the language of war.

Sterne's play on the power of verbal association to block, rather than promote, communication early won him credit as a Lockean.[11] For Locke, "a natural correspondence and connexion" between ideas characterizes normal thought, as he describes its processes in *An Essay concerning Human Understanding*, the work that established the direction of modern epistemology. In a chapter added to the fourth edition, he distinguishes this "natural correspondence" from those misconceptions of "chance or custom" that give rise to mental aberration:

> Ideas that in themselves are not all of a kind, come to be so
> united in some men's minds, that it is very hard to separate them;
> they always keep in company, and the one no sooner at any time
> comes into the understanding, but its associate appears with it;
> and if they are more than two which are thus united the whole
> gang, always inseparable, show themselves together.[12]

Such aberration Locke calls "by so harsh a name as madness," for "opposition to reason deserves that name" (I:528). It is the intrusion of this madness that we have just observed in Toby. More specifically, Tristram tells us as he begins his account of Toby's hobbyhorse, it is not ideas as such, but *words* that cause Toby trouble—the fact that the same words convey different ideas to different people (II.ii.62).

Toby's hobbyhorsical associations, in collision with Walter's through most of the novel and with the Widow Wadman's in Volumes VIII and IX, provide much of the comedy of the book. This emphasis on Toby's hobbyhorse, with the fact that nearly all the other characters (Yorick and Trim excepted) have their own comparable obsessions, implies that such "madness" is more common than Locke seems to allow. With the good-natured tolerance characteristic of him, Tristram asserts from the start that so long as they do not harm other people, he has nothing against hobbyhorses:

> If you come to that, Sir, have not the wisest men in all ages, not
> excepting *Solomon* himself,_____have they not had their
> HOBBY-HORSES_____their running horses,_____their coins and
> their cockle-shells, their drums and their trumpets, their fiddles,
> their pallets,_____their maggots and their butterflies?_____and
> so long as a man rides his HOBBY-HORSE peaceably and quietly
> along the King's highway, and neither compels you or me to get up

behind him,_____pray, Sir, what have either you or I to do with
it?  (I.vii.8)

Some of them, however, *do* harm others: Tristram's satire on the hobbyhorses of public figures and of professionals whose selfish preoccupa-
tions take precedence over their responsibilities is a cutting counterpoint
to the generous warmth and humor we have looked at. But his dominating
point about hobbyhorses seems to be that as no one is immune, we had
better understand their etiology in order to avoid being trapped like the
Shandys.

Tristram can be said to inherit the linguistic naiveté of his uncle and
father and the solipsism it leads to as his fundamental problems. The
verbal sophistication that liberates him emerges from close attention to
his own responses and those of other men and women. His observations
form experience useful in salvaging his damaged family heritage. The
story of the fate of the word *whiskers* at the Court of Navarre is an instance
of how Tristram learns, and transmits his experience with language to us:

> *La Guyol, La Maronette, La Sabatiere,* fell in love with the Sieur
> *de Croix* . . ._____*La Rebours* and *La Fosseuse* knew
> better_____*De Croix* had failed in an attempt to recommend
> himself to *La Rebours;* and *La Rebours* and *La Fosseuse* were
> inseparable.
>
> The queen of *Navarre* was sitting with her ladies . . . as *De
> Croix* passed. . . . He is handsome, said the Lady
> Baussiere._____He has a good mien, said *La Battarelle.*_____He
> is finely shaped, said *La Guyol.*_____I never saw an officer of the
> horse-guards in my life, said *La Maronette,* with two such
> legs_____Or who stood so well upon them, said *La
> Sabatiere*_____But he has no whiskers, cried *La
> Fosseuse*_____Not a pile, said *La Rebours.*   (V.i.241)

Such is the potency of the word *whiskers* that it is soon impossible for the
handsome cavalier to hold up his head—he "found it high time to leave
*Navarre* for want of whiskers"—and the word "in course became indecent" (V.i.243).

The lesson Tristram draws from his parable is one he reiterates, with
variations, from the time the forceps crushes his nose. In every case,
parallels with sexual shapes endow our response to the objects named
with energy, ensuring attention: "There are some trains of certain ideas
which leave prints of themselves about our eyes and eye-brows; and there
is a consciousness of it, somewhere about the heart, which serves but to

make these etchings the stronger———we see, spell, and put them together without a dictionary" (V.i.242). Because Sterne can count on his
readers' participation in sexual interests, whether or not we will admit to
it, words with sexual connotations provide his surest means of teaching us
that language is radically connotative and symbolic.

Sterne wrote in a century that saw the publication of the first dictionaries, with their implication that the main function of language is the
denotation, naming, of objects. Following Locke, even the inner processes
by which objects are perceived are themselves objectified and, as it were,
pinned down with a name. Tristram repeatedly attacks such a conception
of language, insisting that words are defined in use by human beings who
express themselves and communicate with one another. For the ladies at
the Court of Navarre, as for Tristram and us, the connection between facial
hair and more primary sexual characteristics invests first the hair and then
its name with symbolic connotations. In the more famous instance of the
word "nose," correspondences in physiological shape affect the sexual
connection, so that the word carries meanings that can be summoned up
merely by Tristram's insistent emphasis.

The chapter on noses (III.xxii) is a succinct exercise in the power of
context and expressive tone to determine meaning. The more Tristram
attempts to clarify his meaning, the greater the ambiguity:

> I define a nose, as follows [he concludes],———intreating only
> beforehand, and beseeching my readers, both male and female, of
> what age, complexion, and condition soever, for the love of God
> and their own souls, to guard against the temptations and
> suggestions of the devil, and suffer him by no art or wile to put
> any other ideas into their minds, than what I put into my
> definition.———For by the word *Nose*, throughout all this long
> chapter of noses, and in every part of my work, where the word
> *Nose* occurs,———I declare, by that word I mean a Nose, and
> nothing more, or less.   (p. 159)

The last two words of the chapter are a supreme example of Tristram's skill
in teaching us how our minds work through verbal play.[13] Because our
perceptions are inclined to fuse things in our minds through parallels of
some of their qualities, the power of language lies not in its denotative
rigor but rather in connotative and symbolic expressiveness. Sterne's
double-entendres constitute a short course in poetry, initiating the reader
(accustomed to dictionaries) into the principles of symbolism, which is
the mainstay of his effort to communicate with us in *Tristram Shandy*. We
perceive, whether we want to or not, that the word *nose* speaks of more

than one thing at once. Equally important, we engage with Tristram as he speaks the word to us, acknowledging (with amusement or impatience) that what it means is between us.

Sterne's "irresponsible (and nasty) trifling," then, amounts to a concentrated justification of wit, which Hobbes described as the capacity to notice similarities in things otherwise much unlike. Wit requires seeing together, urging recognition of shared perception. For Locke, its value was decisively inferior to that of judgment, which links things on the basis only of marked similarities and separates them by equally marked differences; judgment, then, is the basis of the scientific method. Locke attacks wit and fancy together as "abuses of words" that have no proper use but for trivial ornamentation:

> Since wit and fancy find easier entertainment in the world than dry truth and real knowledge, figurative speeches and allusion in language will hardly be admitted as an imperfection or abuse of it. I confess, in discourses where we seek rather pleasure and delight than information and improvement, such ornaments as are borrowed from them can scarce pass for faults. But yet *if we would speak of things as they are*, we must allow that all the art of rhetoric, besides order and clearness; all the artificial and figurative application of words eloquence hath invented, are for nothing else but to insinuate wrong ideas, move the passions, and thereby mislead the judgment; and so indeed are perfect cheats: and therefore, however laudable or allowable oratory may render them in harangues and popular addresses, they are certainly, in all discourses that pretend to inform or instruct, wholly to be avoided; and where truth and knowledge are concerned, cannot but be thought a great fault, either of the language or person that makes use of them.   (II:46; emphasis added)

Tristram Shandy knows that to deny wit and fancy the capacity to transmit truth and knowledge is to deny literature the serious place it had traditionally occupied as an enricher and instructor of human experience. He gives his best energies to opposing such a move.

In challenging Locke's view, Sterne takes on what was becoming the dominant modern attitude toward literature. Early in the history of Western thought, Plato had attacked poetry as a seducer of the reason; the Sophists had subverted its prestige in developing a program to divorce rhetoric (the pleasing and persuasive elements of language) from logic (language's claims to truth). But Aristotle effectively countered these concepts by arguing that persuasive and true language can and must be fused, that poetry and rhetoric must be grounded in logic and ethics. Thus understood, poetry "holds up the miror to nature," providing an irreplaceable means of seeing ourselves—as mirrors reflect our own faces, invisible except by indirection. Aristotle's powerful image established and described poetry's power from his time through the Renaissance. It is cited in sixteenth-century defenses of poetry (like Sidney's) against the incursions of the Puritans. And its force is typically buttressed by support from Horace's description of poetry as "*dulce et utile.*" The latter retained its influence into the eighteenth century, translated into French by Boileau, for instance (in his much-quoted *Art Poetique*), as "*plaire et instruire,*" and into English as to "instruct by pleasing."

But Locke, the Royal Society that adopted his view, and the whole tendency of empirical philosophy and modern science were all pushing out wit and establishing judgment as the only means to truth. As we have seen, *Tristram Shandy* implicitly opposes this usurpation from its opening page. Then in the "Author's Preface" that Tristram snatches time to write in the middle of Volume III, Sterne directs a full-scale attack against the conception of literature that would reduce his novel (and all others) to mere entertainment. His tone, as usual, is playful, but perhaps more than usually direct:

> All I know of the matter is,——when I sat down, my intent was
> to write a good book; and as far as the tenuity of my
> understanding would hold out,——a wise, aye, and a
> discreet,——taking care only, as I went along, to put into it all
> the wit and judgment (be it more or less) which the great author
> and bestower of them had thought fit originally to give
> me,——so that, as your worships see,——'tis just as God
> pleases.  (III.xx.140)

The critics of his first two volumes agree, he says, that there may be some wit in them, "but no judgment at all . . . for that wit and judgment in this world never go together; inasmuch as they are two operations differing from each other as wide as east is from west." Tristram knows precisely where to lay the blame for this heresy and how to deal with it: "So, says *Locke,*——so are farting and hickuping, say I" (III.xx.141).

His means of retaliation is emblematic of the whole preface—and of the whole novel. The crude but effective figure of speech brilliantly makes his point that wit can reveal truth. Continuing, he argues that wit and judgment are inseparable, that to place one above the other is a modern error. Illustrations, he says, serve mainly to "clarify the understanding, previous to the application of the argument itself, in order to free it from any little motes, or specks of opacular matter, which if left swimming therein, might hinder a conception and spoil all" (III.xx.141). Wit makes it possible to appreciate the infinite connective parallels in creation; judgment distinguishes them, elucidating significant differences, deciding which similarities matter more and less.

Tristram's preface calls attention to itself as a parody of the usual novelistic preface. While it performs the function of such an essay, describing the purpose and method of the larger work, it does so without recourse to the discursive and logical language typical of prefatory essays. In his first two volumes, Sterne had exercised his reader in reasoning by analogy. In the preface he floods us with images that figure forth what the book is about. Tristram justifies his use of witty illustrations *with* an illustration: "wiping the looking glass clean." He defends the inseparability of wit and judgment by leaping up and pointing to the knobs on the back of his chair:

> _____Here stands *wit,*_____and there stands *judgment,* close beside it, just like the two knobbs I'm speaking of. . . . You see, they are the highest and most ornamental parts of its *frame,*_____as wit and judgment are of *ours,* and like them, too, indubitably both made and fitted together, in order as we say in all such cases of duplicated embellishments,_____to *answer one another.* (III.xx.146)

The reader who has been attentive to Tristram through the first two volumes will by this time hear several meanings even in the word "answer." The most obvious in the context of the paragraph—ornamental symmetry—is deepened by the larger context of our experience in the first two volumes. There, "answer" has proved to mean response, lively, irresistible engagement with what we hear from Tristram. To answer is to be in conversation, in communication, in connection.

He sustains the metaphor through two more long paragraphs, weaving an argument radically dependent on the figurative power of language: "It is by these observations, and a wary reasoning by analogy in that kind of argumentative process, which *Suidas* calls *dialectick induction,*——that I draw and set up this position as most true and veritable" (III.xx.144). Calling wit and judgment the "top ornaments of the mind of man, which crown the whole entablature," he asks "who does not wish . . . to be, or to be thought at least master of the one or the other, and indeed of both of them, if the thing seems any way feasible, or likely to be brought to pass" (III.xx.146–47). The reason that men of influence have so surprisingly forgone the effort to gain credit for both wit and judgment is not really hard to find. The "graver gentry," so grave indeed as to have no hope of gaining credit for wit, "raised a hew and cry against the lawful owners." Even "the great *Locke*, who was seldom outwitted by false sounds,—was nevertheless bubbled here" (III.xx.147).

Thus self-centered egoism, with the humorlessness it invariably breeds, is as always the enemy of true Shandeism. This combination, in its determination to eradicate wit, has established "the Magna Charta of stupidity." Tristram appears content that he has proved to us our capacity to learn through metaphor and symbol, aware that he has engaged us in a conversational quest for meaning. In the same tone with which he had expressed his tolerance of hobbyhorse riders at the outset of the book, he sidesteps the graver gentry whom he has just anatomized for us: "I have no abhorrence whatever, nor do I detest and abjure either great wigs or long beards,_____any further than when I see they are bespoke and let grow on purpose to carry on . . . imposture_____for any purpose,_____peace be with them;_____mark only [he stresses the moral with a pointing hand],_____I write not for them" (III.xx.147).

The redemption of the vital human function of wit underwrites Sterne's double-entendre as a means of exploring with the reader the connections between mind and body. It instills purpose into the central structural metaphors of both *Tristram Shandy* and *A Sentimental Journey,* making words like "hobbyhorse" and "journey" into a kind of vigorous shorthand standing for a rich range of experience that the reader and narrator share. Finally, his redemption of verbal wit spills over to illuminate physical gesture as well: Walter Shandy awkwardly reaching across his coat to extricate a handkerchief from his pocket, Corporal Trim dropping a hat to indicate death's descent, or Tristram jumping up in frustration to hurl a blotted page into the fire all speak a body language inseparable from the metaphoric verbal one.

"A man and his HOBBY-HORSE," says Tristram as he launches into his description of Toby's,

> tho' I cannot say that they act and re-act exactly after the same manner in which the soul and body do upon each other: Yet doubtless there is a communication between them of some kind, and my opinion rather is, that there is something in it more of the manner of electrified bodies,_____and that by means of the heated parts of the rider, which come immediately into contact with the back of the HOBBY-HORSE._____By long journies and much friction, it so happens that the body of the rider is at length fill'd as full of HOBBY-HORSICAL matter as it can hold;_____so that if you are able to give but a clear description of the nature of

the one, you may form a pretty exact notion of the genius and character of the other.   (I.xxiv.55)

Tristram elsewhere repeats that the hobbyhorse does not constitute the entire character, remarking for example that Toby's moral behavior transcends his hobbyhorse. But as he sets about "drawing Toby's character from his HOBBY-HORSE," he emphasizes the physical connection suggested by the metaphor: a man's obsession is especially like horseback riding in the excitement it arouses, partaking of sexual stimulation. Later he speaks of Toby posting down to his bowling green—the site of his fortifications—like a lover eager to join his mistress.

Such descriptions have been read as reducing hobbyhorsical mankind to mechanisms, with sexual desire—simple or sublimated—as the key to the machine. That interpretation seems to be encouraged by Tristram's pronouncement upon Corporal Trim's story about falling in love with the Fair Beguine "quite suddenly" as she massaged the upper part of his leg: "Whether the corporal's amour terminated precisely in the way my uncle *Toby* described it, is not material; it is enough that it contain'd in it the essence of all the love-romances which ever have been wrote since the beginning of the world" (VIII.xxii.406). But what we have seen of the transformation of the merely material into wit suggests that such a mechanical view of hobbyhorses (and of love) is inadequate. While Tristram steadily insists that "soul and body" interpenetrate one another (thus mocking hypocrites who deny their own sexual nature), his emphasis on the elaborate construction of Toby's hobbyhorse directs attention to its complexity. Its sources in Toby's physical (and probably sexual) wound are simple. But equally, the resultant structure—illustration, game, raison d'être—is richly multifarious. In the figure of the hobbyhorse, soul and body mesh in a child's game, with the wonder and subtlety of the connection presented for our contemplation as surely as its childishness.

A related image, that of the journey, is as important as the hobbyhorse to the structure of *Tristram Shandy*—even more so in *A Sentimental Journey*—and to Sterne's vision of the human situation. Neither image is new. The *Oxford English Dictionary* shows that "hobbyhorse" was in common use as a name for a child's toy or preoccupation long before Sterne expanded it; the journey is an ancient image figuring forth human life. Consistent with his larger intention of revealing the familiar to us in a new light, Sterne revivifies the metaphor—biblical, Homeric—in recounting Tristram's run from Death in Volume VII. Drawing on parallels he had begun to explore in his sermons,[14] Sterne invests the image with intensity by starting Tristram's journey as a race against Death, that "son of a whore [who] has found out my lodgings" (IX.i.336).

Tristram marks the image as his own, transforming it unforgettably, by his means of eluding Death. He is able to slip away because Death finds himself uniquely abashed by his victim's nonchalance and humor. Addressing his own high spirits, Tristram says: "In no one moment of my existence, that I remember, have ye once deserted me . . . when DEATH himself knocked at my door_____ye bad him come again; and in so gay a tone of careless indifference, did ye do it, that he doubted of his commission_____ 'There must certainly be some mistake in this matter,' quoth he" (IX.i.335).

Aware that Death's setback is certain to be temporary, Tristram resolves to fly while he can. The verbs he chooses to describe his plan are themselves images that only Shandean high spirits could apply to a travel cure:

> Then by heaven! I will lead him a dance he little thinks
> of_____for I will gallop, quoth I, without looking once behind me
> to the banks of the *Garonne;* and if I hear him clattering at my
> heels_____I'll scamper away to mount *Vesuvius*_____from
> thence to *Joppa,* and from *Joppa* to the world's end, where, if he
> follows me, I pray God he may break his neck_____ . . . .
>     Allons! said I; the post boy gave a crack with his whip_____off
> I went like a cannon, and in half a dozen bounds got into
> *Dover.*  (IX.i.436)

Starting like this, Tristram pulls the reader along through a volume that identifies witty agility as a lifesaving power, with good humor (again) as *the* capacity necessary to stay alive.

In *A Sentimental Journey,* travel as an image figuring spiritual development is, if anything, more prominent than in Volume VII of *Tristram Shandy.* Gardner Stout has studied the ways in which Yorick's journey to health evokes seventeenth-century Puritan accounts of spiritual pilgrimage, notably John Bunyan's *Pilgrim's Progress* (Introduction, pp. 38–40). While this world is a very different kind of test for Bunyan's Christian than it is for Sterne's, their movement through its landscape provides both with chances to reveal their spiritual fiber. If Christian is struggling through on his way to heaven, Yorick too seeks a better world in "NATURE, and those affections which rise out of her, which make us love each other_____and the world, better than we do" (p. 219). Stout concludes that Yorick's "travels may be said to combine the 'seventeenth-century ideal of *pélerinage de l'ame'* with the 'eighteenth century ideal of cosmopolitanism and sociability,' for by traveling with him the reader can develop the faculties essential to participation in this joyful religion." As I remarked earlier, sentiment is to the *Journey* what Tristram's opinions are to his life: "incontestably the sunshine." To journey with Tristram and with Yorick is to invest travel with spirits, and high spirits with a spirituality they had never revealed before Sterne.

Finally, Sterne's success at bringing physical nature (man's included) to function as a sign of the spiritual allows the extension of metaphoric language beyond words—to gesture. "A man's body and his mind, with the utmost reverence to both I speak it, are exactly like a jerkin, and a jerkin's lining;_____rumple the one_____you rumple the other" (III.iv.114). From this principle it follows that attitudes, in the sense of posture and gesture, indicate attitudes of mind and spirit. In both novels Sterne calls for our close attention to them.

Corporal Trim and his hat will serve to represent jerkin's lining and jerkin. When word of the death of Tristram's brother Bobby reaches Shandy Hall, it sends their father into a paroxysm expressed through quotation of ancient authorities on the brevity of life and the transiency of things. In the kitchen the response differs. "My young master in *London* is dead! said Obadiah" (V.vii.252), and each of the servants thinks his or her own thoughts. Tristram remarks, "Well might *Locke* write a chapter upon the imperfections of words"—for to Susannah, "dead" summons up only thoughts of the green satin dress she will get when her mistress goes into mourning. To Obadiah, Bobby's death means that the master will invest his money in "stubbing the ox-moor" instead of a grand tour for his son, and "we shall have a terrible piece of work of it." Their unanimous creatural self-concern is uttered with massive simplicity by the scullery maid as she scours a fish kettle: "He is dead! said *Obadiah*,_____he is certainly dead!_____So am not I, said the foolish scullion."

But for Tristram this self-concern constitutes as well a brute self-awareness; by now we may anticipate that even such material will serve as a base for expansion. While the word "dead" remained nearly dead for all of them, a metaphorical gesture stirs them to move out of themselves. Corporal Trim is again the effective rhetorician:

> Are we not here now, continued the corporal, (striking the end of his stick perpendicularly upon the floor, so as to give an idea of health and stability)_____and are we not_____(dropping his hat upon the ground) gone! in a moment!_____'Twas infinitely striking! *Susannah* burst into a flood of tears._____We are not stocks and stones._____*Jonathan, Obadiah*, the cook-maid, all

melted._____The foolish fat scullion herself . . . was rous'd with it. (V.vii.253)

Tristram comments, perhaps not just hyperbolically, that to understand and master persuasive rhetoric as Trim has done would enable a speaker to rally support for "the preservation of our constitution in church and state." Perhaps he means that properly to understand how people connect with things, and the mind with the body, would ensure both social and personal integration.

He concludes by again emphasizing that it is the inseparability of mind and body that involves us in a gesture like Trim's, moves us, and leads us out (the root meaning of *educare*). We are "but men cloathed with bodies, and governed by our imaginations." Given those facts, we cannot be unaffected by what stimulates the senses. Furthermore, "of all the senses, the eye . . . has the quickest commerce with the soul,_____gives a smarter stroke, and leaves something more inexpressible upon the fancy, than words can either convey_____or sometimes get rid of" (V.vii.253). As it is their common mortality that has encroached upon Trim's audience through their eyes, it seems that death, like sex, is another of those "certain ideas which leave prints of themselves about our eyes and eyebrows . . . a consciousness of it, somewhere about the heart" (V.i.242). Locke also considered vision preeminent among our sensory faculties. But Tristram parts company with him to show that what sight connects us with, and how it happens, radically contradicts Locke's assumptions about the connection between language, speaker, and listener. Like "hobbyhorse" and "journey"—to use them once more as representative of Sterne's purposes with language—Trim's hat comes to hold for his watchers and for the reader a lively experience even in the face of death.

---

## III

Sterne's anticonventional narrative structures and his antiempirical mobilization of language may thus be said to constitute the chief means to the "experience" of narrator and reader in *Tristram Shandy* and *A Sentimental Journey.* Hans-Georg Gadamer distinguishes literary experience so conceived as corollary to *all* experience rather than an event discrete unto itself:

> Inasmuch as we encounter the work of art in the world and a world in the individual work of art, this does not remain a strange universe into which we are magically transported for a time.

> Rather, we learn to understand ourselves in it, and that means that we preserve the discontinuity of the experience in the continuity of our existence. Therefore it is necessary to adopt an attitude to . . . art that does not lay claim to immediacy, but corresponds to the historical reality of man. The appeal to immediacy, to the genius of the moment, to the significance of the "experience," cannot withstand the claim of human existence to continuity and unity of self-understanding. The experience of of art must not be side-tracked into the uncommittedness of aesthetic awareness. . . . Art is knowledge and the experience of the work of art is a sharing of this knowledge.[15]

While each event, each moment, in a text has its own identity, literary moments are not qualitatively different from others. Such a conception of art deprives it of the "magic" with which it is endowed by more Romantic theories, but it ratifies vital connections between art and the rest of life of the kind we have explored in discussing the preface in *Tristram Shandy*. In such a view, reading provides intense (and in that limited sense "immediate") experiences which take their shape against the background of the experience we bring to them, issuing in perspectives that in turn shape our further experience.

A.D. McKillop's description of Tristram Shandy as narrator suggests that the relationship I have just described between readers and what they read parallels that of the narrator and what he tells: Tristram Shandy is "both inside and outside the moment; he is not only the knower of English empirical philosophy, but the philosopher who writes with confidence about the knower."[16] Such conceptions of the relations between reader, narrator, and work return us to the crucial function of conversation as a model for narrative in Sterne's novels. Here is Tristram's most direct pronouncement on the subject:

> Writing, when properly managed, (as you may be sure I think mine is) is but a different name for conversation: As no one, who knows what he is about in good company, would venture to talk all;_____so no author, who understands the just boundaries of decorum and good breeding, would presume to think all: The truest respect which you can pay to the reader's understanding, is to halve this matter amicably, and leave him something to imagine, in his turn, as well as yourself. (II.xi.77)

As we have seen, leaving the reader "something to imagine" is precisely the function of Sterne's witty language and digressive structure. His vision—and use—of a language rooted in physical human nature and of digressions (Tristram's opinions, Yorick's sentiment) that impede conventional narrative progress aim to persuade the reader to "think as well as read" (I.xx.42).[17] That is, they make it almost impossible for a reader to ignore Sterne's narrators as speakers with their own sometimes baffling but always definite points of view on any subject they introduce. Simultaneously, Sterne's language makes it hard for readers to avoid trying to locate and articulate their own relations to what they find themselves involved in. "Never in the annals of fiction," says James Swearingen, "is the awareness of the integrity of the reader more explicit and sensitive than here."[18]

Iser's theoretical analysis of the reading process and Swearingen's study of reflexivity, both phenomenological in their approaches, provide terms especially useful for appreciating the purposive nature of conversation in Sterne's novels. Iser begins by stressing that reading a literary text is conversational in that it involves text and reader in mutual creation of the literary work, which "must lie halfway between the two":

> The convergence of text and reader brings the literary work into existence, and this convergence can never be precisely pinpointed, but must always remain virtual, as it is not to be identified either with the reality of the text or with the individual disposition of the reader. . . .
>
> It is the virtuality of the work that gives rise to its dynamic nature, and this in turn is the precondition for the effects that the work calls forth. As the reader uses the various perspectives offered him by the text in order to relate the patterns . . . to one another, he sets the work in motion, and this very process results ultimately in the awakening of responses within himself.
> (*Implied Reader*, 274–75)

Swearingen uses a phenomenological term to describe the points of view of the two parties to a conversation; he calls them "horizons" (*Reflexivity*, 10). While conversation fuses the horizons, such mingling takes place only to the degree that the differing points of view have first been defined and understood by the participants: "Detaching himself from his own orientation, attempting to suspend his own historical conditioning insures a reader's *failure* as a conversationalist" (p. 11; my emphasis).

Iser situates the origins of the dynamic nature of the process in "gaps" which—again as in conversation—we are invited to fill in from our own direction. Without these "elements of indeterminacy, the gaps in the text, we should not be able to use our imagination" (*Implied Reader*, 283).[19]

Probably the best Sternean endorsement of this view of reading is found in a letter to one of his own readers who had sent him a double-handled walking stick, calling it "shandean statuary." Sterne responded:

> Your walking stick is in no sense more *shandaic* than in that of
> its having *more handles than one*_____The parallel breaks only
> in this, that in using the stick, every one will take the handle
> which suits his convenience. In *Tristram Shandy*, the handle is
> taken which suits their passions, their ignorance or sensibility.
> There is so little true feeling in the *herd* of the *world*, that I wish
> I could have got an act of parliament, when the books first
> appear'd, "that none but wise men should look into them." It is
> too much to write books and find heads to understand them. . . .
> A true feeler always brings half the entertainment with him. His
> own ideas are only call'd forth by what he reads, and the
> vibrations within, so entirely correspond with those excited, 'tis
> like reading *himself* and not the *book*. (*Letters*, 411)

The distinction Sterne makes between the "herd" and the "true feeler" is of the greatest importance: the ignorant reader forces the text to fit his assumptions; the better response begins with *inward* movement ("vibrations") that issues in defining the self through the text.

The letter serves to introduce the fundamental purpose of narrative as conversation. In a relationship where to speak and to listen are also to interpret, what begins as a means of knowing results in "a mode of being" (*Reflexivity*, 12). Swearingen defines "Tristram's ultimate aim in his book and ours in reading" as articulating "the close relation between understanding an 'other'—person, event, text, or tradition—and understanding oneself" (p. 14). Similarly, for Iser, "the production of the meaning of literary texts . . . does not merely entail the discovery of the unformulated, which can then be taken over by the active imagination of the reader; it also entails the possibility that we may formulate ourselves and so discover what had previously seemed to elude our consciousness" (*Implied Reader*, 294).

Such analyses of conversation in its relation to the reading process reveal that when, as we found in our discussion of Tristram's preface, Sterne "holds up the mirror to nature," he does so through an art conceived as alive and moving. If Aristotle's formulation of the function of poetry was usually taken to mean that great literature is a kind of static warehouse of "truth," both Tristram and Yorick transform the concept, engaging the reading in a demonstrative experience of art *as* truth.

Sterne is extremely resourceful in engaging the reader's participation in his narrator's quest after his own nature. His most direct means involves Tristram in writing problems that turn out to have ontological implications for the reader as well. We have already encountered some of these in considering the way Tristram chooses to begin his "life and opinions." While he presented himself as assured in the manner of his setting forth, we have seen that in raising the issue of suitable starting places, he makes it a question with more than literary implications. Where does a life—my life?—really begin? Once underway, he reverts periodically to the question of what is suitable for inclusion, and in doing so pushes the "true feeler" to explore the boundaries of his own selfhood:

> O ye POWERS! (for powers ye are, and great ones too)_____which enable mortal man to tell a story worth the hearing,_____that kindly shew him, where he is to begin it,_____and where he is to end it,_____what he is to put into it,_____and what he is to leave out,_____how much of it he is to cast into shade,_____and whereabouts he is to throw his light! . . .
>
> I beg and beseech you . . . that wherever, in any part of your dominions it so falls out, that three several roads meet in one point . . . that at least you set up a guide-post, in the center of them, in mere charity to direct an uncertain devil, which of the three he is to take. (III.xxiv.151)

Such a passage, putting into question what makes up the *story* of a life, simultaneously questions what makes up life itself. Telling and reading *are* interpreting.

This conjunction becomes more intense when telling is placed in an adversary relation against the time available to do it. If, once again, an adjunct of Sterne's program is to instill new life into time-worn cliché, then *ars longa, vita brevis* opens in an unexpected direction as Tristram complains how impossibly little time he has to get so much down on paper: "I am this month one whole year older than I was this time twelve-month; and having got . . . almost into the middle of my fourth volume_____and no farther than to my first day's life_____ 'tis demonstrative that I have three hundred and sixty-four days more life to write just now, than when I first set out" (IV.xiv.207).

*Ars longa* has always meant that art lasts a long time compared to a human life. Grumbling that it *takes* a long time (never mind whether it will last) provides a laugh for those who summon up the implied cliché, while at the same time the crazily formidable narrative goal lures us again to consider the relation between event and interpretation in our own lives.

Later he turns from humorous concern about whether his book will "swim down the gutter of Time" toward Posterity (*ars longa* in the traditional sense) to carry us suddenly into poignant awareness of how brief life really is:

> I will not argue the matter: Time wastes too fast: every letter I trace tells me with what rapidity Life follows my pen; the days and hours of it, more precious, my dear *Jenny*, than the rubies about thy neck, are flying over our heads like light clouds of a windy day, never to return more_____every thing presses on_____whilst thou art twisting that lock,_____see! it grows grey; and every time I kiss thy hand to bid adieu, and every absence which follows it, are preludes to that eternal separation which we are shortly to make._____
> _____Heaven have mercy upon us both!   (IX.xi.430)

Thus artistic problems of narrative inclusion (the resistance of the narrative medium to life) fuse with existential problems (the resistance of life's own medium—time—to life), forcing ontological thoughtfulness.

The "true feeler" will stand in need of all the good-humored acceptance of life that Tristram and Yorick have fostered. For Tristram and Yorick exist to make us laugh and make us willing to explore serious questions about ourselves. We have already noticed many of these questions in studying Sterne's purpose with language and structure. Overall, it is perhaps not too much to say that these questions and purposes are in the service of integration for both narrator and reader. Certainly the interdependence of body and mind that pervades both *Tristram Shandy* and *A Sentimental Journey* tests us as readers, with the aim in the long run of making us accept ourselves as we are and be the better for it. As Sterne says in one of his sermons, " 'Tis one step towards acting well, to think worthily of our nature" (*Sermons*, I:82). But such self-respect is, as we have seen, won (if at all) at the cost of almost steady embarrassment and frequent pain. Like Tristram, whose pitiful body has "been the continual sport of what the world calls Fortune" (I.v.6), the reader of Sterne's novels has the chance to come to terms with the body—or spend a lifetime complaining about it.

But reconciling mind with body is not the only reconciliation Sterne attempts in his two long conversations with the reader. In *A Sentimental Journey* even more explicitly than in *Tristram Shandy*, he implicates us with his narrator in confronting the obdurate problems that human society, as well as individual human nature, pose to the traveler through life's foreign landscapes. The problem of communication takes on further urgency where one's native tongue is itself alien. Yorick confronts the fact that he is without a passport in a country at war with his own; he glimpses the possibility of imprisonment. And of course he skirts all perils by his wit, his subtle empathy, and the privileged position that allows him to exercise them. Recognizing that he *is* so privileged, we should also acknowledge that anyone who reads his *Journey* enjoys (by definition?) some comparable resources. Again, the presence in Yorick's route of a "herd" of travelers with all the same privileges, who nonetheless cannot or will not summon his wit and sympathy, places his *choice* of them in strong relief. And the bitter refusal of Smelfungus and Mundungus to do anything but rail against the abundant beauty through which they pass makes Yorick's participation in the peasants' gesture of grace (in the next to last chapter of the book) a profound acknowledgment of life's value even in a world that has given him his share of troubles:

> It was not till the middle of the second dance, when, from some pauses in the movement wherein they all seemed to look up, I fancied I could distinguish an elevation of spirit different from that which is the cause or the effect of simple jollity._____In a word, I thought I beheld *Religion* mixing in the dance_____but as I had never seen her so engaged, I should have look'd upon it now, as one of the illusions of an imagination which is eternally misleading me, had not the old man, as soon as the dance ended, said, that this was their constant way . . . after supper was over . . . to dance and rejoice; believing, he said, that a chearful and contented mind was the best sort of thanks to heaven that an illiterate peasant could pay_____
> _____Or a learned prelate either, said I.   (pp. 283–84)

Once again Sterne has so constructed his dialogue with the reader that it is impossible to deny the relevance of the alternatives offered—gratefulness vs. bitterness—regardless of what we think about heaven.

By their nature, the existential contradictions Sterne works and plays at reconciling are all linked with one another: the difficulty of comprehending our life story, compounded by the persistence of time in piling on more and more for us to interpret, results in the first place from conflicting impulses of mind and body—all of which make life seem as much damnation as blessing. The most inclusive and daunting contradiction of all is the presence of death in the midst of life—the most intimidating challenge to living fully. Sterne takes it on implicitly in the same early chapter of *Tristram Shandy* that tells us the date of his hero's birth: "I can truly say, that from the first hour I drew my breath . . . to this, that I can now scarce draw it at all, for an asthma I got in scating against the wind in *Flan-*

*ders;*———I have been the continual sport of what the world calls Fortune" (I.v.6). That shadow is the darkest that Tristram confronts. He faces it with the same comic vision that encompasses such "pitiful misadventures and cross accidents" as his crushed nose and extreme circumcision. Introducing the threat of death, he refuses to exploit its tragic potential, opting instead for the mock-heroic. When much later he refers again to his illness, it is to comment that his most recent attack resulted from laughing too hard—as usual, at one of life's incongruities:

> To this hour art thou not tormented with the vile asthma thou gattest in skating against the wind in *Flanders*? and is it but two months ago, that in a fit of laughter, on seeing a cardinal make water like a quirister (with both hands) thou brakest a vessel in thy lungs, whereby, in two hours, thou lost as many quarts of blood; and hadst thou lost as much more, did not the faculty tell thee———it would have amounted to a gallon?———
> (VIII.vi.384)

Sidestepping the ultimate danger with that final humorous prevarication is precisely the opposite of ignoring the threat's reality.

The extra-fictional connection of Tristram's illness with Sterne's own tuberculosis contributes to intensify that reality. As early as his Cambridge days, Sterne had been afflicted—he woke one morning to find he had "bled the bed full"—and his lungs never healed. Even a reader unacquainted with the facts of Sterne's life might start to sense an autobiographical reference in this ominous note as it is repeatedly inserted among the private and relatively small-scale trials of Tristram. Swearingen remarks that the voices of Sterne and Tristram "are neither equivalent nor clearly discriminated. One senses that the living voice must often be speaking from his own experience. . . . The problems encountered in the process of writing, for example, are not fictional problems, one is convinced, even if they are the ostensible concerns of Tristram" (*Reflexivity,* 4). Death, in the circumstantial guise of a "vile asthma," begins to stand out as a concern insinuating itself beyond the fiction toward the author and back again. Thus the reader also, more and more enmeshed in a web of conversation bonding him with the narrator, finds it impossible to distance the threat or extricate himself from the issues raised by its presence.

The fact that Yorick and Tristram, too, "are neither equivalent nor clearly discriminated" has the effect of emphasizing the role of death as threat and motivator. The story of Yorick's destruction by the solemn and vindictive targets of his humor is told within the first dozen chapters of *Tristram Shandy:* his descent from Hamlet's dead court jester, his generosity of spirit, his death with a joke on his lips, his grave marked "Alas, poor YORICK!"—and Tristram's two black pages. Then he is resurrected to play out at length the part his brief tragicomedy had prepared us for: Tristram's clearest exemplum of a life well lived. To say the least, Yorick's cheerful acceptance of life's blows, including the final one, fuses him with Tristram as both offer brilliant resistance to death's dominion.

And then consider some of the further autobiographical interweaving of Sterne, Tristram, and Yorick. Having begun Tristram's tale, including the short life and death of Yorick, in the first volumes of *Tristram Shandy*, and having published volumes of his sermons as those of "Mr. Yorick," Sterne (whose own life was steadily more well known) broke the retrospective patterns established in his novel to leap into Tristram's adult travels in Volume VII. Such a break calls attention to Sterne's direct experience by the urgency with which illness and danger of death suggest a motivation not only of Tristram's journey but of his author's decision to grasp it as subject for his work. And finally, in choosing to retell his own and Tristram's journey as Yorick's *Sentimental Journey*, Sterne infuses the sentimental with the dangerous, and Yorick's urgent pursuit of life partakes of Tristram's earlier escape from death.

By this time, readers of Sterne who have come through *Tristram Shandy* and gone on to *A Sentimental Journey* will be occupied with uncertainty about where they have arrived. Conception, asthma, humor, death, unexpected journeys—Sterne's aim is to submerge us in them and get us to swim in them, or transcend them. Learning to swim is a more modest conception than transcendence. Either will suffice to suggest the vision Sterne makes available through good-natured travel in the world and humorous reflection in art. The vision, transcendence, mode of motion in a foreign medium—all are epitomized in a passage from the midst of Tristram's travels:

_____Now this is the most puzzled skein of all_____for in this last chapter, as far at least as it has helped me through *Auxerre*, I have been getting forwards in two different journies together, and with the same dash of the pen_____for I have got entirely out of *Auxerre* in this journey which I am writing now, and I am got half way out of *Auxerre* in that which I shall write hereafter _____ There is but a certain degree of perfection in every thing; and by pushing at something beyond that, I have brought myself into such a situation, as no traveller ever stood before me; for I am this moment walking across the market-place of *Auxerre* with my father and my uncle *Toby*, in our way back to dinner _____ and I am this moment also entering *Lyons* with my post-chaise broke into a thousand pieces——and I am moreover this moment in a handsome pavillion built by *Pringello*, upon the banks of the *Garonne*, which Mons. *Sligniac* has lent me, and where I now sit rhapsodizing all these affairs.

——Let me collect myself, and pursue my journey. (VII.xxviii.362)

And yet it must be admitted that there are readers for whom the experience Sterne offers remains uncompelling. For some, the invitations to good-humored participation in a joint search for self-definition may seem merely a mocking challenge. Appeals to our confidence may lead no further than the next embarrassing encounter with one of our own false assumptions or one of the narrator's dirty jokes. Responses to Sterne were from the start, and they remain, very strong and very mixed. A perceptive reader like Horace Walpole could find that the first volumes of *Tristram* "make one smile two or three times at the beginning, but in recompense make one yawn for two hours,"[20] and he goes on to comment on the "odd coupling" of the sermon in the first volume with a good deal of bawdy. A few laughs paid for with a great deal of boredom, an unlikable mixture of high sentiment and low talk—these are descriptions of how many readers still feel.

Coleridge, who loved Sterne's works, nevertheless describes (in appreciating them) some elements that may add up to a negative effect on many readers:

> A sort of *knowingness*, the wit of which depends, first on the modesty it gives pain to; or secondly, the innocence and innocent ignorance over which it triumphs; or thirdly, on a certain oscillation in the individual's mind between the remaining good and the encroaching evil of his nature, a sort of dallying with the devil, a fluxionary act of combining courage and cowardice . . . so that the mind has in its own white and black angel the same or similar amusements as might be supposed to take place between an old debauchee and a prude. . . . We have only to suppose society *innocent*—and [these effects are] equal to a stone that falls in snow; it makes no sound because it excites no resistance. [These effects account] for nine tenths [of our response]; the remainder rests on its being an offence against the good manners of human nature itself.[21]

I am not concerned here to show again the ways in which Sterne works to place these various affronts to the reader in the service of "experience"; rather, what Coleridge appreciates, simply (or complexly) puts off many readers.

Women readers may find Sterne's approach to them (especially in *Tristram Shandy*) as prudes and hypocrites hard to get beyond, regardless of how strong a case one makes for interpreting that treatment as aimed at the prudish in *all* of us, of both sexes. And the fact that both Tristram and Yorick sketch their female characters first as libidinous and mostly mindless may turn away female readers altogether. (On this score, Swearingen's appraisal of the role of Elizabeth Shandy in her son's story does more than anything else I know to reassess her much-maligned character.)

Along with what can easily be taken as misogynist in Sterne, a general air of masculine impotence—or at least disability—hangs over the novels, from Walter Shandy's premature ejaculation right to the last act of Yorick's journey: "So that when I stretch'd out my hand, I caught hold of the Fille de Chambre's" (p. 291). Toby Shandy—in Swearingen's words, "the man of feeling with the wound upon the groin" (*Reflexivity*, 215)—is in so many ways a model of sympathy that one may come to the conclusion that sentiment is achieved only at the cost of sexual potency and action. Some of Yorick's sexual contretemps encourage that equation, as does Tristram's acknowledgment of his own incapacity (at least temporarily) with his "dear *Jenny*" (VII.xxix.363). To distinguish Tristram the narrator, who sees such failures and discontinuities as the symptoms of a malaise his work exists to heal, may not be enough to redeem him—for many readers—as a character crippled by an infirmity that pervades his world.

Such reservations, or revulsions, may come between many readers and the kind of experience I have described, believing that it coheres in the manifold means by which Sterne seeks us out and engages our participation. My own purpose has been to show how Sterne's books come to *matter* for a reader. In other words, to corroborate one of Walter Shandy's many statements that mean more than he knows: "Every thing in this world, said my father, is big with jest,_____and has wit in it, and instruction too,_____if we can but find it out" (V.xxxii,276).

## Notes

1. References are to *Tristram Shandy*, ed. Howard Anderson (New York: Norton, 1980), and to *A Sentimental Journey*, ed. Gardner D. Stout, Jr.

222

(Berkeley: Univ. of California Press, 1967), and to Stout's Introduction in the latter.

2. J. Paul Hunter, "Response as Reformation: *Tristram Shandy* and the Art of Interruption," *Novel* 4 (1971), 133.

3. Tristram Shandy's two names imply the dialectic between tragic fact and comic treatment in his "life and opinions."

4. See William Bowman Piper, *Laurence Sterne* (New York: Twayne, 1966).

5. *Letters of Laurence Sterne*, ed. Lewis P. Curtis (Oxford: Clarendon Press, 1935), 231.

6. Tobias Smollett, *Travels through France and Italy*, ed. Thomas Seccombe (London: Oxford Univ. Press, 1935), 235–36.

7. *The Sermons of Mr. Yorick*, 2 vols. (Oxford: Basil Blackwell, 1927), I:29.

8. Wolfgang Iser, *The Implied Reader: Patterns of Communication in Prose Fiction from Bunyan to Beckett* (Baltimore: Johns Hopkins Univ. Press, 1974), 24.

9. *Selected Letters of Samuel Richardson*, ed. John Carroll (Oxford: Clarendon Press, 1964), 341.

10. F. R. Leavis, *The Great Tradition* (Garden City, N.Y.: Doubleday, 1954), 11.

11. See Kenneth MacLean, *John Locke and English Literature of the Eighteenth Century* (New Haven, Conn.: Yale Univ. Press, 1936).

12. John Locke, *An Essay concerning Human Understanding*, ed. Alexander Campbell Fraser, 2 vols. (Oxford: Clarenden Press, 1894), I:529.

13. Cf. Ian Watt, Introduction to *Tristram Shandy* (Boston: Houghton Mifflin, 1965), xxv; and Richard A. Lanham, *"Tristram Shandy": The Games of Pleasure* (Berkeley: Univ of California Press, 1973).

14. Cf. Stout, Introduction, p. 47, n. 64.

15. Hans-Georg Gadamer, *Truth and Method* (New York: Seabury Press, 1975), 86–87.

16. A. D. McKillop, *The Early Masters of English Fiction* (Lawrence: Univ. of Kansas Press, 1956), 210.

17. Earlier in the same chapter, Tristram has explained that his aim in sending "the lady" reader back to see if she can discover a clue to his mother's religion is "to rebuke a vicious taste which has crept into thousands besides herself,———of reading straight forwards, more in quest of the adventures, than of the deep erudition and knowledge which a book of this cast, if read over as it should be, would infallibly impart with them" (I.xx.41).

18. James Swearingen, *Reflexivity in "Tristram Shandy": An Essay in Phenomenological Criticism* (New Haven, Conn.: Yale Univ. Press, 1977), 11.

19. Iser remarks a few pages earlier that the "unwritten" in the text, which "stimulates the reader's creative participation," had been noticed by Virginia Woolf in her study of Jane Austen (pp. 275–76). In *The Common Reader*, 1st ser. (London: Hogarth Press, 1957), 174, Woolf wrote: "Jane Austen is thus a mistress of much deeper emotion than appears upon the surface. She stimulates us to supply what is not there. What she offers is, apparently, a trifle, yet is composed of something that expands in the reader's mind and endows with the most enduring form of life scenes which are outwardly trivial."

20. *Horace Walpole's Correspondence with Sir David Dalrymple*, ed. W. S. Lewis, Charles H. Bennett, and Andrew G. Hoover (New Haven, Conn.: Yale Univ. Press, 1951), 66.

21. *Coleridge's Miscellaneous Criticism*, ed. Thomas M. Raysor (Cambridge, Mass.: Harvard Univ. Press, 1936), 121.

# Alistair M. Duckworth

# Jane Austen's Accommodations

I

> With all the chances against her of house, hall,
> place, park, court, and cottage, Northanger
> turned up an abbey.

So Catherine Morland exults, while wondering that her friends, the Tilneys, are not elated by a home that surely has "long, damp passages . . . narrow cells and ruined chapel" (*Northanger Abbey*, 141).[1] In fact, Northanger Abbey is the *dernier cri* in modern improvements. Caring for "no furniture of a more modern date than the fifteenth century" (*NA*, 182), Catherine is dismayed to find "furniture in all the profusion of modern taste," a smoke-free Rumford fire-place, and a breakfast room with a set of Staffordshire china. Her apartment has a Bath stove, mahogany wardrobes, and neatly painted chairs. True, the kitchen is the original kitchen of the convent, but even here General Tilney's "improving hand had not loitered . . . every modern invention to facilitate the labour of the cooks, had been adopted within this, their spacious theatre"(*NA*, 183). Outside in the grounds, Catherine is shown a huge kitchen garden, countless walls, a "whole village of hot-houses," and much more. Northanger has pineapples in its plantations and French bread in its ovens. The General is conspicuous in his modernism, resembling Count Rumford in his inventiveness, or Pope's Timon in the grandiosity of his conceptions.[2] Surely there is more to Jane Austen's untypically detailed descriptions of house and grounds than the aim of deflating the heroine's "gothic" preconceptions.

General Tilney is, in fact, a modern rather than gothic tyrant, a member of the wealthy gentry voraciously intent on extending his power and riches through arranging an advantageous matrimonial alliance for his son. This explains his deference to Catherine at Northanger and, later, at Woodston parsonage. Woodston is a "new-built substantial stone house, with . . . semi-circular sweep and green gates" (*NA*, 212). Disappointed at Catherine's apparent lack of enthusiasm, the General suggests a bow window as an improvement. His solicitude vanishes, of course, when he discovers

225

that Catherine is not the heiress he has assumed. She is dismissed immediately from the Abbey, forced to borrow money from Eleanor, and, after a journey of seventy miles, unattended, eventually returns home to the Fullerton parsonage, a "heroine in a hack post-chaise" (*NA*, 232).

Within the parody of the gothic novel that is the obvious genre of *Northanger Abbey*, another drama is played out, the drama of an innocent girl of modest means abroad in society. That there are horrors enough in this scenario is a hidden message of the novel. Alongside the delight Jane Austen took in spoofing *The Mysteries of Udolpho*, and in exposing the social hypocrisies of Bath society, there are even in this buoyant early work intimations of concern for the predicament of the single woman in a materialistic world. Jane Austen was in her twenty-fourth year when she first composed the novel in 1799 and may already have seen the writing on the wall. Within two years she would be forced to leave her own parsonage home at Steventon for residence in Bath, and (despite the report of her fainting away on being abruptly told by her mother of the intended move) she is likely to have known of her father's plans to retire, relinquish his livings to his eldest son, and remove with his wife and two daughters to another place—one appropriate to a reduced income. What domestic destiny lay ahead? What were Jane Austen's own chances of "house, hall, place, park, court and cottage"? In Bath the Austens stayed first in Sidney Place and Green Park Buildings and then, after Mr. Austen's death, in smaller houses in Gay Street and Trim Street. In 1806, Mrs. Austen and her two daughters shared a house with Frank Austen and his wife in Castle Square, Southampton, and in 1809, mother and daughters took up residence in Chawton Cottage, a house recently inhabited by the Chawton Manor steward and said to have been a "posting-inn" in the past.

Jane Austen ended up in a cottage, then. For apart from visits such as those to her brother Edward in Kent and to her brother Henry in London, she would stay at Chawton for the rest of her life, revising the novels she wrote in the late 1790's—published as *Sense and Sensibility* (1811), *Pride and Prejudice* (1813), and *Northanger Abbey* (1818)—and composing the novels of her maturity: *Mansfield Park* (1814), *Emma* (1816), and *Persuasion* (1818). Her domestic destiny was to be a spinster in a cottage, sharing a bedroom with her sister Cassandra and writing her novels in the common sitting room, where, warned by a creaking door, she could slip her papers under the blotting-book before visitors discovered her at her creative work. Without a room of her own, certainly without the £500 a year that Virginia Woolf thought essential to a woman's artistic freedom, she wrote about the sorts of houses she would never be mistress of—Delaford, Pemberley, Mansfield Park, Donwell Abbey—and described women who, through good marriages, acquire comfortable domestic establishments. Three of her heroines—Catherine Morland, Elinor Dashwood, Fanny Price—find accommodation in parsonages, a destiny that I suspect Jane Austen would herself have found congenial. Another three—Marianne Dashwood, Elizabeth Bennet, Emma Woodhouse—become the mistresses of estates varying from the modest to the magnificent. To be mistress of Pemberley, Elizabeth recognizes when that possibility seems remote, would be something. When she does become mistress of the estate, with its park "ten miles round" and its income of £10,000 a year, she can fulfill her aunt Gardiner's dream of a trip around the park in "a low phaeton, with a nice little pair of ponies" (*Pride and Prejudice*, 325). Readers who recall George Stubbs's painting of *Two Cream Ponies, a Phaeton and a Stable Lad* (c. 1785) will gain a sense of the elegance and grace of Elizabeth's married situation.

The fate that Marianne Dashwood escapes, "of remaining . . . for ever with her mother, and finding her only pleasures in retirement and study" (*Sense and Sensibility*, 378), came to none of Jane Austen's heroines, then, but was reserved for herself. Her study, however, was not the study of a scholar but of a novelist unsurpassed in the observation of social manners and in the discrimination of the distinctive signs of social difference. Pushed to the margin, she obtained a lucid perspective on the center of her world, the world of the modest gentry in its relations with the wealthy gentry and with trade and the professions. The exact character of her perspective on society has divided critics for a century. Virginia Woolf believed the "chief miracle" of *Pride and Prejudice* was that it had not been adversely affected by its author's circumstances; Jane Austen wrote "without hate, without bitterness, without fear, without protest, without preaching"; like Shakespeare's, her mind had "consumed all impediments."[3] Others have disagreed, finding hatred in her novels and letters, a criticism of primogeniture, a subversion of patriarchal rule. It is true that she did not always consume impediments with the same success as in *Pride and Prejudice*. But she did effect miracles. Deprived in her life of the house she felt entitled to, afflicted by a sense of restricted social space, she gave her heroines homes ranging from the "snug" to the "commodious." In order to *give* accommodations, however, she had to *make* accommodations. Aware that happy endings are the triumph of fantasy over fact, and that in traditional novels plot is the accomplice of desire, she sought to bring her dreams into acceptable conformity with the exigencies of real life.

Her novels are, therefore, subtle and complex negotiations with the facts of her social experience, as these may be accommodated to inherited fictional traditions. Her heroines are Pamela's daughters in the sense that they marry appropriately and well, implying in the process that the "virtues" of integrity and intelligence will be "rewarded" with a fitting domestic establishment. But while she accommodates her sense of social fact to conventional Richardsonian plot structures and, in so doing, caters to the wishes of her reading public, she also puts "desire"—her own as well as her readers'—in ironical perspective. To this end, for example, she "lays bare" the mechanism of her denouement in *Northanger Abbey*. Her techniques of "desublimation" are not as patent as those later employed by Thackeray, but by foregrounding the artificiality of her conclusion, they serve similar "realistic" goals.[4]

"What probable circumstance could work upon a temper like the General's?" (*NA*, 250) is the question of the final chapter. Henry has followed Catherine to Fullerton and has proposed and been accepted by her, and by her parents, but how are his father's objections to be overcome? Jane Austen concedes that the anxiety "can hardly extend . . . to the bosom of my readers, who will see in the tell-tale compression of the pages before them, that we are all hastening together to perfect felicity" (*NA*, 250). The circumstance that removes the General's objections is the advantageous marriage of Henry's sister Eleanor to a gentleman, whose addresses to her had previously been prevented by "inferiority of situation." His "unexpected accession of title and fortune" removed *that* problem, but Jane Austen can say little else—since the rules of composition forbid the late introduction of characters—except that "this was the very gentleman whose negligent servant left behind him that collection of washing-bills . . . by which my heroine was involved in one of her most alarming adventures" (*NA*, 251). By such parodic means—worthy of Cervantes—Jane Austen brings the pleasure principle into alignment with the reality principle. If it requires such a concatenation of fortuitous events to bring about the marriage of hero and heroine, then we are in the realm of romance still, and should assess the marriage of Henry and Catherine accordingly.

Yet this is perhaps to put it too strongly. Despite the subversion of conventional novelistic endings that the final chapter displays, Jane Austen's conclusion allows "desire" a measure of triumph. Henry's marriage to Catherine finally rests on a realistic basis; the General learns, contrary to the misinformation of John Thorpe, that the Morlands are "in no sense of the word . . . necessitous or poor," that Catherine will have £3,000, and that the Fullerton estate is entirely at the disposal of Catherine's father, and therefore "open to every greedy speculation" (*NA*, 252). Thus, while Catherine may not be entitled to become mistress of the Abbey, she does have a claim on Woodston parsonage. And if she does not merit "the dignity of a countess, with a long train of noble relations in their several phaetons" (*NA*, 232), then neither need she settle for a hack post-chaise. Even while bringing Catherine's expectations down to their proper (architectural) size, Jane Austen claims for Catherine and her other heroines what Othello claims for Desdemona:

> Due reference of place and exhibition
> With such accommodation and besort
> As levels with her breeding.   (*Othello*, I, iii, 237–39)

But at the back of her consciousness there is always the possibility (to allude to Shakespeare again) of the "unaccommodated" woman, reduced to bare, penurious, single existence. Such women appear, in fact, in the novels in secondary roles: Elizabeth Watson in the unfinished fragment, *The Watsons*; Miss Bates in *Emma*; Mrs. Smith in *Persuasion*; and their fates shadow the lives of the heroines, who are all, with the exception of Emma Woodhouse, in uncertain social positions at some point in their lives.

## II

What was there in Jane Austen's background to explain this sense of entitlement shadowed by apprehensions of disinheritance? As recent interpreters have shown, a key to her fictional vision is to be found in the particular circumstances of her social position.[5] On her mother's side Jane Austen was related to nobility, being a great-grandniece of the first Duke of Chandos (though by her time the Chandos peerage was extinct). Her mother was a Leigh of the Leighs of Adlestrop. Stoneleigh Abbey in Warwickshire belonged to a younger, ennobled branch of the family. A magnificent example of that mixture of architectural styles to which the eighteenth century gave the name "Sharawadgi," Stoneleigh comprises the remains of a Cistercian Abbey, an Elizabethan mansion, and a classic west range, which Smith of Warwick added on to the mansion in the years after 1714. It was the one truly imposing country house Jane Austen knew. She visited it in August 1806, shortly after it was inherited by her mother's cousin, the Rev. Thomas Leigh of Adlestrop. So vast was the house (twenty-six bedrooms in the new part alone) that Mrs. Austen humorously suggested he put up signposts. Equally interesting were the grounds, which had remained unaffected by successive waves of landscape improvements in the eighteenth century, and were thus as old-fashioned as the family itself. (Long known for their Tory and Jacobite sympathies, the

Leighs had made their house available to Charles I when he was denied entry to Coventry, and they were just as willing to accommodate the Young Pretender in 1745.)

In 1806, however, the grounds at Stoneleigh were about to be improved. Impressed by the work Humphry Repton had done at Adlestrop—where his "improvements" involved the sweeping away of a seventeenth-century garden, complete with canal, fountain and alcoves—Dr. Leigh planned to invite the controversial landscape architect to redesign his newly acquired property. Undoubtedly he discussed his ideas with the Austen women and, as Mavis Batey has argued, the visit is thus the probable source of the conversation over improvements in chapter six of *Mansfield Park*. Stoneleigh—its Elizabethan parts anyway—may indeed be a model for the fictional Sotherton Court. But Repton appears in a dubious light in the novel, and it may be doubted whether Jane Austen viewed with approval the prospect of his "improvements" at Stoneleigh. How she reacted to his actual improvements is not known. (Repton removed walls, opened vistas, and altered the course of the river Avon; his Red Book (1809), detailing his plans and illustrating his proposed designs, is at Stoneleigh to this day.) In 1806, it may well be that Stoneleigh confirmed her sense of connection to a historical heritage. Jane Austen was no enemy to tasteful improvements but, as I shall argue later, her novels show a fondness for old estates that have evolved naturally over the years, without the aid of the professional improver's hand.[6]

On her father's side, Jane Austen's lineage was less distinguished. George Austen's family descended from Kentish clothiers who had become prosperous and landed, but George's father was a mere surgeon, not a respectable profession in the eighteenth century. His uncle Francis Austen, the solicitor, did become very rich, however, by virtue both of his legal work (including being the agent to the Duke of Dorset at Knole) and of his marriage to not one but two heiresses. At about the time of Jane Austen's birth in 1775, Francis Austen persuaded Lady Falkland, the godmother of his eldest son, to will him a legacy of £100,000.[7] Earlier he had paid his nephew's fees at Tonbridge School (where George obtained a fellowship to St. John's College, Oxford), and had purchased for him, after he took orders, the living at Deane in Hampshire. This became vacant in 1773, providing a welcome addition to the living at nearby Steventon, which another rich relation, Thomas Knight of Godmersham in Kent, had presented to George in 1761.

Despite his combined livings, George Austen was not particularly well off during Jane Austen's childhood. Steventon was valued at £100 a year, and Deane at £110, and though tithes increased his income, he evidently found it necessary to take in pupils and farm his glebe lands. He was able to improve Steventon Rectory, however, so that it became a roomy and comfortable home, as shown in several drawings made by Jane Austen's niece, Anna Lefroy; one sketch shows a front of two stories with dormered attics above.[8] Moreover, he kept a carriage and was a kind of acting squire of Steventon. If his connections with such territorial magnates as Lord Portsmouth and Lord Dorchester were slight, those with such gentry families as the Harwoods of Deane and the Bigg Withers of Manydown were cordial and close.

As she was growing up, Jane Austen occasionally visited great houses like Hurstbourne Park, the home of the third Lord Portsmouth, who had been for a short time a pupil at Steventon; she went there, we know, to the annual ball in November 1800, an occasion graced by the presence of her brother Lieutenant Charles Austen, of the frigate *Endymion*, home from the successful capture of the French ship *Scipio* in a heavy gale. But more usual and congenial were visits to Deane House, Ashe Park, and Manydown. These houses, though on a much smaller scale than Hurstbourne Park—or Hackwood Park, the seat of the Duke of Bolton near Basingstoke—were commodious manor houses dear to Jane Austen's heart. "To sit in idleness over a good fire in a well-proportioned room is a luxurious sensation," she wrote to Cassandra in November 1800, after a "sudden invitation" and a journey in a post-chaise had taken her to Ashe Park.[9]

This was a year before she left for Bath. A year after that removal she returned to Steventon and, while on a visit to Manydown, accepted a proposal of marriage from Harris Bigg Wither, the son and heir, and a man six years her junior. This action, the most precipitant of her life, was almost instantly revoked (the next morning); but can we doubt that it was the appeal of house and establishment in her beloved Hampshire that prompted the acceptance, and the realization that there were certain accommodations she could not make to gain that end that prompted the change of mind? Jane Austen was almost twenty-seven when she rejected Harris Bigg Wither's proposal in December 1802. At the same age, Charlotte Lucas accepts the abominable Mr. Collins, a decision Elizabeth Bennet considers to lack "integrity" (*PP*, 135–36). Marriage throughout the novels is the most important "accommodation" of all, and we may be sure that, like Elizabeth, Jane Austen pondered long over "the difference in matrimonial affairs, between the mercenary and the prudent motive" (*PP*, 153), especially since the answer seemed to assume a double standard. When Elizabeth visits Charlotte at the Hunsford parsonage, she is surprised to discover how well Charlotte has fitted up her house, how successfully she has arranged the rooms so as to be as little bothered by

Collins as possible. But while she gives Charlotte credit for her neat accommodations, she does not alter her view that marriage simply out of desire for an "establishment" is an unprincipled act.[10]

From such a home as the Steventon Rectory, children with the right training, a little luck, and sufficient will could expect to do well—if they were male. The careers of the Austen brothers support this view. James, the eldest, became a clergyman, succeeded his father at Steventon in 1800, and by 1808, with the aid of an allowance from James Leigh Perrot, his mother's rich brother, enjoyed a comfortable annual income of about £1,100. Of George, the second son, little is known except that he was deaf and suffered from fits. Edward, the third son, had the great good fortune of being adopted in his teens by George Austen's kinsman Thomas Knight, and of becoming the heir and eventual owner of estates in Kent (Godmersham) and Hampshire (Chawton). Henry, the fourth son, the most versatile and least dependable, became a banker; as the result of a number of factors, including the failure of wheat prices, his firm—Austen, Maunde and Tilson of London—failed in 1816, and he was declared bankrupt. Edward lost £20,000 as a result; James Leigh Perrot lost £10,000 but was nonetheless able, on his death in 1817, to leave considerable funds and property to his wife, much of which eventually came to James Austen's family. After the bankruptcy, Henry settled into the congenial role of clergyman. The younger sons, Francis and Charles, pursued highly successful careers in the Royal Navy, both ending up as admirals.

Even such a brief sketch of the brothers' careers suggests that the Austens as a family were successful, "at home" in their society, figures of varying consequence in the church, the land, and the naval profession. Aware of her lineage, particularly on her mother's side, and proud of the accomplishments of her brothers (all except Charles older than she), Jane Austen had more than sufficient cause to feel that she had a stake in her country. The origins of her fictional patriotism, expressed so overtly in the praise of "English verdure, English culture, English comfort" in *Emma* (p. 360), were familial, deep, and never—despite provocations—eradicated. The "francophobia" of her novels, too, has a family origin. Jane Austen lived through the French Revolutionary and Napoleonic wars, which touched her family directly. In 1797, Henry married his cousin Eliza, widow of the Comte de Feuillide, who had been guillotined in 1794. Her brothers Frank and Charles were engaged at sea against the French. In 1800, Frank Austen was elevated to the rank of post-captain for his feat of capturing off Marseilles a French ship laden with corn for the forces in Egypt. Later his bravery and efficiency caught the eye of Nelson, but to his disappointment Frank missed the Trafalgar action in 1805. Such connections help explain Jane Austen's nationalism, the strain of cultural affirmation that is genuinely present in her novels; at the same time they put in doubt recent claims by some feminist critics that she was a severe and unremitting critic of the patriarchal system in which she lived.

Feminist criticism of the past decade, however, has valuably focused our attention on Jane Austen's predicament as a woman in her society.[11] In spite of a presumably happy childhood at Steventon—with its pleasures of reading, private theatricals, balls, and visits—she was, along with other women of her time and class, restricted as to opportunities. Her brothers' routes to power, position, money, and success were closed to her, and particularly after her removal from Steventon, her position was insecure. George Austen had very nearly £600 a year on retirement, not a rich income but enough to provide for a comfortable establishment with two maids and a manservant (*Letters*, 99). But on his death the family income from the livings at Deane and Steventon ceased, and Mrs. Austen and her daughters found themselves with a mere £210 a year—and some of this came from a settlement made to Cassandra in 1797 on the death of her fiancé in the West Indies. The Austen brothers rallied round: James, Henry, and Frank each provided an allowance of £50 a year, and the considerably richer Edward came up with £100. Thus the income of the Austen women became £460 a year, a sum sufficient to provide for a fairly comfortable life and a servant. But Jane Austen had become, one suspects, a member of that significant group in English life and letters, the "distressed gentility."

It is easy to be irritated by the plight of this group—to respond with sardonic humor to the appeals that still appear in English Christmas magazines from "The Distressed Gentlefolk's Aid Association." Jane Austen was hardly beneath the poverty line; indeed, her fictional sense of what was financially due to persons of her position was, as R.W. Chapman noted, high. Katherine Mansfield apparently agreed; in a diary entry for February 1914, her comment on the statement in *Sense and Sensibility* that neither Elinor nor Edward was "quite enough in love to imagine that £350 a year would supply them with all the comforts of life" is a simple: "My God!"[12] We may be excused for forgetting in these post-OPEC days how much a pound was worth right up to World War II. One study sets £300 as the lowest limit of a gentlemanly income in the eighteenth century.[13] But even in the 1930s, professional women were lucky to earn £250 a year, as Virginia Woolf angrily pointed out in *Three Guineas*. Woolf also painted a sympathetic portrait of the plight of distressed gentility in Ellie Henderson in *Mrs. Dalloway* (1925), and Ellie Henderson has some features in common with the Jane Austen who was grateful to receive handouts from Edward's adoptive mother, Mrs. Knight (*Letters*, 194); who took gifts ohe had made herself to Godmersham on her visits (*Letters*, 190); and who was forever worrying about how she would get from place to place, or somewhat bitterly aware that until she had a "travelling-purse" of her own she must not expect to determine visits or itineraries (*Letters*, 203).

From an early age, Jane Austen had imagined the condition of the impoverished woman with social claims. The third letter of her juvenile "Collection of Letters" is entitled "From a young Lady in distress'd Circumstances to her freind." The heroine, Maria Williams, has to endure Lady Greville's questioning as she is driven in the latter's carriage to a private ball. Like Lady Catherine's in *Pride and Prejudice*, Lady Greville's aggressive questions are intended to establish the social inferiority of the heroine and her family. She is incensed that the Williamses spend money on candles and on an expensive gown for their daughter: "But I suppose you intend to make your fortune tonight," she charges (*MW*, 156). Like Elizabeth later, Maria shows independence and courage in her "humiliating Situation." The heroine of reduced means abused by a vulgar aristocrat is an encounter that can be traced back at least to Pamela's experiences with Lady Davers in Richardson's novel, but in this particular "exercise," Jane Austen was comically exaggerating possibilities closer to home.

During the years following George Austen's death, Jane Austen shared her mother's expectations of increased income. As she was fond of remarking, "a Legacy is our sovereign good" (*Letters*, 199). Marriage as a means of increased income was now improbable; both Cassandra and Jane were in their thirties, well beyond the "terminal" age for marriage (twenty-seven) suggested by the novels. But there were two hopeful sources of funds. One of these was Mrs. Austen's brother, James Leigh Perrot. The Leigh Perrots were wealthy and childless; James, the eldest Austen son, was considered their natural heir, but it is clear from the letters that Mrs. Austen was in continuous expectation of a legacy from her brother. It never came—not after George Austen's death, when it would have been particularly welcome; not after the "vile compromise" (*Letters*, 316) over the Stoneleigh estate which made Leigh Perrot—who had a legal claim—richer by a sum of £24,000 and £2,000 a year; not even after Leigh Perrot's death in 1817, when there were great expectations from his will.

The other possible source of improved income was Edward Austen. Besides the allowance of £100 a year that he provided after his father's death, in 1809 he offered his mother and sisters a choice of houses on his estates at Chawton and Godmersham. Moreover, he extended his hospitality to his sisters, who went to Godmersham for long stays. Jane Austen's biographers have generally been uncritical of Edward, noting his tendency to ill health and hypochondria but not accusing him of tightfistedness. Yet we may wonder whether he did as much for his mother and sisters as he could. He had become, through his fortunate adoption, "the master of a great gentry estate of the order of Mr. Rushworth's [Sotherton Court],"[14] as well as of Chawton Manor. We can view these estates as they appeared during or just before Jane Austen's time: engravings of W. Watts's views of Godmersham (dating from 1784–85) appear in E. Hasted's *The History and Topographical Survey of the County of Kent* (1799) and are reproduced in Chapman's edition of the *Letters* (facing pp. 168 and 330). Viewing them, we not only get an accurate sense of the setting of houses like Mansfield Park ("so well placed and well screened," Mary Crawford finds, "as to deserve to be in any collection of engravings of gentlemen's seats in the country" [*MP*, 48]), but a sense, too, of the contrasts in Jane Austen's existence: contrasts between "rooms concise [and] rooms distended," as she expressed it in a poem written on the occasion of their moving to Chawton (*Letters*, 266), or between the "vulgar cares" of her normal existence and "the happy Indifference of East Kent wealth" that she conformed to at Godmersham (*Letters*, 336).

Godmersham was what Jane Austen would call a "modern house": that is, a house in the classical style, with a central block (dating from the 1730s) flanked by matching wings. Watts's views show it set in a park improved in the style of Capability Brown. A winding approach skirts a smooth lawn, interspersed with "clumps" of trees; there is a rather aggressively serpentine river with a well-designed bridge; the offices and farm buildings are largely screened from view. It is "complete," as Mary Crawford would say, a visible sign of the prosperity the owner enjoyed as a result of income from agricultural rents. These must have been considerable, as may be suggested by the "Book of Maps containing the Several Estates in the County of Kent belonging to Thomas Knight of Godmersham Park, Esquire" (1789). There are seven plans of the Godmersham estate in the book, as well as detailed maps of "Great Eggerton, Little Eggerton, Pope Street Farm, East Stour, Upper Drucksted, Waltham, Eggering, Crundall Farm, Buckwell Farm," and more (some two dozen farms in all).[15]

Edward's annual income from his estates, as well as that accruing from his marriage contract with Elizabeth Bridges of Goodnestone, Kent, is not known, but at the risk of circular reasoning, it is possible to speculate. The income of the gentry in Jane Austen's fiction ranges from about £600 a year (Willoughby's before his marriage to Sophia Grey) to the noble £12,000 enjoyed by Rushworth at Sotherton. Colonel Brandon of Delaford and Mr. Bennet of Longbourn have £2,000 a year. Henry Crawford draws £4,000 a year from Everingham. The grasping John Dashwoods at Norland, despite their expensive improvements and land purchases, live within an income that may be estimated at about £5,000 or £6,000 a year.

If one assumes that Edward's income was in this range (and David Spring's comparison of Godmersham with Sotherton suggests that it may have been twice as much), then there is an intriguing question to be asked about how Edward Austen interpreted the brilliantly satirical second chapter of *Sense and Sensiblity* on its publication in 1811. John Dashwood's stepmother and half-sisters leave Norland for distant Devonshire, there to live in a cottage with a combined income of £500 a year (close to that of the Austen women). John Dashwood, in the meantime, has given a minimalist interpretation to his father's dying request that he look after them. Abetted by his wife, who has brought a fortune of £10,000 into the family, he progressively reduces his generosity from a gift of £1,000 to each of his three sisters to £500 each, to an annuity of £100 to their mother during her lifetime ("but then if Mrs. Dashwood should live fifteen years, we shall be completely taken in," his wife points out), to occasional gifts of £50, to presents of fish and game, to a final rationalization that his stepmother and sisters will be "comfortable" on their £500 a year. It is a masterly exposure of greed and the failure of a generosity which, if not possessed innately, was obligatory in the circumstances. Could Edward have read it without qualms? It is possible. He did after all provide the annuity of £100.[16]

Chawton Manor was neither so grand nor so modern as Godmersham, nor was the style of its landscape so distinctively fashionable. It was nevertheless a place of some consequence. The Elizabethan house, with Tudor porch and mullioned windows, was set in a modestly improved park, as one may see in Prosser's print (reproduced in the *Letters*, facing p. 304). An even more charming view exists in an anonymous gouache of the house.[17] The Austen women lived, as it were, on the edge of this estate, which was not occupied by Edward during their early years there but rented to a family named Middleton—interesting in view of the family with the same name in *Sense and Sensibility*. Attempts have been made to view Chawton Cottage as "the small house at Chawton," following the example set by Trollope's *The Small House at Allington*; and it is true that the house was not called a cottage at the time and that the Austens seemed to enjoy their house and garden, in which they planted syringas, sweet williams, and columbines. Edward took steps to give the house an air of privacy and quiet. The large drawing room window was blocked up, and the garden was screened from the road by a hornbeam hedge. Even so, in terms of a scale that comprised Hurstbourne Park, Stoneleigh Abbey, Godmersham, Chawton House, and the houses of Ashe, Deane, and

Manydown, Chawton Cottage was not large; its modest dimensions, along with its marginal relation to the great house, may be taken as a metonym for Jane Austen's own reduced and marginal relation to society at the time when she began to write and revise her novels.

## III

Jane Austen's "distressed gentility," I have been suggesting, is a key to the incisive social analysis of her novels. Schooled by her experience in Bath, at Godmersham, and in London, where through Henry and Eliza she came in contact with French émigrée circles (*Letters*, 271–77), she became a keen observer of the nuances of social differences, a discriminating spectator of performances in public places. She measured the ways in which money mattered, particularly in marriage—what Smollett in *Humphry Clinker* had termed "the holy banes of mattermoney." As readers have long sensed and social historians have more recently confirmed, she had an extensive and exact knowledge of incomes; she knew the value of livings and the law of entails; and she knew what fortune would capture the eldest son of a baronet or the younger son of an earl. She had an eye, too, for those "positional goods" that were the signs of, or presumptive claims to, social status.[18]

She had, for example, an eye for a carriage. Carriages were not only the appendages of money and marriage but markers of rank and financial worth. As such, they have an interest well beyond the antiquarian in her life and fiction.[19] As early as 1798, when her father laid down his carriage, she knew the "disconvenience" of not having a conveyance to neighboring balls (*Letters*, 29). What such "disconvenience" could mean is suggested by Lady Greville's remarks to Maria Williams (as Maria stands outside the coach in the wind and cold): "You young ladies who cannot often ride in a Carriage never mind what weather you trudge in, or how the wind shews your legs" (*MW*, 159).

In the instance of carriages as of houses, however, social dispossession led to possession in another—aesthetic—mode. The hero of *Memoirs of Mr. Clifford* (written before Jane was fifteen) travels to London in a "Coach and Four," but he also possesses "a Coach, a Chariot, a Chaise, a Landeau, a Landeaulet, a Phaeton, a Gig, a Whisky, an italian Chair, a Buggy, a Curricle & a Wheelbarrow," as well as "an amazing fine stud of horses. . . . six Greys, 4 Bays, eight Blacks & a poney" (*MW*, 43). Beyond the Rabelaisian parody of the "list," there is here, as in Catherine Morland's list of possible domestic destinies, a spectrum of discriminated social claims and possibilities.

The list is not complete, despite its length. It lacks Mrs. Elton's barouche-landau, by reference to which she lays claim to superior social status; and it does not mention Henry Crawford's barouche, the seating in which causes so much dissension between the Bertram sisters on the trip to Sotherton (*MP* I, ch. 8). But it includes other conveyances that figure, often significantly, in the novels. General Tilney, as one would expect, travels in a fashionable chaise-and-four, with liveried postilions and numerous outriders (*NA*, 156). Lady Catherine travels to Longbourn in similar state to tell Elizabeth she cannot marry Darcy (*PP*, 351). Her sickly daughter "often condescends to drive by [Mr. Collins's] humble abode in her little phaeton and ponies" (*PP*, 67). In the same novel the Bennets have a carriage, but its horses are sometimes needed on the farm. The nouveau riche Bingley has a chaise, and several characters own curricles (the curricle was a fashionable two-wheeled conveyance, drawn by a pair of horses); Darcy drives one when he brings his sister to meet Elizabeth. Henry Tilney has one, too, and when Catherine transfers from the General's chaise to Henry's curricle on the way to Woodston, she is "as happy a being as ever existed" (*NA*, 156). Willoughby drives Marianne to Allenham, unchaperoned, in a curricle (*SS*, 67), but he is, one suspects, living beyond his income. John Thorpe in *Northanger Abbey* covets a curricle but has to make do with a gig, a vehicle drawn by one horse which is appropriate to his income, social status, and driving skills. Other characters who own gigs are the hard-up Sir Edward Denham in *Sanditon*; Mr. Collins, ever anxious to demean himself in *Pride and Prejudice*; and Admiral Croft in *Persuasion*, where the gig signifies not modest means (he is rich enough to rent Kellynch Hall) but his freedom from social vanity and his close partnership with his wife. In the same novel Anne Elliot eventually becomes "mistress of a very pretty landaulette" (*P*, 250). By contrast, in her own life at Chawton, Jane Austen became mistress of a donkey and cart (*Letters*, 475–76, 485).

As she was deprived of the house she desired, so she was deprived of a carriage commensurate with her dreams. The years brought a philosophic mind. She found she could enjoy the "luxury" of riding in Henry's open barouche in the summer of 1813, while admitting that she had "naturally small right to be parading about London in a Barouche" (*Letters*, 312-13). But in her youth she had not been quite so resigned. Everywhere in the juvenilia we can sense her resentment of a world in which social competitiveness and husband-hunting are the norm. With verve and brio she exposes the rationalizations and hypocrisies of this world. Like Mary

Wollstonecraft, she attacks the acquisition of accomplishments by young women of leisure, an attack that continues in the novels. She observes, somewhat obsessively, how important a fair complexion is in marriageable women, a theme that recurs in *Pride and Prejudice*, for example, where Miss Bingley considers Elizabeth "so brown and coarse," but Darcy thinks her only "rather tanned" (*PP*, 270–71). As in the later novels, she criticizes women obsessed with clothes and external appearance, and men addicted to shooting or billiards or overeating.

Again and again, however, her most pointed satire has to do with the importance of money in matters of marriage and position. "In Lady Williams," she writes, "every virtue met. She was a widow with a handsome Jointure & the remains of a very handsome face" (*MW*, 13). Through such nonsequiturs, through zeugma, hyperbole, and mock-Johnsonian antitheses, she exposes the gap between money and morals, desire and decorum. She exaggerates her own social anxieties and for the most part laughs them out of existence. A tailor's daughter leaves her home in Wales in pursuit of a nonpareil, Charles Adams. Her journey ends when she is caught in a man-trap in his grounds. This is not, however, her main worry. Though "possessed of Youth, Beauty, Wit & Merit, & tho' the probable Heiress of [her] Aunts House & business," she fears Charles Adams might think her "deficient in Rank" (*MW*, 21). More often the deficiency is financial. In "The Three Sisters," written when Jane Austen was seventeen, and as brilliant an exposure of sibling competitiveness as one could wish, the following dialogue takes place:

> "Yet how can I hope that my Sister may accept a Man, who cannot make her happy."
> "*He* cannot it is true but his Fortune, his Name, his House, his Carriage will." (*MW*, 61)

"He" is Mr. Watts, and his income of £3,000 a year is, as one of the sisters says, "but six times as much as my Mother's income" (*MW*, 62). Or, we can add, but five times as much as George Austen's probable income at the time of the story.

No one can doubt, reading the minor works, that Jane Austen was a critic of her society. There is a wit, a frankness, a vitality to the exposure of mercenary conduct in the juvenilia that amply justify the attention they have received in recent criticism. But whether they measure the depth of the young Jane Austen's alienation from her patriarchal culture is another question.[20] Her apprehension of social dislocation gives edge to her satire but does not leave her disaffected with her culture. The epistolary *Love and Friendship* (1790), for example, delights in capturing the grotesque shapes that the cult of sensibility can achieve; but it also measures the vicious consequences of selfish individualism, disregard of propriety and of property, disobedience of parents, and an ungrounded faith in the power of love and "elective affinities." However severely Jane Austen attacked social vices, she retained in the juvenile pieces, as in her published fiction, a vision of ideal social modes. The force of humor and irony, indeed, rests on an awareness of the difference between ideal and perverted forms of social conduct, as is surely evident in *Lady Susan*, her brilliant essay in the epistolary mode, of about 1793–94. Lady Susan is a predatory widow quite without a moral sense. She enjoys London, finding existence in a country village "insupportable" (*MW*, 245). She is a coquette, a manipulator, a tyrannical mother, intent on forcing her daughter into a financially re-warding match with a man she detests and, to this end, insistent that her daughter gain "those accomplishments which are now necessary to finish a pretty Woman" (*MW*, 253). She has a regard for her brother-in-law, Charles Vernon—"he is so easily imposed on" (*MW*, 250)—but has eyes for Reginald de Courcy, scion of a noble family, whose "insolent spirit" she means to subdue and whose money and position she plans to acquire. Against her the forces of conventional morality (chiefly Mrs. Charles Vernon) are somewhat dull, as critics have argued (although Letter 12, to Reginald from his father, warning him of his duties to himself, his parents, and his name, is sufficiently dignified and effective). Jane Austen delighted in capturing "the artifice of this unprincipled woman" (like Keats, she could imagine an Iago as well as an Imogen), but the brilliance of her characterization does not imply her covert sympathy. Like Mary Crawford later, Lady Susan joins an amoral character to a witty command of lan-guage. But she is too clever by half, and ends up married to the man she intended for her daughter.

By indicating the moral content of the minor works, we may seek to qualify a recent tendency in Austen criticism to value the juvenilia over the published novels on the grounds of the early works' lack of "organic camouflage."[21] In this view, the magnificent formal achievements of the mature novels tend to be reduced to the status of defence mechanisms, blunting or deflecting what would otherwise be frank attacks on pa-triarchal oppression. Of course, there are dangers also in counterposing a "moral" Jane Austen. On some occasions, her criticism of mercenary conduct seems more like a reflex of her own reduced or threatened circum-stances than a position grounded in moral principle. On other occasions, her satire works in self-protective ways. Critical of aristocrats like Lady Catherine, who appeal to decorum in order to suppress social aspirations, she can make her own appeal to tradition in order to expose "illiterate" and vulgar characters like Lucy Steele and Mrs. Elton, who pose threats from below.[22] Yet she is generally successful in distinguishing the false appeal from the true, and while we may in particular instances question the motives of her appeal to traditional manners and morals, we need not—with Mr. Knightley's characterization in mind—question that Jane Austen sincerely believed in them.

There is both a public and a private thrust to her search for fictional accommodations. Her "public" intention bears some resemblance to the project of Coleridge and other nineteenth-century authors, who sought to heal the breach between "cultivation" and "civilization," culture and society. Her "private" intention, unacknowledged, and sometimes unconsciously in the service of aggression or desire, was to construct a fictional society in which she could feel at home. Herself dispossessed, she sought to possess her world aesthetically. Without a comfortable income, she commanded a precisely discriminated range of incomes in her fiction. The accommodations (and carriages) she missed in life she found in her novels. Her novels are "nests," which she built with the "twigs" of characters and themes (*Letters*, 468). Her formal structures are not the same from novel to novel, and they do not always work—so that it is wrong to insist that her novels are seamless fabrics, organic wholes. Nevertheless, her resolutions are the consequence of authentic searches after accommodation and not, as is sometimes implied, capitulations to conventions, either social or fictional.

## IV

Perhaps the most difficult aspect of Jane Austen's work to describe is the coexistence in her attitude of sincere conservative convictions and a feminine perspective on her society. She has no structural changes to propose in her world, and her social criticism, while it takes sharp focus from her marginal perspective, is not political in the manner of Mary Wollstonecraft. Though she shares Wollstonecraft's distaste for a society which values feminine "refinement" over intelligence, and the appearance more than the reality of chastity, she has no program for rectifying the situation (as Wollstonecraft has, for example in chapter 12 of *A Vindication of the Rights of Woman* (1792), in which she advocates a progressive and co-educational system of national schools). Nor is this merely the difference between novelist and polemical writer; Jane Austen could find accommodation for her ideals within existing structures, as Mary Wollstonecraft could not; accommodations were not always easy to find, as the "dark" lives of Jane Fairfax in *Emma* and Mrs. Smith in *Persuasion* show; but though she occasionally resembles Wollstonecraft in her awareness of women's "enslavement," she shows no signs of advocating alternative roles for women (e.g., those of physicians or businesswomen), as Wollstonecraft does in chapter 9 of *Rights of Woman*. As she seeks homes for her heroines, so, with varying degrees of success, and with some qualifications necessary in a discussion of *Persuasion*, she seeks to invigorate an old society rather than to inaugurate a new.[23]

What was her society, and from what perspective did she criticize it? David Spring has rightly argued that she belonged to "a capitalist money culture" and lived at a time when improving landowners were transforming English agriculture; in the process, they "put an end to a traditional and communal agriculture and a backward, truly reactionary peasantry, thereby promoting the forces of economic individualism in the rural community."[24] But did Jane Austen see it this way? The economic individualism John Dashwood shows in enclosing the Norland common and engrossing East Kingham Farm (*SS*, 225) is evidence of his selfish and mercenary character. In *Emma*, Mr. Knightley provides a better example of an agricultural improver: he shows concern for his sheep, is continually closeted with his steward William Larkins over estate questions, and when his lawyer brother visits, discusses with him questions of drainage, fencing, tree-felling, "and the destination of every acre for wheat, turnips, or spring corn" (*E*, 100). Yet however committed to the improvement of the land, Knightley is opposed to fashionable landscape improvements. Donwell Abbey is unfashionably "low and sheltered"; the house is "rambling and irregular"; the ample gardens stretch down to "meadows washed by a stream, of which the Abbey, with all the old neglect of prospect had scarcely a sight"; there is an "abundance of timber in rows and avenues, which neither fashion nor extravagance had rooted up" (*E*, 358).

All the notations here—the situation and style of the house, the unimproved grounds—are coded signifiers of traditional values. Emma Woodhouse is our observer in this scene, and what she sees is a proleptic expression of the values she will embrace when she marries Knightley. Included in her view is the Abbey-Mill farm, "with all its appendages of prosperity and beauty, its rich pastures, spreading flocks, orchard in blossom, and light column of smoke ascending" (*E*, 360). The Abbey-Mill farm, however, is also the home of Knightley's tenant farmer, Robert Martin, whom Emma will come to recognize as a worthy husband for her protégée, Harriet Smith. Mr. Knightley may well participate in an agrarian capitalist economy, but as his name implies and his actions confirm, he holds to the paternalist values of what E.P. Thompson and others have termed a "moral economy." And in this, it seems to me, he is backed by his author, who, conscious of her maternal ancestry and of her links to an estate like Stoneleigh Abbey, felt an allegiance to the old society.

What is Tory in her outlook is nowhere more evident than in the ideal settings she envisages through much of her fiction as the final accommodations of her heroines. Delaford, the married home of both Dashwood sisters in *Sense and Sensibility*, is one example of this ideal community:

> Delaford is . . . a nice old fashioned place, full of comforts and conveniences; quite shut in with great garden walls that are covered with the best fruit-trees in the country; and such a mulberry tree in one corner! . . . Then, there is a dove-cote, some delightful stewponds, and a very pretty canal; and every thing in short, that one could wish for. . . . it is close to the church. . . . A butcher hard by in the village, and the parsonage-house within a stone's throw. To my fancy, a thousand times prettier than Barton Park, where they are forced to send three miles for their meat. (*SS*, 196–97)

Through the garrulity of Mrs. Jennings's description appear certain codes of representation, found elsewhere in Jane Austen's work and in the eighteenth-century novel. Apparently lost in the flow of the discourse, these codes—the enclosing garden walls, fruit-trees, church, parsonage— imply traditional cultural values of continuity, growth, and the interdependence of church and land. One notation, the contrast between Delaford and Barton Park, has classical provenance. The Middletons at Barton Park, who are forced to send three miles for their meat, join a long line of characters from Martial's Bassus ("Baiana nostri villa, Basse, Faustini") onward, who have forsaken the ideal of the self-subsistent community. In contrast, Delaford is an organic social community of the kind Pope admired in "To Bethel" or Smollett in *Humphry Clinker* or, for that matter, Henry James in *English Hours*.[25]

Like Donwell Abbey, Allenham, Sotherton Court, and the Great House at Uppercross, Delaford has escaped the attentions of professional improvers like Kent, Capability Brown, and Humphry Repton. Such places are old-fashioned, and though this is not an invariable virtue (Sotherton Court obviously needs "modern dress," if not of the kind Henry Crawford proposes), an old-fashioned condition usually signifies value in the fiction. Thornton Lacey, the home of Fanny Price before she moves to the Mansfield parsonage, is old-fashioned. "I was suddenly," says Henry Crawford, "in the midst of a retired little village between gently rising hills; a small stream before me to be forded, a church standing on a sort of knoll to my right . . . the Parsonage, within a stone's throw of the said knoll and church" (*MP*, 241). His proposed "improvements" entail the clearing away of the farmyard, the screening of the blacksmith's shop, the reorientation of the house, the creation of a new garden, the damming of the stream: in short, the total transformation of the parsonage into the home of a family "spending from two to three thousand a year" (*MP*, 243). But here he is being impractical, for the living brings in no more than £700. Like his plans for an improved liturgy or improved delivery of sermons (*MP*, 341), Crawford's modernizing plans at Thornton Lacey pose threats to the continuity of a morally grounded traditional society.[26] His sister's response is equally suspect. Disappointed that Edmund Bertram intends to be a resident clergyman at Thornton Lacey, Mary Crawford is "no longer able, in the picture she had been forming of a future Thornton, to shut out the church, sink the clergyman, and see only the respectable, elegant, modernized, and occasional residence of a man of independent fortune" (*MP*, 248). Mary, we recall, had responded to the news of the cessation of prayers in the Sotherton chapel with the remark, "Every generation has its improvements" and had also declared "a clergyman is nothing" (*MP*, 86, 92).

The threats posed by the Crawfords and other materialists and improvers in Jane Austen's fiction are threats to an organic social heritage, grounded in religion: a heritage in which, as Edmund Bertram suggests (*MP*, 92), religious principles, morals, and manners exist in relations of mutual reciprocity. There is no need to be sentimental about this. Jane Austen's values, like those of other conservative writers, are class based and, like the ideal communities she envisioned, ultimately dependent on money. As has been argued, the distinction between country virtue and urban vice is, in historical terms, false, and the ideal of an organic rural community innocent of fiscal "speculation" (and usually set in the past) a mythic reification.[27] Farm rents generally rose in the period, on the estates of improvers and traditionalists alike.[28] We need not seek to elevate Jane Austen's criticism of economic individualism to a set of universal values, but on the other hand, neither need we deny the sincerity of her traditional commitments. Aware of the prosperity resulting from, among other factors, agricultural improvements and increased rents, she criticized the absence of matching moral behavior among the prosperous.

## V

In the instance of her unfinished work *The Watsons*, Jane Austen's criticism is bitter. The fissured society she depicts; the exact notation of social backgrounds, incomes, idiolects; the discrimination among the manners of different sets; the general sense of oppression throughout—all these accord with the date of composition, 1804–05, a period when Jane Austen's fate as a distressed gentlewoman was clearly written (her father died in January 1805). Our point of view on this society is Emma Watson, who (in the words of her brother, the Croydon attorney) has found herself "instead of heiress of 8 or 9,000£, sent back a weight upon [her] family, without a sixpence" (*MW*, 352). Emma's father is a sickly country vicar, too poor to afford a carriage. Her elder sister Elizabeth is twenty-eight years old (Jane Austen's age in 1804) and a pathetic husband-hunting woman: "I think I could like any good humoured Man with a comfortable Income," she admits, while lamenting that "my Father cannot provide for us, & it is very bad to grow old & be poor & laughed at" (*MW*, 318, 317). Emma's brother Sam is "only a Surgeon" (like Jane Austen's paternal grandfather), a fact that militates against his suit with the Edwards's only daughter, who "will have at least ten thousand pounds" (*MW*, 321). Her other brother, Robert, has been luckier, having married the daughter of the attorney to whom he had been clerk; she (a vicious piece of goods) has a fortune of £6,000 and can therefore look on Emma with "Triumphant Compassion" (*MW*, 349). Emma's other sister, Margaret, also unmarried, has become a sycophant to those with money and is fretful and querulous with members of her family. Elizabeth believes that "if Margt had had a thousand or fifteen hundred pounds, there was a young man who wd have thought of her" (*MW*, 353).

By what mechanisms of plot and theme was *The Watsons* to transcend its gloomy analysis of the economic calculus at work? At the ball, Emma finds herself, "she knew not how, seated amongst the Osborne set," and when Miss Osborne reneges on her promise to dance with Master Blake, "Emma did not think, or reflect;—she felt and acted" (*MW*, 330). Like Mr. Knightley's act of dancing with Harriet Smith (*E*, 328), Emma's action bespeaks not only excellent manners but goodness, and it gains her the attention of Lord Osborne, Tom Musgrave, and Mr. Howard, the clergyman at Osborne Castle. Had the fragment been finished, Emma would surely have married Mr. Howard (whose worth is signified, briefly, by the excellence of his sermon delivery), after rejecting Lord Osborne and, perhaps, Tom Musgrave. Lord Osborne is a patrician hero whose pride, unlike that of Darcy, is too ingrained to be improved; and Musgrave, like Willoughby and Wickham, is an attractive false hero whose social aspirations overcome his attraction to a heroine without a dowry.

Since the plot of *The Watsons* is clear enough, one may suggest that the fragment was left unfinished not merely because the heroine was too

"low,"[29] but because the task of closing the social rifts so bitterly represented was too great. The emphasis is oppressively on the plight of distressed gentility, and society as a possible arena of values does not
substantially appear through the agencies of character or setting.

There is a bitterness and oppression present, too, in her first published
work, *Sense and Sensiblity* (1811). Like *Pride and Prejudice* (1813), this
novel seeks to define an ideal relation between the individual and society
through the accommodation of opposed terms. Behind both works (completed in early versions in the 1790s[30]) is a century of debate over whether
man is naturally selfish, as Hobbes and Mandeville had argued, or naturally social and benevolent, as the Third Earl of Shaftesbury had suggested
when he posited an innate moral sentiment. Jane Austen was hardly the
first to see that—in the world as given—sense, prudence, circumspection,
even a touch of *astutia serpentis* were needful (in this general sense she
follows the example of Fielding). Her attitudes were formed in the context
of anti-Jacobin polemic, however, and she had greater inducements than
earlier novelists to express a conservative suspicion of idealistic conceptions of human nature.[31]

The success with which these early novels accommodate individual
and social claims is by no means equal. Whereas *Pride and Prejudice* (like
*Emma*) largely contains its criticisms within an affirmation of cultural
heritage, *Sense and Sensibility* (like *Mansfield Park*) leaves many readers
with a sense of a discordance between meaning and form. As in *The
Watsons*, there is a bitter indictment of a world vitiated by economic
individualism and—despite its completed plot—a failure to dramatize a
convincing moral alternative to this world. The marriages of Marianne to
Colonel Brandon, and of Elinor to Edward Ferrars, with both sisters
"accommodated" at Delaford (in house and parsonage respectively), are
not convincing. The heroes in particular do not carry the weight of moral
authority she successfully invests in Darcy and Knightley. But the heroines pose problems, too. Elinor, the exemplar of "sense" in its best forms,
the advocate of traditional values, and the upholder of manners as an
expression of such values is successful to some extent; hers is the consciousness the reader has continual access to, and her solitary courage in
maintaining integrity in a world of moral corruption connects her with
Fanny Price and Anne Elliot, who in later novels find themselves similarly
placed. Yet Elinor's characterization is not always perfectly pitched, and
her hewing to traditional ways can seem on occasions brittle and formulaic, even insincere. Her sister, Marianne, is the vulnerable
spokeswoman for "sensibility," that misguided belief in the holiness of
the heart's affections, which leads her (at the age of seventeen) to voice her

criticisms tactlessly in public, to disregard decorum (as in her correspondence with Willoughby, to whom she is not engaged), to act insensitively (as on her unchaperoned trip to Allenham), and to endanger her own life by so pledging herself to Willoughby ("I felt myself . . . to be as solemnly engaged to him, as if the strictest legal covenant had bound us to each other" [SS, 188]) that when he rejects her in pursuit of an heiress, she finds no reason to live.

As regards Marianne, Jane Austen's rhetoric is clear: sensibility as a program of living is false. Yet to read the novel mainly as an exposure of Rousseauist sentimentalism seems somehow beside the point. Marianne's outbursts, as the testimony of many readers confirms, are sometimes admirable expressions of sincerity (perhaps in spite of her author's rhetoric); in some instances—as in her spirited defense of Elinor's "very pretty pair of screens" against the curt, dismissive praise of Mrs. Ferrars (SS, 235)—Marianne's protests serve as a safety valve for the reader's own pent-up disgust. Moreover, Marianne's sensibility is not what endangers the world depicted in the novel; her sensibility endangers no one so much as herself. What endangers the world of Sense and Sensibility is "sense," semantically debased from its associations with the Christian humanist virtue of prudence and now too often descriptive of attitudes of venal self-interest.

In Chapter 11 of the second volume, Elinor, on a mission to sell her mother's jewels, meets her brother in Gray's of Sackville Street. Everything in the dialogues that follow confirms the deep dyed materialism of the man. Mistakenly believing Colonel Brandon to be in love with his sister, John Dashwood tells Elinor he wishes that Brandon's income (£2,000) were twice as much for her sake. (His own income from Norland is £4,000 a year.) When Elinor denies Colonel Brandon's interest in her, he counsels a policy of "sense": "the smallness of your fortune may make him hang back; his friends may all advise him against it. But some of those little attentions and encouragements which ladies can so easily give, will fix him, in spite of himself" (SS, 223). He tells of an alliance between Edward Ferrars and the Hon. Miss Morton with £30,000. To make this an "equal alliance," Mrs. Ferrars promises to settle on Edward a thousand a year. He laments his own expenses caused by enclosures, land purchases, and improvements. Elinor keeps her "concern and censure to herself." In his conduct traditional obligations have been eradicated as surely as the old walnut trees at Norland during his improvements. We are in the world of Goldsmith's Traveller, where

As nature's ties decay,

> As duty, love and honour fail to sway,
> Fictitious bonds, the bonds of wealth and law,
> Still gather strength, and force unwilling awe.
> (*The Traveller*, 349–52)

Impervious to Elinor's irony, John Dashwood persists in valuing people in proportion to the extent of their income. Like the Steele sisters, he knows the price of everything. Like his wife, he has the mind of an actuary. Having seen Marianne looking pale and sickly—the consequence of Willoughby's repudiation—he questions "whether Marianne *now*, will marry a man worth more than five or six hundred a-year, at the utmost" (*SS*, 227).

Yet Marianne, in the end, finds herself "in a new home, a wife, the mistress of a family, and the patroness of a village" (*SS*, 379). Like the journey of Catherine Morland from the Fullerton parsonage to the Woodston parsonage by way of Bath and Northanger, the journey of the Dashwood sisters takes them from one enclosure of values at Norland to another at Delaford by way of London. But in her illness Marianne had begged that her mother not "go round by London . . . I shall never see her, if she goes by London" (*SS*, 311), and for many readers the "London" habits of the novel, like the "Croydon" habits in *The Watsons*, have been so forcefully described that the happy conclusion does not convince. Against all the odds (to adopt the "betting" language characteristic of the speech of the John Dashwoods, of Willoughby, of Lucy Steele), Marianne through her marriage gains the "competence" she had ingenuously estimated (£2,000 a year), while Elinor through her marriage gains rather less than her practical estimate of "wealth" (£1,000 a year) (*SS*, 91).[32]

---

## VI

*Pride and Prejudice* succeeds where *Sense and Sensibility* fails. As mistress of Pemberley, Elizabeth Bennet is the most lavishly rewarded of Jane Austen's heroines, and the novel she so delightfully inhabits is the happiest of her author's works. How are we to explain this? Did Jane Austen achieve her affirmative vision through ignoring, for once, the mercenary and competitive character of her society? By no means. The financial and social registers are as precise here as ever. Fitzwilliam Darcy has £10,000 a year, a beautifully improved estate, a London house, and influence at court. His friend Bingley has inherited a fortune of nearly £100,000, but the money was made in trade; he rents rather than owns

Netherfield, and his social roots—as Jane Bennet discovers to her dismay—are shallow. Mr. Bennet is landed and has a considerable income of £2,000 a year; but he has saved nothing over the years, his estate is entailed on Mr. Collins, and the five Bennet daughters can look forward to little more than £50 a year each from their share of the settlement of £5,000 made on Mrs. Bennet at marriage. Mr. Bennet is a gentleman, as Elizabeth will proudly remind Lady Catherine. Mrs. Bennet's origins and relations are less well established. Her father was an attorney, who left her £4,000; her sister is married to a Meryton attorney; and her brother is engaged in trade in London, where he lives in unfashionable Gracechurch Street. The Bennets' neighbor, Sir William Lucas, had been "formerly in trade" also, his knighthood the result of an address made to the king while mayor of Meryton. Sir William is not rich, which explains his daughter's prudential decision to marry that ogre, Mr. Collins. One consequence of the marriage is that Charlotte will eventually be mistress of Longbourn, a fact that leads her mother, Lady Lucas, "to calculate with more *interest* than . . . before, how many years longer Mr. Bennet was likely to live" (*PP*, 122, italics added).

In one way, *Pride and Prejudice* is closer to home than any of the novels, the mixed social claims of the Bennet parents bearing a reverse relationship to those of Jane Austen's own, and the representation of a family in danger of "degradation" having some relevance to Jane Austen's own apprehensions of a déclassé state. Yet as Virginia Woolf suggested, the novel is raised to a level of comic power where humor, wit, and intelligence triumph over social obstacles and pettiness. Elizabeth and Darcy are kin to Beatrice and Benedick (particularly in their witty conversations at Netherfield). Elizabeth, to test Virginia Woolf's comparison to *Antony and Cleopatra*, is kin to Cleopatra. When her sister Jane is ill, Elizabeth walks to Netherfield, "crossing field after field at a quick pace, jumping over stiles and springing over puddles with impatient activity, and finding herself at last within view of the house, with weary ancles, dirty stockings, and a face glowing with the warmth of exercise" (*PP*, 32). Did Virginia Woolf recall Enobarbus's memory of Cleopatra?

> I saw her once
> Hop forty paces through the public street;
> And having lost her breath, she spoke, and panted
> That she did make defect perfection,
> And breathless, power breathe forth.[33]

Jane Austen confessed that she considered Elizabeth "as delightful a creature as ever appeared in print" (*Letters*, 297); but even the obnoxious characters are delightful in this novel. The Rev. Mr. Collins descends from a line of moralizing clerics like Dr. Bartlett in *Sir Charles Grandison*, of whose piety he is a splendid parody.[34] Lady Catherine, too, is a type (the *grande dame*), but perhaps the best compliment we can pay to her characterization is to suggest that without her, Oscar Wilde could not have created Lady Bracknell. The danger the critic faces is that he will weigh down this superbly comic novel with ponderous analysis; yet the alternative—a sense of wonder before the book's comic power—is empty praise. For Jane Austen's comedy not only serves and rests on a confident moral vision but emerges from an aesthetic intelligence unequaled in the English novel.

The novel's formal excellence does not disguise its social criticism but includes it within a vision of a worthy society. The plot works first to humble Darcy's patrician pride and then to chasten Elizabeth's antisocial prejudices. In the process a most satisfying structural balance is achieved: if Elizabeth suffers at the beginning from her mother's vulgar behavior at Netherfield, Darcy is later embarrassed by his aunt's rudeness at Rosings. Ill manners are not peculiar to one social level. Nor for that matter is poor taste, as Rosings, the "gaudy" opposite of the "elegant" Pemberley, reveals. Nor, finally, is sexual immorality. Elizabeth's hopes are dashed by the news of her sister Lydia's elopement with Wickham; but in bringing this affair to a successful resolution, Darcy is guiltily aware that he has suppressed the fact of his own sister's earlier elopement with Wickham. Thus Elizabeth's hypothetical definition of "connubial felicity" (*PP*, 312) will, in fact, be fulfilled. By "her ease and liveliness," Darcy's "mind" will be "softened, his manners improved"; and from "his judgment, information, and knowledge of the world," she will receive "benefit of greater importance" (*PP*, 312).

In achieving its *concordia discors* the union of Darcy and Elizabeth defines what is absent from the other marriages in the novel. Mr. and Mrs. Bennet are incompatible opposites, a cause of humor and (increasingly for Elizabeth) of regret. Lydia and Wickham are alike in their appetites, irresponsibility, and rashness. Collins and Charlotte are alike in their prudent, self-serving acceptance of a marriage of convenience. Jane and Bingley are alike in a better sense; yet, though pleasant and unsuspicious by nature, they would never have married if left to themselves. Only in the marriage of Darcy and Elizabeth do we have a vital union that gives assurance that the gap between debased "sense" and morality can be crossed. Such a union is absent from *Sense and Sensibility*. We need not deny that their marriage fulfills the fantasy of sexual compatibility across social and economic divisions. Elizabeth, too, is an offspring of Pamela (or of Harriet Byron). What disarms the charge of fantasy fulfilment, however, is the moral authority the novel gains through its continual moral discriminations.

Jane Austen fills every rift with ore. Her dialogues, summaries, descriptions all carry thematic supercargo. Reading, writing, smiles, laughter, music, art, running, walking, silence, noise: these are only some of the apparently "anodyne data" that pepper the novel's discourse, permitting the author to distinguish between moral and immoral behavior, to measure attitudinal extremes, and to define accommodative norms.[35]

Consider, again, the visit to Netherfield. Elizabeth's instinctive response to her sister's illness is, of course, admirable, a demonstration of her selfless concern as well as of her superior moral character among the Bennets: her mother's scheming is the cause of Jane's cold in the first place; her father's disengagement is no help; her sisters, Kitty and Lydia, agree to accompany her on the walk, but only "as far as Meryton," where they hope to meet the officers. Yet it is not quite enough to admire Elizabeth's action. We can discount, of course, the jealous criticisms of the Bingley sisters, who object to her "wild" appearance, her "petticoat, six inches deep in mud," and the very idea of her "scampering about the country" (PP, 35–36). And we surely prefer Bingley's response to the episode: he has not noticed the dirty petticoat and excuses Elizabeth's actions on the grounds of her affection for Jane. But we have also to assess Darcy's divided response: he admits he would not wish to see his sister "make such an exhibition," and yet, to the disappointment of Miss Bingley, his admiration of Elizabeth's "fine eyes . . . brightened by the exercise" has increased.

We are asked to read the episode both realistically, in terms of its psychological disclosure, and thematically, as a means of normative definition. Both Bingley and his sisters are "prejudiced" here, their positive and negative interpretations preceding a true judgment of the event; only Darcy (whose uncle was a judge) is judicious. This is not to say that his criticism exposes Elizabeth's behavior; because it is morally motivated, her vigorous, instinctive, socially unconventional action is, on this occasion, censureproof. Yet Miss Bingley's charge that Elizabeth has shown a "sort of conceited independence, a most country town indifference to decorum" (PP, 36), does more than reveal her jealous resentment. Other "independent" characters—like Elizabeth's sister Lydia, given to instinctive self-gratification, "wild" behavior, noisy laughter, indecorous "scampering" here and here—are open to censure. Even Elizabeth herself, when she prejudicially accepts Wickham's version of the history of his relationship with Darcy, can culpably ignore the "rules" of decorum in a misguided reliance on "first impressions."

In the Netherfield episode Elizabeth's "primitive" behavior is obviously preferable to the "civilized" rectitude of the Bingley sisters; and elsewhere in the novel, in Mary Bennet's bookish erudition, in Collins's formulaic pedantry, in Darcy's own grave insistence on punctilio and rules (all these characters go by the book, we might say), the uses of "civilization" to suppress spontaneity and exclude individual aspirations are laughed out of court. But *Pride and Prejudice* is, in the end, a very civilized novel. It calls for a worthy "marriage" of individual behavior and social conventions; it asks that the rules be informed by individual commitment; it requires the continuous exercise of active and intelligent (rather than formulaic) judgment. Darcy's admiration of Elizabeth's fine eyes represents his accessibility to what is worthy in her individualist position; she will learn that inherited social and moral principles are worthy of her commitment. The thematic marriage repeatedly implied from the beginning is confirmed by the marriage of the sexes at the end; and, by a superb accommodation of themes, Jane Austen justifies Elizabeth's final accommodations at Pemberley.

## VII

*Mansfield Park*, the first of the Chawton novels, composed between February 1811 and June 1813, is not an accommodative novel in the manner of *Pride and Prejudice*, nor can its heroine, Fanny Price—timid, unassertive, physically weak—be said to invigorate her adoptive culture when she becomes mistress of the Mansfield parsonage. In this novel, vigor describes not the heroine, as in *Pride and Prejudice* and *Emma*, but the anti-heroine, Mary Crawford, whose "London" values are finally expelled from the park. Lionel Trilling recognized the affront Fanny poses to many modern readers but went on to argue that the "almost perverse rejection of Mary Crawford's vitality in favor of Fanny's debility lies at the very heart of the novel's intention."[36]

Trilling's view of the novel's rhetoric is surely right. Jane Austen consistently exposes the danger of any union with the Crawfords. Especially in the beautifully choreographed sequences in the first volume (the visit to Sotherton and the theatricals episode), her serious, even Christian, intention is conveyed through dialogue and setting. Walking through the grounds of Sotherton, the Bertrams and the Crawfords leave accustomed "paths"; enter a moral "wilderness"; follow "winding," "serpentine," and "circuitous" ways; and break social bounds. Acting in *Lovers' Vows*, they impersonate dramatic roles that prefigure their future errors, while failing to fulfill the responsibilities of their given or chosen roles (elder son, clergyman, affianced woman). In turning "house" ("my father's house") into "theatre," they endanger the moral fabric of their inheritance as surely as Maria Bertram risks tearing her gown, when—"so far from the house already"—she squeezes past the gate and crosses the ha-ha with Henry Crawford rather than wait for her fiancé, who is "so long fetching [the] key" (*MP*, 97–100). None of the other novels reaches quite the same level of symbolic resonance, or the same command of double entendre in description and dialogue; none more successfully foreshadows its conclusion; and with Tom Bertram chastened by illness, Maria exiled following her adultery and divorce, and the Crawfords banished, no conclusion is less accommodating.

Yet running beneath rhetorical "intention" there is a stream of fantasy in *Mansfield Park*, which may partly account for its perennial ability to offend readers, especially those who have a Nietzschean suspicion of the Christian ethic. At the still center of the moving world sits Fanny Price, the Christian heroine, the meek woman who inherits the Mansfield earth, "the lowest and the last" (*MP*, 221) who becomes first, the object of charity who—Sir Thomas finally recognizes—is "the daughter that he wanted" (*MP*, 472). The fantasy fulfilled in *Mansfield Park* is not erotic but social and moral, the fantasy of a society saved from corruption by the fidelity of its least powerful, most marginal figure. As usual, Jane Austen seeks to "desublimate" her final union (*MP*, 470) and, as at the end of *Sense and Sensibility*, to concede that her fictional distribution of rewards and punishments achieves patterns of unrealistic neatness (*MP*, 468–69). But social fantasy persists in the novel, along with social anxieties that are, as usual, expressed in descriptions of accommodations and interiors. At every stage, Fanny's social options are defined and limited by the physical space she inhabits. On arrival at Mansfield as a child of ten, she is "placed" (in more than one sense) "in the little white attic . . . so near Miss Lee [the governess], and not far from the girls, and close by the housemaids" (*MP*, 910). By age eighteen, she has "artlessly" annexed the East Room, thus making up for "the deficiency of space and accommodation" in the attic (*MP*, 151). In the East Room, Fanny's position is still marginal, but she has more than Jane Austen had in Chawton Cottage: space for privacy and withdrawal, "a room of her own" where she can pursue her interests in plants and works of charity, read Crabbe and Johnson, and hang her transparencies of Tintern Abbey and the Lake District. Fanny in the East Room represents the kind of life Jane Austen might have led had Edward taken her into the household at Godmersham; her existence surely also mirrors that of many single women in the period, with "good" connections and reduced means. But in *Mansfield Park*, Jane Austen imagines social possibilities both better and worse than the East Room. Fanny's journey to the better possibility (the Mansfield parsonage) involves a trip to the worse (her old home in Portsmouth).

The Portsmouth episode (*MP*, 375–447) is the single most problematic sequence in Jane Austen. Like Emma Watson, Fanny returns home and, out of a consciousness formed in a spacious and elegant adoptive environment, finds her home not only deficient in decorum but a cause of disgust: "She sat in a blaze of oppressive heat, in a cloud of moving dust; and her eyes could only wander from the walls marked by her father's head, to the table cut and knotched by her brothers, where stood the tea-board never thoroughly cleaned, the cups and saucers wiped in streaks, the milk a mixture of motes floating in thin blue, and the bread and butter growing every minute more greasy than even Rebecca's hands had first produced it" (*MP*, 439).

In having Fanny repudiate her noisy, disordered home (where "felicity" is defined as escaping from the "evil" of Henry Crawford's having to dine in her father's house), Jane Austen serves up a dish that is harder to swallow, for many readers, than "Rebecca's puddings and Rebecca's hashes" (*MP*, 413). In having her discover in her sister Susan an "innate" taste for "the genteel and the well-appointed" (*MP*, 419), she strikes a false note. And in allowing her "a review of the two houses," she provides a nostalgic retrospect in which the moral anarchy of Mansfield, and Fanny's sufferings there, are largely suppressed in an unconvincing picture of elegance, propriety, and regularity (*MP*, 391–92).

The rhetorical intention of the episode is to reveal the collapse of the Mansfield society during Fanny's banishment; in Portsmouth she becomes the absent center of reference and values, the confidante—through letters—of Lady Bertram, Edmund and Mary Crawford. But as the descriptions of the Price household reveal, the rhetorical and structural ironies of the episode accompany, perhaps cover, a nightmare vision of claustrophobia, oppression, and dirt. The subtext of Fanny's Portsmouth experience is a living-through of the possibility of real social distress, glimpsed elsewhere in Miss Bates's dark and narrow staircase in *Emma*, and described in fuller and more threatening detail in Mrs. Smith's restricted accommodations, noisy parlor, and dark bedroom in *Persuasion*.[37] In having Fanny experience the horror (however temporary) of this fate, Jane Austen complicates her heroine's role, which is otherwise to be the rock and guardian of traditional values. Fanny's double role is perhaps at the heart of *Mansfield Park's* problem. In its "public"intention, the novel brilliantly imagines the dangers posed to inherited cultural structures (an estate, the Anglican liturgy, the English language itself) by the irresponsibility and materialism of its heirs. But in its "private" apprehensions, it takes a rather too "masochistic" interest in Fanny's weakness and suffering.

This dimension of the novel is evident throughout in the character of Mrs. Norris, who warrants comparison with Snow White's stepmother, the scheming and sadistic Queen.[38] Mrs. Norris's enmity to Fanny is constant: she opposes her getting a horse, visiting Sotherton, dining out; she ensures that there is no fire for her in the East Room; she tries to prevent the ball in her honor; and she is incensed when Crawford proposes to her. Her bitter opposition to Fanny's rise, however, is not simply a fairytale given; it originates in her sense of insulted ambition. As eldest of the three Ward sisters, she has seen a younger sister marry a baronet, her fortune of £7,000 being "at least three thousand pounds short of any equitable claim" (*MP*, 3). Some six years later, she herself marries the Rev. Mr. Norris, who, "with scarcely any private fortune," is given the Mansfield living. Mr. and Mrs. Norris begin "their career of conjugal felicity with very little less than a thousand a year" (*MP*, 3). (This is a comfortable income in Jane Austen's scale, close to that enjoyed by Jane Austen's brother James, before Leigh Perrot's will made him richer.) But when Fanny is fifteen, Mr. Norris dies, and the Mansfield living devolves on Dr. Grant. Her income reduced, Mrs. Norris moves to the White House, refusing to take Fanny with her on the grounds that she has "barely enough to support [herself] in the rank of gentlewoman" (*MP*, 29). Once again, the financial details are precise, allowing us to estimate what Mrs. Norris sets as a minimum income for a gentlewoman, as well as the income lost to Edmund as a result of his elder brother's extravagance.[39]

Mrs. Norris is a brilliant portrait of a woman, embittered in her own social experience, who seeks to prevent the "encroachments" of her indigent niece and others who reveal the "folly" of "stepping out of their rank" (*MP*, 221). Her own rise blocked, she compensates by associating with those, like Maria, whose position and prospects are splendid. By economizing over the years, she almost doubles her principal; by "sponging," she increases her stock. We can understand her attraction for feminist critics. She is the most energetic of Jane Austen's villains—arranging, contriving, directing, dictating, managing, projecting, promoting, planting, improving, walking, and so on, throughout the novel. Jane Austen observes that she would have managed nine children on a small income better than her sister, Mrs. Price. But it is misguided to view her sympathetically. While her strategies are understandable, they are hardly admirable. Jane Austen imagines her psychology brilliantly, not to sympathize with her but to expose the selfishness of her schemes and "spirit of activity."

## VIII

With a fortune of £30,000, the heroine of *Emma* (1816) lacks Mrs. Norris's motives for displaying a "spirit of activity" and pursuing schemes and promotions. Emma is richer than Mary Crawford, who considers her £20,000 more than enough to catch the eldest son of a baronet, and far richer than Anne Elliot, daughter of a spendthrift baronet, who will be lucky to receive her portion of £10,000. Financially secure, Emma nevertheless bears a superficial resemblance to Mrs. Norris, who loves to manage and direct. Like Mrs. Norris, she is a matchmaker, taking credit for the marriage of her governess, Miss Taylor, to Mr. Weston and promoting matches for her friend Harriet Smith with, successively, Mr. Elton, Frank Churchill, and an "unnamed" gentleman who turns out (to her chagrin) to be Mr. Knightley. She exaggerates the social claims of Harriet (who becomes a kind of surrogate for herself in search of a husband), at the same time depressing the social claims of Robert Martin, the worthy tenant farmer and proper suitor for Harriet's hand. She also opposes the encroachments of the aspiring Eltons and Coles. Her snobbery in these instances aligns her with Mrs. Norris, but in spite of such resemblances, she is no real kin to that "officious" character. Her activity poses no final danger to her society; like Elizabeth Bennet, she chooses to accommodate her energies within social bounds. Her self-limitation is not, any more than Elizabeth's, abject or conformist; in accepting her culture, she invigorates and improves it.

The community in which Emma finds accommodations for her wit and vitality is a traditional community, ideally characterized by its members' adherence to public structures of manners and morals. The consistent exemplar of this community is Mr. Knightley, whose Donwell Abbey, as we have seen, is a metonym for a moral economy operating according to unwritten rules and inherited obligations. Throughout the novel Mr. Knightley the gentleman is opposed to Frank Churchill the gallant. At the end of the first volume, the terms of their opposition appear in Knightley's response to Churchill's "letter of excuse" for yet another failure to pay a promised visit to his father and his father's new bride. In Knightley's view, Churchill has failed to do his "duty," which "a man can always do, if he chuses . . . not by manoeuvring and finessing, but by vigour and resolution" (*E*, 146). Knightley's judgments are uncompromising, but not seriously flawed by his incipient jealousy of a possible rival. "Your amiable young man," he tells Emma, "can be amiable only in French, not in English. He may be very 'aimable,' have very good manners, and be very agreeable; but he can have no English delicacy towards the feelings of other people; nothing really amiable about him" (*E*, 149).

Endorsing Mr. Knightley's code of conduct, Jane Austen extends and complicates the contrast between Knightley's "open" world of work, truth, and social obligation and Churchill's "closed" world of games, duplicity, and selfishness. Though the tone of *Emma* remains comic, something of *Mansfield Park*'s seriousness is communicated by the vocabulary of secrecy, deceit, hypocrisy, double-dealing, mystery, finesse, equivocation and even "espionage" (*E*, 399) that attaches to Churchill's games and maneuvers. Trivial and amusing as his "whims" and "freaks" may seem, they carry implications of cultural treachery. Secretly engaged to Jane Fairfax, he has presented himself as "disengaged." Greatly given to talk, he has misled and deceived. By misusing "communication," he has endangered "community."[40]

As social and moral norm, Knightley is not to everyone's taste, and in recent years a number of critics have sought to deny or qualify readings of *Emma* as a novel about the heroine's moral education.[41] Certainly, *Emma* is more than this, but to the considerable extent that it describes Emma's change of attitude—a change described in a vocabulary of "penance" (*E*, 141, 182) and "mortification" (*E*, 376)—the novel expresses Jane Austen's commitment to a traditional morality. As an heiress, Emma does not at first consider the problems of distressed gentlewomen to be of much concern. She airily informs Harriet that "a single woman, with a very narrow income, must be a ridiculous, disagreeable old maid! the proper sport of boys and girls" (*E*, 85). And on Box Hill she fulfills her prophecy by indeed making Miss Bates the object of her "sport" (*E*, 370). But Emma's insult is neither "proper" nor "amiable"; caught up in Churchill's world of games, she fails to observe that "English delicacy towards the feelings of other people," which Knightley had earlier found to be lacking in Churchill's behavior.

The Box Hill episode suggests that Jane Austen's "solution" to the predicament of the poor single woman is a traditional appeal to the gentry's sense of social obligation. Such a solution would not have satisfied Mary Wollstonecraft, and—for many readers—does not accommodate the difficulties presented by Jane Fairfax's situation. Jane's difficulties are partly the consequence of her having placed herself beyond the reach of traditional forms of help. Trapped in her clandestine engagement to Churchill, never securely confident that he will fulfill his promise, Jane contemplates with horror a future in which she must seek employment at "offices for the sale—not quite of human flesh—but of human intellect" (E, 300). At such moments, the shadow of another story darkens the summer romance of *Emma*, but the substance of that story had to await Charlotte Bronte's telling in *Jane Eyre* and *Villette*.

Jane Fairfax's story allows for the exploration of other difficulties in *Emma*—the difficulty, for example, of accommodating nouveau riche aspirations in a settled community. Waiting for Churchill's decision, Jane has to endure the insufferable and officious intermeddling in her affairs of Mrs. Elton, née Augusta Hawkins, the younger of two daughters of a Bristol merchant. In Emma's infuriated responses to Mrs. Elton's "pert pretension and under-bred finery" (E, 279), a good deal of the novel's humor resides. Her anger is expelled in a flurry of plosives directed against Mrs. Elton's "pique and pretension" (E, 182), her "pic-nic Parade" (E, 352), which suggest that her antagonism results not so much from a moral position as from a sense of her own insulted priority in Highbury. A moral opposition there is to Mrs. Elton, however, in Knightley, who here as elsewhere bears the burden of Jane Austen's trust in a gentry version of noblesse oblige. Bringing his gifts of apples to the Bates household, thoughtfully providing his carriage for their conveyance, Mr. Knightley "naturally" exemplifies both the form and spirit of the gentry life, which (as Jane Austen believes) an *arriviste* like Mrs. Elton can only "artificially" and unsuccessfully imitate. Even as we recognize the ideological assumptions here, we delight in the counterpoint achieved between Mr. Knightley's manners and Mrs. Elton's ill-breeding—as for example during the absurd alfresco strawberry party that Mrs. Elton takes it upon herself to "manage" at Donwell Abbey (E, III, ch. 6).

*Emma* may contain yet another kind of accommodation: the accommodation of the creative artist in a communal society. Emma is an "imaginist" (E, 335), who seeks to improve upon the actual, as in her portrait of Harriet (E, 47–48), or who uses her creative imagination to invest an everyday view, like the street scene visible from Ford's, with aesthetic order and meaning (E, 233). Adept at word games and puzzles, she is also a superb mimic, capable of imitating (with cruel accuracy) the scattered thoughts and uncoordinated syntax of Miss Bates (E, 225). As Jane Austen was well aware, verbal wit can endanger communal values—this is the lesson of Box Hill. Even earlier, Emma had resolved on "repressing imagination all the rest of her life," following the fiasco of her scheme to have Harriet marry Elton (E, 142). She does not keep her resolve, of course, for if she were to do so, she would impugn her author's own vocation. Jane Austen's task in *Emma* is to marry Emma's "wit" to Knightley's "wisdom," not to eradicate her wit—to distinguish and expose the false uses of the imagination while affirming society's hospitality to the true. To this end she involves herself in a curious paradox: while exposing the social dangers of Churchill's duplicity, as author she creates a duplicitous discourse. *Emma* is a good example of Roland Barthes's classic plot, in which the reader (at least on a first reading) is prevented from discovering the "hermeneutic" secret (here Churchill's engagement to Jane) by a series of false or partial clues, dissimulations, snares, and delays.[42]Churchill's equivocations with Emma and other characters parallel Jane Austen's equivocations with the reader. Indeed, as readers we have yet to sound all the depths of her tricks, secrets, and double-dealing in the novel. In pursuing this paradox, we can find in *Emma* an interest beyond its affirmative social and moral meanings, but we need not argue that the paradox introduces a fissure between her aesthetic and moral commitments. Even Mr. Knightley, "open" as he is, can (as we are amused to observe) adopt a measure of art in promoting, directing, and arranging the marriage of Harriet and Robert Martin, which confirms in this novel the viability of an organic community. In something of the same way, Jane Austen's art in *Emma* works in the service of her social ideals.

## IX

The success with which *Emma* accommodates its imaginative heroine in a traditional community invites us to read Jane Austen's conservative commitment as a sincere response rather than a conventional cover or camouflage. Unlike *Emma*, however, *Persuasion* (1818) does not bring its heroine to a defined social place and role; and in the last novel the attitude to social heritage differs subtly, if not in the end radically, from that communicated in the earlier novels. Though Anne Elliot becomes the wife of Captain Wentworth and the delighted mistress of a "very pretty landaulette," she has (as her status-obsessed sister Mary observes with satisfaction) "no Uppercross-hall before her, no landed estate, no headship of a family" (*P*, 250). *Persuasion* marks a new direction in Jane Austen's search for accommodations. Her deliberate decision not to provide Anne with abbey, house, hall, place, park, or cottage on her marriage to a man who has gained a fortune of £25,000 from prize money does not indicate— as the failure to finish *The Watsons* did—an oppressed sense of insurmountable difficulties to be overcome. The nature of the problem has changed, as has the kind of accommodation sought.

One way to describe the new direction of *Persuasion* is to compare Anne Elliot's role with that of Fanny Price. Like Fanny, Anne is often made aware of her "own nothingness" (*P*, 42). Fanny, however, becomes involved despite herself in issues of social importance at Sotherton, Mansfield, and Thornton Lacey, defending traditional "grounds" from the injuries of selfish improvements, innovative behavior, and materialistic ways. When she becomes the mistress of the Mansfield parsonage, she redeems her society. In *Persuasion*, by contrast, "place" is no longer there to be defended, since Sir Walter Elliot, the "foolish spendthrift baronet, who had not had principle or sense enough to maintain himself in the situation in which Providence had placed him" (*P*, 248), has rented his ancestral home and moved to Bath, where, to Anne's sorrow, he feels "no degradation in his change" (*P*, 138). Kellynch Hall will never be Anne's to "improve," nor is she to find a home like Uppercross (of which she could have been mistress one day, had she accepted Charles Musgrove's proposal of marriage).

Uppercross mansion, with "its high walls, great gates, and old trees, substantial and unmodernized" (*P*, 36), exists at the heart of the kind of organic community Jane Austen had described in her positive pictures of places like Delaford and Thornton Lacey. But in *Persuasion* the viability of its "old English style" is put in some question. Charles Musgrove, heir to the estate, has introduced improvements in the community in the form of a farmhouse "elevated into a cottage," complete with "viranda, French windows, and other prettinesses" (*P*, 36). Meanwhile, within the great house the Musgrove girls have created an air of confusion in the old-fashioned, wainscoted parlor, by furnishing it with a pianoforte, harp, flower stands, and "little tables placed in every direction" (*P*, 40). The ancestral portraits seem "to be staring in astonishment" at "such an overthrow of all order and neatness" (*P*, 40). Yet despite her exposure of the selfishness of the younger generation, Jane Austen does not adopt a censorious attitude. In this respect, *Persuasion* differs from earlier works in which the desire of Mary Crawford to new-furnish Mansfield (*MP*, 48) or of Marianne Dashwood to new-furnish Allenham (*SS*, 69) were suspect signs of "modern manners" to be repudiated by the reader.

Anne's task in *Persuasion* is not, then, to reclaim Kellynch (debased beyond Anne's powers of recovery by her father's extravagance, otiosity, and absurd pride in rank) but to discover new possibilities of accommodation for herself. Thus in conversation with Mr. Elliot, her false suitor, she proclaims herself "too proud to enjoy a welcome which depends so entirely upon place" (P, 151), while later she assures Wentworth that "every fresh place would be interesting to me" (P, 184). The novel provides Anne with a number of "fresh" possibilities of accommodation, which are associated not with the stabilities of the land (Winthrop, the future home of Henrietta Musgrove is significantly described as an "indifferent" place, "without beauty and without dignity" [P, 85]) but with the risks and uncertainties of life at sea or among sailors. Mrs. Croft knows "nothing superior to the accommodations of a man of war," having lived with her husband Admiral Croft in no fewer than five ships, crossed the Atlantic four times, and been once to the East Indies (P, 68–70).[43] Ashore, the Crofts are tenants of Kellynch, where their improvements include the removal of a number of large looking glasses from Sir Walter's dressing room. They drive an unfashionable gig and, while in Bath, live in lodgings that are none the worse, as the Admiral tells Anne, "for putting us in mind of those we first had at North Yarmouth. The wind blows through one of the cupboards just in the same way" (P, 170). Described as "generally out of doors together . . . dawdling about in a way not endurable to a third person" (P, 73), the Crofts are the most successful portrait of seasoned "connubial felicity" in Jane Austen's work. Their partnership in life, no less than in their style of driving the gig (P, 92), provides Anne with a model of marriage, an exemplary way of responding to an existence in which the waters are not always smooth.

A second naval family, the Harvilles, provides another positive example. Anne meets Captain Harville in Lyme shortly before Louisa Musgrove's disastrous leap from the steps on the Cobb calls into question the nature of her "fortitude." Suffering from a severe wound, Harville reveals a more estimable form of fortitude in his modest house near the Cobb. Its rooms are so small that Anne is at first astonished that he can think them "capable of accommodating so many." But her astonishment gives way to pleasure deriving from "all the ingenious contrivances and nice arrangements of Captain Harville, to turn the actual space to the best possible account, to supply the deficiencies of lodging-house furniture, and defend the windows and doors against the winter storms to be expected" (P, 98). In his illness, Captain Harville has at least set his house in order; and we are surely asked to discover in his usefulness, active employment, and positive outlook an exemplary response to reduced social expectations. Like Mrs. Smith in her even worse circumstances in Westgate Buildings, Harville responds not only with resolution and independence but with "elasticity of mind" (P, 154). Without fortune or carriage or spacious accommodations, Harville extends an "uncommon" degree of hospitality to the visitors in Lyme, whereas the Elliots in Bath, in sycophantic pursuit of their aristocratic relations and guiltily aware of their own reduced style of living, have altogether abandoned "old fashioned notions" of "country hospitality" (P, 219).

So consistent is the contrast between the landed and the naval characters in *Persuasion*, and so consistent the preference for the latter, that critics (myself included) have been led to make excessive historical claims concerning the new directions of the novel. We should not see the renting of Kellynch Hall as a doom-laden portent of the decline of the landed order; nor should we see in the energy and initiative of the naval characters implications as to the arrival on the social scene of a new, perhaps "bourgeois," class.[44] As Jane Austen's own family showed, a modest but well-connected gentry family could more than adequately fill both landed and naval roles in the period. Nor should we see *Persuasion*'s new directions as a contradiction of the traditional values embodied in the character of Mr. Knightley. It is true that in her last completed novel, Jane Austen reexamines both the idea of the gentleman and the role of manners. But in repudiating Sir Walter's definition of the gentlemen—which excludes sailors on the grounds that they are without property, have to work, and are exposed to inclement weather that ravages their looks—she does not abandon her trust in gentlemanly behavior; and in consistently presenting the hypocritical Mr. Elliot as a man of "polished" manners, she does not renounce her faith in morally informed manners as a medium of social intercourse.

The contrast between land and sea in *Persuasion* works not to announce a new social leadership but rather to open new possibilities of accommodation for the marginal woman. What if our hopes of landed entitlement are disappointed—is this the end of the world? "Desire" is, of course, fulfilled in the marriage of Anne to Wentworth, but the dependence on marriage for the closure of the novel's plot is not escapist, in view of the positive examples of the Crofts, the Harvilles, Mrs. Smith, and Anne herself, who in the lonely period before her rapprochement with Wentworth showed stoicism, self-reliance, and above all "usefulness" in her social relations.

Even the most interesting of *Persuasion*'s new directions, its new attitude to nature, needs careful description. Sister of a great landowner, Jane Austen had always shown (like Fanny on her trip to Sotherton) a proprietary interest in "the appearance of the country, the bearings of the roads, the difference of soil, the state of the harvest, the cottages, the cattle" (*MP*, 80). In her last works, however, nature begins to express states of consciousness, as her heroines respond to atmospheric conditions and seasonal moods.[45] On the walk to Winthrop, for example, Anne's "autumnal" feelings of loss and loneliness find consolation in "the view of the last smiles of the year upon the tawny leaves and withered hedges" (P, 84). But such "romanticism" is closer to that expressed in the sonnets of Charlotte Smith (1784) and William Lisle Bowles (1789) than to that of Wordsworth or Coleridge, and unlike Captain Benwick's romantic attitudes, it is never allowed to become self-indulgent. Even so, Anne's feelings for the natural scene mark a new emphasis in Jane Austen's response to the land, which is no longer viewed mainly as a place to be inhabited by the heroine in a responsible social role but as a possible source of alternative emotional consolation.

Like *Persuasion*, Jane Austen's unfinished fragment *Sanditon*, written in the winter before her death on 18 July 1817, also shows signs of a more private interest in nature. *Sanditon* describes with remarkable brio the transformation of an old village into a seaside resort for valetudinarians. Mr. Parker and Lady Denham are partners in this speculative enterprise, which brilliantly captures aspects of the rootless, fashion-seeking Regency era.[46] Mr. Parker makes of his inheritance "his Mine, his Lottery, his Speculation & his Hobby Horse" (MW, 372). He moves from his old house—like Donwell Abbey, unfashionably low and sheltered but "rich in . . . Garden, Orchard & Meadows"—to a new house, to which he gives the topical name of Trafalgar House. Trafalgar House lacks a kitchen garden and shade trees, is exposed to winter storms, and is built near a cliff "on the most elevated spot on the Down" (MW, 379, 384). Jane Austen's satire is in the eighteenth-century tradition of Horace Walpole, who, in a letter to Montagu (15 June 1768), wrote: "How our ancestors would laugh at us, who knew there was no being comfortable, unless you had a high hill before your nose, and a thick warm wood at your back! Taste is too freezing a commodity for us, and depend upon it will go out of fashion again."[47] It seems clear that the lofty and precarious location of Mr. Parker's new house was intended to prefigure the crash of his speculative ventures, but what is remarkable about *Sanditon* is Jane Austen's sang-froid in face of the "improvements" she describes. Here, after all, is the theme of *Mansfield Park*, but *Sanditon's* heroine is unlikely to play Fanny's role of social redeemer, or even of social conscience. Like Emma, she responds aesthetically to the external scene, finding "amusement enough in standing at her ample Venetian window, & looking over the miscellaneous foreground of unfinished Buildings, waving Linen, & tops of Houses, to the Sea, dancing & sparkling in Sunshine & Freshness" (MW, 384). Charlotte Heywood is like previous heroines in emerging from a traditional rural home into the glare of a materialistic world, but her accommodation to this world is more detached, more self-contained; she finds the Sanditon

264

scene "very striking—and very amusing—or very melancholy, just as Satire or Morality might prevail" (*MW*, 396). And rather than being critical of Sanditon's "modern" developments, she views them "with the calmness of amused curiosity" (*MW*, 384). *Sanditon* is a remarkable work by a woman about to move into her last accommodations in College Street, Winchester. In its satire of hypochondria, it announces itself to be on the side of life and health; and in its presentation of the heroine, it arouses our curiosity. Like Mr. Knightley in his early concern for Emma, we "wonder what will become of her" (*E*, 40). More than in her future husband, we are interested in the home she would have found.[48]

***

### Notes

1. All page references to Jane Austen's fiction are to *The Novels of Jane Austen*, ed. R.W. Chapman, 3rd ed., 5 vols. (London: Oxford Univ. Press, 1932–34), or to *The Works of Jane Austen: Minor Works*, ed. R.W. Chapman, rev. B.C. Southam (London: Oxford Univ. Press, 1954, rev. 1969). Where appropriate, novels will be indicated by the initial letters of their titles; *MW* stands for *Minor Works*.

2. Brian Southam, "*Sanditon*: The Seventh Novel," in *Jane Austen's Achievement*, ed. Juliet McMaster (London: Macmillan, 1976), 12–16; Christopher Kent, " 'Real Solemn History' and Social History," in *Jane Austen in a Social Context*, ed. David Monaghan (Totowa, N.J.: Barnes & Noble, 1981), 98–99.

3. *A Room of One's Own* (1929; rpt. New York: Harcourt Brace, 1957), 71.

4. For an analysis of Jane Austen's denouements, see Lloyd W. Brown, *Bits of Ivory: Narrative Techniques in Jane Austen's Fiction* (Baton Rouge: Louisiana State Univ. Press, 1973), 199–235; for a consideration of the dialectic played out between realism and desire in *Northanger Abbey*, see George Levine, *The Realistic Imagination* (Chicago: Univ. of Chicago Press, 1981), 61–80.

5. Brigid Brophy, "Jane Austen and the Stuarts," in *Critical Essays on Jane Austen*, ed. B.C. Southam (London: Routledge & Kegan Paul, 1968), 21–38; David Spring, "Interpreters of Jane Austen's Social World," in *Jane Austen: New Perspectives*, ed. Janet Todd (New York: Holmes & Meier, 1983), 53–72. For biographical details I am mainly indebted to R.W. Chapman, *Facts and Problems* (Oxford: Clarendon Press, 1948); George Holbert Tucker, *A Goodly Heritage: A History of Jane Austen's Family* (Manchester: Carcanet New Press, 1983); and John Halperin, *The Life of Jane Austen* (Brighton: Harvester Press, 1984; Baltimore: Johns Hopkins Univ. Press, 1984).

6. Mavis Batey, "Jane Austen at Stoneleigh Abbey," *Country Life* 160 (30 December 1976), 1974–75. Jane Austen's negative use of Repton in *Mansfield Park* troubles scholars who consider his philosophy of tasteful improvement to be close to hers. Along with such predecessors as Dryden, Cowper, and Burke, however, she had a conservative distrust of "improvements," which may explain her (perhaps unfair) treatment of Repton; see Alistair M. Duckworth, "Improvements," in *The Jane Austen Handbook*, ed. J. David Grey et al. (a

forthcoming Scribner publication). It is also possible, as Tucker suggests, that she disliked what she saw of Repton's work at Adlestrop (*Goodly Heritage*, 58).

7. David Waldron Smithers, *Jane Austen in Kent* (Westerham, Kent: Hurtwood Publications, 1981), 17.

8. Two sketches of Steventon Rectory are included in F.B. Pinion's valuable *Jane Austen Companion* (London: Macmillan, 1973), facing p. 18.

9. *Jane Austen's Letters to her Sister Cassandra and Others*, ed. R.W. Chapman, 2d ed. (London: Oxford Univ. Press, 1964), 84. Subsequent page references to the letters are given in the text.

10. For an excellent treatment of the question, see Stuart M. Tave, *Some Words of Jane Austen* (Chicago: Univ. of Chicago Press, 1973), 131–41.

11. The liveliest expression of the vigorous recent movement of feminist criticism of Jane Austen's fiction may be found in Sandra M. Gilbert and Susan Gubar, *The Madwoman in the Attic: The Woman Writer and the Nineteenth-Century Literary Imagination* (New Haven, Conn.: Yale Univ. Press, 1979).

12. *Journal of Katherine Mansfield*, ed. John Middleton Murry (New York: McGraw-Hill, 1927), 5.

13. G.E. Mingay, *English Landed Society in the Eighteenth Century* (London: Routledge & Kegan Paul, 1963).

14. Spring, "Interpreters," 63.

15. *Godmersham Park Sale Catalogue* (London: Christie, 1983), II: 7, item 2003.

16. It should be added that little resentment toward Edward Austen or Mrs. Knight appears in the letters, whereas there is a good deal of resentment expressed toward James Austen and his wife, Mary. Not only had they usurped Jane Austen's childhood home; they seem to have been parsimonious as well. There is also no cause to question Edward's generosity after 1814, when a lawsuit over the ownership of Chawton, followed by Henry's bankruptcy (in 1816) severely depleted his funds.

17. Reproduced in Marghanita Laski, *Jane Austen and Her World* (London: Thames and Hudson, 1969), 72–73. The same work includes contemporary views of Stoneleigh Abbey, Godmersham, and Manydown.

18. Spring, "Interpreters," 61.

19. Readers with antiquarian interests will delight in Chapman's copious illustrations of carriages in *The Oxford Illustrated Jane Austen* (i.e., the standard text); F.B. Pinion has a more critical interest, to which I am indebted; see *A Jane Austen Companion*, 28–29.

20. Gilbert and Gubar, *Madwoman*, 117.

21. Ibid., 153.

22. For Jane Austen's defense of the gentry against pressures from above and below, see David Monaghan, *Jane Austen: Structure and Social Vision* (Totowa, N.J.: Barnes & Noble, 1980), 7, and elsewhere.

23. For a different view of Jane Austen in relation to Mary Wollstonecraft, see Margaret Kirkham, *Jane Austen, Feminism and Fiction* (Brighton: Harvester Press, 1983).

24. Spring, "Interpreters," 64–65.

25. Proposing that "the walk to church from a beautiful country-house, of a lovely summer afternoon, may be the prettiest possible adventure," Henry James also described the Warwickshire countryside as expressing "imperturbable

British Toryism." The fact that this was a conservative county, he said, was "written in the hedgerows. . . . Of course the owners of these things were conservative; of course they were stubbornly unwilling to see the harmonious edifice of their constituted, convenient world the least bit shaken" (*English Hours*, ed. Leon Edel [Oxford: Oxford Univ. Press, 1981], 117, 120; "In Warwickshire" was written in 1877).

26. Alistair M. Duckworth, *The Improvement of the Estate: A Study of Jane Austen's Novels* (Baltimore: Johns Hopkins Univ. Press, 1974), 38–54.

27. Raymond Williams, *The Country and the City* (London: Oxford Univ. Press, 1973).

28. Terry Lovell, "Jane Austen and Gentry Society," in *Literature, Society and the Sociology of Literature*, ed. Francis Barker et. al. (Colchester: Univ. of Essex, 1977), 120.

29. James Edward Austen-Leigh's opinion in *A Memoir of Jane Austen* (London: R. Bentley, 1870).

30. According to Cassandra's memorandum, *First Impressions* (the original of *Pride and Prejudice*) was begun October 1796 and ended August 1797; *Sense and Sensibility* was begun November 1797.

31. Marilyn Butler, *Jane Austen and the War of Ideas* (Oxford: Clarendon Press, 1975).

32. Even with Colonel Brandon's generous gift of the Delaford living, worth £200 a year, Edward and Elinor face the prospect of beginning married life on £350 a year—the living plus income from his £2,000 and her £1,000. Mrs. Ferrars eventually gives Edward £10,000, which brings their income up to a comfortable but certainly not wealthy £750 a year. This sum would suffice only for "*menus plaisirs*" in the worldly London life of the Crawfords (*MP*, 226). I suspect that Jane Austen's own youthful anticipations may have hovered between "a competence" of £1,000 a year and "wealth" of £2,000 a year; the income of Edmund and Fanny at the end of *Mansfield Park* is between these limits.

33. *Antony and Cleopatra*, II.ii.236–240. When Mr. Gardiner's letter describing the resolution of the Lydia-Wickham affair arrives at Longbourn, Elizabeth runs across the lawn to her father and, "*panting* for breath," eagerly asks, "What news?" (*PP*, 301, italics added).

34. Henrietta Ten Harmsel, *Jane Austen: A Study in Fictional Conventions* (The Hague: Mouton, 1964), 83.

35. For a discussion of the thematic use of "anodyne data" in classic fiction, see Roland Barthes, *S/Z*, trans. Richard Miller (New York: Hill and Wang, 1974), 22–23.

36. Lionel Trilling, "*Mansfield Park*," in *The Opposing Self* (1955); reprinted in *Jane Austen: A Collection of Critical Essays*, ed. Ian Watt (Englewood Cliffs, N.J.: Prentice-Hall, 1963), 128.

37. Sidney Ives has suggested that the squalor of the Price household owes its origin to Jane Leigh Perrot's experiences (and her epistolary description of the same) in the Scaddings household, Ilchester. She was held there, at her own expense, in the autumn and winter of 1799–1800, while awaiting trial on the charge of shoplifting (of which she was acquitted). See *The Trial of Mrs. Leigh Perrot* (Boston: Club of Odd Volumes, 1980), 13–15, 29–32.

38. Gilbert and Gubar, *Madwoman*, 172.

39. If we assume that, like her sister Lady Bertram, Mrs. Norris has a fortune of £7,000, or £350 a year, then by subtracting this from "very little less than a thousand a year," we can estimate the Mansfield living as bringing in about £600 a year (since Mr. Norris has "scarcely any private fortune"). After Mr. Norris's death, however, his widow will have, according to Sir Thomas, £600 a year (*MP*, 29). This means that she has raised her principal to £12,000, which suggests in turn that over her married life of roughly twenty years, she must have saved something like £200 a year. These details not only illuminate Mrs. Norris's character as an "economist" ("I must live within my income, or I shall be miserable" [*MP*, 30] but also allow for a retrospective criticism of Mr. Bennet in *Pride and Prejudice*, who is unable to save anything from his £2,000 a year.

40. Alistair M. Duckworth, " 'Spillikins, Paper Ships, Riddles, Conundrums, and Cards': Games in Jane Austen's Life and Fiction," in *Jane Austen: Bicentenary Essays*, ed. John Halperin (London: Cambridge Univ. Press, 1975), 292–96.

41. Recent critics who dispute moral interpretations of *Emma* include Julia Prewitt Brown, *Jane Austen's Novels: Social Change and Literary Form* (Cambridge, Mass.: Harvard Univ. Press, 1979), who finds "the drive toward cooperation" in Jane Austen to be dictated by "anthropological" rather than by moral imperatives; Susan Morgan, *In the Meantime: Character and Perception in Jane Austen's Fiction* (Chicago: Univ. of Chicago Press, 1980), who values the perceptual and the epistemological dimensions of *Emma* over the ethical; and Bernard J. Paris, *Character and Conflict in Jane Austen's Novels: A Psychological Approach* (Detroit: Wayne State Univ. Press, 1978), who proposes that Emma's education may be viewed, in Horneyan terms, as Jane Austen's glorification of self-effacement as a strategy of living.

42. Barthes, *S/Z*, 75–76 and passim.

43. One wonders whether the eight hundred sailors crammed between decks in Nelson's *Victory* would agree with Mrs. Croft's opinion respecting the superiority of a man-of-war's accommodations.

44. For David Spring's strictures, see "Interpreters," 65–66.

45. A. Walton Litz, *Jane Austen: A Study of her Artistic Development* (London: Chatto and Windus, 1965), 150–69.

46. Southam, "*Sanditon*," 1–26.

47. *Horace Walpole's Correspondence with George Montagu*, ed. W.S. Lewis and Ralph S. Brown, Jr. (New Haven: Yale Univ. Press, 1941), II, 262.

48. I wish to thank John Fain, John Halperin, Sidney Homan, Sidney Ives, Donald Justice, and Bernard J. Paris for their helpful comments.

# Jack D. Durant

# Books about the Early English Novel: A Survey and a List

Even though the Copyright Act of Queen Anne (1710–1814) entitled the University Library, Cambridge, to a free copy of every new title entered in the Stationers' Register, the authorities of the library apparently saw for the English novel a very bleak future: between 1740 and 1780 they did not keep or claim, according to J.C.T. Oates, a single registered novel except *Sir Charles Grandison.*[1] This oversight was largely repaired—at great expense—by the middle of the nineteenth century, when the "Novel Room" of the library "was one of the most frequented places in it and a memorably impressive sight to lady visitors."[2] And by the middle of the twentieth century, as the following list of books indicates, the early English novel had become a favorite subject of academic critics. In fact, the titles included here—books written in English during the twentieth century on the general subject of the eighteenth-century novel, not about one novelist only—indicate that as a subject of professional study, the early English novel has come into its own during the five middle decades of the twentieth century, between 1930 and 1980. These decades, plus a lustrum on each side, have asked the questions most immediate to the subject.

Of course, no such question claims more immediacy than the one asking what the novel is; and while not really deceived about the complexity of the matter, most literary historians have acceded to definitions similar to that offered by E.A. Baker in his ten-volume *History of the English Novel* (item 7 of the present list): "A prose story, picturing real life, or something corresponding thereto, and having the unity and coherence due to a plot or scheme of some kind or to a definite intention and attitude of mind on the part of the author" (I:11). By way of suggesting that the novel is a tradition and not a coherently developing genre, Edward Wagenknecht, in his *Cavalcade of the English Novel* (87), defines it simply as its own history, and Walter Allen, in *The English Novel: A Short Critical History* (3), sees it as an interplay of art and ideas, a mixture of the timely and timeless. But while asserting the novel's variety and aesthetic richness, these historians make no quarrel with its persistent properties:

prose, fiction, formal integrity, some illusion of reality. In his *Introduction to the English Novel* (41), Arnold Kettle formulates a definition virtually identical to that offered by Baker, though adding the important property of length; in *The English Novel: A Panorama* (76), Lionel Stevenson, remarking that the novel is the first literary type not to require speculation about a murky past, discusses each of its received properties in turn, including its length. Its definition, at least in broad descriptive terms, has found a tentative consensus, for all that its aesthetic continues a subject of closely reasoned debate.

The question of why the form emerged when it did, however, enjoys no such consensus. Ian Watt, in his celebrated *Rise of the Novel* (88), roots the phenomenon in new apprehensions of individual human worth and of the struggle of the individual against economic and social realities. Diana Spearman, in *The Novel and Society* (74), challenges this theory on grounds that the first novels do not represent their own time in any sociologically attestable way; nor do they depict middle-class economic struggle, since the earlier eighteenth century nurtured little concept of a middle class. Instead, she holds, the novel originated in the genius of individual writers who brought superb new quality to previously existing narrative forms. Quite recently, Lennard Davis, in *Factual Fictions: The Origins of the English Novel* (21), has also rejected Watt's theory, arguing that social changes cannot affect literary changes as by osmosis. He suggests that the novel came into being as "a form of defense against censorship, power, and authority" (p. 222); it is a "discourse" unifying news, ideology, history, fact, and fiction. Other theorists see it to originate in reaction, if not in defense. To Frederick R. Karl (36) the novel is an "adversary literature" rising to represent new and often dangerous ideas; to Arnold Kettle (41) it is a bourgeois reaction to feudal rigidity; but to Robert Scholes and Robert Kellogg (66), it is a phenomenon not of reaction but of reconciliation, a new synthesis of two primordial narrative traditions, the "empirical" and the "fictional." The emergence of the novel continues to be a vexed question.

The middle decades of the twentieth century have produced several studies exploring relationships between the novel and other literary forms and modes. In *The Role of Personal Memoirs in English Biography and Novel* (51), John Campbell Major claims for the memoir significant force in the development of two types of fiction before 1740 (amorous intrigue and historical fiction), and he places it in the background of Defoe's techniques of "lying like the truth" in personalized history and historical fiction. Philip Babcock Gove's *Imaginary Voyage in Prose Fiction* (28) first analyzes at length a taxonomy of the imaginary voyage in the eighteenth century, then provides in an annotated checklist 215 instances of it published between 1700 and 1800. Percy G. Adams's *Travelers and Travel-Liars, 1660–1800* (2), while not specifically about the novel, suggests how travel books written with the conscious purpose of deceiving participate in the development of the novel by applying the devices of fiction. Adams's more recent book, *Travel Literature and the Evolution of the Novel* (1), confronts the question directly; it frees both forms from close generic confinement and identifies the qualities they share in their concurrent and continuing evolutions. In the earlier of two twentieth-century books about the novel and the epic, E.M.W. Tillyard (80) sees epic properties in no eighteenth-century novel after Defoe. Such a work as *Tom Jones*, he says, lacks the sustained intensity required of epic and reflects the "manners" rather than the "soul" of a generation. But Thomas E. Maresca (52) credits Fielding with restoring the epic, under the guise of the novel, to the culturally central place it had once held. Fielding discards the outmoded forms of the epic and rediscovers the human nature of the epic hero; he welds epic meaning to epic action.

In discussing the relationship of the novel to the mode of satire, Ronald Paulson, in *Satire and the Novel in Eighteenth-Century England* (59), emphasizes that while the great age of English satire gave place to the great age of the novel, the two forms are not continuous. Rooted in different epistemologies, they represent different perspectives upon morality: one judgmental, the other sympathetic. Nevertheless, the novel accommodates such satiric conventions as the Juvenalian isolated protagonist; and as Paulson demonstrates in *The Fictions of Satire* (58), narrative satires of the Swiftian sort—themselves fictional constructs with stories, plots, and character relationships—merge gradually with the satiric novels of Fielding, Smollett, and Sterne. Emphasizing the differences between satire and the novel, especially of attitude, Susan Auty, in *The Comic Spirit of Eighteenth-Century Novels* (6), perceives an antisplenetic drive, a tendency to demonstrate what is risible rather than ridiculous in human conduct; she traces the vitality of these novels to their crusade against melancholy, waged by means of laughter.

In addition to these several books about the novel in relation to other literary forms and modes, the twentieth century has also produced books about the novel in its manifestations before 1740 and (in one instance) during the single decade of the 1740s. Charlotte Morgan, in *The Rise of the Novel of Manners* (57), after surveying English prose fiction published between 1600 and 1740, concludes that the narrative practices of this period lead directly to the work of Richardson: the epistolary form, the theme of virtue in distress, the deluded girl, the gentlemanly rake, the sentimental narrative. Reaching back yet further, Margaret Schlauch, in *Antecedents of the English Novel 1400–1600* (65), draws upon the received definition of the novel to discuss novelistic attributes in narrative texts from Chaucer to Deloney. John J. Richetti, concentrating on the first four decades of the eighteenth century, explains the popularity of Defoe and Richardson in terms of the ideological myths giving form to such popular narrative types as criminal biography, whore biography, rogue biography, travel literature, and scandal chronicles. In *Popular Fiction before Richardson: Narrative Patterns 1700–1739* (62), Richetti identifies the heroes and heroines of these narratives as individuals daring to survive in the secular world by rejecting or disregarding providential design; in thus opposing specific reality and generalized moral convention, popular narratives help to prepare the main tradition of the novel. Focusing directly upon the *Novels of the 1740s* (11), Jerry Beasley demonstrates that by bringing a special imaginative intensity to bear upon familiar materials, the major novelists of that decade earned the attention accorded them by history; they accommodated their work to as many popular types as possible and rang brilliant variations on the conventions of these types.

Critics inquiring into the distinctive forms taken by the novel during the eighteenth century have ranged widely and provided comprehensive coverage of the subject. By examining the epistolary novel, they have determined that Richardson was less an innovator than a perfecter (22, 70) and that the epistolary mode in later eighteenth-century fiction occurred usually in third rate literature (12). They have distilled from countless picaresque narratives the formal and thematic conventions of the novel of roguery (5, 18, 56). In scrutinizing the novel of sentiment, they have explored its backgrounds (27, 91) and sifted its worth, sometimes to find it stifled by its own misdirected aesthetics (42) and sometimes to see it corrupted not by intrinsic frailty but by philosophically bankrupt practitioners (16). They have chronicled the oriental tale (20) and the magazine novel (53), and discovered in the burlesque novel a necessary balance for the serious one (67). They have offered sweeping surveys of the pedestrian and the perishable in fiction (82), and most of all they have reveled in the gothic novel, charting its place in larger literary movements (61), explaining the psychology of its appeal (77), relating it to other traditions of fiction (90), and effusing the glories of its history (86).

Still other critics have chosen to analyze the literary dynamics of the novel: the social, intellectual, and psychological realities shaping its features and driving its aims. These dynamics usually involve the individual adjusting to some problematic aspect of experience. In fact, Dorothy Van Ghent, in *The English Novel: Form and Function* (85), declares it the procedure of the novel to individualize and organize human experience by isolating the principles of coherence in an event. In *Imagining a Self: Autobiography and Novel in Eighteenth-Century England* (73), Patricia Meyer Spacks identifies the obsession underlying both novel and autobiography as the individual's search for a consistent identity. Leo Braudy, in *Narrative Form in History and Fiction* (15), sees novelists and historians of the eighteenth century apprehending in a new way the effects of time on the individual life; and John Dussinger, in *The Discourse of the Mind in Eighteenth-Century Fiction* (24), perceives behind the dynamics of some novels (the Richardsonian ones more than the Fieldingesque) a fear that individual identity is transient and false. Focusing more narrowly upon formal dynamics, Sheldon Sacks, in *Fiction and the Shape of Belief* (64), explains how novelists use fictional actions to assert personal beliefs, opinions, and prejudices. Eric Rothstein, in *Systems of Order and Inquiry in Later Eighteenth-Century Fiction* (63), demonstrates the formal procedures by which novelists work within received epistemological systems while yet confronting the limitations of these systems; and Robert Donovan, in *The Shaping Vision* (23), explores the inner form inhering in the novelist's view of experience, the narrative "valence" containing from the outset of a novel the formal possibilities available to it. Douglas Brooks, in *Number and Pattern in the Eighteenth-Century Novel* (17), suggests that the more artistically aware novelists turned to numerological conventions in patterning their fiction.

Of course, the eighteenth-century novel asserts yet another kind of dynamic in the relationship it invites between narrator and reader. Insisting that the narrators can never wholly disappear—however fervently some critics may wish them to—Wayne Booth, in *The Rhetoric of Fiction* (14), admires the phenomenon in much eighteenth-century fiction in which the narrator so legitimates his or her character as to make it indispensable to the narrative. In *Limits of the Novel* (31), David Grossvogel argues that the continuing process of conditioning fictions to new relationships between reader and author accounts for the evolution of the novel, and several other critics also explore these relationships in the eighteenth-century novel. In *The Impossible Observer* (83), Robert Uphaus examines the means whereby novelists require their readers to participate in the creative process by responding not just objectively but affectively to the fiction. Wolfgang Iser, in *The Implied Reader* (35), theorizes upon literary effects and responses by noticing how reader involvement coincides with the production of meaning; and John Preston, in *The Created Self* (60), analyzes the "self" generated by the reader of an eighteenth-century novel, a fictional self but one with whom the actual reader is willing to cooperate. Taking a historical view of the subject, Q.D. Leavis, in her *Fiction and the Reading Public* (45), finds the two sorts of reader nurtured separately by Bunyan and Mrs. Behn brought together by the periodical essays and so prepared for the arrival of the novel in the 1740s.

By the end of the eighteenth century, readers of the novel had become—at least to some novelists—ready targets for indoctrination, and twentieth-century books have studied the address of the novel to such great political and cultural themes as the French Revolution (29), the American Revolution (33), the Jacobin movement (39), and the Industrial Revolution (43). Books have also assessed the novel's sense of itself during the eighteenth century by examining reviews and critical essays from the period (79) or by collecting commentary on the subject written by the novelists themselves (8)[3] or their contemporaries (89). Such commentary records the ebb and flow of what one twentieth-century critic, Robert Alter, calls a series of great traditions (4), despite the judgment of another, F.R. Leavis, that the English novel before Jane Austen falls short of true greatness (44).

In books about the novelists themselves, A.D. McKillop devotes his *Early Masters of English Fiction* (50) to the literary careers of Defoe, Richardson, Fielding, Smollett, and Sterne. Bridget MacCarthy, in two books about women writers, first demonstrates that women played a significant part in preparing the way for Richardson (49), then argues that they gradually made the novel their own by directing it toward the world as they perceive it (48). More recently, Hazel Mews has also emphasized the importance of the distinctive female awareness to the development of the novel; women novelists, she writes, did not establish a separate tradition but added comprehensiveness and sensitivity to the main tradition (54). Her book studies woman's changing social role as it affects the work of major women novelists.

Like MacCarthy and Mews, Nancy Miller observes that the novel has always been associated with women; but in *The Heroine's Text* (55) she discusses not female writers but female characters, analyzing novels of eighteenth-century England and France as fictions of a feminine destiny, some leading their heroines from "nothing" to "all" (the euphoric texts), others from "all" to "nothing" (the dysphoric texts). Also concentrating upon female characters, Janet Todd (81) analyzes types of female friendship in eighteenth-century English and French novels. Robert Utter and Gwendolyn Needham, in *Pamela's Daughters* (84), first isolate the traits of character apparent in Richardson's Pamela, then examine these traits separately as they manifest themselves in fictional heroines after Richardson. In books about male characters and character types, Kenneth Slagle discusses the English country squire in eighteenth-century fiction

(72), and Homai Shroff examines, against sociological backgrounds, the idea of the gentlemen (69).

Having asked questions, then, about the nature and origin of the English novel, about its forms, its dynamics, its practitioners, its characters, and its kinships with other literary traditions, twentieth-century critics and scholars have clearly brought it into its own as a subject of professional study. So rich and complex are the currents of criticism that Arthur Sherbo (68) has gone so far as to base his book-length study almost wholly upon reactions to other printed criticism as he reexamines such subjects as Fielding's narrator, the implied reader in Fielding, the moral basis of *Joseph Andrews*, and imagery in *Moll Flanders*. And bibliographers, of course, have assisted scholars by compiling catalogues and checklists of early English fiction (9, 13, 47) and by gathering under one cover the titles of books and articles about the subject (10, 25). To one such gathering, Jerry Beasley's *English Fiction, 1660–1800: A Guide to Information Sources* (10), the present list is very much indebted.

The list excludes books mainly about a single novelist and collections of essays by diverse hands. It includes several books germane to but not specifically about the general subject of the early English novel. A one-sentence annotation purposes to suggest the expository focus of each entry.

1. Adams, Percy G. *Travel Literature and the Evolution of the Novel.* Lexington: Univ. Press of Kentucky, 1983.

    Points relationships in structure, subject, language, tone, and philosophy between two amorphous and continuously evolving literary forms.

2. _____. *Travelers and Travel-Liars, 1660–1800.* Berkeley: Univ. of California Press, 1962.

    Surveys the objects, methods, and effects of travel books written with the conscious purpose of deceiving.

3. Allen, Walter. *The English Novel: A Short Critical History.* New York: Dutton, 1954.

    Presents the novel not as a phenomenon that "progresses" but as a form that successfully combines the timely and timeless.

4. Alter, Robert. *Fielding and the Nature of the Novel.* Cambridge, Mass.: Harvard Univ. Press, 1968.

    Discusses Fielding's novels as vivid models of the form.

5. _____. *Rogue's Progress: Studies in the Picaresque Novel.* Cambridge, Mass.: Harvard Univ. Press, 1964.

Inquires not into the history of the picaresque but its inner nature and distinctive vision.

6. Auty, Susan G. *The Comic Spirit of Eighteenth-Century Novels.* Port Washington, N.Y.: Kennikat, 1975.

Analyzes the critical implications of the novel's antisplenetic spirit.

7. Baker, Ernest A. *The History of the English Novel.* 10 vols. London: Witherby, 1924–39.

Defines the novel and traces its history. (An eleventh volume was added by Lionel Stevenson in 1967.)

8. Barnett, George, ed., *Eighteenth-Century British Novelists on the Novel.* New York: Appleton-Century-Crofts, 1968.

Collects statements by twenty-six novelists.

9. Beasley, Jerry C. *Check List of Prose Fiction Published in England, 1740–1749.* Charlottesville: Univ. Press of Virginia, 1972.

10. _____. *English Fiction, 1660–1800: A Guide to Information Sources.* Detroit: Gale, 1978.

Provides brief annotations of articles and books.

11. _____. *Novels of the 1740s.* Athens: Univ. of Georgia Press, 1982.

Explains the achievements of the major novelists in terms of the literary milieu.

12. Black, Frank Gees. *The Epistolary Novel in the Late Eighteenth Century: A Descriptive and Bibliographical Study.* Eugene: Univ. of Oregon Press, 1940.

Chronicles the decline of the epistolary mode.

13. Block, Andrew. *The English Novel, 1740–1850: A Catalogue Including Prose Romances, Short Stories and Translations of Foreign Fiction.* London: Dawsons of Pell Mell, 1961.

Provides an alphabetical listing.

14. Booth, Wayne C. *The Rhetoric of Fiction.* Chicago: Univ. of Chicago Press, 1961.

Examines authorial control in fiction and vindicates self-conscious narration.

15. Braudy, Leo. *Narrative Form in History and Fiction: Hume, Fielding, and Gibbon.* Princeton: Princeton Univ. Press, 1970.

Explores the effects on narrative form of new apprehensions of time and man's relation to it.

16. Brissenden, R.F. *Virtue in Distress: Studies in the Novel of Sentiment from Richardson to Sade.* New York: Barnes & Noble, 1974.

Defines sentimentalism and isolates distinguishing characteristics of the novel of sentiment.

17. Brooks, Douglas. *Number and Pattern in the Eighteenth-Century Novel: Defoe, Fielding, Smollett, and Sterne.* London: Routledge & Kegan Paul, 1973.

Describes numerically based spatial patterns in the work of these novelists.

18. Chandler, Frank Wadleigh. *The Literature of Roguery.* 2 vols. Boston: Houghton Mifflin, 1907.

Defines the literature of roguery; then traces its progress from Spain through France to England.

19. Church, Richard. *The Growth of the English Novel.* London: Methuen, 1951.

Compares the evolution of the novel to a vegetal growth from seedbed to massive forest.

20. Conant, Martha Pike. *The Oriental Tale in England in the Eighteenth Century.* New York: Columbia Univ. Press, 1908.

Studies the oriental tale in England from 1704 to 1786.

21. Davis, Lennard J. *Factual Fictions: The Origins of the English Novel.* New York: Columbia Univ. Press, 1983.

Rejects old theories of the origins of the novel and posits new ones.

22. Day, Robert Adams. *Told in Letters: Epistolary Fiction before Richardson.* Ann Arbor: Univ. of Michigan Press, 1966.

Discovers that "earlier fiction had anticipated Richardson's novels in all but their total effect."

23. Donovan, Robert Alan. *The Shaping Vision: Imagination in the English Novel from Defoe to Dickens.* Ithaca: Cornell Univ. Press, 1966.

Pursues the inner form that precedes the structure and outer (generic) form of a novel.

24. Dussinger, John A. *The Discourse of the Mind in Eighteenth-Century Fiction.* The Hague: Mouton, 1974.

Examines the effect on fiction of confusion about the relationships between mind and body.

25. Dyson, A.E. *The English Novel: Select Bibliographical Guides.* London: Oxford Univ. Press, 1974.

Contains bibliographic essays on major eighteenth-century novelists.

26. Forsyth, William. *The Novels and Novelists of the Eighteenth Century, in Illustration of the Manners and Morals of the Age.* London: Kennikat, 1970.

Not seen.

27. Foster, James R. *History of the Pre-Romantic Novel in England.* New York: Modern Language Association, 1949.

Roots the sentimental novel in deistic thinking reinforced by latitudinarian and low-church theology.

28. Gove, Philip Babcock. *The Imaginary Voyage in Prose Fiction: A History of its Criticism and a Guide for its Study, with an Annotated Check List of 215 Imaginary Voyages from 1700 to 1800.* New York: Columbia Univ. Press, 1941.

Analyzes the taxonomy of imaginary voyage fiction.

29. Gregory, Allene. *The French Revolution and the English Novel.* New York: Putnam's, 1915.

Discusses against a background of idealistic philosophies the novelists who wrote about the French Revolution.

30. Greiner, Walter F., ed. *English Theories of the Novel. Vol. 2: Eighteenth Century.* Tübingen: Niemeyer, 1970.

Collects commentary on the aesthetics of the novel written between 1700 and 1797.

31. Grossvogel, David I. *Limits of the Novel: Evolutions of a Form from Chaucer to Robbe-Grillet.* Ithaca: Cornell Univ. Press, 1968.

Holds that the evolution of the novel turns upon evolving reader-author relationships.

32. Heidler, Joseph Bunn. *The History, from 1700 to 1800, of English Criticism of Prose Fiction.* Urbana: Univ. of Illinois Press, 1928.

Considers criticism written by English writers and the better-known continental ones.

33. Heilman, Robert Bechtold. *America in English Fiction 1760–1800: The Influence of the American Revolution.* Louisiana State University Studies no. 33. Baton Rouge: Louisiana State Univ. Press, 1937.

Draws conclusions from 450 British novels.

34. Horner, Joyce M. *The English Women Novelists and Their Connection with the Feminist Movement (1688–1797).* Smith College Studies in Modern Languages, vol. 11, no. 1–3 (1929–30). Northampton, Mass.: Smith College, 1930.

Credits early women novelists with expanding women's rights and asserting status for themselves as "Mental Females."

35. Iser, Wolfgang. *The Implied Reader: Patterns of Communication in Prose Fiction from Bunyan to Beckett.* Baltimore: Johns Hopkins Univ. Press, 1974.

Analyzes the literary effects of reader participation.

36. Karl, Frederick R. *The Adversary Literature, The English Novel in the Eighteenth Century: A Study in Genre.* New York: Farrar, Straus &

Giroux, 1974.

Sees the novel as upsetting familiar assumptions about life and society.

37. _____. *A Reader's Guide to the Development of the English Novel in the Eighteenth Century.* London: Thames & Hudson, 1975.

Reissues item 36 above.

38. _____. *A Reader's Guide to the Eighteenth-Century English Novel.* New York: Noonday, 1974.

Reissues item 36 above.

39. Kelly, Gary. *The English Jacobin Novel, 1780–1805.* Oxford: Clarendon, 1976.

Shows the Jacobin novelists as developing a unity of design in which character originates in external circumstances.

40. Kermode, Frank. *The Sense of an Ending: Studies in the Theory of Fiction.* New York: Oxford Univ. Press, 1967.

Sees the sense of form in literary fiction as analogous to the cosmic "fictions" of beginning, middle, and end.

41. Kettle, Arnold. *An Introduction to the English Novel.* 2 vols. London: Hutchinson, 1951 (revised 1967).

Chronicles the novel along two broad lines of concept: life and pattern.

42. Kiely, Robert. *The Romantic Novel in England.* Cambridge, Mass.: Harvard Univ. Press, 1972.

Perceives for the romantic novel an aesthetic unable to express transport and blurred by political concerns.

43. Kovacevic, Ivanka. *Fact into Fiction: English Literature and the Industrial Scene, 1750–1850.* Leicester: Leicester Univ. Press, 1975.

Provides commentary valuable to the milieu of the eighteenth-century novel but not specifically related to it.

44. Leavis, F.R. *The Great Tradition.* London: Chatto and Windus, 1948.

Omits eighteenth-century fiction from the Great Tradition but provides valuable critical touchstones.

45. Leavis, Q.D. *Fiction and the Reading Public.* London: Chatto and Windus, 1932.

Studies (anthropologically) the phenomenon of the best seller and the character of the public it appeals to.

46. Le Tellier, Robert Ignatius. *An Intensifying Vision of Evil: The Gothic Novel (1764–1820) as a Self-Contained Literary Cycle.* Salzburg: Univ. of Salzburg, 1980.

Follows the gothic novel from a latent sense of the demonic in the world to an overt acknowledgment of it.

47. McBurney, William Harlin. *A Check List of English Prose Fiction, 1700–1739.* Cambridge, Mass.: Harvard Univ. Press, 1960.

 Lists 337 titles, about a third of which are translations.

48. MacCarthy, Bridget G. *The Later Women Novelists, 1744–1818.* New York: William Salloch, 1948.

 Extends item 49 (below) to show women writers gradually guiding the directions of the novel.

49. ———. *Women Writers: Their Contribution to the English Novel, 1621–1744.* Cork, Eng.: Cork Univ. Press, 1944.

 Surveys the participation of women in various forms of narrative fiction.

50. McKillop, Alan Dugald. *The Early Masters of English Fiction.* Lawrence: Univ. of Kansas Press, 1956.

 Discusses the literary careers of Defoe, Richardson, Fielding, Smollett, and Sterne.

51. Major, John Campbell. *The Role of Personal Memoirs in English Biography and Novel.* Philadelphia: Univ. of Pennsylvania Press, 1934.

 Shows how English and French memoirs affect biography and the early novel.

52. Maresca, Thomas E. *Epic to Novel.* Columbus: Ohio State Univ. Press, 1974.

 Traces "the process by which the novel replaced the epic as the major literary form in English."

53. Mayo, Robert D. *The English Novel in the Magazines, 1740–1815. With a Catalogue of 1375 Magazine Novels and Novelists.* Evanston, Ill.: Northwestern Univ. Press, 1962.

 Chronicles the history of the magazine novel.

54. Mews, Hazel. *Frail Vessels: Women's Role in Women's Novels from Fanny Burney to George Eliot.* London: Athlone, 1969.

 Studies the major women novelists as affected by woman's changing social role.

55. Miller, Nancy K. *The Heroine's Text: Readings in the French and English Novel, 1722–1782.* New York: Columbia Univ. Press, 1980.

 Studies eight novels as presenting "the fiction of a feminine destiny."

56. Miller, Stuart. *The Picaresque Novel.* Cleveland: Case Western Reserve Univ. Press, 1967.

 Constructs an "ideal genre type" for the picaresque novel.

57. Morgan, Charlotte E. *The Rise of the Novel of Manners: A Study of English Prose Fiction Between 1600 and 1740.* New York: Columbia Univ. Press, 1911.

Organizes a descriptive history according to broad narrative types: chivalric romance, classical romance, etc.

58. Paulson, Ronald. *The Fictions of Satire*. Baltimore: Johns Hopkins Univ. Press, 1967.

Examines the fictional constructs by which satire frequently expresses itself.

59. _____. *Satire and the Novel in Eighteenth-Century England*. New Haven, Conn.: Yale Univ. Press, 1967.

Traces the stages by which the great age of satire evolved into the great age of the novel.

60. Preston, John. *The Created Self: The Reader's Role in Eighteenth-Century Fiction*. New York: Barnes & Noble, 1970.

Sees what we value in a novel as being related to what it asks us to do or be.

61. Railo, Eino. *The Haunted Castle: A Study of the Elements of English Romanticism*. London: Routledge & Kegan Paul, 1927.

Discusses the major gothic writers and comments upon prevailing gothic themes.

62. Richetti, John J. *Popular Fiction before Richardson: Narrative Patterns, 1700–1739*. Oxford: Clarendon Press, 1969.

Explains the popularity of Defoe and Richardson in terms of the ideological myths that gave form to popular narrative types.

63. Rothstein, Eric. *Systems of Order and Inquiry in Later Eighteenth-Century Fiction*. Berkeley: Univ. of California Press, 1975.

Demonstrates that novels apparently different from one another share the formal procedures by which they address epistemological systems.

64. Sacks, Sheldon. *Fiction and the Shape of Belief: A Study of Henry Fielding with Glances at Swift, Johnson and Richardson*. Berkeley: Univ. of California Press, 1964.

Analyzes the expectations established by the major types of fiction in which beliefs are asserted: satire, apologue, and "action" (which includes the novel).

65. Schlauch, Margaret. *Antecedents of the English Novel, 1400–1600 (from Chaucer to Deloney)*. Warsaw: Polish Scientific, 1963.

Discusses novelistic attributes in early narrative texts.

66. Scholes, Robert, and Robert Kellogg. *The Nature of Narrative*. New York: Oxford Univ. Press, 1966.

Strips away predispositions to narrative art and subjects the phenomenon of narrative to historical reexamination.

67. Shepperson, Archibald Bolling. *The Novel in Motley: A History of the Burlesque Novel in English*. Cambridge, Mass.: Harvard Univ. Press, 1936.

     Represents the burlesque novel as an effective medium of criticism and a necessary counterpoise to the development of other types.

68. Sherbo, Arthur. *Studies in the Eighteenth Century Novel*. East Lansing: Michigan State Univ. Press, 1969.

     Remarks the distinctiveness of eighteenth-century novelists by reexamining received opinions of them.

69. Shroff, Homai J. *The Eighteenth Century Novel: The Idea of the Gentleman*. New Delhi: Arnold-Heinemann, 1978.

     Examines the English class system as viewed by philosophers and novelists.

70. Singer, Godfrey Frank. *The Epistolary Novel: Its Origin, Development, Decline, and Residuary Influence*. Philadelphia: Univ. of Pennsylvania Press, 1933.

     Surveys the epistolary mode in fiction before Richardson and after.

71. Skilton, David. *The English Novel: Defoe to the Victorians*. New York: Barnes & Noble, 1977.

     Describes the novel as an anti-Tory, bourgeois progressivist phenomenon.

72. Slagle, Kenneth Chester. *The English Country Squire as Depicted in English Prose Fiction from 1740 to 1800*. Philadelphia: Univ. of Pennsylvania Press, 1938.

     Finds the squire heroized in some works but denigrated in others, either for the promotion of social reform or from the novelist's personal distaste for the class.

73. Spacks, Patricia Meyer. *Imagining a Self: Autobiography and Novel in Eighteenth Century England*. Cambridge, Mass.: Harvard Univ. Press, 1976.

     Shows how novels and autobiographies convey doubts about character identity and ways of dealing with these doubts.

74. Spearman, Diana. *The Novel and Society*. London: Routledge & Kegan Paul, 1966.

     Minimizes the influence of sociological factors on the emergence of the novel.

75. Steeves, Harrison R. *Before Jane Austen: The Shaping of the English Novel in the Eighteenth Century*. New York: Holt, Rinehart & Winston, 1965.

Considers the eighteenth century to represent the novel in its experimental phase.

76. Stevenson, Lionel. *The English Novel: A Panorama*. Boston: Houghton Mifflin, 1960.

Explains the emergence of the novel and traces its history.

77. Summers, Montague. *The Gothic Quest: A History of the Gothic Novel*. London: Fortune, 1938.

Justifies gothic fiction as escape literature.

78. Tarr, Mary Muriel. *Catholicism in Gothic Fiction*. Washington, D.C.: Catholic Univ. of America Press, 1946.

Finds Catholic materials in gothic fiction to serve as sources of the sublime and as targets of deistical attack.

79. Taylor, John Tinnon. *Early Opposition to the English Novel: The Popular Reaction from 1760 to 1830*. New York: King's Crown, 1943.

Shows that the reputation of the novel fell far behind its growing readership.

80. Tillyard, E.M.W. *The Epic Strain in the English Novel*. London: Chatto and Windus, 1958.

Assigns to the epic a communal or chronic quality and perceives this quality in Defoe but not Fielding.

81. Todd, Janet M. *Women's Friendship in Literature: The Eighteenth-Century Novel in England and France*. New York: Columbia Univ. Press, 1980.

Analyzes types of female friendship in the novel.

82. Tompkins, J.M.S. *The Popular Novel in England, 1770–1800*. London: Constable, 1932; rpt. Lincoln: Univ. of Nebraska Press, 1961.

Notes trends in content and form emergent in popular novels of the later eighteenth century.

83. Uphaus, Robert W. *The Impossible Observer: Reason and the Reader in Eighteenth-Century Prose*. Lexington: Univ. Press of Kentucky, 1979.

Analyzes techniques whereby novelists involve readers in the creative process.

84. Utter, Robert P., and Gwendolyn B. Needham. *Pamela's Daughters*. New York: Macmillan, 1937.

Traces attributes of Pamela's character in later fictional heroines.

85. Van Ghent, Dorothy. *The English Novel: Form and Function*. New York: Rinehart, 1953.

Analyzes representative novels on the conviction that the value of the novel for us is the only value that matters.

86. Varma, Devendra P. *The Gothic Flame: Being a History of the Gothic Novel in England, Its Origins, Efflorescence, Disintegration, and Residuary Influences.* London: Arthur Barker, 1957.

    Describes the "gothic spirit"; then traces the gothic novel from Walpole through the nineteenth century.

87. Wagenknecht, Edward. *Cavalcade of the English Novel.* New York: Holt, 1943; rev. 1954.

    Sees the tradition of the novel not as a coherent development but as the successive achievements of literary geniuses.

88. Watt, Ian P. *The Rise of the Novel: Studies in Defoe, Richardson, and Fielding.* Berkeley: Univ. of California Press, 1957.

    Recognizes in the early novel a set of procedural conventions responding to new apprehensions of individual human worth.

89. Williams, Ioan M., ed. *Novel and Romance 1700–1800: A Documentary Record.* London: Routledge & Kegan Paul, 1970.

    Reprints 101 documents containing critical comments on the novel.

90. Wilt, Judith. *Ghosts of the Gothic: Austen, Eliot, and Lawrence.* Princeton: Princeton Univ. Press, 1980.

    Studies the gothic as a tradition of fiction that curves out from the main tradition but never separates from it.

91. Wright, Walter Francis. *Sensibility in English Prose Fiction, 1760–1814: A Reinterpretation.* Urbana: Univ. of Illinois Press, 1937.

    Draws distinctions between novels of sensibility and "realistic" novels.

---

**Notes**

1. J.C.T. Oates, "Cambridge and the Copyright Act of Queen Anne (1710–1814)," in *Quick Springs of Sense: Studies in the Eighteenth Century,* ed. Larry S. Champion (Athens: Univ. of Georgia Press, 1974), 65.

2. Ibid., 66.

3. Miriam Allott's *Novelists on the Novel* (New York: Columbia Univ. Press, 1959), while not limited to eighteenth-century novelists, contains comments by them and by later novelists, all arranged under topic headings.

# Contributors

HOWARD P. ANDERSON is Professor of English at Michigan State University. Besides earlier studies of Sterne, he has published essays on Richardson and Fielding and on the Gothic fiction of the eighteenth century. He is editor or coeditor of *The Familiar Letter in the Eighteenth Century* (Univ. of Kansas Press, 1966), *Studies in Criticism and Aesthetics, 1660-1800* (Univ. of Minnesota Press, 1967), M.G. Lewis's *The Monk* (Oxford Univ. Press, 1973), and Sterne's *Tristram Shandy* (Norton, 1979).

JACK M. ARMISTEAD, Professor of English at the University of Tennessee, is the editor of *Restoration: Studies in English Literary Culture, 1660–1700* and of *Scientific Awakening in the Restoration* (AMS Press, 1985–    ). He is the author of *Nathaniel Lee* (Twayne Series, 1979), *Four Restoration Playwrights* (G.K. Hall, 1984), and articles about Dryden, Addison, Poe, and other English and American writers.

PAULA R. BACKSCHEIDER is Associate Professor of English at the University of Rochester. She is author of *A Being More Intense: The Prose Works of Bunyan, Swift, and Defoe* (AMS, 1984), co-author of *An Annotated Bibliography of Twentieth-Century Studies in Women and Literature, 1660–1800* (Garland, 1977), and editor of *Probability, Time and Space in Eighteenth-Century Literature* (AMS, 1979) and of the plays of Charles Gildon (Garland, 1979), Elizabeth Inchbald (Garland, 1980), and Samuel Foote (Garland, 1983). Her many articles have appeared in a variety of major journals.

SHERIDAN BAKER, Professor of English at the University of Michigan, is the former editor of *Papers of the Michigan Academy of Science, Arts, and Letters* (1954-61) and of *The Michigan Quarterly Review* (1964-71). His poems have appeared in the *New Yorker* and other magazines, and he has written *Ernest Hemingway: An Introduction and Interpretation* (Holt, Rinehart, and Winston, 1967), *The Practical Stylist* (Crowell, 1962), *The Essayist* (Crowell, 1963), *The Complete Stylist* (Crowell, 1966), *The Writ-*

*ten Word* (wth Jacques Barzun and I.A. Richards; Newberry House, 1971), *The Practical Imagination* (with Northrup Frye and George Perkins; Harper & Row, 1980), and *The Harper Handbook to Literature* (with Frye and Perkins, 1985). His editions of Fielding's *Shamela* (Univ. of California Press, 1953), *Joseph Andrews* (Crowell, 1972), and *Tom Jones* (Norton, 1973) have been widely used, as have his articles on the novel, American literature, poetics, and literary theory.

JERRY C. BEASLEY is Professor of English at the University of Delaware. His articles and reviews have appeared in many journals and collections of essays. He is the author or editor of five books: *A Check List of Prose Fiction Published in England, 1740–1749* (Virginia, 1972), *English Fiction, 1660–1800: A Guide to Information Sources* (Gale, 1978), *Novels of the 1740s* (Georgia, 1982), *The Plays of Frances Sheridan* (with Robert Hogan; Delaware, 1984), and *The Adventures of Ferdinand Count Fathom,* for *The Works of Tobias Smollett* (Delaware, forthcoming).

MARGARET DOODY is Professor of English at Princeton University. In addition to articles in major journals, she has published *A Natural Passion: A Study of the Novels of Samuel Richardson* (Clarendon Press, 1974), *Aristotle Detective* (Bodley Head, 1978; rpt. Harper & Row, 1980), and *The Alchemists* (Bodley Head, 1980).

ALISTAIR M. DUCKWORTH, Professor of English at the University of Florida, is the author of *The Improvement of the Estate: A Study of Jane Austen's Novels* (Johns Hopkins, 1971) and of numerous other publications on Jane Austen and English novelists of the eighteenth and nineteenth centuries.

JACK D. DURANT is Professor of English at North Carolina State University. He has published articles on Otway, Vanbrugh, Fielding, Goldsmith, and Sheridan and is the author of *Richard Brinsley Sheridan* for the Twayne Series (1975) and *Sheridan: A Reference Guide* (G.K. Hall, 1981).

JAMES E. GILL is Associate Professor of English at the University of Tennessee. He has published articles on theriophily, on Swift, and on Rochester.

DONALD KAY, whose *Short Fiction in "The Spectator"* appeared in 1975 (Univ. of Alabama Press), was Executive Director of the South Atlantic Modern Language Association for seven years and is now associated with Randolph-Macon Woman's College. He has edited or co-edited *The South Atlantic Review* (1978-83), *A Provision of Human Nature: Essays on Fielding and Others* (Univ. of Alabama Press, 1977), and *The Unknown*

*Samuel Johnson* (Univ. of Wisconsin Press, 1983). His articles have appeared in a number of professional journals.

JOHN RICHETTI is Distinguished Professor of English at Rutgers University. He is the author of *Popular Fiction Before Richardson* (Clarendon Press, 1969), *Defoe's Narratives: Situations and Structures* (Clarendon Press, 1975), and most recently, *Philosophical Writing: Locke, Berkeley, Hume* (Harvard Univ. Press, 1983).

# Index

*Account of a most Barbarous and Bloody Murther Committed on Sunday last, An*, 5–6
*Actions of James Butler, An Account of the . . .*, see Defoe, Daniel
Adams, Pauline Serger, xii
Adams, Percy G., vii, xi–xiii, xix, xxxi, 8, 150–51; *Crèvecoeur's Eighteenth-Century Tales in Pennsylvania and New York*, xii; *Early American Literature*, xiii; *Graces of Harmony*, xiii; *Travel Literature and the Evolution of the Novel*, xiii; *Travelers and Travel Liars*, xiii
Addison, Joseph, 11, 52; *Spectator* No. 465, 52
*Advice*, see Smollett, Tobias
Alkon, Paul, xxiii, 62
Allen, Ralph, 124
Allen, Walter, 93–94
Alter, Robert, 123
*Amelia*, see Fielding, Henry
Anderson, Howard, xxviii–xxix; "Structure, Language, Experience In the Novels of Laurence Sterne," 185–223
Anne, Queen of England, 14, 48
*Apology for the Life of Mr. Colley Cibber, An*, see Cibber, Colley
*Apology for the Life of Mrs. Shamela Andrews, An*, See Fielding, Henry
*Arabian Nights*, 119
Ariosto, Ludovico, 133; *Orlando Furioso*, 133
Aristotle, 204–205; 214
Armistead, Jack, xiii
Aubin, Penelope, 29
Austen, Cassandra, 226, 231, 233–34, 236

Austen, Lieutenant Charles, 231–32
Austen, Edward, 226, 232–36
Austen, Eliza, 232
Austen, Francis, 230, 232
Austen, Frank, 226, 232–33
Austen, George, 230, 232–34
Austen, Henry, 226, 232–33, 238
Austen, James, 232–34, 255
Austen, Jane, xxix-xxxi, 61, 100, 103, 225–67; *Emma*, xxx, 226, 229, 232, 242–43, 246, 252, 254, 256–59; *Lady Susan*, 240; *Letters*, 233–35, 237–38, 241, 249; *Love and Friendship*, 239–40; *Mansfield Park*, xxx, 226, 230, 246, 252–57, 263; *Memoirs of Mr. Clifford*, 237–38; *Northanger Abbey*, 225–26; 228, 238; *Persuasion*, xxx–xxxi, 226, 229, 238, 242, 254, 259–63; *Pride and Prejudice*, xxx, 226–27; 234, 238–39, 246, 248–52; *Sanditon*, 238, 263–64; *Sense and Sensibility*, xxx, 226, 233, 236, 243–44, 246–48, 250, 253; *The Watsons*, xxx, 229, 244–46, 248, 259–60
Austen-Leigh, James, 103
*Author's Farce, The*, see Fielding, Henry

Backscheider, Paula R., xxi–xxiii; "Defoe and the Geography of the Mind," 41–65
Baker, Sheridan, xxv–xvi; "Fielding: The Comic Reality of Fiction," 109–42
Barbauld, Elizabeth, xxxi
Barker, Jane, 29, 100
Barth, John, 158

Barthes, Roland, 259
Batey, Mavis, 230
Battestin, Martin C., 112, 116, 123–24, 135
Baxter, Richard, 52
Beasley, Jerry C., xxvi–xxviii; "Smollett's Art: The Novel as 'Picture,'" 143–84
Beckett, Samuel, 94
Bellow, Saul, 158
Bertram, Edmund, 244
Blake, William, 90
Blanchard, Frederic T., 133
Blount, Martha, 31
Boccaccio, Giovanni, 10
Boileau-Despréaux, Nicolas, 205; Art Poetique, 205
Booth, Wayne C., 128–29, 133
Bowles, William Lisle, 263
Boyd, Elizabeth, 24; The Happy Unfortunate: or, the Female Page, 24–28
Bradshaigh, Lady, 68, 97
Bridges, Elizabeth, 235
British Magazine, see Smollett, Tobias
Brontë, Charlotte, 258; Jane Eyre, 258; Villette, 258
Brown, Capability, 235, 243
Brown, Tom, 118; trans. Comical Romance, 118
Bunyan, John 4–5, 52, 96, 209; Grace Abounding to the Chief of Sinners, 45; Pilgrim's Progress, xx, 4, 199, 209
Burney, Fanny, xxxi, 58, 103
Butt, John, 133

Captain Singleton, see Defoe, Daniel
Carlyle, Alexander, 145
Cervantes, Saavedra, Miguel de, 113, 115–119, 124, 128, 146, 228; Don Quixote, xxvii, 83, 146, 161, 166
Champion, The, see Fielding, Henry
Chandler, F.W., 6–7
Chandos, Duke of, 229
Chapman, R.W., 233, 235
Charles I, King of England, 230
Chaucer, Geoffrey, 10
Chesterfield, Philip Dormer Stanhope, fourth Earl of, 111
Chetwood, William: The Voyages, Dangerous Adventures, and Imminent Escapes of Captain Richard Falconer, 8–10, 45–46

Cibber, Colley, xxv, 111–14
Clarissa; or The History of a Young Lady, see Richardson, Samuel
Coffee-House Politician, The, see Fielding, Henry
Coleridge, Samuel Taylor, 220–21, 241, 263
Coley, William B., 134, 135
Complete English Tradesman, see Defoe, Daniel
Congreve, William, 125
Conjugal Lewdness, see Defoe, Daniel
Consolidators, The, see Defoe, Daniel
Coolidge, John S., 134
Covent-Garden Journal, 120, 131
Crabbe, George, 253
Crane, R.S., 126
Crèvecoeur, St. Jean de, xii; Voyage dans la haute Pensylvanie et dans l'état de New York: xii
Critical Review, 195
Cross, Wilbur L., 117, 125, 132
Cruel Mother, The, 6
Curry, Kenneth, xii

Dampier, William, 44; Voyages, 45
Daphnis and Chloe, 118
David Simple, "Preface" to, see Fielding, Henry
Davis, Lennard, 7–8
Davis, Richard Beale, xii–xiii
Davys, Mary, 30–33; The Reform'd Coquet, 30–33
Day, Robert A., 29
Dedeyan, Charles, xiii
Defoe, Daniel, xx, xxi–xxiii, 3, 4, 7, 8–10, 41–65, 109, 121, 126, 149, 177; An Account of the . . . Actions of James Butler, 48; Captain Singleton, 49–50; The Complete English Tradesman, 56; Conjugal Lewdness, 56; The Consolidator, 55; Due Preparations for the Plague, 53; An Essay on the History and Reality of Apparitions, 53; The Family Instructor, 56; The Four Years Voyages of Captain Roberts, 49–50; Further Adventures of Robinson Crusoe, 44, 46, 49–50, 52, 61; A General History of the Robberies and Murders of the most notorious Pyrates, 7–8; The History and Remarkable Life of

Defoe, Daniel (cont.)
the Truly Honourable Col. Jacque
(Jack), 10, 49–50, 53, 55, 60; A
Journal of the Plague Year, 53–56,
59, 62; Memoirs of a Cavalier, 56,
59, 60, 62; Memoirs of John Duke
of Melfort, 48; The Memoirs of
Majr. Alexander Ramkins, 48;
Moll Flanders, xxii, 6, 22, 46–48,
53, 55, 58–60; The Political
History of the Devil, 53; Religious
Courtship, 56; Robinson Crusoe,
xxi, xxiii, 8–9, 41–46, 48–53,
56–57, 59–60, 62, 148, 177;
Roxana, xxiii, 55, 59–60; The
Storm, 55
Dickens, Charles, 41, 57
Diderot, Denis, 69, 103
Digeon, Aurelien, 120, 121, 124
Don Quixote in England, see Fielding,
Henry
Doody, Margaret, xxiii–xxv; "Saying
'No,' Saying 'Yes': The Novels of
Samuel Richardson," 67–108
Dorchester, Lord, 231
Duckworth, Alistair, xxix–xxxi; "Jane
Austen's Accommodations,"
225–67
Due Preparations for the Plague, see
Defoe, Daniel
Durant, Jack, xxxi; "Books About the
Early English Novel: A Survey and
a List," 269–84
Dyson, A.E., 121

Earle, Peter, 49
Ehrenpreis, Irvin, 126
Eliot, George, 61, 103
Emma, see Austen, Jane
Essay on the History and Reality of
Apparitions, An, see Defoe,
Daniel
Eugene of Savoy, Prince, 163–64

Falkland, Lady, 230
Familiar Letters, see Richardson,
Samuel
Family Instructor, The, see Defoe,
Daniel
Faulkner, William, 158
Ferdinand Count Fathom, The
Adventures of, see Smollett,
Tobias

Feuillide, Comte de, 232
Fielding, Henry, xxiii, xxv–xxvi, 3–4,
11, 31, 58, 61, 67–68, 92, 94, 97,
103, 109–42, 143, 146, 148, 160,
162, 167, 171, 177, 246; Amelia,
xxv, xxvi, 97, 109, 120–21,
130–35; An Apology for the Life of
Mrs. Shamela Andrews, xxv,
112–17; The Author's Farce, xxv,
109, 111, 125, 133; The
Champion, xxv, 111–12, 116; The
Coffee-House Politician, The
Wedding Day, 125, 132; "Preface"
to David Simple, 122; Don
Quixote in England, 116–20, 124;
The Grub Street Opera, 110; The
Historical Register, 111; Jonathan
Wild, 109, 120–22, 130–32; Joseph
Andrews, xxv–xxvi, 98, 109,
111–16, 120, 122, 124–25, 128,
130, 133, 135, 167; Journey from
This World to the Next, 120;
Letters, 133; The Lottery, 124;
Love in Several Masques, xxv,
110–11, 124; The Masquerade,
109, 131; Miscellanies, 120–22,
130; The Modern Husband,
132–33; Pasquin, 111; "Preface,"
Plutus, the God of Riches, 123; A
Short Account of God's Dealings
with the Reverend Mr. George
Whitefield, 112–13; The Temple
Beau, 124, 132; Tom Jones, xxv,
xxvi, 68, 94, 98, 109–11, 115,
117–18, 120, 122–31, 133, 135,
143, 148, 171, 177; Tom Thumb,
109–10; Tragedy of Tragedies,
110; The Universal Gallant, 124
Fielding, Sarah, xxxi
Floris and Blancheflour, 133
Flynn, Carol Houlihan, 93
Forced Virgin, The; or the Unnatural
Mother, 23–4
Foucault, Michel, 7
Four Year Voyages of Captain Roberts,
The, see Defoe, Daniel
Freud, Sigmund, 94
Further Adventures of Robinson
Crusoe, see Defoe, Daniel

Gadamer, Hans-Georg, 211–12
Garrick, David, 150, 160
Gasset, Ortega y, 62

Gay, John, 31, 110–11, 120; *The Beggar's Opera*, 110–11, 120
*General History of the Robberies and Murders of the Most Notorious Pyrates, A, see* Defoe, Daniel
George I, King of England, 48
Ghent, Dorothy Van, 92
Gildon, Charles, 10–11; *The Golden Spy*, 10–11; *The Post-Man Robb'd of his Mail*, 11
Gill, James E., "Introduction," xix–xxxi
Goethe, Johan Wolfgang von, 103
Goldberg, Homer, 117
Golden, Morris, 94, 98; *Richardson's Characters*, 94
Goldsmith, Oliver, 166, 247–48; *The Vicar of Wakefield*, 148
Gordon, John, 144–45
Green, Martin, 9
Griffith, R.H., xii
Griffiths, Ralph, 194, 198; *Monthly Review*, 194
*Grub Street Opera, The, see* Fielding, Henry

Haage, Richard, 125
Handel, George Frederick, 159
Hardy, Thomas, 61, 63
Harrington, James, 54
Harris, John, 44; *Navigantium Atque Itinerantium Bibliotheca*, 44
Harrison, Bernard, 123
Hasted, E., 235; *History and Topographical Survey of the County of Kent, The*, 235
Hatfield, Glenn W., 121
Haywood, Eliza, xxi, 16–23; *The British Recluse*, 18; *The Distress'd Orphan; or, Love in a Mad House*, 16; *The Fatal Secret; or Constancy in Distress*, 16, 19; *The Force of Nature; or, the Lucky Disappointment*, 16; *Idalia: or, the Unfortunate Mistress*, 16; *The Injur'd Husband; or, the Mistaken Resentment*, 16; *Lasselia; or, the Self-Abandon'd*, 16; *Love in Excess*, 16–18, 22; *Love-Letters on All Occasions Lately passed between Persons of Distinction*, 16; *Memoirs of Certain Islands Adjacent to the Kingdom of Utopia*, 16; *The Mercenary Lover:*

Haywood, Eliza (*cont.*) *or, the Unfortunate Heiresses*, 19–20; *Philidore and Placentia: or L'Amour trop Delicat*, 16; *Secret Histories, Novels and Poems*, 17
Heliodorus, 93; *Aethiopica*, 93
Heller, Joseph, 158
Hervey, John, Lord, 113–14
Hill, Aaron, 73, 92
Hilles, Frederick W., 124
*Historical Register, The, see* Fielding, Henry
*History and Adventure of an Atom, The, see* Smollett, Tobias
*History and Adventure of Gil Blas of Santillone*, trans., *see* Smollett, Tobias
*History and Remarkable Life of the Truly Honourable Col. Jacque (Jack), The, see* Defoe, Daniel
Hobbes, Thomas, 54, 190, 246
Hodges, John C., xii
Hogarth, William, xxvi, 119, 143–44; *Industrious Apprentice*, 143; *Rake's Progress*, 143
Homer, 187, 208; *Iliad*, 187
Horace (Quintus Horatius Flaccus), 114, 186, 187, 205; *Ars Poetica*, 187
Hornberger, Theodore, xii
Hume, David, xxvi, 135
*Humphry Clinker, The Expedition of, see* Smollett, Tobias
Hunter, J. Paul, 45; *Reluctant Pilgrim*, 45
Hutchens, Eleanor, 127

Iser, Wolfgang, 199, 213–14

James, Henry, 54, 61, 68, 103, 243; *English Hours*, 243
Jehlen, Myra, 18
Jensen, Gerard Edward, 131
Job, 51
Johnson, Maurice, 127, 133
Johnson, Samuel, 11–12, 75, 253; *Dictionary*, 11–12
Jonah, 57
*Jonathan Wild, see* Fielding, Henry
*Joseph Andrews, see* Fielding, Henry
*Journal of the Plague Year, A, see* Defoe, Daniel
*Journey from this World to the Next, see* Fielding, Henry

Joyce, James, 54, 62–63, 68, 96, 113, 129, 158; *Ulysses*, 113, 133
Jung, Karl, 93

Keats, John, 68, 129, 240
Kinkead-Weekes, Mark, 94
Knickerbocker, Kenneth, xii
Knight, Charles A., 130
Knight, Thomas, 230, 232, 235
Knox, Robert, 44; *An Historical Relation of Ceylon*, 44

La Calprenède, Gauthier de Costes de, 134; *Cassandra*, 134
Laclos, Mlle [Lesage], 103
*Lady Susan, see* Austen, Jane
Langer, Susanne K., 126
*La Picara*, 47
*Lay-Monk*, 11
Leavis, F.R., 200; *The Great Tradition*, 200
Lefroy, Anna, 231
Leigh, Rev. Thomas, 229
LePage, Peter V., 135
LeSage, Alain René, 119, 146–47, 149, 160; *History and Adventures of Gil Blas of Santillane*, 146–47, 149
*Letters, see* Austen, Jane; Fielding, Henry, Sterne, Laurence
*Life of Lazarillo de Tormes, The*, 147, 149
Lillo, George, 121
Locke, John, 54, 201, 203–205, 207, 210–11; *An Essay concerning Human Understanding*, 201, 204–205
*London Times*, 54
Lorrain, Paul, 6, 7; *The Ordinary of Newgate's Account of the Life, Conversations, Birth and Education, of Thomas Ellis, and Mary Goddard*, 6, 48
*Lottery, The, see* Fielding, Henry
*Love and Friendship, see* Austen, Jane
*Love in Several Masques, see* Fielding, Henry
*Lovers Tales: In Several New Surprising and Diverting Stories*, 20–22
Lucian (Lucianus Samosatensis), 120
Lyttelton, George, 111, 122, 129–30, 160

McBurney, W.H., 5, 69
McKillop, A.D., 128–29, 212
Macmillan, Alexander, 63
Mandeville, Bernard, 246
Manley, Mary, xx–xxi, 12–16; *Secret History of Queen Zarah and the Zarazians*, xx, 12–13; *Secret Memoirs and Manners of several Persons of Quality, of Both Sexes from the new Atlantis*, 13–17
Mansfield, Katherine, 233
*Mansfield Park, see* Austen, Jane
Maresca, Thomas, 118
Marivaux, Pierre Carlet de, 119
Marlborough, John Churchill, Duke of, 119, 163, 164
Marlborough, John Churchill, Duke of, and Sarah Churchill, Duchess of, 14
Marlborough, Sarah Churchill, Duchess of, 13, 119
*Masquerade, The, see* Fielding, Henry
*Memoirs of a Cavalier, see* Defoe, Daniel
*Memoirs of John Duke of Melfort, see* Defoe, Daniel
*Memoirs of Majr. Alexander Ramkins, The, see* Defoe, Daniel
*Memoirs of Mr. Clifford, see* Austen, Jane
Meredith, George, 63
Middleton, Rev. Mr. Conyers, 113–14; *Life of Cicero*, 113
Miller, Henry Knight, 129–30
Miller, Nancy, 76
*Miscellanies, see* Fielding, Henry
Misson, Captain, 8
*Modern Husband, The, see* Fielding, Henry
*Moll Flanders, see* Defoe, Daniel
Montague, Lady Mary Wortley, 109, 131, 133
Morley, John, 63
*Mysteries of Udolpho*, 226

*Northanger Abbey, see* Austen, Jane
Novak, Maximillian E., 53

Osborn, John, 71–72
Ovid (Publius Ovidius Naso), 19
Oxford English Dictionary (OED), 208

*Pamela: or, Virtue Rewarded, see* Richardson, Samuel

*Pamela II, see* Richardson, Samuel
*Paradise Lost*, 52
*Pasquin, see* Fielding, Henry
Paulson, Ronald, 118
*Peregrine Pickle, see* Smollett, Tobias
*Perfidious P, The*, 29–30
Perrot, James Leigh, 232, 234, 255
Perry, Ruth, 18, 33
*Persuasion, see* Austen, Jane
Pinter, Harold, 94
Plato, 204
*Plutus, the God of Riches*, "Preface,"
    *see* Fielding, Henry
*Political History of the Devil, The, see*
    Defoe, Daniel
Pope, Alexander, 31, 43, 109–12, 114,
    123, 129, 145, 243; *Dunciad*,
    109–10; *An Essay on Man*, 123;
    *Imitation of Horace*, 111–12, 114
Portsmouth, Lord, 213
Powers, Lyall H., 123, 131
Preston, John, xxvi
Price, Martin, 122
*Pride and Prejudice, see* Austen, Jane
Pritchett, V.S., 93
Proust, Marcel, 96

Quin, James, 160, 175

Rabelais, François, 237
*Rambler 97, see* Richardson, Samuel
Rawson, C.J., 29
Red Book, 229
*Regicide, The, see* Smollett, Tobias
Reiss, Timothy J., 58
*Religious Courtship, see* Defoe, Daniel
*Reproof, see* Smollett, Tobias
Repton, Humphry, 230, 243
Ribble, Frederick G., 134
Richardson, Samuel, xxiii–xxv, 3, 4,
    19, 29, 58, 62, 67–109, 114–17,
    119, 121, 126, 146, 149, 162, 173,
    177, 200, 228; *Clarissa; or, The
    History of a Young Lady*, xxiv, 19,
    70, 83–97, 98, 102–103, 173, 177;
    *Familiar Letters*, 73; *The History
    of Sir Charles Grandison*,
    xxiv–xxv, 67, 83, 96–103, 250;
    *Pamela: or Virtue Rewarded*, xxiv,
    58, 73–82, 83, 92, 113–15, 119,
    148; *Pamela II*, xxiv, 82–84;
    *Rambler 97*, 100
Richetti, John, xix–xxi, 45, 69;
    "Popular Narrative in the Early

Richetti, John (*cont.*)
    Eighteenth Century: Formats and
    Formulas," 3–39
Rivington, Charles, 71–72
Roberts, Bartho, 8
*Robinson Crusoe, see* Defoe, Daniel
Rochester, John Wilmot, second Earl
    of, 19
*Roderick Random, The Adventures of*,
    *see* Smollett, Tobias
Rothstein, Eric, 113–14
Rousseau, Jean-Jacques, 54, 69, 83,
    103, 247; *Émile*, 83; *Julie ou la
    Nouvelle Héloise*, 83
Rowe, Elizabeth, 29
Rowlandson, Thomas, 146
*Roxana, see* Defoe, Daniel
Ruskin, John, 98

Sanders, Norman, xiii
*Sanditon, see* Austen, Jane
Scarron, Paul, 7, 115, 117–19; *Romant
    Comique*, 118
Scott, Sir Walter, 62, 68
*Sense and Sensibility, see* Austen,
    Jane.
*Sentimental Journey, A, see* Sterne,
    Laurence
*Sermons of Mr. Yorick, see* Sterne,
    Laurence
Shaftesbury, Anthony Ashley Cooper,
    third Earl of, 246
Shakespeare, William, 68, 192, 227;
    *Antony and Cleopatra*, 249; *King
    Lear*, 92; *A Midsummer Night's
    Dream*, 192; *Othello*, 229; *Romeo
    and Juliet*, 192; *Twelfth Night*,
    100
*Shamela, see* Fielding, Henry
Shaw, George Bernard, 92
Sheppard, Jack, 6
Sherburn, George, 110, 133
Sheridan, Richard Brinsley, 170; *The
    Rivals*, 170
Shesgreen, Sean, 118
*Short Account of God's Dealings with
    the Reverend Mr. George
    Whitefield, A, see* Fielding, Henry
Sidney, Sir Philip, 4, 114, 205; *Arcadia*,
    4, 114
*Sir Charles Grandison, The History of*,
    *see* Richardson, Samuel
*Sir Launcelot Greaves, see* Smollett,
    Tobias

Smith, Captain Alexander, 6–7;
  *History of the Lives and
  Robberies of the Most Noted
  Highway-Men*, 6–7
Smith, Charlotte, 263
Smollett, Archibald, 144
Smollett, Tobias, xxvi–xxviii, 67,
  143–84, 195, 237, 243; *The
  Adventures of Ferdinand Count
  Fathom* xxvii–xxviii, 98, 143, 148,
  158–59, 162–66, 168–69, 175; *The
  Adventures of Roderick Random*,
  xxvi–xxvii, 98, 144–61, 163–64,
  168, 175, 177; *Advice*, 145; *British
  Magazine*, 166; *The Expedition of
  Humphry Clinker*, xxvii–xxviii,
  143, 146, 148, 153, 158, 163, 166,
  168–78, 195, 237, 243; *The
  History and Adventures of an
  Atom*, 168; *History and
  Adventures of Gil Blas of
  Santillane*, trans., 146, 159;
  *Peregrine Pickle*, xxvii, 148,
  158–63, 165, 175, *The Regicide*,
  144–45, 157, 159, 164, 175;
  *Reproof*, 145; *Sir Launcelot
  Greaves*, xxvii, 148, 159, 166–67;
  *Travels through France and Italy*,
  168, 195, 197
Speck, W.A., 48
*Spectator, The*, 11
Spilka, Mark, 117
Spring, David, 236, 242
Staël, Mme de, 69
Starr, G.A., 45, 48; *Defoe and Spiritual
  Autobiography*, 45
Steele, Richard, 11
Sterne, Laurence, xxiii, xxviii–xxix,
  62, 177, 185–223; *Letters*, 214;
  *The Life and Opinions of Tristram
  Shandy*, xxviii–xxix, 177, 185–87,
  189, 190, 194, 199–221, *A
  Sentimental Journey*, xxviii–xxix,
  185, 187–89, 193–99, 207, 209,
  211, 216–17, 219; *Sermons of Mr.
  Yorick*, 198, 216
Stevick, Philip, 126
Stewart, Bain Tate, xiii
Stinstra, Johannes, 72–73
Stirling, William, 145
*Storm, The, see* Defoe, Daniel
Stout, Gardner, 194–95, 209
*Strange and Wonderful news from
  Lincolnshire*, 48

Stuart, Charles Edward, the Young
  Pretender ("Bonnie Prince
  Charlie"), 163–64, 230
Stuart, James, the "Pretender," 48
Stubbs, George, 227; *Two Cream
  Ponies, a Phaeton and a Stable
  Lad*, 227
Stuber, Florian, 83, 93
Swearingen, James, 213–14, 218, 221
Swift, Jonathan, 10, 94, 109, 110;
  *Gulliver's Travels*, 10, 94, 110, 194

*Tatler, The*, 11
Taylor, Dick, Jr., 117
Teach, Captain Edward, 8
Temple, Sir William, 43
*Temple Beau, The, see* Fielding, Henry
Thackery, William Makepeace, 228
Thaler, Alwin, xiii
Thomas, D.S., 135
Thompson, E.P., 242–43
Thomson, James, 92
*Tom Jones, see* Fielding, Henry
*Tom Thumb, see* Fielding, Henry
*Tragedy of Tragedies, see* Fielding,
  Henry
*Travels through France and Italy, see*
  Smollett, Tobias
*Treacherous Confidence, The; or,
  Fortune's Change*, 22–23
Trilling, Lionel, 252
*Tristram Shandy, The Life and
  Opinions of, see* Sterne, Laurence
Trollope, Anthony, 103, 236; *The
  Small House at Allington*, 236
*Tryal and Conviction of several
  Reputed Sodomites, The*, 6

*Universal Gallant, The, see* Fielding,
  Henry

Virgil, 131; *Aeneid*, xxvi, 131, 133
*Voyage to the New Island of Fonseca*,
  44

Walpole, Horace, 220, 263
Walpole, Sir Robert, xxv, 111, 112,
  120–21
Warner, William Beatty, 70
*Watsons, The, see* Austen, Jane
Watt, Ian, 4, 126
Watts, W., 235
*Wedding Day, The, see* Fielding, Henry
Wendt, Allan, 131, 135

Wesley, John, 112
Whitefield, Rev. George, 112–13
Whitman, Walt, 129
Wild, Jonathan, 6
Wilde, Oscar, 250
William I, King of England, 48
*Williamson's Memoirs, Mr.*, 43
Wilson, Angus, 103
Wither, Harris Bigg, 231

Wollstonecraft, Mary, 241–42; *A Vindication of the Rights of Women*, 214–42
Woods, Charles, 112
Woolf, Virginia, 68, 226–27, 249; *Three Guineas*, 233
Wordsworth, William, 263
Wright, Andrew, 124
Wright, Nathalia, xiii

*The First English Novelists* was composed into type on a Mergenthaler Linotron 202 digital phototypesetter in nine point Trump Medieval with three point spacing between the lines. The book was designed by Cameron Poulter, composed by Typecraft Company, printed offset by Thomson-Shore, Inc., and bound by John H. Dekker & Sons. The paper on which the book is printed embodies acid-free characteristics for an effective life of at least three hundred years.

THE UNIVERSITY OF TENNESSEE PRESS : KNOXVILLE